In Our Own Words

Readings on the Psychology of Women and Gender

In Our Own Words

Readings on the Psychology of Women and Gender

Mary Crawford
West Chester University of Pennsylvania

Rhoda Unger
Montclair State University

The McGraw-Hill Companies, Inc.

New York   St. Louis   San Francisco   Auckland   Bogotá   Caracas
Lisbon   London   Madrid   Mexico City   Milan   Montreal   New Delhi
San Juan   Singapore   Sydney   Tokyo   Toronto

McGraw-Hill

A Division of The **McGraw·Hill** *Companies*

WOMEN AND GENDER
Readings on the Psychology of Women and Gender

Copyright © 1997 by The McGraw-Hill Companies, Inc. All rights reserved. Printed in the United States of America. Except as permitted under the United States Copyright Act of 1976, no part of this publication may be reproduced or distributed in any form or by any means, or stored in a data base or retrieval system, without the prior written permission of the publisher.

Acknowledgments appear on pages 379–381 and on this page by reference.

ISBN 0-07-065929-x

2 3 4 5 6 7 8 9 0 DOC DOC 9 0 9 8

This book was set in Palatino by Ruttle, Shaw & Wetherill, Inc.
The editor was Beth Kaufman; the editing manager was Peggy Rehberger;
the production supervisor was Annette Mayeski.
The design manager was Joseph A. Piliero; the cover was designed by Joan Greenfield.
Project supervision was done by Ruttle, Shaw & Wetherill, Inc.
R. R. Donnelley & Sons Company was printer and binder.

Library of Congress Cataloging-in-Publication Data

In our own words : readings on the psychology of women and gender /
  [compiled by] Mary Crawford, Rhoda Unger.
      p.   cm.
   Includes bibliographical references and index.
   ISBN 0-07-065929-X
   1. Women—Psychology.   2. Feminist psychology.   3. Sex
(Psychology)   4. Sex role.   I. Crawford, Mary (Mary E.)   II. Unger,
Rhoda Kesler.
   HQ1206.I595   1997
   155.6'33—dc20   96–38653

http://www.mhcollege.com

About the Editors

MARY CRAWFORD is Professor of Psychology and Women's Studies at West Chester University of Pennsylvania. She has held the Jane W. Irwin Chair in Women's Studies at Hamilton College, served as Distinguished Visiting Teacher/Scholar at Trenton State College, and directed the graduate program in women's studies at the University of South Carolina. She received her Ph.D. in experimental psychology from the University of Delaware. Professor Crawford is active in the Division on the Psychology of Women of the American Psychological Association as well as many regional and national groups concerned with gender equity. Her publications include the books *Gender and Thought; Talking Difference: On Gender and Language;* and *Women and Gender: A Feminist Psychology.* In addition to her scholarly works, she has written on women's issues in popular periodicals such as MS. Magazine.

RHODA UNGER is Professor of Psychology at Montclair State University in New Jersey. She received her Ph.D. in experimental psychology from Harvard University. Professor Unger was the first recipient of the Carolyn Wood Sherif Award from the Division on the Psychology of Women of the American Psychological Association. She is also the recipient of two distinguished publication awards and a distinguished career award from the Association for Women in Psychology. She has been active in various feminist organizations within psychology since 1972 and has lectured extensively in the United States and abroad. She is currently the North American editor of the international journal *Feminism & Psychology.* Professor Unger is the author or editor of six previous books, including *Representations: Social Constructions of Gender; Women, Gender, and Social Psychology; Female and Male;* and *Women and Gender: A Feminist Psychology.*

For Our Mothers and Their Stories

Contents

Part Three
MAKING MEANING

Part Four
MAKING A LIVING: WOMEN, WORK, AND ACHIEVEMENT

Part Five
MAKING CONNECTIONS

Part Six
MAKING OUR LIFEPATHS

Preface

In the past two decades, feminist psychology has grown and matured. In the process, it has enlarged psychological theory, research, and practice and developed new, transformative ways of thinking about women and gender relations. Truly, we are living at an exciting time for teaching and learning about the psychology of women and gender.

In the more than twenty years that each of us has been teaching in this area, we have noticed that when students first begin to learn about the psychology of women and gender, they make sense of it by looking for stories that capture the realities of living in a gendered world. They want to learn about people, and they want to hear the individual voices of girls and women. They seek narrative—unique accounts that capture shared experiences. By listening to the viewpoints of others, students interpret and make meaning of their own experiences, both positive and negative.

Students want models of resistance and rebellion, and evidence of social change for the better, to balance the depressing data on prejudice and discrimination. Often, they seek this evidence independently. Many teachers have noticed that courses in the psychology of women and gender generate a sort of "dialogue by clipping." By the end of the second week of class, the contributions start coming in. A student shares a "Cathy" cartoon strip. Another brings in a news-magazine story on women executives. A third offers her copy of a feminist detective novel, and a fourth her favorite Marge Piercy poem. They want to know what their classmates and teacher think of these counternarratives.

The need for sense-making through narrative may be universal. And for students, beginning to learn about psychology can be frustrating. They may turn to narrative at least in part to compensate for psychology's limitations. In working with students, we have identified several causes of their frustration with conventional psychology, and our goal in putting together this collection is to address each of them.

First, psychology can seem distanced and cold to the beginning student. Psychology's methods most often involve making inferences from group data. Many of its most respected studies involve decontextualized laboratory manipulations. While experienced psychologists know that group data and controlled settings are important in establishing reliable and valid evidence about the topics we study, students may find such research alienating. Moreover, psychological research historically has oversampled white people, college students, and males. For women and people of color, finding those who are like oneself represented in the theories and empirical studies of psychology has not been easy.

Another source of frustration is that much of what students learn in their psychology of women and gender courses is discouraging. Research, by definition, can only describe and analyze what is past. To be sure, statistics about violence against women, the wage gap, and other issues provide important documentation of sexism. Experimental studies of attributions, stereotypes, and so on reveal the workings of gender under the laboratory lens. But these kinds of research may also arouse feelings of helplessness and despair. Indeed, we do still live in a sexist world. But that is only part of the picture.

In this collection, we attempt to meet students' needs for women's stories and to enrich the study of women and gender. The women who have written these essays differ in age, sexual orientation, social class, race/ethnicity, sensibility, and opinion. In choosing selections, we have been mindful of the need to teach critical thinking about women and gender. When students read the accounts in this collection, their ability to think critically about psychological knowledge grows. Learning about how one woman has experienced skin color and beauty, for example, can bring about a deeper understanding of the strengths and limitations of standard psychological research on attractiveness. Hearing a mother's perspective on the issues involved in bringing up daughters gives new meaning to research on gender role socialization. Seeing an old issue from a new perspective is perhaps one of the great moments in learning, a moment that can be brought about through the unique stories of the diverse women in this collection.

We offer *In Our Own Words,* then, to share with a new generation our belief that psychology is about very real, very human issues; to demonstrate concretely that women are a diverse group with many divergent viewpoints and experiences; and to help students learn to think critically about psychological research and women's lives. To that end, we have drawn on the richness and diversity of women's own voices as they tell about their lives. The individual selections and the organization of the book reflect our goals.

ORGANIZATION OF THIS BOOK

The selections in this book are grouped into six sections that reflect our perspective on gender as a social construction. Part I, Making Our Voices Heard: Historical Perspectives, recounts the experiences of women who have made scholarship their life's work. Part II, The Making of a Woman: Bodies, Power, and Society, explores women's understanding of the cultural meanings of the female body. In Part III, Making Meaning, women create their own reconstructions of meanings on issues as varied as sexuality and the SAT. Part IV, Making A Living: Women, Work, and Achievement, provides the accounts of diverse women in the work force and contrasts them with media images of working women. In Part V, Making Connections, women speak of the nontraditional families, friendships, and helping relationships they create. Finally, Part VI, Making Our Lifepaths, looks at developmental issues for diverse girls and women across the lifespan.

Each part is introduced by a short essay that shapes an approach to critical reading of the individual selections, inviting the student reader to engage in dialogue with each author, to compare the divergent viewpoints of the various authors, and to think critically about the implications of their views. A brief Afterword invites reflection on how the differences in women's lives are shaped by social class, sexual orientation, race/ethnicity, and age cohort.

USING THIS BOOK

In selecting and grouping the narratives for *In Our Own Words*, our goal was to provide a varied collection centered around the main conceptual issues usually addressed in courses on women and gender. Therefore, we chose the six general themes described above, rather than tying the topics to any particular textbook's organization. The collection can stand on its own or be used as a flexible adjunct to any current textbook on women and gender. In writing our own text (*Women and Gender: A Feminist Psychology*, 2nd edition, 1996), we tried to give voice to the experiences and thoughts of individual women as well as to synthesize feminist research. We plan to use *In Our Own Words* in conjunction with our text, and we hope that other instructors who have adopted *Women and Gender* will find *In Our Own Words* a valuable and engaging addition to their syllabus. We also expect that it will find a place in introductory women's studies, introductory psychology, sociology of gender, and developmental psychology courses.

Because most of the readings, and all of the introductory essays, are quite short, each part can be assigned as a unit. A section of readings might be used to complement or to replace a textbook chapter. Alternatively, selections can be assigned individually or in groupings different from ours. Because this is an anthology of wonderfully unique voices, the organization we have imposed is, in a sense, arbitrary. Each author's voice can stand on its own.

Most of the pieces could be read in conjunction with more than one of the topics commonly addressed in courses on women and gender. Kate Bornstein's radical essay on her life as a transsexual could be read as part of a discussion on gender schemas and stereotypes, sexuality, biological aspects of gender, or personality development. Carol Tomlinson-Keasey's essay on a gifted woman who was one of the participants in Terman's famous study could be read in conjunction with the topic of adult development, intelligence, or achievement or as an example of women's history in biography. These two examples are typical of the essays in this collection: each has many points of connection to psychological issues and allows for many readings that uncover multiple meanings.

The works in this collection were discovered by students, colleagues, and friends, as well as by our own efforts. We are especially grateful to three feminist psychologists who provided constructive reviews of our preliminary set of readings and made suggestions for works that, in some cases, we were able to include: Elizabeth R. Cole of Northeastern University, Patricia Connor-Greene of Clemson University, and Patricia Donat of Mississippi University for Women. We also thank our ace editor at McGraw-Hill, Beth Kaufman. Beth is more than just an editor; she is a one-woman cheering section and an active feminist contributor to this volume.

Mary Crawford classroom-tested an earlier version of this collection at the University of South Carolina in 1992 and 1993; students' detailed comments on the readability and appeal of the selections were invaluable in making final choices. Finally, to the students who, over the years, have given us photocopies of articles and essays with stick-on notes urging us to "Read this, you'll love it," we send a warm collective thanks. Some of you will find your favorites here.

Mary Crawford and Rhoda Unger

In Our Own Words

Readings on the Psychology of Women and Gender

PART ONE

Making Our Voices Heard: Historical Perspectives

Just a few generations ago, white, privileged men were the only people thought to be capable of creating knowledge and governing society. For women, making one's voice heard has meant resisting core beliefs of western culture that do not accord us full intellect and agency. These beliefs have been expressed in societal forces that tell women that we are not clever enough, not motivated enough, and simply not good enough—or if we are, we shouldn't be. Women have faced sex discrimination in access to education, in hiring and promotion, and in judgments about our work. The cumulative effect is a powerful message that women should forget about our dreams of achievement and stay in the place assigned to us.

Women have always resisted staying "in their place." Yet the young women in each new generation may believe themselves to be alone in their struggle, because they do not know about the strong women who came before them. Although not everyone wants to earn a Ph.D., do scientific research, or write novels, each of us is faced with the task of achieving our full potential, and each of us needs to find the courage to take ourselves seriously.

In this group of readings you will learn about six women—four psychologists, a mathematician, and a writer—who tried to find ways to make a contribution to society. We chose the stories that appear here because we believe that hearing our foremothers' stories can help women find their own voices. That each of them took different paths and used different tactics reflects their specific situations. As you read their stories, you may want to think about how their social class, ethnicity, and the era they live(d) in shaped their choices.

When Rhoda Unger and I (M.C.) decided to write our own stories as part of this collection, we agreed it would not be easy. Why might psychologists, who specialize in human behavior, find it difficult to write about their own lives? We decided that each of us should write her own account without consulting with the other.

When we traded "first drafts," we were astonished at the similarities in our stories. We have been friends for years; our first extended professional contact was in 1988, when Rhoda spoke at a conference I organized, and we started work together on *Women and Gender* in 1989. We had talked about some similarities in our personal histories: that each of us was the first in her family to go to college, for example, and that each of us had switched from experimental to social psychology along the way. But neither of us had ever expressed to the other just how lonely we were as aspiring young students, how "different" we felt, or how difficult it was to combine marriage, motherhood, and our work. Why do you think that these parts of women's history often remain invisible? Each of us describes various roadblocks we encountered. How do personal and social structural factors interact in creating these roadblocks? What were some sources of encouragement and support for each of us along the way?

We next move back in time to Mary Whiton Calkins, a pioneering woman psychologist. Calkins' story is given voice by Laurel Furumoto, a feminist psychologist who did her graduate studies in the same psychology department at Harvard where Calkins had done hers some eighty years earlier. In Calkins' day, psychology was a new field of study; its power structure (and that of higher education in general) was exclusively male. How did influential men both help and hinder her? Do you think it would be possible (or necessary) for a young woman to seek out one of the "great men" of the field for tutoring today? How did Calkins' social class and family background shape her experience? Look for both opportunities and constraints.

Naomi Weisstein, an experimental psychologist, writes in her own distinctively witty and ironic voice about her graduate school days at Harvard. How was her second-class status as a woman conveyed to her? How was her experiential world different from that of the male graduate students? When Weisstein began searching for jobs, she encountered nepotism rules that forbade hiring related people in the same institution. How did these rules selectively affect women? She describes an academic hierarchy in which women were at the bottom rung and men almost always at the top. Do such gendered hierarchies still exist? (You might want to look at your own psychology department and tally the proportion of women among the instructors and the full professors.) Moving from Harvard to an "unknown" university, how did Weisstein's opportunities further decline? How does she explain her survival against the odds?

We have started with the stories of four women in psychology because most readers of this book will be students of psychology and other social sciences. But women in other fields have stories to tell, too. Emmy Noether and bell hooks are women from a prototypically "male" field, mathematics, and a prototypically "female" field, English, respectively.

Emmy Noether's story is told by Mary Crawford, who stumbled on her existence while researching an article on women scientists. Crawford then went to Bryn Mawr College, where Noether spent the last years of her life, and found materials for her story hidden away in the archives. Noether, like Calkins, struggled to gain access to a field in which the power structure was exclusively male. How did her family background provide her with a "head start" in mathematics? What sacrifices did she make to be able to study and teach mathematics? How was she dependent on the good will of influential men? Why did she leave her native Germany for the United States, and how did her life change as a result? Albert Einstein called Noether a genius, yet many of her colleagues seemed more concerned with her appearance than her mind. Think about what the life of a female genius in mathematics might be like today.

bell hooks, a feminist theorist, academic, and writer, describes being "terrorized" by racism and sexism as an African American undergraduate and graduate student majoring in English. She eloquently describes how, in the academic hierarchy we have discussed, students are on the ultimate bottom rung. How did the hierarchy function to silence students' protests about racist and sexist treatment? How did students from privileged class backgrounds (mostly white) and those from working class backgrounds (mostly people of color) experience the pattern of abuse differently? What coping strategies did hooks and others use? Like white women before them, black women are now a tiny minority of college and university professors. Have you ever had a black woman for a teacher?

Some interesting commonalties emerge when the six stories are considered together. Elite universities—Harvard, Stanford, Göttingen—figure in several of them. Do you think that similar barriers exist at less lofty institutions? Women's colleges play an important positive role: for Calkins and Weisstein, the college was Wellesley; for Noether, Bryn Mawr. Why have women's colleges historically been so important, and what function might they serve today?

A feminist truism is the saying, "Anonymous was a woman." Mary Crawford had to dig into archival records to learn about Emmy Noether, who contributed to the mathematics of relativity. Laurel Furumoto says that as a graduate student she learned little about her predecessor's achievements. Mary Whiton Calkins invented the paired associate technique, developed an influential theory of the self, was president of both the American Psychological Association and the American Philosophical Association, and published prolifically throughout a long career. Were her life and work discussed in any of your psychology textbooks? Looking back over these stories, what were some of the ways that each woman was denied credit and recognition for her work? Do these means of "erasing" women's achievements still occur?

The stories of these six women span a period of some 100 years, from the 1890s to the present. During this time, women's access to educational and professional resources has changed a great deal. Today, women are no longer denied degrees from prestigious universities, and they are more visible as researchers, intellectuals, and teachers. Many students think that gender equality now exists, and that all a woman needs to succeed is intelligence and motivation. Clearly, all of the women in these histories possess these characteristics. Yet Naomi Weisstein insists that they are not enough: "Many have had extraordinary strength and *not* survived." She argues that women are still in danger of having our full humanity denied. How might social structures be changed so that women's potential to contribute to society can be achieved, no matter what their social class or color?

Claiming the Right to Know:
A Personal History

When I was growing up, there seemed to be no women out in the world. Maybe I got an overdose of patriarchy at an early age. First of all, it was the 1950s, and the women I knew were all full-time homemakers. Aside from Aunt Tacy Jane, a cashier in a supermarket, and Aunt Ruth, a seamstress, none of them had a dime of her own in her pocket.

My father was an Air Force sergeant. I grew up on and around military bases. When my family went to church on Sunday, the priest stood with his back to the congregation and chanted the Mass in Latin in homage to a trinity of male gods. Even the servers at Mass were always boys.

Okay, I found a few straws to grasp. At the age of five, I became a big fan of Dale Evans. Never mind that she was second-in-command to Roy Rogers— she had her own horse, a lasso, and a gun! I cajoled a cowgirl outfit from my parents and spent hours fantasizing giving orders from atop my palomino. In third grade, my class read "Trees," by Joyce Kilmer. I loved this poem ("I think that I shall never see/A poem lovely as a tree . . ."), and I thought how wonderful it must be to write something in a book for children to read. I wanted to be Joyce Kilmer, woman writer. Unfortunately, I later discovered that Kilmer was a man.

Moving on, I discovered Nancy Drew, the answer to my brother's Hardy Boys mysteries. Nancy was way cool, with her roadster, her smarts, and her boyfriend. In high school, I stumbled on Margaret Mead. Her *Coming of Age in Samoa* dazzled me. From it I began to learn how people are shaped by culture, and—equally important—that a woman could be smart and tough enough to go off by herself and discover something new about the world. And I heard about Golda Meir, Prime Minister of the new state of Israel. In fact, Meir provided me with one of my first moments of feminist awakening. Confronted with a suggestion in parliament to reduce crime and sexual assault by restricting the hours women could travel in public, Meir replied that it would be better to restrict the men, who were committing the crimes.

The parental guidance I remember was composed of "don'ts," from "Don't talk back," to "Don't get pregnant before you're married." Education was seen as a way up the ladder of social class for boys, not girls. Of course, a girl could always try to become an honorary male by studying hard and going on to college—but a "bookworm" was likely to end up an "old maid." In high school, I developed an advanced case of cynicism, making sarcastic remarks about stupid housewives, grubby little kids, and dumb husbands, and declaring dramatically, I Will Never Marry. The bookworm wanted to be prepared in case nobody ever asked!

My SAT scores were the best in the class. The boy with the next-best scores went on to Harvard; I went to a nearby branch of a state college. Did I perceive this as an injustice? Absolutely not. I felt wildly lucky to be going to college at all. I was the first person in my family to do so, and I did not appreciate the fine nuances involved in comparing Harvard and State Teachers' College. I just got out of town as fast as I could.

I wish I had known while I was growing up about all the other women who have struggled to find their place in the world. Though I write about it lightly now, I can easily remember the doubts, the lack of confidence, the uncertainty and confusion I experienced. Who was I; what could I become? I was afraid and shy much of the time. I was chronically ambivalent, dreaming of being a writer or a scientist yet doubting whether I was smart enough to do much of anything. Most of all, I just felt lonely.

I graduated from college with a degree in music education, not because I had any great talents in this direction, but because teaching music was considered a tolerable deviance for women. I did like music, and I wanted to lead a high school chorus or symphonic band. The only jobs I was offered were part-time elementary music teaching. A few years of listening to third-graders play scales on their little plastic recorders was more than enough of that.

I discovered psychology later, as a returning student in my late twenties. It was then that I came to appreciate the power of making knowledge—in, of all places, "stat class." I loved learning how to design a study to find out something new about the world. It was hard, to be sure—correlations, regressions, t tests, analyses of variance, interactions, sampling distributions—but I loved the power of it. It felt like I was learning the passwords to a secret society. I would become one of the chosen few, the Scientists. It never occurred to me to question why there were so few women in my classes or textbooks, or why "women's issues" were never the topic of research. I had found what I was good at doing, and I would become an honorary man.

Not that there weren't reminders of my marginality as I proceeded to become an experimental psychologist:

- I am a graduate student at my first professional conference. Of course, there are ten times as many men there as women. On an elevator, I see a man whose presentation I had attended earlier in the day. It was about tonic immobility, a reaction that can be seen in birds and some other animals, in which they go limp and "play dead" when they are attacked. Turning to the man, I remark that I enjoyed his presentation. He launches into a routine about how the technique works with women, too: just grab 'em by the neck and they go limp and stop resisting. He continues his extended rape joke until the elevator doors open.

- I am about to collect the data for my Ph.D. dissertation when the faculty member in charge of the animal laboratory decides that certain grad students (me) should not have access to animal subjects, which are to be reserved for faculty and selected grad students (his). I protest in vain. Then I find that half the animals are being discarded. Nobody wants the female rats, it seems; all of the researchers think that their hormonal cycles will mess up the data. I snag the female rats and run my dissertation study (they do not mess up the data).

- I start my first job, team-teaching Introductory Psychology with my husband, also a brand-new Ph.D. We decide that we will debate issues in class, so that students can learn critical thinking. I'll start off as the leader with my husband as respondent, and later in the semester we will switch. We think we are doing just great. Then the dean's wife tells me that a student has described our class to her as "the one where the woman talks and the man corrects her when she's getting it wrong."

- I move on to a larger university. When I sign the contract as an assistant professor, it specifies exactly how many articles per year I must publish and what journals they must be in. Later, I find that no male hired by the department, before or after, has ever had such a contract. It is assumed that the men will know where and when to publish their research, and that rigid rules would stifle their creativity. With the help of a female department chair, I got a contract like the men's.

- The year I apply for promotion to full professor, five women and fifteen men apply. One-third of the men, and none of the women, get promoted. With the other women, I file a complaint. Two years later, the university settles in our favor.

In 1975, I started to get involved in Women's Studies by teaching a mini-course in Psychology of Women. The discovery that there was no research on women in the field that claimed to be "the science of human behavior" was galvanizing. I began to realize that psychology, my intellectual home, had serious flaws, and that the problem extended to all knowledge. Although I did not read her words until much later, I had come to the same realization as the poet Adrienne Rich: what I learned in college and graduate school was

> how *men* have perceived and organized their experience, their history, their ideas of social relationships, good and evil, sickness and health, etc. When you read or hear about "great issues," "major texts," "the mainstream of Western thought," you are learning about what men, above all white men, in their male subjectivity, have decided is important (1979:232).

At this time, the women's movement was growing, and I got involved in various kinds of political and social activism. Meanwhile, my experimental work was starting to get published and noticed. Rather than bringing me satisfaction, my dual identities as activist and psychologist seemed at odds with each other. More and more, my research seemed like a series of intellectual puzzles that had no connection to the rest of my life. In the laboratory, I studied abstract theories of conditioning, accepting the assumption that the principles were similar for rats and humans. In the "real world," I perceived injustice everywhere and sought to understand the reasons for it. I became aware of sexual harassment, wife battering, media stereotyping, and other kinds of sexism that were just then being named by the women's movement. Also, trying to build a marriage between equal partners and bring up my children in non-sexist ways made me much more aware of social pressures to conform to traditional gender roles. (For another chapter in this story, see "Two Jobs, Three Kids, and Her 2000-Mile Commute," in Part V.) I began to ask myself why I was doing a kind of psychology that had so little to say about the real problems of women. I turned to social psychology and the study of women/gender to make my personal and professional life congruent and to begin using my skills as a psychologist on behalf of social change.

Finding my second intellectual home in the psychology of women has expanded my thinking and also has given me a new vantage point for looking at psychology. From women's studies, I have learned that laboratory research using experimental and statistical techniques is not the only route to knowledge. I have learned how radically a research agenda can change when you start to ask, "Where are the women?" Each question about women and their lives leads to another, more daring question, which leads to developing new methods for finding answers, until you have followed a path that leaves most of psychology behind.

I still value my early work and training in psychology. From it, I learned how to go about scientific inquiry systematically and responsibly. However, my beliefs about what are the important questions in psychology, and the best ways to go about answering them, have changed. So I stand both within and outside the "mainstream" of psychology, enjoying the contradictions of feeling both marginal and at the center.

When I hear that in a survey of APA members, Division 35 (Psychology of Women) was ranked 33rd out of 40 in importance, I feel marginal. Conversely, women now earn more than half the Ph.D.s in psychology—the days of professional conferences with ten times as many men as women are over. Women's studies, with programs in more than 600 universities around the country, is not going to fade away. Division 35 and the Association for Women in Psychology provide a home that women have never had before in psychology's history. In being part of these changes, I believe that I am at the center of a revolution. Shifting from margin to center and back gives a unique double vantage point. Articulating this "double vision" is, I think, one of the most important contributions of feminist psychology.

It is not easy for me to write about my own struggles to get an education and to be treated fairly in my profession. Part of the training a psychologist receives is to learn how to conceal oneself, the better to speak as an expert on other people. And even now there is a part of me that believes that the loneliness and difficulties I have experienced must have been partly my fault. Living a prosperous and contented life today, it would be easier to forget how hard it has been to get here. From women's studies I have learned, though, that if I am to take my students seriously, I must be honest with myself and them. There is always a new generation of young women trying to claim their right to an education, and they need to hear from those who have gone before. Knowledge is power.

Reference

Rich, A. (1979). Claiming an education. In *On lies, secrets and silences: Selected prose 1966–1978* (pp. 231–235). New York: Norton.

Making a Feminist:
A Personal History

I never planned to study women or gender. Most of the women in my generation did not. There were no courses, no journals, and little history. Most of us had forgotten that there had ever been a first wave of feminism in the 1920s, and, if we remembered, we considered it to be irrelevant to our lives and work.

Looking back, it is hard to remember how lonely I felt in most academic/professional contexts. I started college in 1956, graduate school in 1960, and my professional career (my first full-time position) in 1966. There are figures about the percentage of women who participated in the American Psychological Association's annual conventions during these years—10.8 percent in 1956 and 13.9 percent in 1966. But I am not sure these numbers convey the isolation of women psychologists within the university environment and, especially, when we ventured into the "outside world" of professional meetings.

During conferences women were invisible except as potential sexual partners. Invitations for dinner at these meetings (even when one paid for oneself) seemed to be taken as invitations for sexual trysts afterwards. Although we were visible as potential sexual partners, we were completely invisible as professional colleagues. In 1966 I went to a meeting with my husband (who is not a psychologist) just after getting married. I was on the job market at the time. We became involved in a number of conversations in which senior men asked my husband what I did (I was right there at the time!). He was even offered a position at a prestigious university because he was a good listener for the distinguished professor who was holding forth at the time. Needless to say, when he indicated that he was not professionally qualified, the position was not offered to me.

Most of the feminist psychologists who were professionally active during this period have their own "war stories." But most of us were socialized to believe that personal history was irrelevant for us as objective social scientists. Some, like myself, have internalized that belief, and it is only recently that I have begun to reveal myself in my scholarly papers. I am still very uncomfortable in doing so.

Nevertheless, the first personal comments I ever made in a professional context (in 1985) seem quite revealing:

> Rhoda Kesler Unger regards herself as having been marginal throughout her professional career. She was the only woman in her year in the Experimental Psychology program at Harvard from which she received her Ph.D. She is a Professor of Psychology at Montclair State College and an active researcher in a primarily teaching institution. She is a feminist married to her first and only husband, with whom she is rearing two teen-aged daughters. . . . She believes that marginality explains her scholarly concerns as well as expanding their perspective. (In O'Leary, Unger, & Wallston, 1985, p. xii.)

Actually, my perceptions of marginality date from earlier in my life. Like many other feminist academics of my acquaintance, I am from a working-class background. I was the first member of my family to go to college. Graduate school was not even part of our awareness. The elementary school system that I attended could be characterized as "inner city" even then. And I was a bookish "ugly duckling" who was beloved by my teachers but ignored by my peers.

My experiences during my elementary and high school years had led me to believe that hard work paid off. When I performed very well academically at Brooklyn College, I saw no reason to believe that I could not do as well in a Ph.D. program. In some ways my marginalization had sheltered me from the sexism of the 1950s. Because there was no one in my family with whom to compare myself in terms of class mobility, I ignored gender constraints as well. As Naomi Weisstein—a classmate in graduate school—has eloquently related, Harvard was quite an awakening in this regard!

I have since learned from male classmates that they perceived the years of graduate school as dehumanizing too, but at the time, they did not confide this. The style at Harvard was "academic macho," which meant pretending that one neither studied nor worried and passed examinations through innate brilliance. The male faculty (of course, there was not a single female to be found) took on the most promising (and arrogant) male graduate students as apprentices. However, they did not want female apprentices because they believed that women could not achieve professional "stardom." Women were to be tracked into teaching positions. In my second year of graduate school, they did not offer me the usual research assistantships that my surviving male classmates received. Instead, they found me a teaching assistantship at MIT, where a graduate program in psychology was being started and they did not have enough graduate students of their own to teach undergraduate sections. The male graduate students, however, were taught to write grant proposals, conduct research, and give professional presentations.

The faculty at Harvard did not seem to believe that training women for their doctorates involved any responsibility for them afterward. As I found out accidentally later on, letters of recommendation could contain potential bombshells. For example, one faculty member from whom I had received "*A*'s" wrote that I was argumentative (I had once criticized his changing his name to what I perceived as a less Jewish one, and I was outspoken in his seminars), and another stated that I was "ambitious" (I was, but "highly motivated" might have been a less loaded term). These letters resulted in a "stress interview" for a postdoctoral position in which I was asked whether I got along with other women (which seems ironic now) instead of what kind of research I was interested in. I must have given the "right answers," because I did get the position.

Of course, I was left to find my own job after receiving my Ph.D. The field was still expanding then, so teaching positions were not hard to find. Positions at elite research institutions (comparable to those that almost all my male classmates obtained) were not available for women in experimental psychology. The percentage of women in this subdiscipline at the time was less than 10 percent. Most of the women could be found in teaching institutions or as research associates at large universities where their husbands were employed. I found myself a position at a teaching institution.

My political views were not particularly popular at this university, where I was one of the first two young women hired by the psychology department. My personal style was also rather "hippie" at the time. For example, I had long straight hair down to my waist (I did wear it up for classes). One of the senior women in the department was unhappy with my style, which she thought would lead the students to not respect me. She requested that I cut my hair before she would let me teach graduate courses. I was still politically naive and somewhat arrogant (I thought my professional credentials were more important than my appearance), so I laughed, told the story to others, and did not cut my hair. I also did not get tenure.

I would not suggest that there was a direct connection between hairstyle and tenure. However, my experience is indicative of the dilemmas encountered by at least one young female faculty member during a period when the "rules" were changing. There were a lot of double binds around. For example, I thought I could combine a career and children—rare among earlier generations of women academics (who were sometimes penalized professionally if they even married). I tried to time my pregnancies to coincide with academic vacations. Unfortunately, I miscalculated on my first pregnancy and was informed that insurance regulations would not permit me to teach at the institution during late pregnancy. My graduate seminar met at my home for a few weeks—much to the displeasure of higher authorities.

Moreover, no one during my graduate training had ever pointed out to me how difficult it would be to maintain a career in physiological psychology and have any semblance of a normal family life. The facts that animals had to be fed every day or that brain operations could not be interrupted for family emergencies were not seen as relevant when the researchers were male. The practical problems that I encountered trying to do such research combined with the increasing irrelevance I found in studies of the caudate nucleus in rats (on which I had done my Ph.D. dissertation) moved me to reconsider my research goals.

During this time I had become involved in developing curricular materials for a course in the psychology of women. When I did not receive tenure in 1972, I moved to Montclair State University, where I have remained. When I interviewed at Montclair, I was much more aware of potential political problems in decisions about promotion and tenure than I had been six years earlier. During the hiring interview, I announced that I was in the process of shifting fields from physiological to social psychology and that I was interested in developing a course on the psychology of women for the institution. There was much ignorance about the area, but not too much hostility, and I was hired. Some of the questions asked were amusing and, in hindsight, predictable. They included: "Don't we cover the area in human sexuality?" "Will we have a comparable class in the psychology of men?" "Is there enough material for such a course?" And, "Who will teach this course if you do not?" The answer to the latter question was a chorus from all the other women in the room. Obviously, Montclair was a much more comfortable academic environment for me than my previous institution had been.

While I was beginning my career and having children (two daughters, one born in 1968 and one in 1970), other women were entering psychology and also encountering sexism on both personal and professional levels. Book titles were unabashedly sexist, positions were advertised for men only, and if women were interviewed for positions, they were routinely asked about their marital and childbearing plans.

The Association for Women in Psychology (AWP) began from informal conversations at meetings of graduate students and younger academic women who, like myself, had been influenced by popular feminists. It was an enormous relief to share experiences with other women who were having difficulty getting positions, were underemployed, and, somewhat later, were encountering difficulties obtaining tenure. We also shared stories about the difficulties of finding mentors, juggling roles, sexual harassment, and the alienation we felt from being in a virtually all-male environment.

We had long, emotional conversations about current problems and future plans. Our friendships transcended geography and subdisciplinary affiliation. They served as the nucleus for more formal networks as women in psychology became increasingly politically organized.

Involvement with feminist organizations within psychology helped to give legitimacy to research on women. We were able, for example, to develop journals such as the *Psychology of Women Quarterly* and *Sex Roles*. Our goals, as first stated, were not, however, particularly activist in nature. Instead, the organizers of APA's Division on the Psychology of Women stressed the scientific value of scholarship on women.

Today it is important to me to be *both* a scholar and an activist. This was not always true. I cannot say that I was a feminist from the earliest point of my professional life. Unlike my classmate Naomi Weisstein, it took me a while longer to identify the fundamental sexism of psychology and in academia as a whole. Until graduate school the meritocratic system seemed to have worked for me. I blamed my growing sense of alienation from psychology on my own inadequacies as a person and as a researcher.

I became a feminist through writing my first textbook (published in 1975). I became a feminist as I read more and more sources needed to write this text. I recognized that my own experiences of injustice were shared by others and were grounded in structural processes rather than personal inadequacies.

The book was driven by passion. We wanted to demonstrate that psychological research could illuminate the way sexual inequality was produced and maintained and to show that such inequality had no basis in fact. We believed in the power of science to effect social change.

The writing of a feminist textbook twenty years after the first one is more of a political act. Mary Crawford and I want to move psychology beyond its narrow concern with laboratory research. At the same time, we wish to use such research to examine women and gender. This forces us to use the scholarly base of traditional psychology while attempting to deconstruct that tradition. I have not lost hope that we can do both.

Many of you reading this story are probably surprised by the notion that I continue to view myself as an "outsider." This is partly a consequence of my early history, but it is also attributable to some deeply held beliefs that I share with other social activists. I have found that many influential feminists have a contradictory view of themselves and the world. They recognize that authority is not synonymous with truth, that people are not always rational, and that chance is important in human affairs. Conversely, they also possess a deep conviction that their actions can change reality. This contradictory view is what gives them the wisdom to understand social injustices and the energy to challenge them. My own ability to balance contradictory behaviors such as involvement in both traditional scholarship and movements for social change is nourished by my identification with marginality. It is my hope that I will always retain such an identification.

Reference

O'Leary, V. E., Unger, R. K., & Wallston, B. S. (Eds.) (1985). *Women, gender, and social psychology*. Hillsdale, N.J.: Erlbaum.

Laurel Furumoto

Mary Whiton Calkins (1863–1930) Fourteenth President of the American Psychological Association

When I was a graduate student in the Department of Psychology at Harvard University, I learned two things from my adviser about Mary Whiton Calkins. One was that, contrary to popular belief, she, rather than Georg Müller and Alphons Pilzecker, was the inventor of the paired-associate technique. The other was that she declined to accept a Radcliffe Ph.D. on the grounds that she had done all of her graduate work at Harvard. This second fact seemed to amuse my adviser a great deal, whereas it simply puzzled me. I could not understand why it was so important where her work had been done. Now, almost fifteen years later, I have come to appreciate the principle involved.

Calkins did postgraduate work at Harvard in the 1890s under William James, Josiah Royce, and Hugo Münsterberg. She took seminars with Royce and James and conducted experimental work in Münsterberg's laboratory, the results of which formed the basis of a doctoral dissertation on association which she presented to the Department of Philosophy. She was given an oral examination by the members of this department who subsequently communicated to the president and fellows of Harvard College that she had completed all the requirements for the Ph.D. However, she was not granted the degree; the presumptive basis for this decision being that Harvard does not grant degrees to women.

Several years later, after Radcliffe College had been founded, plans were made to offer a Radcliffe Ph.D. to Calkins and three other women who had undertaken graduate studies at Harvard but were denied the Ph.D. because of their sex.[1] In the spring of 1902, after approval by Harvard and Radcliffe, Dean Agnes Irwin of Radcliffe wrote to Calkins offering her the degree. The following is part of Calkins's reply:

> I hope that I may make quite clear to you my reasons for declining to accept the honor of the Radcliffe doctor's degree. I sincerely admire the scholarship of the three women to whom it is to be given and I should be very glad to be classed with them. I furthermore think it highly probable that the Radcliffe degree will be regarded, generally, as the practical equivalent of the Harvard de-

gree. And, finally I should be glad to hold the Ph.D. degree, for I occasionally find the lack of it an inconvenience, and now that the Radcliffe Ph.D. is offered, I doubt whether the Harvard degree will ever be open to women.

On the other hand, I still believe that the best ideals of education would be better served if Radcliffe College refused to confer the doctor's degree. You will be quick to see that, holding this conviction, I cannot rightly take the easier course of accepting the degree.[2]

The contents of this letter, coupled with Calkins's firmly held belief that there were no inherent sex differences in qualities of mind, lead me to believe that she refused the degree on the principle that the Harvard Ph.D. should be awarded for graduate work done at Harvard and that the sex of the recipient was irrelevant; that is, she believed that Harvard should not discriminate against women in granting degrees.

Aside from an autobiographical chapter,[3] most of which she devoted to a discussion of her system of self-psychology, there has been very little published about the life of Mary Whiton Calkins, fourteenth president of the American Psychological Association. One of the aims of the present article is to describe briefly her family background, career, and contributions to psychology. A corollary aim is to give a chronicle of Calkins's graduate education because of the insights into American psychology in the 1890s which it provides, as well as the way in which it illustrates the difficulties encountered by a woman pursuing graduate work in psychology during that era.

Mary Whiton Calkins was born in 1863, the eldest of five children in the family of Charlotte and Wolcott Calkins. The family was extremely close-knit, and the most salient and persuasive theme in Calkins's life was her steadfast devotion to her family. In 1880 the family—father, mother, two daughters, and three sons—moved from Buffalo, New York, where Calkins had spent her childhood, to Newton, Massachusetts. Here her father, a Congregational clergyman, assumed the ministry of a new church and built a house which remained Calkins's home for the rest of her life.

Both her parents traced their lineage back to the early settlers in this country. Her father's family, of Welsh origin, first arrived here in 1638, and her mother was of triple Mayflower descent.[4] Wolcott Calkins was characterized by his youngest son, Grosvenor, in the following way: "Father's strongest characteristics [were] . . . complete . . . confidence in his ability to deal personally with almost any mechanical or construction project and a resolute determination to carry through his projects in the face of any obstacles."[5]

These traits of "confidence" and "resolute determination" were also apparent in Wolcott Calkins's ideas about education. He felt that much time was lost in ordinary schooling and alternately pushed his children ahead in school at certain points and removed them at others in order to have them tutored or to take them to Europe where they learned foreign languages by being boarded out with French and German families. He firmly believed that prolonged and constant exposure was the only way to acquire a foreign language. That he acted on this belief is indicated by his son Grosvenor: "In order to give her an early knowledge of German, no other language was used in the home for five or six years following my sister Mary's birth."[6] As a consequence of his educational program, all the Calkins children entered college with advanced standing, graduated at the usual age after attending for only three years, and could read and speak fluently both French and German.

Unfortunately, there is less detailed information available about Calkins's mother, Charlotte. The image that emerges is of a patient, sensitive, intelligent, and physically very frail, but resolute, woman who was devoted to her family. It is also clear that the relationship between Calkins and her mother was remarkably warm, close, and enduring.

Calkins's middle brother, Raymond, noted in his journal that his sister's departure for Smith College in the fall of 1882 was the first break in the family circle.[7] Another, unexpected and tragic, soon followed when Calkins's sixteen-year-old sister, Maude, became seriously ill during that same fall, and after months of suffering, died in the spring of 1883. Presumably because of her grief and a reluctance to leave her family at this time, Calkins remained at home the following academic year studying and taking private lessons in Greek. She reentered Smith in the fall of 1884 with senior standing and graduated with the class of 1885 having concentrated in classics and philosophy. The following year she remained at home tutoring her brothers and studying on her own.

In May 1886, the entire family set out on a journey to Europe, traveling first in England and then France. Wolcott Calkins returned to his pastoral duties in Massachusetts in the fall while the rest of the family went to Germany and set up winter quarters in Leipzig. Here Mary Calkins became acquainted with an instructor from Vassar College who invited Calkins to accompany her on a trip to Greece. The two left in early winter, traveled through Italy, and then proceeded to Greece. During their several months in Greece, Calkins took the opportunity to study modern Greek.

After sixteen months in Europe, the family returned home. Calkins took a position at Wellesley College, a recently founded liberal arts college for women, where she taught Greek for the next three years. Referring to her time in Italy and Greece, her brother Raymond commented in his journal, "She was then preparing to teach Greek to private pupils, if a college position did not offer. But as a result of father's interview with Miss Freeman, then President at Wellesley, an appointment as Instructor in Greek there was offered and accepted. She entered upon that work as soon as we returned home."[8]

Soon after Calkins began teaching at Wellesley, she happened to borrow a volume on the history of Greece from a professor in the philosophy department. When she went to the professor's quarters to get the book, Calkins noticed her collection of philosophy books and confided to the professor "her deep interest in that subject and her ardent desire for an opportunity to continue her study of it."[9]

Two unrelated factors combined to provide Calkins the opportunity to fulfill her desire. One of these was the explicitly acknowledged aim of the fledgling institution to keep abreast of the latest developments in the liberal arts and sciences. Therefore, in the late 1880s, about a decade after the founding of Wilhelm Wundt's laboratory and just as the first crop of American psychological laboratories was beginning to spring up, Wellesley College began to feel the need to represent the new experimental psychology, complete with laboratory, in its curriculum. As was generally true in that period, the instruction in psychology was to be carried on within the philosophy department.

LAUREL FURUMOTO
*Mary Whiton Calkins
(1863–1930)
Fourteenth President
of the American
Psychological
Association*

The second circumstance that could make a promising young teacher in the Greek department a candidate for founding a laboratory of psychology was the scarcity of academically qualified women. The recruiting policy of one of Wellesley College's early presidents has been summarized as follows: "Find the right person; preparation can be discussed later."[10] It was in this spirit that the professor to whom Calkins had expressed her interest in philosophy recommmended to the president of the college that she consider Calkins for the proposed psychology position. Early in 1890, the president agreed to recommend Calkins for the position on the condition that she first prepare herself by studying psychology for a year.

Accepting this proposition, Calkins considered where she might undertake a year of study. Her correspondence from this period indicates that she sought advice from a number of people. She wrote to one of her former instructors at Smith College asking him whether he would advise her to study abroad and, if so, with whom. Or, she inquired, whether he thought she should work in this country "with Dr. Ladd of New Haven, or with Professor James of Harvard, or with Dr. Hall at Worcester."[11] The instructor replied that he would recommend that she study in Germany if women were allowed the same privileges as men. The same sentiment was expressed by another of her former instructors, who wrote, "Germany is a good place to study . . . [but] . . . whether you could have the privilege of attending lectures or obtaining private instruction in psychology and philosophy in any of the German universities outside of Zurich, I do not know."[12]

Another letter to Calkins regarding study in Göttingen had a distinctly discouraging tone: "A common friend of ours, Miss Molly Knox, has asked me to give you my opinion about a woman's chances of study at the University of Göttingen. I wish I might encourage you; but past experience has proved to me the utter uselessness of trying to enlighten the authorities, at least, in our generation."[13]

Calkins also must have considered going to Michigan to study with John Dewey. A letter Dewey wrote to Calkins in May 1890 outlined the offerings in psychology and philosophy at the University of Michigan and indicated that he hoped to meet with her to discuss things in more detail during a trip to the Boston area that summer.[14]

A Smith classmate of Calkins, Anna A. Cutler, was doing graduate work in psychology at Yale with G. T. Ladd. In a letter to Calkins dated May 1890, Cutler wrote:

> He [Ladd] knows of no reason why you could not take courses 2, 3, 4, & 8 with himself, if you chose. 6 & 7 are undergraduate courses likely to be crowded by men. He would have to ask advice before admitting any women to the Physiolog.[ical] Psychol.[ogy]. I think he would be glad to arrange some way by which you could get that course if possible. . . . He would be very glad to have a côterie of women as students under him, and as he said yesterday "I am glad to put myself out to help any earnest woman especially one who is going to teach."[15]

After Cutler had consulted further with Ladd, she wrote again to Calkins with additional information:

LAUREL FURUMOTO
*Mary Whiton Calkins
(1863–1930)
Fourteenth President
of the American
Psychological
Association*

He said among other things that the Physiolog.[ical] Psychol.[ogy] course next year is to be taken by a very few men, and that you would be allowed to attend as a guest (that being an undergraduate course you could open your mouth only after decree of the Faculty & Corporation. The P.[ost] G.[raduate] courses you can take as full a part in as you choose. We were invited to read papers this year).[16]

Calkins did not take advantage of the opportunity to study at Yale under Ladd's direction or at Michigan with Dewey. Perhaps it was because she was reluctant to leave her family, or because neither institution had a psychological laboratory. In one of her letters Cutler mentioned the lack of a "regular psycholog.[ical] laboratory" at Yale,[17] and Dewey revealed in his letter that he did not know how much laboratory work there might be in connection with the course in physiological psychology because there was "no regular psychophysical laboratory."[18]

It was important to Calkins that she spend part of her year studying physiological psychology, at that time roughly synonymous with the new experimental psychology. It is also quite probable that she thought it important to undertake her work in physiological psychology in an institution with a psychological laboratory. If so, in the United States in 1890, she would have been limited to less than a dozen institutions. Harvard was among the handful of those with a psychological laboratory, and it was also within commuting distance of her family home.

In late spring of 1890, it was to Harvard that Calkins turned seeking permission to enter Philosophy 20a and b in the academic year 1890–1891. Philosophy 20a was a seminar in physiological psychology taught by William James; Philosophy 20b, a seminar on Hegel, was taught by Josiah Royce. Both James and Royce were eager to welcome Calkins into their seminars, but President Charles Eliot refused to give them permission to do so because official policy prohibited the admission of women to Harvard courses.

In a letter to Calkins expressing his regret over the enforcement of this policy, James inquired, "Can't you get to Worcester almost as easily as to Cambridge? Stanley Hall's Psychological department ought to be the best in the world."[19]

Calkins heeded James's advice about seeking instruction in Hall's department, but she did not give up on Harvard. Nor did James immediately give up on Eliot. At the end of May he wrote to Calkins:

I have been attacking the President again on the subject you know of. He tells me that the overseers are so sensitive on the subject that he dares take no liberties. He received such a "tremendous wigging" from them a few years ago for winking at just this thing, that he is forced now to be strict. . . . I think that in justice to him you should know these facts.[20]

James's desire to be fair to Eliot did not prevent him from expressing his feelings about Calkins being "kept out. . . . Enough to make dynamiters of you and all women."[21]

It was not to dynamite but to a petition that Calkins turned next in a renewed attempt to get permission to enter James's and Royce's seminars. In July 1890, Calkins's father submitted a petition to the Corporation of Harvard

University, supported by a letter from the president of Wellesley College, requesting that his daughter be allowed to take courses with James and Royce. The phrasing of the petition minimized the coeducational aspect and was framed in terms of one institution (Wellesley College) asking a favor from another institution (Harvard University), this favor being "postgraduate and professional instruction for one who is already a member of a college faculty."[22] On 1 October 1890, Harvard voted to permit Calkins to attend Philosophy 20a and b during that year. It was specifically noted in the Harvard Corporation records that in accepting this "privilege" she would not become a student of the university entitled to registration.[23]

Two days after the decision, James wrote to Calkins welcoming her into his seminar:

> My students 4 in number seem of divergent tendencies and I don't know just what will come of the course. Having published my two rather fat tomes, I shan't lecture, but the thing will probably resolve itself into advice and possibly some experimentation. Our evening meetings have been provisionally fixed for Thursdays at 7:15. Will you please come if you can next Thursday at seven so as to have a little talk in advance, or rather come at 1/2 past six and take tea.[24]

Thus began Calkins's graduate career in psychology at Harvard. She attended James's seminar which turned into a tête-à-tête as the other members dropped away early in the term leaving only her and James at either side of a library fire with his "two rather fat tomes." Calkins recalled, "The *Principles of Psychology* was warm from the press; and my absorbed study of those brilliant, erudite, and provocative volumes, as interpreted by their writer, was my introduction to psychology."[25]

In addition to attending James's and Royce's seminars during her year of preparation in psychology, Calkins also arranged to do some work as a private school pupil with E. C. Sanford at Clark University. She undertook some dream research with him, the results of which he reported at the first annual meeting of the American Psychological Association in 1892.[26]

In the fall of 1891, Calkins returned to Wellesley College as an instructor in psychology and taught a new offering in the Department of Philosophy: psychology approached from the physiological standpoint. The college catalog for the year 1891–1892 included a description of the new psychological laboratory:

> Students in Physiological Psychology have the use of models and plates of the brain, dissecting instruments, a pressure balance, a color wheel, a perimeter, a Wheatstone stereoscope, apparatus for experiments in simultaneous contrast, reaction-times apparatus, a stopwatch, and other simple appliances. Required experiments are chiefly in sensation, space perception, and reaction-times, sensational and intellectual.[27]

The report of the president of the college for that year indicated that fifty-four students had elected the new physiological psychology course. It also noted that Calkins had expressed "her indebtedness to Dr. Sanford of Clark University for invaluable counsel, and for personal superintendence of the construction of part of the apparatus" for the new psychological laboratory.[28]

During this undoubtedly strenuous year of teaching and setting up a laboratory, Calkins also actively sought a place where she could undertake further study in psychology. Letters from Sanford, Royce, and James, all written in February 1892, offered her advice in this matter. The contents of the letters suggest that she was considering, among other possibilities, studying under Frank Angell at Cornell and Hugo Münsterberg at Freiburg.

Sanford wrote:

> Assuming . . . that you are going to study next year, should it be Cornell or Europe? I say Europe. Why? Because . . . a European Ph[.]D[.] will do you more good I believe than an American one, I don't think that my J.[ohns]H.[opki]N.[s] Ph[.]D[.] is quite so impressive to the average person in authority as a Leipzig one would be. . . . Also I saw when at Harvard the other day a picture of Münsterberg and his seminary—among the rest a lady! I infer that she was a student, and think there is ground for the inference. . . . They are beginning to wake up over there, the more shame to John Hopkins and Clark—an ineffable shame that you can't get a fellowship in your own country in institutions given to advanced work.[29]

Royce, on the other hand, advised her to take her next year at Cornell if she could get a fellowship. He urged her not to postpone further study too long, issuing the following caution: "One who teaches too steadily before reaching the studious maturity which one's ideals had planned, becomes too easily content with one's limitations."[30]

From James came a plea to delay as long as possible the decision of where to undertake further study. He affirmed that Münsterberg had had a woman student the previous year and advised Calkins to wait a bit longer before making a decision with the reassurance that more information would soon become available about the relative advantages of the various schools.[31] At the end of April 1892, a letter from James to Calkins announced that Münsterberg would be coming to Harvard the following academic year.[32]

Another petition was submitted to Harvard, this time by Calkins in her own behalf, and was approved on 9 January 1893. Calkins was advised that she would be welcome to attend the instruction of Professor Münsterberg in his laboratory as his guest but not as a registered student of the university.[33] Calkins recalled her plans to study with Münsterberg as follows: "In the very fall of 1892, when I had planned to ask admission to his Freiburg Laboratory, he came instead to Harvard; and for parts of three years I worked under his inspiring direction in the old Psychology Laboratory of Dane Hall."[34] During 1893 and the first half of 1894, Calkins taught at Wellesley College and worked in Münsterberg's laboratory. In the academic year 1894–1895, she went on leave from the college to devote herself full time to the work at Harvard.

From 1892 on, Calkins was a steady contributor to the psychological literature. In that year she published her first paper on association, which grew out of the seminar she took with James.[35] Also in 1892, there appeared a description of the new course in experimental psychology at Wellesley College.[36] In 1893, her work with Sanford on dreams[37] and research on mental forms[38] done in the Wellesley laboratory were reported. The first of a series of papers communicating minor studies undertaken in the Wellesley laboratory appeared in

21

LAUREL FURUMOTO
Mary Whiton Calkins
(1863–1930)
Fourteenth President
of the American
Psychological
Association

1894.[39] Also published in that year was the first of a series of reports on work she had done in Münsterberg's laboratory: experiments on association using the paired-associate technique which she had invented.[40]

In October 1894, Münsterberg wrote to the president and fellows of Harvard College inquiring if there were a chance that Calkins might be admitted as a candidate for the Ph.D. The following is an excerpt from his letter:

> With regard to her ability, I may say that she is the strongest student of all who have worked in the laboratory in these three years. Her publications and her work here do not let any doubt to me that she is superior also to all candidates of the philosophical Ph.D. during the last years. More than that: she is surely one of the strongest professors of psychology in this country. . . . the Harvard Ph.D. attached to the name of Mary W. Calkins would mean not only a well deserved honor for her, but above all an honor for the philosophical department of Harvard University.[41]

The Harvard Corporation records for 29 October 1894 note that Münsterberg's request was considered and refused.[42]

In the spring of 1895, Calkins presented her thesis—"An Experimental Research on the Association of Ideas"—to the Department of Philosophy at Harvard. The thesis was approved by the members of the department, and after conducting an informal and unauthorized Ph.D. examination of the candidate, her examiners forwarded a communication to the president and fellows of Harvard College. It read in part: "At the examination, held May 28, 1895, before Professors Palmer, James, Royce, Münsterberg, Harris, and Dr. Santayana it was unanimously voted that Miss Calkins satisfied all the customary requirements for the degree."[43] The communication was duly noted in the Harvard Corporation records for 10 June 1895.[44]

Her graduate studies successfully accomplished, except for the lack of a degree, Calkins returned to Wellesley College in the autumn of 1895 as Associate Professor of Psychology and Philosophy. Over the next five years there appeared in the psychological literature a steady stream of studies from the Wellesley College psychological laboratory communicated by Calkins.[45]

One of these reports is of more than usual interest because it appears to have touched off the first controversy over sex differences in cognitive processes in the psychological literature.[46] In 1891, Joseph Jastrow reported the results of a study he had conducted with female and male college students in his psychology class at the University of Wisconsin. He instructed his students to write out 100 words as rapidly as possible, and he then analyzed the lists thus produced. Among his conclusions were the following: ". . . the feminine traits revealed by this study are an attention to the immediate surroundings, to the finished product, to the ornamental, the individual, and the concrete; while the masculine preference is for the more remote, the constructive, the useful, the general, and the abstract."[47]

An attempted replication of Jastrow's study by one of Calkins's students produced results interpreted as contradictory to his. Following the publication of this study, there was a heated exchange between Calkins[48] and Jastrow[49] with Jastrow criticizing the replication for its inexactness and Calkins commenting on the impossibility of making valid distinctions between masculine and feminine intellect when one cannot eliminate the effect of the environment.

During this period Calkins also published two more papers reporting the results of her work on association in Münsterberg's laboratory, including the work that would have been her doctoral thesis.[50] In 1900 there appeared the first of a series of papers in which she developed her ideas about psychology as a science of self,[51] and the following year her first book, *An Introduction to Psychology*,[52] was published. . . .

23

LAUREL FURUMOTO
Mary Whiton Calkins
(1863–1930)
Fourteenth President
of the American
Psychological
Association

Calkins published prolifically in both psychology and philosophy; four books and well over a hundred papers are divided fairly evenly between the two disciplines. Her work in psychology tends to cluster in the first half of her career, while her concern with philosophy was a continuing thread that became increasingly prominent after the last of her experimentally based work was published in 1900. This shift in emphasis is reflected in her election to the presidencies of the American Psychological Association in 1905 and the American Philosophical Association in 1918.

It is generally acknowledged that Calkins's philosophical thinking, in the idealist tradition, was strongly influenced by her teacher Josiah Royce. She was a proponent of personalism, "that philosophy which makes personality the ultimate reality in the universe."[60] It is worth noting that all of her work in philosophy as well as psychology came to center around the importance of self.

In 1929, after a teaching career spanning forty-two years, Calkins retired from Wellesley College. It was said that she planned to devote her time to writing and enjoying the companionship of her mother, but less than one year later she was dead, the victim of an inoperable cancer. She left behind a prodigious amount of published work in psychology and philosophy and a carefully thought out system of self-psychology. Aside from the presidency of APA, the eminence that Calkins achieved as a psychologist can be judged by the fact that when in 1903 a list of fifty leading psychologists in the United States was arranged in order of distinction, Calkins ranked twelfth on the list.[61] She had been the recipient of many academic and professional honors, but one which she believed she had rightly earned—the Harvard Ph.D.—perpetually eluded her grasp.

More than three decades after Münsterberg and the other members of her thesis committee had failed in their efforts to persuade Harvard to grant Calkins the Ph.D., a group of her colleagues renewed the effort. In 1927, Christian A. Ruckmick, a psychologist at the University of Iowa who had become acquainted with Calkins when he was teaching for a short time in the department at Wellesley, sent a letter to President Abbot Lowell of Harvard containing a petition on behalf of Calkins signed by a number of psychologists and philosophers who were Harvard graduates.[62]

The petition outlined Calkins's career at Harvard and commented on "her subsequent achievements as a constructive psychologist and philosopher of outstanding international reputation." It concluded by recommending that Harvard grant her the degree of doctor of philosophy and was signed by a group of thirteen Harvard graduates, many of whom were professors of psychology at prestigious institutions. Among the names on the list were R. S. Woodworth, R. M. Yerkes, and E. L. Thorndike. Less than two weeks after Ruckmick had mailed the petition to Harvard, Lowell's secretary sent him a reply indicating that the recommendation had been considered, and it was decided "that there was no adequate reason" for granting Calkins the degree.[63]

Although this belated attempt to secure the Harvard Ph.D. for Calkins had failed, the attempt itself was an impressive tribute to her reputation as a scholar. The petition with its list of signatures, many of acknowledged leaders in the field of psychology, must have provided some consolation to Calkins. For, unquestionably, to be the inspiration for a testimonial of this kind is a far rarer and more remarkable honor than to be the recipient of a Harvard Ph.D.

The author wishes to thank the family of Mary W. Calkins for their generosity in making available to her letters, journals, and scrapbooks which provided much of the documentation for this paper. She also wishes to thank Elizabeth S. Goodman, State University College, Fredonia, N.Y., for helpful comments on an earlier draft of this paper. The assistance of the Amherst College Archives, the Boston Public Library, the Harvard University Archives, the Radcliffe College Archives, the Smith College Archives, and the Wellesley College Archives in providing background information and documentation is gratefully acknowledged. Permission from Alexander R. James is also gratefully acknowledged to reprint portions of the letters of William James.

Notes

1. Minutes of the meeting of the Radcliffe Academic Board, 10 April 1902. Radcliffe College Archives, Cambridge, Mass.
2. Calkins to Irwin, 30 May 1902, Radcliffe College Archives.
3. Mary W. Calkins, in *History of Psychology in Autobiography*, ed. C. Murchison (Worcester, Mass.: Clark University Press, 1930), 1: 31–62.
4. Raymond Calkins, "Mary Whiton Calkins," in *In Memoriam: Mary Whiton Calkins (1863–1930)* (Boston: Merrymount Press, 1931), pp. 1–19.
5. Grosvenor Calkins, "Notes from Father's Log."
6. Ibid.
7. Raymond Calkins, "Volume 1 (1869–1890)."
8. Ibid.
9. R. Calkins, "Mary Whiton Calkins," p. 7.
10. Ibid., p. 8.
11. Calkins to Charles Edward Garman, 22 February 1890, Amherst College Archives, Amherst, Mass.
12. H. N. Gardiner to Calkins, 1 May 1890.
13. M. L. Perrin to Calkins, 12 July 1890.
14. Dewey to Calkins, 28 May 1890.
15. Cutler to Calkins, 28 May 1890.
16. Cutler to Calkins, 5 June 1890.
17. Cutler to Calkins, 28 May 1890.
18. Dewey to Calkins, 28 May 1890.
19. James to Calkins, 24 May 1890.
20. James to Calkins, 29 May 1890.
21. James to Calkins, 30 July 1890.
22. Wolcott Calkins, Petition to the Corporation of Harvard University, 1 July 1890, Harvard University Archives, Cambridge, Mass.
23. Corporation Records, 1 October 1890, Harvard University Archives.
24. James to Calkins, 3 October 1890.
25. Calkins, *History of Psychology in Autobiography*, p. 31.
26. Michael M. Sokal, "APA's First Publication: Proceedings of the American Psychological Association, 1892–1893," *American Psychologist* 28 (1973): 277–292.
27. "Calendar of Wellesley College (1891–1892)," Wellesley College Archives, Wellesley, Mass.

28. Helen A. Shafer, "President's Report," (1892), Wellesley College Archives.
29. Sanford to Calkins, 16 February 1892.
30. Royce to Calkins, 17 February 1892.
31. James to Calkins, 14 February 1892.
32. James to Calkins, 29 April 1892.
33. Eliot to Calkins, 9 January 1893.
34. Calkins, *History of Psychology in Autobiography*, p. 33.
35. Mary W. Calkins, "A Suggested Classification of Cases of Association," *Philosophical Review* 1 (1892): 389–402.
36. Mary W. Calkins, "Experimental Psychology at Wellesley College," *American Journal of Psychology* 5 (1892): 260–271.
37. Mary W. Calkins, "Statistics of Dreams," *American Journal of Psychology* 5 (1893): 311–343.
38. Mary W. Calkins, "A Statistical Study of Pseudo-chromesthesia and Mental Forms," *American Journal of Psychology* 5 (1893): 439–464.
39. Mary W. Calkins, "Wellesley College Psychological Studies," *Educational Review* 8 (1894): 269–286.
40. Mary W. Calkins, "Association I." *Psychological Review* 1 (1894): 476–483.
41. Münsterberg to President and Fellows of Harvard College. 23 October 1894, Harvard University Archives.
42. Corporation Records, 29 October 1894, Harvard University Archives.
43. Royce, Palmer, James, Santayana, Münsterberg, and Harris to President and Fellows of Harvard College, 29 May 1895, Harvard University Archives.
44. Corporation Records, 10 June 1895, Harvard University Archives.
45. Mary W. Calkins, "Minor Studies from the Psychological Laboratory of Wellesley College," *American Journal of Psychology* 7 (1895): 86–107; idem, "Wellesley College Psychological Studies," *Pedogogical Seminary* 3 (1895): 319–341; idem, "Wellesley College Psychological Studies," *Psychological Review* 2 (1895): 363–367; idem, "Minor Studies from the Psychological Laboratory of Wellesley College," *American Journal of Psychology* 7 (1896): 405–411; idem, "Short Studies in Memory and Association from the Wellesley Laboratory," *Psychological Review* 5 (1898): 451–462; idem, "Wellesley College Psychological Studies," ibid. 7 (1900): 580–591.
46. Calkins, "Wellesley College Psychological Studies," *Psychological Review,* 1895.
47. Joseph Jastrow, "A Study in Mental Statistics," *New Review* 5 (1891): 559–568.
48. Mary W. Calkins, "Community of Ideas of Men and Women," *Psychological Review* 3 (1896): 426–430.
49. Joseph Jastrow, "Community of Ideas of Men and Women," *Psychological Review* 3 (1896): 68–71.
50. Mary W. Calkins, "Association: An Essay Analytic and Experimental," *Psychological Review Monograph Supplement Number 2* (1896): 1–56; idem, "Association II," *Psychological Review* 3 (1896): 32–49.
51. Mary W. Calkins, "Psychology as Science of Selves," *Philosophical Review* 9 (1900): 490–501.
52. Mary W. Calkins, *An Introduction to Psychology* (New York: Macmillan, 1901).

• • •

60. E. S. Brightman, "Mary Whiton Calkins: Her Place in Philosophy," in *In Memoriam,* p. 45.
61. James McKeen Cattell and Jacques Cattell, eds. *American Men of Science: A Biographical Directory*, 5th ed. (New York: Science Press, 1933).
62. Ruckmick to Lowell, 4 June 1927.
63. F. W. Hunnewell to Ruckmick, 16 June 1927.

LAUREL FURUMOTO
Mary Whiton Calkins
(1863–1930)
Fourteenth President
of the American
Psychological
Association

Naomi Weisstein

"How can a little girl like you teach a great big class of men?" the Chairman Said, and Other Adventures of a Woman in Science

I am an experimental psychologist. I do research in vision. The profession has for a long time considered this activity, on the part of one of my sex, to be an outrageous violation of the social order and against all the laws of nature. Yet at the time I entered graduate school in the early sixties, I was unaware of this. I was remarkably naive. Stupid, you might say. Anybody can be president, no? So, anybody can be a scientist. Weisstein in Wonderland. I had to discover that what I wanted to do constituted unseemly social deviance. It was a discovery I was not prepared for: Weisstein is dragged, kicking and screaming, out of Wonderland and into Plunderland. Or Blunderland, at the very least.

What made me want to become a scientist in the first place? The trouble may have started with *Microbe Hunters*,[1] de Kruif's book about the early bacteriologists. I remember reading about Leeuwenhoek's discovery of organisms too small to be seen with the naked eye. When he told the Royal Society about this, most of them thought he was crazy. He told them he wasn't. The "wretched beasties" were there, he insisted; one could see them unmistakably through the lenses he had so carefully made. It was very important to me that he could reply that he had his evidence: evidence became a hero of mine.

It may have been then that I decided that *I* was going to become a scientist, too. I was going to explore the world and discover its wonders. I was going to understand the brain in a better and more complete way than it had been understood before. If anyone questioned me, I would have my evidence. Evidence and reason: my heroes and my guides. I might add that my sense of ecstatic exploration when reading *Microbe Hunters* has never left me through all the years I have struggled to be a scientist.

As I mentioned, I was not prepared for the discovery that women were not welcome in science, primarily because nobody had told me. In fact, I was supported in thinking—even encouraged to think—that my aspirations were perfectly legitimate. I graduated from the Bronx High School of Science in New

[1]Paul de Kruif, *Microbe Hunters* (New York: Harcourt, Brace & World, 1926).

York City where gender did not enter very much into intellectual pursuits; the place was a nightmare for everybody. We were all, boys and girls alike, equal contestants; all of us were competing for that thousandth of a percentage point in our grade average that would allow entry into one of those high-class out-of-town schools, where we could go, get smart, and lose our New York accents.

I ended up at Wellesley, and this further retarded my discovery that women were supposed to be stupid and incompetent: the women faculty at Wellesley were brilliant. (I learned later on that they were at Wellesley because the schools that had graduated them,—the "very best" schools where you were taught to do the very best research—couldn't, or didn't care to, place them in similar schools, where they could continue their research.) So they are our brilliant unknowns, unable to do research because they labor under enormous teaching loads, unable to obtain the minimal support necessary for scholarship—graduate students, facilities, communication with colleagues. Whereas I was ignorant then about the lot of women in the academy, others at Wellesley knew what it was like. Deans from an earlier, more conscious feminist era would tell me that I was lucky to be at a women's college where I could discover what I was good at and do it. They told me that women in a man's world were in for a rough time. They told me to watch out when I went on to graduate school. They said that men would not like my competing with them. I did not listen to the deans, however; or, when I did listen, I thought what they were telling me might have been true in the nineteenth century, but not then, in the late fifties.

So my discovery that women were not welcome in psychology began when I got to Harvard, on the first day of class. That day, the entering graduate students had been invited to lunch with one of the star professors in the department. After lunch, he leaned back in his chair, lit his pipe, began to puff, and announced: "Women don't belong in graduate school."

The male graduate students, as if by prearranged signal, then leaned back in their chairs, puffed on their newly bought pipes, nodded, and assented: "Yeah."

"Yeah," said the male graduate students. "No man is going to want you. No man wants a woman who is more intelligent than he is. Of course, that's not a real possibility, but just in case. You are out of your *natural* roles; you are no longer feminine."

My mouth dropped open, and my big blue eyes (they have since changed back to brown) went wide as saucers. An initiation ceremony, I thought. Very funny. Tomorrow, for sure, the male graduate students will get it.

But the male graduate students never were told that they didn't belong. They rapidly became trusted junior partners in the great research firms at Harvard. They were carefully nurtured, groomed, and run. Before long, they would take up the white man's burden and expand the empire. But for me and for the other women in my class, it was different. We were shut out of these plans; we were *shown* we didn't belong. For instance, even though I was first in my class, when I wanted to do my dissertation research, I couldn't get access to the necessary equipment. The excuse was that I might break the equipment. This was certainly true. The equipment was eminently breakable. The male graduate students working with it broke it every week; I didn't expect to be any different.

27

NAOMI WEISSTEIN
"How can a little girl
like you teach a great
big class of men?"

I was determined to collect my data. I had to see how the experiment I proposed would turn out. If Harvard wouldn't let me use its equipment, maybe Yale would. I moved to New Haven, collected my data at Yale, returned to Harvard, and was awarded my Ph.D. in 1964, and afterward could not get an academic job. I had graduated Phi Beta Kappa from Wellesley, had obtained my Ph.D. in psychology at Harvard in two and one half years, ranked first in my graduate class, and I couldn't get a job. Yet most universities were expanding in 1964, and jobs were everywhere. But at the places where I was being considered for jobs they were asking me questions like—

"How can a little girl like you teach a great big class of men?" At that time, still unaware of how serious the situation was, I replied, "Beats me. I guess I must have a talent."

and

"Who did your research for you?" This last was from a famous faculty liberal at another school, who then put what I assume was a fatherly hand on my knee and said in a tone of deep concern, "You ought to get married."

Meanwhile, I was hanging on by means of a National Science Foundation postdoctoral fellowship in mathematical biology, at the University of Chicago, and attempting to do some research. Prior to my second postdoctoral year, the University of Chicago began negotiations with me for something like a real job: an instructorship jointly in the undergraduate college and the psychology department. The negotiations appeared to be proceeding in good faith, so I wrote to Washington and informed them that I would not be taking my second postdoctoral year. Then, ten days before classes began, when that option as well as any others I might have taken had been closed, the person responsible for the negotiations called to tell me that, because of a nepotism rule—my husband taught history at the University of Chicago—I would not be hired as a regular faculty member. If I wanted to, I could be appointed lecturer, teaching general education courses in the college; there was no possibility of an appointment in psychology. The lectureship paid very little for a lot of work, and I would be teaching material unconnected with my research. Furthermore, a university rule stipulated that lecturers (because their position in the university was so insecure) could not apply for research grants. He concluded by asking me whether I was willing to take the job; ten days before the beginning of classes, he asked me whether I was willing to take the only option still available to me.

I took the job, and "sat in," so to speak, in the office of another dean, until he waived the restriction on applying for research grants. Acknowledging my presence, he told a colleague: "This is Naomi Weisstein. She hates men."

I had simply been telling him that women are considered unproductive precisely because universities do their best to keep women unproductive through such procedures as the selective application of the nepotism rule. I had also asked this dean whether I could read through the provisions of the rule. He replied that the nepotism rule was informal, not a written statute—flexibility being necessary in its application. Later, a nepotism committee set up partly in response to my protest agreed that the rule should stay precisely as it was: that it was a good idea, should not be written out, and should be applied selectively.

Lecturers at major universities are generally women. They are generally married to men who teach at these major universities. And they generally labor under conditions which seem almost designed to show them that they don't belong. In many places, they are not granted faculty library privileges; in my case, I had to get a note from the secretary each time I wanted to take a book out for an extended period. Lecturers' classrooms are continually changed; at least once a month, I would go to my assigned classroom only to find a note pinned to the door instructing me and my class to go elsewhere: down the hall, across the campus, out to Gary, Indiana.

In the winter of my first year, notices were distributed to all those teaching the courses I was teaching, announcing a meeting to discuss the next year's syllabus. I didn't receive the notice. As I was to learn shortly, this is the customary way a profession that prides itself on its civility and genteel traditions indicates to lecturers and other "nuisance personnel" that they're fired: they simply don't inform them about what's going on. I inquired further. Yes, my research and teaching had been "evaluated" (after five months: surely enough time), and they had decided to "let me go" (a brilliant euphemism). Of course, the decision had nothing to do with my questioning the nepotism rules and explaining to deans why women are thought unproductive.

I convinced them to "let me stay" another year. I don't know to this day why they changed their minds. Perhaps they changed their minds because it looked like I was going to receive the research grant for which I had applied, bringing in money not only for me, but for the university as well. A little while later, Loyola University in Chicago offered me a job.

So I left the University of Chicago. I was awarded the research grant and found the Psychology Department at Loyola at first very supportive. The chairman, Ron Walker, was especially helpful and especially enlightened about women at a time when few academic men were. I was on my way, right? Not exactly. There is a big difference between a place like Loyola and a place with a heavy commitment to research—any large state university, for example—a difference that no amount of good will on the part of an individual chairman could cancel out. The Psychology Department was one of the few active departments at Loyola. The other kinds of support one needs to do experimental psychology—machine and electrical shops, physics and electrical engineering departments, technicians, a large computer—were either not available or were available at that time only in primitive form.

When you are a woman at an "unknown" place, you are considered out of the running. It was hard for me to keep my career from "shriveling like a raisin" (as an erstwhile colleague predicted it would). I was completely isolated. I did not have access to the normal channels of communication, debate, and exchange in the profession—those informal networks where you get the news, the comment and the criticism, the latest reports of what is going on. I sent my manuscripts to various people for comment and criticism before sending them off to journals; few replied. I asked others working in my field to send me their prepublication drafts; even fewer responded. Nobody outside Loyola informed me about special meetings in my area of psychology, and few inside Loyola knew about them. Given the snobbery rife in academic circles (which has eased lately since jobs are much harder to find and thus even "outstanding" young male graduates from the "best" schools may now be found at places formerly beneath their condescension), my being at Loyola almost automatically disqualified me from the serious attention of professional colleagues.

The "inner reaches" of the profession, from which I had been exiled, are not just metaphorical and intangible. For instance, I am aware of two secret societies of experimental psychologists in which fifty or so of the "really excellent" young scientists get together regularly to make themselves better scientists. The ostensible purpose of these societies is to allow these "best and brightest" young psychologists to get together to discuss and criticize each other's work; they also function, of course, to define who is excellent and who is not, and to help those defined as excellent to remain so, by providing them with information to which "outsiders" in the profession will not have access until much later (if at all).

But the intangibles are there as well. Women are treated in ways men hardly ever experience. Let me give you one stunning example. I wrote up an experiment I thought was really good and its results, which were fascinating, and sent the paper to a journal editor whose interests I knew to be close to what was reported in my paper. The editor replied that there were some control conditions that should be run, and some methodological loose ends, so they couldn't publish the paper. Fair enough. He went on to say that they had much better equipment over there, and they would like to test my ideas themselves. Would I mind? I wrote them back, told them I thought it was a bit unusual, asked if they were suggesting a collaboration, and concluded by saying that I would be most happy to visit with them and collaborate on my experiment. The editor replied with a nasty letter explaining to me that by suggesting that they test my ideas themselves, they had merely been trying to help me. If I didn't want their help in this way, they certainly didn't want mine, that is, they had had no intention of suggesting a collaboration.

In other words, what they meant by "did I mind" was: Did I mind if they took my idea and did the experiment themselves? As we know, instances of taking someone else's idea and pretending it's your own are not at all uncommon in science. The striking thing about this exchange, however, was that the editor was arrogant enough, and assumed that I would be submissive enough, so that he could openly ask me whether I would agree to this arrangement. Would I mind? No, of course not. Women are joyful altruists. We are happy to give of ourselves. After all, how many good ideas do you get in your lifetime? One? Two? Why not give them away?

Generally, the justification for treating women in such disgraceful ways is simply that they are women. Let me give another spectacular example. I was promised the use of a small digital laboratory computer, which was to be purchased on a grant. The funds from the grant would become available if a certain job position entailing administration of this grant could be filled. I was part of the group which considered the candidates and which recommended appointing a particular individual. During the discussions of future directions of this individual's work, it was agreed that he would of course share the computer with me. He was hired, bought the computer, and refused me access to it. I offered to put in money for peripherals which would make the system faster and easier for both of us to work with, but this didn't sway him. As justification for his conduct, the man confessed to the chairman that he simply couldn't share the computer with me: he has difficulty working with women. To back this up, he indicated that he'd been "burned twice." Although the chairman had previously been very helpful and not bothered in the least about women, he accepted that statement as an explanation. Difficulty in working with women was not a problem this man should work out. It was *my* problem. Colleagues thought no worse of him for this problem; it might even have raised him in their estimation. He obtained tenure quickly, and retains an influential voice in the department. Yet if a woman comes to *any* chairman of *any* department and confesses that she has difficulty working with men, she is thought pathological.

What this meant for me at the time was that my research was in jeopardy. There were experimental conditions I needed to run that simply could not be done without a computer. So there I was, doing research with stone-age equipment, trying to get by with wonder-woman reflexes and a flashlight, while a few floors below, my colleague was happily operating "his" computer. It's as if we women are in a totally rigged race. A lot of men are driving souped-up, low-slung racing cars, and we're running as fast as we can in tennis shoes we managed to salvage from a local garage sale.

Perhaps the most painful of the appalling working conditions for women in science is the peculiar kind of social-sexual assault women sustain. Let me illustrate with a letter to *Chemical and Engineering News* from a research chemist named McGauley:

> There are differences between men and women . . . just one of these differences is a decided gap in leadership potential and ability . . . this is no reflection upon intelligence, experience, or sincerity. Evolution made it that way. . . . Then consider the problems that can arise if the potential employee, Dr. Y (a woman) [*sic*: he could at least get his chromosomes straight] will be expected to take an occasional business trip with Dr. X. . . . Could it be that the guys in shipping and receiving will not take too kindly to the lone Miss Y?[2]

Now what is being said here, very simply, and to paraphrase the Bible, is that women are trouble. And by trouble, McGauley means sexual trouble. Moreover, somehow, someway, it is our fault. *We* are provoking the guys in shipping and receiving. Women are universally assigned by men, first—no matter who the women are or what they have in mind—to sexual categories. Then, we are accused by men of taking their minds away from work. When feminists say that women are treated as sex objects, we are compressing into a single, perhaps rhetorical phrase, an enormous area of discomfort, pain, harassment, and humiliation.

This harassment is especially clear at conventions. Scientific meetings, conferences, and conventions are harassing and humiliating for women because women, by and large, cannot have male colleagues. Conversations, social relations, invitations to lunch, and the like are generally viewed as sexual, not professional, encounters if a woman participates in them. It does not cross many men's minds that a woman's motivation may be entirely professional.

I have been at too many professional meetings where the "joke" slide was a woman's body, dressed or undressed. A woman in a bikini is a favorite with past and perhaps present presidents of psychological associations. Hake showed such a slide in his presidential address to the Midwestern Psychological Association, and Harlow, past president of the American Psychological As-

[2]T. J. McGauley, letter to *Chemical and Engineering News*, December 7, 1970, pp. 8–9.

sociation, has a whole set of such slides, which he shows at the various collo-quia to which he is invited. This business of making jokes at women's bodies constitutes a primary social-sexual assault. The ensuing raucous laughter expresses the shared understanding of what is assumed to be women's primary function—to which we can always be reduced. Showing pictures of nude and sexy women insults us: it puts us in our place. You may think you are a scientist, it is saying, but what you really are is an object for our pleasure and amusement. Don't forget it.

I could continue recounting the horrors, as could almost any woman who is in science or who has ever been in science, but I want to stop now and ask: What conclusions can we draw from my experience? What does it all add up to?

Perhaps we should conclude that persistence will finally win out. Or that life is hard, but cheerful struggle and a "sense of humor" may make it bearable. Or perhaps we should search back through my family, and find my domineering mother and passive father or my domineering father and passive mother, to explain my persistence. Perhaps, but all these conclusions are beside the point. The point is that none of us should have to face this kind of offense. The point is that we must change this man's world and this man's science.

How will other women do better? One of the dangers of this kind of narrative is that it may validate the punishment as it singles out the few survivors. The lesson appears to be that those (and only those) with extraordinary strength will survive. This is not the way I see it. Many have had extraordinary strength and have *not* survived.

Much of the explanation for my professional survival has to do with the emergence and growth of the women's movement. I am an experimental psychologist, a scientist. I am also a feminist. I am a feminist because I have seen my life and the lives of women I know harassed, dismissed, damaged, destroyed. I am a feminist because without others I can do little to stop the outrage. Without a political and social movement of which I am a part—without feminism—my determination and persistence, my clever retorts, my hours of patient explanation, my years of exhortation amount to little. If the scientific world has changed since I entered it, it is not because I managed to become an established psychologist within it. Rather, it is because a women's movement came along to change its character. It is true that as a member of that movement, I have acted to change the character of the scientific world. But without the movement, none of my actions would have brought about change. And now, as the strength of the women's movement ebbs, the old horrors are returning. This must not happen.

Science, knowledge, the search for fundamental understanding is part of our humanity. It is an endeavor that seems to give us some glimpse of what we might be and what we might do in a better world. To deny us the right to do science is to deny us our humanity. We shall not have our humanity denied.

Emmy Noether:
She Did Einstein's Math

It was 1915. For years young mathematicians around the world had been hearing the same advice from their mentors: "Pack your suitcase and take yourself to Göttingen."

I like to think of her arriving at the Göttingen train station in Germany, wearing stout shoes and a sturdy serge dress with a token bit of lace at the collar, carrying a worn satchel. A rare intelligence and singleness of purpose shone in the eyes behind her little round spectacles. Though the men who would be her colleagues sometimes dwelt more on her appearance than her skills—one described her as an energetic and very nearsighted washerwoman—she knew they needed her knowledge in their work on the general theory of relativity. Emmy Noether was determined to seize her chance.

Emmy had absorbed mathematics all her life, growing up in a swirl of discussions on algebraic functions. Her father Max was professor of mathematics at the University of Erlangen when she was born in 1882, and his close friend and colleague Paul Gordan, whom Emmy knew from early childhood as "uncle," then mentor, supervised her doctoral dissertation. Gordan's interest was in formal algebraic processes; Noether's thesis, "On Complete Systems of Invariants for Ternary Biquadratic Forms," was very much the product of his influence. The famous mathematician Hermann Weyl, her colleague, called it an "awe-inspiring piece of work"; she would later move so far beyond it that she'd dismiss it as "a jungle of formulas."

Gordan's algebra provided the initial discipline that honed her genius. In her twenties she had already published half a dozen papers and occasionally substituted for her father at lectures. By the time she moved to Göttingen she was ready to take a place beside David Hilbert and Felix Klein, two of the great mathematicians of the era who welcomed and eagerly began to work with her.

Noether's forte was invariant theory. An algebraic equation is said to be *transformed* when every x in it is replaced by y-2. A geometric figure in a plane can be transformed, too, for example, by stretching it. But some aspects of an equation or a geometric shape remain unchanged during transformation—and these *invariants* can provide extremely significant information.

Despite its name, relativity is really a theory of invariants. It is concerned largely with how physical processes such as motion will appear to observers located at different places and traveling at various speeds in various directions. Some things will look different—in the classic example, if you are sitting in the dining car of a train, the vase of flowers on your table appears to be immobile in front of you; to a worker along the tracks it flashes by. Some things will look the same to different observers, however, and it is the discussion of these particular invariants that begins the subject of relativity.

Einstein had already created his grand plan for the theory of relativity, but it had yet to be laid out in concrete mathematical form. Hilbert and Klein were interested in mathematical realizations of Einstein's ideas. Noether's skills and knowledge were crucial to progress in the area because Einstein had initially underestimated the complexity of the mathematics that would be required to express the fundamental laws of physics.

Hermann Weyl describes Göttingen University as "a great center for the passionate scientific life." Unfortunately, this was exceeded by the professors' passion for retaining an all-male faculty. Hilbert's efforts to obtain a post for Noether were met with implacable resistance, more from Göttingen's philosophers and historians than from its mathematicians. In *Hilbert* (Springer-Verlag, 1970), author Constance Reid describes his struggle:

> They argued formally: "How can it be allowed that a woman become a Privatdozent [lecturer]? She can then become a member of the University Senate. Is it permitted that a woman enter the Senate?" They argued informally: "What will our soldiers think when they return to the University and find that they are expected to learn at the feet of a woman?"

Hilbert declared in a faculty meeting: "I do not see that the sex of the candidate is an argument against her admission as Privatdozent. After all, we are a university, not a bathhouse." But his indignation was to no avail. Emmy Noether's lectures were simply announced under Hilbert's name.

I imagine her striking off on one of her "mathematical walks" through the narrow streets of Göttingen. Wild gesticulations punctuate her analysis of some abstruse point. Students cluster, chicks to her mother hen. She loves these students, pokes into their personal lives, steers them to the most fruitful research questions. As she plumps along, she tosses off ideas that will become a dissertation for this student, a seminal paper for that one, the start of a new research area and lasting fame for another. The faculty calls the recipients of this intellectual generosity "the Noether boys"; they are her family.

Perhaps it was her own upbringing in a loving, stable, and cultured family that formed her genuine goodheartedness. Weyl remembers her as "warm like a loaf of bread . . . a broad, comforting, vital warmth." All who knew her remember her essential kindness and generosity of spirit.

Still, her students cannot have had an easy time in class. Even her friend Weyl admits that her lectures were a bit erratic and enormously demanding. The problem lay in her phenomenal imagination and her habit of puzzling out brand-new solutions to problems in mid-lecture. One student remembers the day she was to teach a standard proof of a classical theorem. Just before class she brainstormed a unique proof based entirely on concepts and axioms rather than on calculations. Of course the proof wasn't entirely thought out, but the intrepid Noether planned to develop it "on her feet" as she lectured. After entering one blind alley after another (and thoroughly confusing her students), Noether, overcome with rage at the intractability of the problem, threw her chalk to the floor, stamped on it, shouted, "There, I'm forced to do it the way I don't want to!" and then calmly and flawlessly taught the traditional proof.

She was at her best only when she was free to move beyond traditional themes and present her own work in progress. Sometimes she lectured on the same topic semester after semester, probing into unsolved problems more deeply each time. To the students who could give themselves entirely to Noether's paths of thought, she was "an inspired teacher."

Noether worked for six years without pay or formal status before being appointed *Nichtbeamteter ausserordentlicher Professor,* a position whose importance is inversely related to the length of its title. It means, roughly, a "nontenured irregular faculty member." She was also given a contract to teach abstract algebra, with an extremely modest stipend.

Emmy Noether's work, like much of modern mathematics, deals with abstractions of abstractions and is not easily reduced to everyday language. She was 38 years old when her first ground-breaking work, a paper on differential operators, was published in 1920. It marked the beginning of her development of conceptual axiomatics as a powerful research tool. The goal of the axiomatic method is to clarify an area of study by splitting problems into smaller parts and stripping them of inessential features to reveal their basic underlying logic. The art lies in being able to perceive the most fruitful ways of partitioning the problems.

Noether's strengths as a mathematician lay in her ability to think in abstractions, rather than resort to concrete examples, and to visualize remote connections. She strove to simplify, purify, and unify areas of theory. Weyl was awed by her "mighty imagination." Einstein agreed, writing: "In the realm of algebra, in which the most gifted mathematicians have been busy for centuries, she discovered methods which have proved of enormous importance in the development of the present-day younger generation of mathematicians." Noether, he stated, was a "creative mathematical genius."

Noether held her modest place in the official hierarchy at Göttingen for 11 years. In 1930 her friend Hermann Weyl joined the faculty and tried to win a promotion for her: "I was ashamed to occupy such a preferred position beside her whom I knew to be my superior as a mathematician in many respects." His efforts failed. "Tradition, prejudice, external considerations weighted the balance against her scientific merits and scientific greatness, by that time denied by no one. She was without doubt the strongest center of mathematical activity at Göttingen, considering both the fertility of her scientific research program and her influence upon a large circle of pupils." Yet even her editing of Germany's scholarly journal of mathematics went officially unacknowledged.

The Göttingen school, once described as a perpetual international congress of mathematicians, was utterly destroyed by the Nazi takeover of 1933. Emmy Noether—liberal, pacifist, Jewish, woman professor—hadn't a hope of staying on, though Weyl, Hilbert, and others flooded the Ministry of Education with testimonials on her behalf. Weyl vividly recalls that "her courage, her frankness, her unconcern about her own fate . . . were in the midst of all the hatred and meanness, despair, and sorrow surrounding us, a moral solace." Finally, she left for Bryn Mawr College in the United States. And Weyl joined Einstein at the Institute for Advanced Study in Princeton, where the two welcomed Noether's visits and guest lectures.

Emmy Noether had her huge desk shipped to Bryn Mawr from Germany and settled into a joyous life of work with women students and friends. "Our lives were intertwined, like a family," says former student Grace Shover Quinn of Noether, her four graduate students, and Anna Wheeler (head of the mathematics department). "I remember many cups of tea at Emmy's apartment," says Quinn, "and of course the mathematical walks. Those walks were the bane of our lives—Emmy was rotund, with thick glasses, rather unconventional-looking, and spoke loudly and in a strange mix of English and German." Completely absorbed in a mathematical point, she would stop suddenly in mid-street, leaving her students to nudge her to the curb.

Her satisfaction with her new life was evident even to those outside the little circle. A colleague recalls: "Work was only the core of her relation to students. She looked on the world with direct friendliness and unfeigned interest, and she wanted them to do the same. Mathematical meetings at the University of Pennsylvania, at Princeton, at New York, began to watch for the little group, slowly growing, which always brought something of the freshness and buoyance of its leader."

For the first time in her life, Emmy Noether began to receive the respect and recognition due her. She was 53, and, according to Weyl, at the summit of her creative power. "Her far-reaching imagination and her technical abilities . . . had come to a perfect balance; she had eagerly set to work on new problems." No one was prepared for her sudden death on April 14, 1935, of complications following surgery.

Weyl's eulogy, delivered at Bryn Mawr shortly after her death, is a moving remembrance of her personality as well as her work. Yet, like many of his colleagues, he still seemed unable to reconcile himself to the reality of "woman" and "mathematician" in the same body. Acknowledging her evident genius, he was forced to deny her "femininity":

> It was only too easy for those who met her for the first time, or had no feeling for her creative power, to consider her queer and to make fun at her expense. She was heavy of build and loud of voice, and it was often not easy for one to get the floor in competition with her. . . . In everyday life she was most unassuming and utterly unselfish: she had a kind and friendly nature. Nevertheless she enjoyed the recognition paid her; she could answer with a bashful smile like a young girl to whom one had whispered a compliment. No one could contest that the Graces had stood by her cradle; but if we in Göttingen often chaffingly referred to her as "der Noether" [with the masculine article], it was also done with a respectful recognition of her power as a creative thinker who seemed to have broken . . . the barrier of sex.

But Weyl remains puzzled: what sort of woman was she? "Essential aspects of human life remained undeveloped in her, among them, I suppose, the erotic . . . the strongest source of emotions, raptures, desires, and sorrows, and conflicts."

I wonder about the inner life of Emmy Noether. We know nothing of her "emotions and conflicts." Even her letters are about mathematics, with only a phrase or two of personal news appended. But judging from the memories of her colleagues, she survived as woman and scholar through her generosity of spirit. Meanness, discrimination, and misogyny completely escaped her notice. As Weyl says, "she did not believe in evil—indeed it never entered her mind that it could play a role among men." From Noether we have no angry words, only the abstract beauty of her work.

MARY CRAWFORD
Emmy Noether: She Did Einstein's Math

Black and Female: Reflections on Graduate School

Searching for material to read in a class about women and race, I found an essay in *Heresies: Racism is the Issue* that fascinated me. I realized that it was one of the first written discussions of the struggles black English majors (and particularly black women) face when we study at predominately white universities. The essay, "On Becoming A Feminist Writer," is by Carole Gregory. She begins by explaining that she has been raised in racially segregated neighborhoods but that no one had ever really explained "white racism or white male sexism." Psychically, she was not prepared to confront head-on these aspects of social reality, yet they were made visible as soon as she registered for classes:

> Chewing on a brown pipe, a white professor said, "English departments do not hire Negroes or women!" Like a guillotine, his voice sought to take my head off. Racism in my hometown was an economic code of etiquette which stifled Negroes and women.
>
> "If you are supposed to explain these courses, that's all I want," I answered. Yet I wanted to kill this man. Only my conditioning as a female kept me from striking his volcanic red face. My murderous impulses were raging.

Her essay chronicles her struggles to pursue a discipline which interests her without allowing racism or sexism to defeat and destroy her intellectual curiosity, her desire to teach. The words of this white male American Literature professor echo in her mind years later when she finds employment difficult, when she confronts the reality that black university teachers of English are rare. Although she is writing in 1982, she concludes her essay with the comment:

> Many years ago, an American literature professor had cursed the destiny of "Negroes and women." There was truth in his ugly words. Have you ever had a Black woman for an English teacher in the North? Few of us are able to earn a living. For the past few years, I have worked as an adjunct in English. Teaching brings me great satisfaction; starving does not. . . . I still remember the red

color of the face which said, "English departments do not hire Negroes or women." Can women change this indictment? These are the fragments I add to my journal.

Reading Carole Gregory's essay, I recalled that in all my years of studying in English department classes, I had never been taught by a black woman. In my years of teaching, I have encountered students both in English classes and other disciplines who have never been taught by black women. Raised in segregated schools until my sophomore year of high school, I had wonderful black women teachers as role models. It never occurred to me that I would not find them in university classrooms. Yet I studied at four universities—Stanford, University of Wisconsin, University of Southern California, and the University of California, Santa Cruz—and I did not once have the opportunity to study with a black woman English professor. They were never members of the faculty. I considered myself lucky to study with one black male professor at Stanford who was visiting and another at the University of Southern California even though both were reluctant to support and encourage black female students. Despite their sexism and internalized racism, I appreciated them as teachers and felt they affirmed that black scholars could teach literature, could work in English departments. They offered a degree of support and affirmation, however relative, that countered the intense racism and sexism of many white professors.

Changing hiring practices have meant that there are increasingly more black professors in predominately white universities, but their presence only mediates in a minor way the racism and sexism of white professors. During my graduate school years, I dreaded talking face-to-face with white professors, especially white males. I had not developed this dread as an undergraduate because there it was simply assumed that black students, and particularly black female students, were not bright enough to make it in graduate school. While these racist and sexist opinions were rarely directly stated, the message was conveyed through various humiliations that were aimed at shaming students, at breaking our spirit. We were terrorized. As an undergraduate, I carefully avoided those professors who made it clear that the presence of any black students in their classes was not desired. Unlike Carole Gregory's first encounter, they did not make direct racist statements. Instead, they communicated their message in subtle ways—forgetting to call your name when reading the roll, avoiding looking at you, pretending they do not hear you when you speak, and at times ignoring you altogether.

The first time this happened to me I was puzzled and frightened. It was clear to me and all the other white students that the professor, a white male, was directing aggressive mistreatment solely at me. These other students shared with me that it was not likely that I would pass the class no matter how good my work, that the professor would find something wrong with it. They never suggested that this treatment was informed by racism and sexism; it was just that the professor had for whatever "unapparent" reason decided to dislike me. Of course, there were rare occasions when taking a course meant so much to me that I tried to confront racism, to talk with the professor; and there were required courses. Whenever I tried to talk with professors about racism, they always denied any culpability. Often I was told, "I don't even notice that you are black."

In graduate school, it was especially hard to choose courses that would not be taught by professors who were quite racist. Even though one could resist by naming the problem and confronting the person, it was rarely possible to find anyone who could take such accusations seriously. Individual white professors were supported by white-supremacist institutions, by racist colleagues, by hierarchies that placed the word of the professor above that of the student. When I would tell the more supportive professors about racist comments that were said behind closed doors, during office hours, there would always be an expression of disbelief, surprise, and suspicion about the accuracy of what I was reporting. Mostly they listened because they felt it was their liberal duty to do so. Their disbelief, their refusal to take responsibility for white racism made it impossible for them to show authentic concern or help. One professor of 18th century literature by white writers invited me to his office to tell me that he would personally see to it that I would never receive a graduate degree. I, like many other students in the class, had written a paper in a style that he disapproved of, yet only I was given this response. It was often in the very areas of British and American literature where racism abounds in the texts studied that I would encounter racist individuals.

Gradually, I began to shift my interest in early American literature to more modern and contemporary works. This shift was influenced greatly by an encounter with a white male professor of American literature whose racism and sexism was unchecked. In his classes, I, as well as other students, was subjected to racist and sexist jokes. Any of us that he considered should not be in graduate school were the objects of particular scorn and ridicule. When we gave oral presentations, we were told our work was stupid, pathetic, and were not allowed to finish. If we resisted in any way, the situation worsened. When I went to speak with him about his attitude, I was told that I was not really graduate school material, that I should drop out. My anger surfaced and I began to shout, to cry. I remember yelling wildly, "Do you love me? And if you don't love me then how can you have any insight about my concerns and abilities? And who are you to make such suggestions on the basis of one class?" He of course was not making a suggestion. His was a course one had to pass to graduate. He was telling me that I could avoid the systematic abuse by simply dropping out. I would not drop out. I continued to work even though it was clear that I would not succeed, even as the persecution became more intense. And even though I constantly resisted.

In time, my spirits were more and more depressed. I began to dream of entering the professor's office with a loaded gun. There I would demand that he listen, that he experience the fear, the humiliation. In my dreams I could hear his pleading voice begging me not to shoot, to remain calm. As soon as I put the gun down he would become his old self again. Ultimately in the dream the only answer was to shoot, to shoot to kill. When this dream became so consistently a part of my waking fantasies, I knew that it was time for me to take a break from graduate school. Even so I felt as though his terrorism had succeeded, that he had indeed broken my spirit. It was this feeling that led me to return to graduate school, to his classes, because I felt I had given him too much power over me and I needed to regain that sense of self and personal integrity that I allowed him to diminish. Through much of my graduate school career, I was told that "I did not have the proper demeanor of a graduate student." In one graduate program, the black woman before me, who was also subjected to racist and sexist aggression, would tell me that they would say she was not as smart as me but she knew her place. I did not know my place. Young white radicals began to use the phrase "student as nigger" precisely to call attention to the way in which hierarchies within universities encouraged domination of the powerless by the powerful. At many universities the proper demeanor of a graduate student is exemplary when that student is obedient, when he or she does not challenge or resist authority.

During graduate school, white students would tell me that it was important not to question, challenge, or resist. Their tolerance level seemed much higher than my own or that of other black students. Critically reflecting on the differences between us, it was apparent that many of the white students were from privileged class backgrounds. Tolerating the humiliations and degradations we were subjected to in graduate school did not radically call into question their integrity, their sense of self-worth. Those of us who were coming from underprivileged class backgrounds, who were black, often were able to attend college only because we had consistently defied those who had attempted to make us believe we were smart but not "smart enough"; guidance counselors who refused to tell us about certain colleges because they already knew we would not be accepted; parents who were not necessarily supportive of graduate work, etc. White students were not living daily in a world outside campus life where they also had to resist degradation, humiliation. To them, tolerating forms of exploitation and domination in graduate school did not evoke images of a lifetime spent tolerating abuse. They would endure certain forms of domination and abuse, accepting it as an initiation process that would conclude when they became the person in power. In some ways they regarded graduate school and its many humiliations as a game, and they submitted to playing the role of subordinate. I and many other students, especially non-white students from non-privileged backgrounds, were unable to accept and play this "game." Often we were ambivalent about the rewards promised. Many of us were not seeking to be in a position of power over others. Though we wished to teach, we did not want to exert coercive authoritarian rule over others. Clearly those students who played the game best were usually white males and they did not face discrimination, exploitation, and abuse in many other areas of their lives.

Many black graduate students I knew were concerned about whether we were striving to participate in structures of domination and were uncertain about whether we could assume positions of authority. We could not envision assuming oppressive roles. For some of us, failure, failing, being failed began to look like a positive alternative, a way out, a solution. This was especially true for those students who felt they were suffering mentally, who felt that they would never be able to recover a sense of wholeness or well-being. In recent years, campus awareness of the absence of support for international students who have many conflicts and dilemmas in an environment that does not acknowledge their cultural codes has led to the development of support networks. Yet there has been little recognition that there are black students and other non-white students who suffer similar problems, who come from backgrounds where we learned different cultural codes. For example, we may learn that it is important not to accept coercive authoritarian rule from someone who is not a family elder—hence we may have difficulties accepting strangers assuming such a role.

Not long ago, I was at a small party with faculty from a major liberal California university, which until recently had no black professors in the English department who were permanent staff, though they were sometimes visiting scholars. One non-white faculty member and myself began to talk about the problems facing black graduate students studying in English departments. We joked about the racism within English departments, commenting that other disciplines were slightly more willing to accept study of the lives and works of non-white people yet such work is rarely affirmed in English departments where the study of literature usually consists of many works by white men and a few by white women. We talked about how some departments were struggling to change. Speaking about his department, he commented that they have only a few black graduate students, sometimes none, that at one time two black students, one male and one female, had been accepted and both had serious mental health problems. At departmental meetings, white faculty suggested that this indicated that black students just did not have the wherewithal to succeed in this graduate program. For a time, no black students were admitted. His story revealed that part of the burden these students may have felt, which many of us have felt, is that our performance will have future implications for all black students and this knowledge heightens one's performance anxiety from the very beginning. Unfortunately, racist biases often lead departments to see the behavior of one black student as an indication of the way all black students will perform academically. Certainly, if individual white students have difficulty adjusting or succeeding within a graduate program, it is not seen as an indication that all other white students will fail.

The combined forces of racism and sexism often make the black female graduate experience differ in kind from that of the black male experience. While he may be subjected to racial biases, his maleness may serve to mediate the extent to which he will be attacked, dominated, etc. Often it is assumed that black males are better able to succeed at graduate school in English than black females. While many white scholars may be aware of a black male intellectual tradition, they rarely know about black female intellectuals. African-American intellectual traditions, like those of white people, have been male-dominated. People who know the names of W.E.B. Dubois or Martin Delaney may have never heard of Mary Church Terrell or Anna Cooper. The small numbers of black women in permanent positions in academic institutions do not constitute a significant presence, one strong enough to challenge racist and sexist biases. Often the only black woman white professors have encountered is a domestic worker in their home. Yet there are no sociological studies that I know of which examine whether a group who has been seen as not having intellectual capability will automatically be accorded respect and recognition if they enter positions that suggest they are representative scholars. Often black women are such an "invisible presence" on campuses that many students may not be aware that any black women teach at the universities they attend.

Given the reality of racism and sexism, being awarded advanced degrees does not mean that black women will achieve equity with black men or other groups in the profession. Full-time, non-white women comprise less than 3 percent of the total faculty on most campuses. Racism and sexism, particularly on the graduate level, shape and influence both the academic performance and employment of black female academics. During my years of graduate work in English, I was often faced with the hostility of white students who felt that because I was black and female I would have no trouble finding a job. This was usually the response from professors as well if I expressed fear of not finding employment. Ironically, no one ever acknowledged that we were never taught by any of these black women who were taking all the jobs. No one wanted to see that perhaps racism and sexism militate against the hiring of black women even though we are seen as a group that will be given priority, preferential status. Such assumptions, which are usually rooted in the logic of affirmative action hiring, do not include recognition of the ways most universities do not strive to attain diversity of faculty and that often diversity means hiring one non-white person, one black person. When I and other black women graduate students surveyed English departments in the United States, we did not see masses of black women and rightly felt concerned about our futures.

Moving around often, I attended several graduate schools but finally finished my work at the University of California, Santa Cruz where I found support despite the prevalence of racism and sexism. Since I had much past experience, I was able to talk with white faculty members before entering the program about whether they would be receptive and supportive of my desire to focus on African-American writers. I was given positive reassurance that proved accurate. More and more, there are university settings where black female graduate students and black graduate students can study in supportive atmospheres. Racism and sexism are always present yet they do not necessarily shape all areas of graduate experience. When I talk with black female graduate students working in English departments, I hear that many of the problems have not changed, that they experience the same intense isolation and loneliness that characterized my experience. This is why I think it is important that black women in higher education write and talk about our experiences, about survival strategies. When I was having a very difficult time, I read *Working It Out*. Despite the fact that the academics who described the way in which sexism had shaped their academic experience in graduate school were white women, I was encouraged by their resistance, by their perseverance, by their success. Reading their stories helped me to feel less alone. I wrote this essay because of the many conversations I have had with black female graduate students who despair, who are frustrated, who are fearful that the experiences they are having are unique. I want them to know that they are not alone, that the problems that arise, the obstacles created by racism and sexism are real—that they do exist—they do hurt but they are not insurmountable. Perhaps these words will give solace, will intensify their courage, and renew their spirit.

PART TWO

The Making of a Woman: Bodies, Power, and Society

You may be tired of the oft-repeated feminist message that in our society (as well as many others) a woman's value is defined by the attractiveness of her body. We hope these readings will bring you new insights. As you read them, think about the following questions: What does beauty (or its perceived lack) mean to individual women from ethnically diverse groups? Who has the power to determine standards of attractiveness? What happens to women who violate these standards? Finally, what is the role of choice for the women whose voices you are reading? We hope their stories will help you recognize that women are not passive victims of social forces. Personal choices support resistance as well as submission to oppression.

Judith Ortiz Cofer's story forces us to think about the relative nature of attractiveness. Under what circumstances was her skin color defined as light or dark? Under what circumstances was she defined as short or tall? Was she free to construct her own definitions of her physical body? Is there a difference in the crite-

ria by which she was judged as intelligent rather than beautiful? Which perception was more important to her as a young adolescent? And, which view of herself did she internalize as a permanent part of her adult identity?

Eugenia Kaw's extensive interviews with Asian American women who have chosen to have cosmetic surgery on their eyes show us how views of beauty are race and class based. Do you agree with those who argue that such expensive and uncomfortable surgery is an acquiescence to societal oppression? Or do you agree with those women who state that they have made a personal choice to improve an unattractive feature and increase their chances of career advancement? You also might want to think about how these arguments about individual and collective action relate to other kinds of body standards such as weight. What happens to women who cannot or will not conform? But what price is paid by women who strive to meet rigid societal standards?

The conversations that Michelle Fine and Pat Macpherson (a professor of social psychology and a professor of English) share with us touch on appearance issues discussed in the previous stories, but also show us the complexities of dealing with individual women's stories. These are conversations with four ethnically diverse adolescent girls who are struggling both with self-definitions and definitions imposed by society. You might try to think about what is similar about these girls and what is different. This is particularly important because the girls vary in class and ethnicity as well as age. How do these variables interact with gender to influence the way they see themselves as well as the way others see them?

Fine and Macpherson suggest that these girls' struggles involve the definition of femininity and resistance, and that their definition of feminism appears to involve resistance to domination by individual males in their lives. Look for other possible sources of conflict. How do these individualistic definitions differ from more collective strategies advocated by feminists of an earlier generation? How are these women's struggles framed by their particular ethnic and class-based realities? Recognizing that choices are constrained shows us just how tricky it is to evaluate whether any one choice is better than any other.

Nancy Datan's personal account of how she reacted to advice on "restoring her femininity" after a mastectomy highlights some of the same double binds as the other women's stories. Does flouting rules about one's appearance represent a "failure of socialization"? Are private consciousness and public display related? Is denial psychologically healthy or destructive? Who defines us? What does it mean when one defines oneself as a victim or a survivor?

Ynestra King's (a feminist philosopher and ecofeminist) disability is much less severe than that described by Datan, but it provides her with a unique vantage point—she is defined as "able-bodied" when seated and "disabled" when she is moving around. In some ways, her experiences of "passing" are similar to the experiences of individuals of color who look "white" or the cross-sex gender presentations of transsexual individuals. From her observations, can you determine whether a woman's body is ever irrelevant? Why might all disabled women be thought to "look alike"? Because many of us will become disabled at some point in our lives, it is important for the individual and society to distinguish between realistic needs for assistance and the need for autonomy and self-esteem. How might definitions provided by feminism help to negotiate this disparity?

Alice Mayall (an undergraduate when she did this research) and Diana Russell bring us evidence about an "underground" form of defining women—the images found in pornography. These female researchers represent women looking at the making of meaning. The images they describe may make you physically sick, but they are read and enjoyed by a large number of men. Imagine the effect they have— for example, what role they might play if a regular reader is called as a jury member in a rape trial. You also might think about how these ugly images are made acceptable and how racism and sexism reinforce each other. What role can women play when they conduct research in this area?

Gloria Steinem is one of the best-known writers among second-wave feminists. Her celebration of women's varied bodies shows how women can take the making of meaning into their own hands. Who decides what is beautiful and what is an honorable scar? How do cultural standards impose barriers between women of differing ages, ethnicities, and social class? How can we translate knowledge into power?

These readings demonstrate that all women are not alike. We hope they will help you to understand that you must look at external circumstances to understand an individual woman's choices in terms of their meaning to herself. Resistance, too, takes many forms. As a final question, think about the relationship between various ways of resisting domination and the many varieties of feminism. Do you still believe that any one approach is the best?

The Story of My Body

Migration is the story of my body.

—VICTOR HERNANDEZ CRUZ

1. SKIN

I was born a white girl in Puerto Rico, but became a brown girl when I came to live in the United States. My Puerto Rican relatives called me tall; at the American school, some of my rougher classmates called me "skinny-bones" and "the shrimp," because I was the smallest member of my classes all through grammar school until high school, when the midget Gladys was given the honorary post of front-row center for class pictures and scorekeeper, bench warmer in P.E. I reached my full stature of five feet even in sixth grade.

I started out life as a pretty baby and learned to be a pretty girl from a pretty mother. Then at ten years of age I suffered one of the worst cases of chicken pox I have ever heard of. My entire body, including the inside of my ears and in between my toes, was covered with pustules that, in a fit of panic at my appearance, I scratched off of my face, leaving permanent scars. A cruel school nurse told me I would always have them—tiny cuts that looked as if a mad cat had plunged its claws deep into my skin. I grew my hair long and hid behind it for the first years of my adolescence. This was when I learned to be invisible.

2. COLOR

In the animal world it indicates danger: The most colorful creatures are often the most poisonous. Color is also a way to attract and seduce a mate. In the human world color triggers many more complex and often deadly reactions. As a Puerto Rican girl born of "white" parents, I spent the first years of my life

47

hearing people refer to me as *blanca*, white. My mother insisted that I protect myself from the intense island sun because I was more prone to sunburn than some of my darker, *triqeno* playmates. People were always commenting within my hearing about how my black hair contrasted so nicely with my "pale" skin. I did not think of the color of my skin consciously, except when I heard the adults talking about complexion. It seems to me that the subject is much more common in the conversation of mixed-race peoples than in mainstream U.S. society, where it is a touchy and sometimes even embarrassing topic to discuss, except in a political context. In Puerto Rico I heard many conversations about skin color. A pregnant woman could say "I hope my baby doesn't turn out *prieto* (slang for dark or black) like my husband's grandmother, although she was a good-looking *negra* in her time." I am a combination of both, being olive-skinned—lighter than my mother yet darker than my fair-skinned father. In America, I am a person of color, obviously a Latina. On the island I have been called everything from a *paloma blanca*, after the song (by a black suitor), to *la gringa*.

My first experience of color prejudice occurred in a supermarket in Paterson, New Jersey. It was Christmastime and I was eight or nine years old. There was a display of toys in the store where I went two or three times a day to buy things for my mother who never made lists but sent for milk, cigarettes, a can of this or that, as she remembered from hour to hour. I enjoyed being trusted with money and walking half a city block to the new, modern grocery store. It was owned by three good-looking Italian brothers. I liked the younger one with the crew-cut blond hair. The two older ones watched me and the other Puerto Rican kids as if they thought we were going to steal something. The oldest one would sometimes even try to hurry me with my purchases, although part of my pleasure in these expeditions came from looking at everything in the well-stocked aisles. I was also teaching myself to read English by sounding out the labels in packages: L&M cigarettes, Borden's homogenized milk, Red Devil potted ham, Nestlé's chocolate mix, Quaker oats, and Bustelo coffee, Wonder bread, Colgate toothpaste, Ivory soap, and Goya (makers of products used in Puerto Rican dishes) everything—these are some of the brand names that taught me nouns. Several times this man had come up to me wearing his bloodstained butcher's apron and, towering over me, had asked in a harsh voice whether there was something he could help me find. On the way out I would glance at the younger brother who ran one of the registers and he would often smile and wink at me.

It was the mean brother who first referred to me as "colored." It was a few days before Christmas and my parents had already told my brother and me that since we were in *los estados* now, we would get our presents on December twenty-fifth instead of *Los Reyes, Three Kings Day*, when gifts are exchanged in Puerto Rico. We were to give them a wish list that they would take to Santa Claus, who apparently lived in the Macy's store downtown—at least that's where we had caught a glimpse of him when we went shopping. Since my parents were timid about entering the fancy store, we did not approach the huge man in the red suit. I was not interested in sitting on a stranger's lap anyway. But I did covet Susie, the talking schoolteacher doll that was displayed in the center aisle of the Italian brothers' supermarket. She talked when you pulled a string on her back. Susie had a limited repertoire of three sentences: I think she could say: "Hello, I'm Susie Schoolteacher; two plus two is four," and one other thing I cannot remember. The day the older brother chased me away, I was reaching to touch Susie's blond curls. I had been told many times, as most children have, not to touch anything in a store that I was not buying. But I had been looking at Susie for weeks. In my mind, she was my doll. After all, I had put her on my Christmas wish list. The moment is frozen in my mind as if there were a photograph of it on file. It was not a turning point, a disaster, or an earthshaking revelation. It was simply the first time I considered—if naively—the meaning of skin color in human relations.

I reached to touch Susie's hair. It seems to me that I had to get on tiptoe since the toys were stacked on a table and she sat like a princess on top of the fancy box she came in. Then I heard the booming "Hey, kid, what do you think you're doing!" spoken very loudly from the meat counter. I felt caught although I knew I was not doing anything criminal. I remember not looking at the man, but standing there feeling humiliated because I knew everyone in the store must have heard him yell at me. I felt him approach and when I knew he was behind me, I turned around to face the bloody butcher's apron. His large chest was at my eye level. He blocked my way. I started to run out of the place, but even as I reached the door I heard him shout after me: "Don't come in here unless you gonna buy something. You PR kids put your dirty hands on stuff. You always look dirty. But maybe dirty brown is your natural color." I heard him laugh and someone else too in the back. Outside in the sunlight I looked at my hands. My nails needed a little cleaning as they always did since I liked to paint with watercolors, but I took a bath every night. I thought the man was dirtier than I was in his stained apron. He was also always sweaty—it showed in big yellow circles under his shirt sleeves. I sat on the front steps of the apartment building where we lived and looked closely at my hands, which showed the only skin I could see, since it was bitter cold and I was wearing my quilted play coat, dungarees, and a knitted navy cap of my father's. I was not pink like my friend Charlene and her sister Kathy who had blue eyes and light-brown hair. My skin is the color of the coffee my grandmother made, which was half milk, *leche con café* rather than *café con leche*. My mother is the opposite mix. She has a lot of café in her color. I could not understand how my skin looked like dirt to the supermarket man.

I went in and washed my hands thoroughly with soap and hot water, and, borrowing my mother's nail file, I cleaned the crusted watercolors from underneath my nails. I was pleased with the results. My skin was the same color as before, but I knew I was clean. Clean enough to run my fingers through Susie's fine gold hair when she came home to me.

3. SIZE

My mother is barely four feet eleven inches in height, which is average for women in her family. When I grew to five feet by age twelve, she was amazed and began to use the word tall to describe me, as in: "Since you are tall, this dress will look good on you." As with the color of my skin, I didn't consciously think about my height or size until other people made an issue of it. It is around the preadolescent years that in America the games children play for fun become fierce competitions where everyone is out to "prove" they are better than others. It was in the playground and sports fields that my size-related problems began. No matter how familiar the story is, every child who is the last chosen for a team knows the torment of waiting to be called up. At the Paterson, New Jersey, public schools that I attended, the volleyball or softball game was the metaphor for the battlefield of life to the inner city kids—the black kids vs. the Puerto Rican kids, the whites vs. the blacks vs. the Puerto Rican kids; and I was 4F, skinny, short, bespectacled, and apparently impervious to the blood thirst that drove many of my classmates to play ball as if their lives depended on it. Perhaps they did. I would rather be reading a book than sweating, grunting, and running the risk of pain and injury. I simply did not see the point in competitive sports. My main form of exercise then was walking to the library, many city blocks away from my barrio.

Still, I wanted to be wanted. I wanted to be chosen for the teams. Physical education was compulsory, a class where you were actually given a grade. On my mainly all-A report card, the C for compassion I always received from the P.E. teachers shamed me the same as a bad grade in a real class. Invariably, my father would say: "How can you make a low grade *for playing games*?" He did not understand. Even if I had managed to make a hit (it never happened), or get the ball over that ridiculously high net, I already had a reputation as a "shrimp," a hopeless nonathlete. It was an area where the girls who didn't like me for one reason or another—mainly because I did better than they on academic subjects—could lord it over me; the playing field was the place where even the smallest girl could make me feel powerless and inferior. I instinctively understood the politics even then; how the *not* choosing me until the teacher forced one of the team captains to call my name was a coup of sorts—there you little show-off, tomorrow you can beat us in spelling and geography, but this afternoon you are the loser. Or perhaps those were only my own bitter thoughts as I sat or stood in the sidelines while the big girls were grabbed like fish and I, the little brown tadpole, was ignored until Teacher looked over in my general direction and shouted, "Call Ortiz," or worse, "Somebody's got to take her."

No wonder I read Wonder Woman comics and had Legion of Super Heroes daydreams. Although I wanted to think of myself as "intellectual," my body was demanding that I notice it. I saw the little swelling around my once-flat nipples; the fine hairs growing in secret places; but my knees were still bigger than my thighs and I always wore long or half-sleeve blouses to hide my bony upper arms. I wanted flesh on my bones—a thick layer of it. I saw a new product advertised on TV. Wate-On. They showed skinny men and women before and after taking the stuff, and it was a transformation like the 97-pound weakling turned into Charles Atlas ads that I saw on the back cover of my comic books. The Wate-On was very expensive. I tried to explain my need for it in Spanish to my mother, but it didn't translate very well, even to my ears—and she said with a tone of finality, eat more of my good food and you'll get fat—anybody can get fat. Right. Except me. I was going to have to join a circus someday as "Skinny Bones," the woman without flesh.

Wonder Woman was stacked. She had a cleavage framed by the spread wings of a golden eagle and a muscular body that has become fashionable with women only recently. But since I wanted a body that would serve me in P.E., hers was my ideal. The breasts were an indulgence I allowed myself. Perhaps the daydreams of bigger girls were more glamorous, since our ambitions are filtered through our needs, but I wanted first a powerful body. I daydreamed of leaping up above the gray landscape of the city to where the sky was clear and blue, and in anger and self-pity I fantasized about scooping my enemies up by their hair from the playing fields and dumping them on a barren asteroid. I would put the P.E. teachers each on their own rock in space too where they would be the loneliest people in the universe since I knew they had no "inner resources," no imagination, and in outer space, there would be no air for them to fill their deflated volleyballs with. In my mind all P.E. teachers have blended into one large spiky-haired woman with a whistle on a string around her neck and a volleyball under one arm. My Wonder Woman fantasies of revenge were a source of comfort to me in my early career as a shrimp.

I was saved from more years of P.E. torment by the fact that in my sophomore year of high school I transferred to a school where the midget, Gladys, was the focal point of interest for the people who must rank according to size. Because her height was considered a handicap, there was an unspoken rule about mentioning size around Gladys, but of course there was no need to say anything. Gladys knew her place: front-row center in class photographs. I gladly moved to the left or to the right of her, as far as I could without leaving the picture completely.

4. LOOKS

Many photographs were taken of me as a baby by my mother to send to my father who was stationed overseas during the first two years of my life. With the army in Panama when I was born, he later joined the navy and traveled often on tours of duty. I was a healthy, pretty baby. Recently I read that people are drawn to big-eyed round-faced creatures, like puppies, kittens, and certain other mammals and marsupials, koalas for example, and, of course, infants. I was all eyes, since my head and body, even as I grew older, remained thin and small-boned. As a young child I got a lot of attention from my relatives and many other people we met in our barrio. My mother's beauty may have had something to do with how much attention we got from strangers in stores and on the street. I can imagine it. In the pictures I have seen of us together, she is a stunning young woman by Latino standards: long, curly black hair and round curves in a compact frame. From her I learned how to move, smile, and talk like an attractive woman. I remember going into a bodega for our groceries and being given candy by the proprietor as a reward for being *bonita*, pretty.

I can see in the photographs and I also remember that I was dressed in the pretty clothes, the stiff, frilly dresses, with layers of crinolines underneath, the glossy patent leather shoes, and, on special occasions, the skull-hugging little hats and the white gloves that were popular in the late fifties and early sixties. My mother was proud of my looks, although I was a bit too thin. She could dress me up like a doll and take me by the hand to visit relatives, or go to the Spanish mass at the Catholic church, and show me off. How was I to know that she and the others who called me pretty were representatives of an aesthetic that would not apply when I went out into the mainstream world of school?

In my Paterson, New Jersey, public schools there were still quite a few white children, although the demographics of the city were changing rapidly. The original waves of Italian and Irish immigrants, silk-mill workers and laborers in the cloth industries, had been "assimilated." Their children were now the middle-class parents of my peers. Many of them moved their children to the Catholic schools that proliferated enough to have leagues of basketball teams. The names I recall hearing still ring in my ears: Don Bosco High vs. St. Mary's High, St. Joseph's vs. St. John's. Later I too would be transferred to the safer environment of a Catholic school. But I started school at Public School Number 11. I came there from Puerto Rico, thinking myself a pretty girl, and found that the hierarchy for popularity was as follows: pretty white girl, pretty Jewish girl, pretty Puerto Rican girl, pretty black girl. Drop the last two categories; teachers were too busy to have more than one favorite per class, and it was simply understood that if there was a big part in the school play, or any competition where the main qualification was "presentability" (such as escorting a school visitor to or from the principal's office), the classroom's public address speaker would be requesting the pretty and/or nice-looking white boy or girl. By the time I was in the sixth grade, I was sometimes called by the principal to represent my class because I dressed neatly (I knew this from a progress report sent to my mother, which I translated for her), and because all the "presentable" white girls had moved to the Catholic schools (I later surmised this part). But I was still not one of the popular girls with the boys. I remember one incident where I stepped out into the playground in my baggy gym shorts and one Puerto Rican boy said to the other: "What do you think?" The other one answered: "Her face is okay, but look at the toothpick legs." The next best thing to a compliment I got was when my favorite male teacher, while handing out the class pictures, commented that with my long neck and delicate features I resembled the movie star Audrey Hepburn. But the Puerto Rican boys had learned to respond to a fuller figure: long necks and a perfect little nose were not what they looked for in a girl. That is when I decided I was a "brain." I did not settle into the role easily. I was nearly devastated by what the chicken-pox episode had done to my self-image. But I looked into the mirror less often after I was told that I would always have scars on my face, and I hid behind my long black hair and my books.

After the problems at the public school got to the point where even non-confrontational little me got beaten up several times, my parents enrolled me at St. Joseph's High School. I was then a minority of one among the Italian and Irish kids. But I found several good friends there—other girls who took their studies seriously. We did our homework together and talked about the Jackies. The Jackies were two popular girls, one blonde and the other red-haired, who had women's bodies. Their curves showed even in the blue jumper uniforms with straps that we all wore. The blonde Jackie would often let one of the straps fall off her shoulder, and although she, like all of us, wore a white blouse underneath, all the boys stared at her arm. My friends and I talked about this and practiced letting our straps fall off our shoulders. But it wasn't the same without breasts or hips.

My final two and a half years at high school were spent in Augusta, Georgia, where my parents moved our family in search of a more peaceful environment. There we became part of a little community of our army-connected relatives and friends. School was yet another matter. I was enrolled in a huge school of nearly two thousand students that had just that year been forced to integrate. There were two black girls and there was me. I did extremely well academically. As to my social life, it was, for the most part, uneventful—yet it is in my memory blighted by one incident. In my junior year, I became wildly infatuated with a pretty white boy. I'll call him Ted. Oh, he was pretty: yellow hair that fell over his forehead, a smile to die for, and he was a great dancer. I watched him at Teen Town, the youth center at the base where all the military brats gathered on Saturday nights. My father had retired from the military and we had all our base privileges—one other reason we had moved to Augusta. Ted looked like an angel to me. I worked on him for a year before he asked me out. This meant maneuvering to be within the periphery of his vision at every possible occasion. I took the long way to my classes in school just to pass by his locker, I went to football games that I detested, and I danced (I too was a good dancer) in front of him at Teen Town—this took some fancy footwork since it involved subtly moving my partner toward the right spot on the dance floor. When Ted finally approached me, "A Million to One" was playing on the jukebox, and when he took me into his arms, the odds suddenly turned in my favor. He asked me to go to a school dance the following Saturday. I said yes, breathlessly, I said yes but there were obstacles to surmount at home. My father did not allow me to date casually. I was allowed to go to major events like a prom or a concert with a boy who had been properly screened. There was such a boy in my life, a neighbor who wanted to be a Baptist missionary and was practicing his anthropological skills on my family. If I was desperate to go somewhere and needed a date, I'd resort to Gary. This is the type of religious nut that Gary was: When the school bus did not show up one day, he put his hands over his face and prayed to Christ to get us a way to get to school. Within ten minutes a mother in a station wagon on her way to town stopped to ask why we weren't in school. Gary informed her that the Lord had sent her just in time to get us there for roll call. He assumed that I was impressed. Gary was even good-looking in a bland sort of way, but he kissed me with his lips tightly pressed together. I think Gary probably ended up marrying a native woman from wherever he may have gone to preach the Gospel according to Paul. She probably believes that all white men pray to God for transportation and kiss with their mouths closed. But it was Ted's mouth, his whole beautiful self that concerned me in those days. I knew my father would say no to our date, but I planned to run away from home if necessary. I told my mother how important this date was. I cajoled and pleaded with her from Sunday to Wednesday. She listened to my arguments, and must have heard the note of desperation in my voice. She said very gently to me: "You better be ready for disappointment." I did not ask what she meant. I did not want her fears for me to taint my happiness. I asked her to tell my father about my date. Thursday at breakfast my father looked at me across the table with his eyebrows together.

My mother looked at him with her mouth set in a straight line. I looked down at my bowl of cereal. Nobody said anything. Friday I tried on every dress in my closet. Ted would be picking me up at six on Saturday: dinner and then the sock hop at school. Friday night I was in my room doing my nails or something else in preparation for Saturday (I know I groomed myself nonstop all week) when the telephone rang. I ran to get it. It was Ted. His voice sounded funny when he said my name, so funny that I felt compelled to ask: "Is something wrong?" Ted blurted it all out without a preamble. His father had asked who he was going out with. Ted had told him my name. "Ortiz? That's Spanish, isn't it?" the father had asked. Ted had told him yes, then shown him my picture in the yearbook. Ted's father had shaken his head. No. Ted would not be taking me out. Ted's father had known Puerto Ricans in the army. He had lived in New York City while studying architecture and had seen how the *spics* lived. Like rats. Ted repeated his father's words to me as if I should understand *his predicament* when I heard why he was breaking our date. I don't remember what I said before hanging up. I do recall the darkness of my room that sleepless night, and the heaviness of my blanket in which I wrapped myself like a shroud. And I remember my parents' respect for my pain and their gentleness toward me that weekend. My mother did not say "I warned you," and I was grateful for her understanding silence.

In college, I suddenly became an "exotic" woman to the men who had survived the popularity wars in high school, who were now practicing to be worldly: They had to act liberal in their politics, in their lifestyles, and in the women they went out with. I dated heavily for a while, then married young. I had discovered that I needed stability more than social life. I had brains for sure, and some talent in writing. These facts were a constant in my life. My skin color, my size, and my appearance were variables—things that were judged according to my current self-image, the aesthetic values of the times, the places I was in, and the people I met. My studies, later my writing, the respect of people who saw me as an individual person they cared about, these were the criteria for my sense of self-worth that I would concentrate on in my adult life.

Eugenia Kaw

"Opening" Faces

The Politics of Cosmetic Surgery and Asian American Women

Ellen, a Chinese American in her forties, informed me she had had her upper eyelids surgically cut and sewed by a plastic surgeon twenty years ago in order to get rid of "the sleepy look," which her naturally "puffy" eyes gave her. She pointed out that the sutures, when they healed, became a crease above the eye which gave the eyes a more "open appearance." She was quick to tell me that her decision to undergo "double-eyelid" surgery was not so much because she was vain or had low self-esteem, but rather because the "undesirability" of her looks before the surgery was an undeniable fact.

During my second interview with Ellen, she showed me photos of herself from before and after her surgery in order to prove her point. When Stacy, her twelve-year-old daughter, arrived home from school, Ellen told me she wanted Stacy to undergo similar surgery in the near future because Stacy has only single eyelids and would look prettier and be more successful in life if she had a fold above each eye. Ellen brought the young girl to where I was sitting and said, "You see, if you look at her you will know what I mean when I say that I had to have surgery done on my eyelids. Look at her eyes. She looks just like me before the surgery." Stacy seemed very shy to show me her face. But I told the girl truthfully that she looked fine and beautiful the way she was. Immediately she grinned at her mother in a mocking, defiant manner, as if I had given her courage, and put her arm up in the manner that bodybuilders do when they display their bulging biceps.

As empowered as Stacy seemed to feel at the moment, I could not help but wonder how many times Ellen had shown her "before" and "after" photos to her young daughter with the remark that "Mommy looks better after the surgery." I also wondered how many times Stacy had been asked by Ellen to consider surgically "opening" her eyes like "Mommy did." And I wondered about the images we see on television and in magazines and their often negative, stereotypical portrayal of "squinty-eyed" Asians (when Asians are featured at all). I could not help but wonder how normal it is to feel that an eye without a crease is undesirable and how much of that feeling is imposed. And

I shuddered to think how soon it might be before twelve-year-old Stacy's defenses gave away and she allowed her eyes to be cut.

The permanent alteration of bodies through surgery for aesthetic purposes is not a new phenomenon in the United States. As early as World War I, when reconstructive surgery was performed on disfigured soldiers, plastic surgery methods began to be refined for purely cosmetic purposes (that is, not so much for repairing and restoring but for transforming natural features a person is unhappy with). Within the last decade, however, an increasing number of people have opted for a wide array of cosmetic surgery procedures, from tummy tucks, facelifts, and liposuction to enlargement of chests and calves. By 1988, two million Americans had undergone cosmetic surgery (Wolf 1991:218), and a 69 percent increase had occurred in the number of cosmetic surgery procedures between 1981 and 1990, according to the ASPRS or American Society of Plastic and Reconstructive Surgeons (n.d.).

Included in these numbers are an increasing number of cosmetic surgeries undergone by people like Stacy who are persons of color (American Academy of Cosmetic Surgery press release, 1991). In fact, Asian Americans are more likely than any other ethnic group (white or nonwhite) to pursue cosmetic surgery. ASPRS reports that over thirty-nine thousand of the aesthetic procedures performed by its members in 1990 (or more than 6 percent of all procedures performed that year) were performed on Asian Americans, who make up 3 percent of the U.S. population (Chen 1993:15). Because Asian Americans seek cosmetic surgery from doctors in Asia and from doctors who specialize in fields other than surgery (e.g., ear, nose, and throat specialists and ophthalmologists), the total number of Asian American patients is undoubtedly higher (Chen 1993:16).

The specific procedures requested by different ethnic groups in the United States are missing from the national data, but newspaper reports and medical texts indicate that Caucasians and nonwhites, on the average, seek significantly different types of operations (Chen 1993; Harahap 1982; Kaw 1993; LeFlore 1982; McCurdy 1980; Nakao 1993; Rosenthal 1991). While Caucasians primarily seek to augment breasts and to remove wrinkles and fat through such procedures as facelifts, liposuction, and collagen injection, African Americans more often opt for lip and nasal reduction operations; Asian Americans more often choose to insert an implant on their nasal dorsum for a more prominent nose or undergo double-eyelid surgery whereby parts of their upper eyelids are excised to create a fold above each eye, which makes the eye appear wider.[1]

Though the American media, the medical establishment, and the general public have debated whether such cosmetic changes by nonwhite persons reflect a racist milieu in which racial minorities must deny their racial identity and attempt to look more Caucasian, a resounding no appears to be the overwhelming opinion of people in the United States.[2] Many plastic surgeons have voiced the opinion that racial minorities are becoming more assertive about their right to choose and that they are choosing not to look Caucasian. Doctors say that nonwhite persons' desire for thinner lips, wider eyes, and pointier noses is no more than a wish to enhance their features in order to attain "balance" with all their other features (Kaw 1993; Merrell 1994; Rosenthal 1991).

Much of the media and public opinion also suggests that there is no political significance inherent in the cosmetic changes made by people of color which alter certain conventionally known, phenotypic markers of racial identity. On a recent Phil Donahue show where the racially derogatory nature of blue contact lenses for African American women was contested, both white and nonwhite audience members were almost unanimous that African American women's use of these lenses merely reflected their freedom to choose in the same way that Bo Derek chose to wear corn rows and white people decided to get tans (Bordo 1990). Focusing more specifically on cosmetic surgery, a *People Weekly* magazine article entitled "On the Cutting Edge" (January 27, 1992, p. 3) treats Michael Jackson (whose nose has become narrower and perkier and whose skin has become lighter through the years) as simply one among many Hollywood stars whose extravagant and competitive lifestyle has motivated and allowed them to pursue cosmetic self-enhancement. Clearly, Michael Jackson's physical transformation within the last decade has been more drastic than Barbara Hershey's temporary plumping of her lips to look younger in *Beaches* or Joan Rivers's facelift, yet his reasons for undergoing surgery are not differentiated from those of Caucasian celebrities; the possibility that he may want to cross racial divides through surgery is not an issue in the article.

When critics speculate on the possibility that a person of color is attempting to look white, they often focus their attack on the person and his or her apparent lack of ethnic pride and self-esteem. For instance, a *Newsweek* article, referring to Michael Jackson's recent television interview with Oprah Winfrey, questioned Jackson's emphatic claim that he is proud to be a black American: "Jackson's dermatologist confirmed that the star has vitiligo, a condition that blocks the skin's ability to produce pigment . . . [however,] most vitiligo sufferers darken their light patches with makeup to even the tone. Jackson's makeup solution takes the other tack: less ebony, more ivory" (Fleming and Talbot 1993:57). Such criticisms, sadly, center around Michael Jackson the person instead of delving into his possible feelings of oppression or examining society as a potential source of his motivation to alter his natural features so radically.

In this chapter, based on structured, open-ended interviews with Asian American women like Ellen who have or are thinking about undergoing cosmetic surgery for wider eyes and more heightened noses, I attempt to convey more emphatically the lived social experiences of people of color who seek what appears to be conventionally recognized Caucasian features. Rather than mock their decision to alter their features or treat it lightly as an expression of their freedom to choose an idiosyncratic look, I examine everyday cultural images and social relationships which influence Asian American women to seek cosmetic surgery in the first place. Instead of focusing, as some doctors do (Kaw 1993), on the size and width of the eyelid folds the women request as indicators of the women's desire to look Caucasian, I examine the cultural, social, and historical sources that allow the women in my study to view their eyes in a negative fashion—as "small" and "slanted" eyes reflecting a "dull," "passive" personality, a "closed" mind, and a "lack of spirit" in the person. I explore the reasons these women reject the natural shape of their eyes so radically that they willingly expose themselves to a surgery that is at least an hour long, costs one thousand to three thousand dollars, entails administering local anesthesia and sedation, and carries the following risks: "bleeding and hematoma," "hemorrhage," formation of a "gaping wound," "discoloration," scarring, and "asymmetric lid folds" (Sayoc 1974:162–166).

In our feminist analyses of femininity and beauty we may sometimes find it difficult to account for cosmetic surgery without undermining the thoughts and decisions of women who opt for it (Davis 1991). However, I attempt to show that the decision of the women in my study to undergo cosmetic surgery is often carefully thought out. Such a decision is usually made only after a long period of weighing the psychological pain of feeling inadequate prior to surgery against the possible social advantages a new set of features may bring. Several of the women were aware of complex power structures that construct their bodies as inferior and in need of change, even while they simultaneously reproduced these structures by deciding to undergo surgery (Davis 1991:33).

I argue that as women and as racial minorities, the psychological burden of having to measure up to ideals of beauty in American society falls especially heavy on these Asian American women. As women, they are constantly bombarded with the notion that beauty should be their primary goal (Lakoff and Scherr 1984, Wolf 1991). As racial minorities, they are made to feel inadequate by an Anglo American–dominated cultural milieu that has historically both excluded them and distorted images of them in such a way that they themselves have come to associate those features stereotypically identified with their race (i.e., small, slanty eyes, and a flat nose) with negative personality and mental characteristics.

In a consumption-oriented society such as the United States, it is often tempting to believe that human beings have an infinite variety of needs which technology can endlessly fulfill, and that these needs, emerging spontaneously in time and space, lack any coherent patterns, cultural meanings, or political significance (Bordo 1991; Goldstein 1993; O'Neill 1985:98). However, one cannot regard needs as spontaneous, infinite, harmless, and amorphous without first considering what certain groups feel they lack and without first critically examining the lens with which the larger society has historically viewed this lack. Frances C. MacGregor, who between 1946 and 1959 researched the social and cultural motivations of such white ethnic minorities as Jewish and Italian Americans to seek rhinoplasty, wrote, "The statements of the patients . . . have a certain face validity and explicitness that reflect both the values of our society and the degree to which these are perceived as creating problems for the deviant individual" (MacGregor 1967:129).

Social scientific analyses of ethnic relations should include a study of the body. As evident in my research, racial minorities may internalize a body image produced by the dominant culture's racial ideology and, because of it, begin to loathe, mutilate, and revise parts of their bodies. Bodily adornment and mutilation (the cutting up and altering of essential parts of the body; see Kaw 1993) are symbolic mediums most directly and concretely concerned with the construction of the individual as social actor or cultural subject (Turner 1980). Yet social scientists have only recently focused on the body as a central component of social self-identity (Blacking 1977; Brain 1979; Daly 1978; Lock and Scheper-Hughes 1990; O'Neill 1985; Turner 1980; Sheets-Johnstone 1992). Moreover, social scientists, and sociocultural anthropologists in particular, have not yet explored the ways in which the body is central to the everyday experience of racial identity.

METHOD AND DESCRIPTION OF SUBJECTS

In this article, I present the findings of an ethnographic research project completed in the San Francisco Bay Area. I draw on data from structured interviews with doctors and patients, basic medical statistics, and relevant newspaper and magazine articles. The sampling of informants for this research was not random in the strictly statistical sense since informants were difficult to find. Both medical practitioners and patients treat cases of cosmetic surgery as highly confidential, as I later discuss in more detail. To find a larger, more random sampling of Asian American informants, I posted fliers and placed advertisements in various local newspapers. Ultimately, I was able to conduct structured, open-ended interviews with eleven Asian American women, four of whom were referred to me by the doctors in my study and six by mutual acquaintances: I found one through an advertisement. Nine had had cosmetic surgery of the eye or the nose; one recently considered a double-eyelid operation; one is considering undergoing double-eyelid operation in the next few years. The women in my study live in the San Francisco Bay Area, except for two who reside in the Los Angeles area. Five were operated on by doctors who I also interviewed for my study, while four had their operations in Asia—two in Seoul, Korea, one in Beijing, China, and one in Taipei, Taiwan. Of the eleven women in my study, only two (who received their operations in China and in Taiwan) had not lived in the United States prior to their operations.[3] The ages of the Asian American women in my study range from eighteen to seventy-one; one woman was only fifteen at the time of her operation. Their class backgrounds are similar in that they were all engaged in middle-class, white-collar occupations: there were three university students, one art student, one legal assistant, one clerk, one nutritionist, one teacher, one law student, and two doctors' assistants.

Although I have not interviewed Asian American men who have or are thinking of undergoing cosmetic surgery, I realize that they too undergo double-eyelid and nose bridge operations. Their motivations are, to a large extent, similar to those of the women in my study (Iwata 1991). Often their decision to undergo surgery also follows a long and painful process of feeling marginal in society (Iwata 1991). I did not purposely exclude Asian American male patients from my study; rather, none responded to my requests for interviews.

To understand how plastic surgeons view the cosmetic procedures performed on Asian Americans, five structured, open-ended interviews were conducted with five plastic surgeons, all of whom practice in the Bay Area. I also examined several medical books and plastic surgery journals which date from the 1950s to 1990. And I referenced several news releases and informational packets distributed by such national organizations as the American Society of Plastic and Reconstructive Surgeons, an organization which represents 97 percent of all physicians certified by the American Board of Plastic Surgery.

To examine popular notions of cosmetic surgery, in particular how the phenomenon of Asian American women receiving double-eyelid and nose bridge operations is viewed by the public and the media, I have referenced relevant newspaper and magazine articles.

I obtained national data on cosmetic surgery from various societies for cosmetic surgeons, including the American Society of Plastic and Reconstructive Surgeons. Data on the specific types of surgery sought by different ethnic groups in the United States, including Asian Americans, were missing from the national statistics. At least one public relations coordinator told me that such data is unimportant to plastic surgeons. To compensate for this lack of data, I asked the doctors in my study to provide me with figures from their respective clinics. Most told me they had little data on their cosmetic patients readily available.

COLONIZATION OF ASIAN AMERICAN WOMEN'S SOULS: INTERNALIZATION OF GENDER AND RACIAL STEREOTYPES

Upon first talking with my Asian American women informants, one might conclude that the women were merely seeking to enhance their features for aesthetic reasons and that there is no cultural meaning or political significance in their decision to surgically enlarge their eyes and heighten their noses. As Elena, a twenty-one-year-old Chinese American who underwent double-eyelid surgery three years ago from a doctor in my study, stated: "I underwent my surgery for personal reasons. It's not different from wanting to put makeup on . . . I don't intend to look Anglo-Saxon. I told my doctor, 'I would like my eyes done with definite creases on my eyes, but I don't want a drastic change.' " Almost all the other women similarly stated that their unhappiness with their eyes and nose was individually motivated and that they really did not desire Caucasian features. In fact, one Korean American woman, Nina, age thirty-four, stated she was not satisfied with the results of her surgery from three years ago because her doctor made her eyes "too round" like that of Caucasians. One might deduce from such statements that the women's decision to undergo cosmetic surgery of the eye and nose is harmless and may be even empowering to them, for their surgery provides them with a more permanent solution than makeup for "personal" dissatisfactions they have about their features.

However, an examination of their descriptions of the natural shape of their eyes and nose suggests that their "personal" feelings about their features reflect the larger society's negative valuation and stereotyping of Asian features in general. They all said that "small, slanty" eyes and a "flat" nose suggest, in the Asian person, a personality that is "dull," "unenergetic," "passive," and "unsociable" and a mind that is narrow and "closed." For instance, Elena said, "When I look at other Asians who have no folds and their eyes are slanted and closed, I think of how they would look better more awake." Nellee, a twenty-one-year-old Chinese American, said that she seriously considered surgery for double eyelids in high school so that she could "avoid the stereotype of the 'oriental bookworm' " who is "dull and doesn't know how to have fun." Carol, a thirty-seven-year-old Chinese American who received double eyelids seven years ago, said: "The eyes are the window of your soul . . . [yet] lots of oriental people have the outer corners of their eyes a little down, making them look tired. [The double eyelids] don't make a big difference in the size of our eyes but they give your eyes more spirit." Pam, a Chinese American, age forty-four, who received double-eyelid surgery from another doctor in my study, stated, "Yes, Of course. Bigger eyes look prettier. . . . Lots of Asians' eyes are so small they become little lines when the person laughs, making the person look sleepy." Likewise, Annie, an eighteen-year-old Korean American woman who had an implant placed on her nasal dorsum to build up her nose bridge at age fifteen, said: "I guess I always wanted that sharp look—a look like you are smart. If you have a roundish kind of nose it's like you don't know what's going on. If you have that sharp look, you know, with black eyebrows, a pointy nose, you look more alert. I always thought that was cool." The women were influenced by the larger society's negative valuation of stereotyped Asian features in such a way that they evaluated themselves and Asian women in general with a critical eye. Their judgments were based on a set of standards, stemming from the eighteenth- and nineteenth-century European aesthetic ideal of the proportions in Greek sculpture, which are presumed by a large amount of Americans to be within the grasp of every woman (Goldstein 1993:150, 160).

Unlike many white women who may also seek cosmetic surgery to reduce or make easier the daily task of applying makeup, the Asian American women in my study hoped more specifically to ease the task of creating with makeup the illusion of features they do not have as women who are Asian. Nellee, who has not yet undergone double-eyelid surgery, said that at present she has to apply makeup everyday "to give my eyes an illusion of a crease. When I don't wear make-up I feel my eyes are small." Likewise, Elena said that before her double-eyelid surgery she checked almost every morning in the mirror when she woke up to see if a fold had formed above her right eye to match the more prominent fold above her left eye: "[on certain mornings] it was like any other day when you wake up and don't feel so hot, you know. My eye had no definite folds, because when Asians sleep their folds change in and out—it's not definite." Also, Jo, a twenty-eight-year-old Japanese American who already had natural folds above each eye but wishes to enlarge them through double-eyelid surgery, explained:

> I guess I just want to make a bigger eyelid [fold] so that they look bigger and not slanted. I think in Asian eyes it's the inside corner of the fold [she was drawing on my notebook] that goes down too much. . . . Right now I am still self-conscious about leaving the house without any makeup on, because I feel just really ugly without it. I try to curl my eyelashes and put on mascara. I think it makes my eyes look more open. But surgery can permanently change the shape of my eyes. I don't think that a bigger eyelid fold will actually change the slant but I think it will give the perception of having less of it, less of an Asian eye.

For the women in my study, their oppression is a double encounter: one under patriarchal definitions of femininity (i.e., that a woman should care about the superficial details of her look), and the other under Caucasian standards of beauty. The constant self-monitoring of their anatomy and their continuous focus on detail exemplify the extent to which they feel they must measure up to society's ideals.

In the United States, where a capitalist work ethic values "freshness," "a quick wit," and assertiveness, many Asian American women are already disadvantaged at birth by virtue of their inherited physical features which society associates with dullness and passivity. In this way, their desire to look more spirited and energetic through the surgical creation of folds above each eye is of a different quality from the motivation of many Anglo Americans seeking facelifts and liposuction for a fresher, more youthful appearance. Signs of aging are not the main reason Asian American cosmetic patients ultimately seek surgery of the eyes and the nose; often they are younger (usually between eighteen and thirty years of age) than the average Caucasian patient (Kaw 1993). Several of the Asian American women in my study who were over thirty years of age at the time of their eyelid operation sought surgery to get rid of extra folds of skin that had developed over their eyes due to age; however, even these women decided to receive double eyelids in the process. When Caucasian patients undergo eyelid surgery, on the other hand, the procedure is almost never to create a double eyelid (for they already possess one); in most cases, it is to remove sagging skin that results from aging. Clearly, Asian American women's negative image of their eyes and nose is not so much a result of their falling short of the youthful, energetic beauty ideal that influences every American as it is a direct product of society's racial stereotyping.

The women in my study described their own features with metaphors of dullness and passivity in keeping with many Western stereotypes of Asians. Stereotypes, by definition, are expedient caricatures of the "other," which serve to set them apart from the "we"; they serve to exclude instead of include, to judge instead of accept (Gilman 1985:15). Asians are rarely portrayed in the American print and electronic media. For instance, Asians (who constitute 3 percent of the U.S. population) account for less than 1 percent of the faces represented in magazine ads, according to a 1991 study titled "Invisible People" conducted by New York City's Department of Consumer Affairs (cited in Chen 1993:26). When portrayed, they are seen in one of two forms, which are not representative of Asians in general; as Eurasian-looking fashion models and movie stars (e.g., Nancy Kwan who played Suzy Wong) who already have double eyelids and pointy noses; and as stereotypically Asian characters such as Charlie Chan, depicted with personalities that are dull, passive, and nonsociable (Dower 1986; Kim 1986; Ramsdell 1983; Tajima 1989). The first group often serves as an ideal toward which Asian American women strive, even when they say they do not want to look Caucasian. The second serves as an image from which they try to escape.

Asian stereotypes, like all kinds of stereotypes, are multiple and have changed throughout the years; nevertheless they have maintained some distinct characteristics. Asians have been portrayed as exotic and erotic (as epitomized by Suzie Wong, or the Japanese temptress in the film *The Berlin Affair*), and especially during the U.S. war in the Pacific during World War II, they were seen as dangerous spies and mad geniuses who were treacherous and stealthy (Dower 1986; Huhr and Kim 1989). However, what remains consistent in the American popular image of Asians is their childishness, narrow-mindedness, and lack of leadership skills. Moreover, these qualities have long been associated with the relatively roundish form of Asian faces, and in particular with the "puffy" smallness of their eyes. Prior to the Japanese attack on Pearl Harbor, for instance, the Japanese were considered incapable of planning successful dive bombing attacks due to their "myopic," "squinty" eyes; during the war in the Pacific, their soldiers were caricatured as having thick horn-rimmed glasses through which they must squint to see their targets (Dower 1986). Today, the myopic squinty-eyed image of the narrow-minded Asian persists in the most recent stereotype of Asians as "model minorities" (as epitomized in the Asian exchange student character in the film *Sixteen Candles*). The term *model minority* was first coined in the 1960s when a more open-door U.S. immigration policy began allowing an unprecedented number of Asian immigrants into the United States, many of whom were the most elite and educated of their own countries (Takaki 1989). Despite its seemingly complimentary nature, *model minority* refers to a person who is hardworking and technically skilled but desperately lacking in creativity, worldliness, and the ability to assimilate into mainstream culture (Huhr and Kim 1989; Takaki 1989). Representations in the media, no matter how subtle, of various social situations can distort and reinforce one's impressions of one's own nature (Goffman 1979).

Witnessing society's association of Asian features with negative personality traits and mental characteristics, many Asian Americans become attracted to the image of Caucasian, or at least Eurasian, features. Several of the women in my study stated that they are influenced by images of fashion models with Western facial types. As Nellee explained: "I used to read a lot of fashion magazines which showed occidental persons how to put makeup on. So I used to think a crease made one's eyes prettier. It exposes your eyelashes more. Right now they all go under the hood of my eyes." Likewise, Jo said she thought half of her discontent regarding her eyes is a self-esteem problem, but she blames the other half on society: "When you look at all the stuff that they portray on TV and in the movies and in Miss America Pageants, the epitome of who is beautiful is that all-American look. It can even include African Americans now but not Asians." According to Jo, she is influenced not only by representations of Asians as passive, dull, and narrow-minded, but also by a lack of representation of Asians in general because society considers them un-American, unassimilable, foreign, and to be excluded.

Similar images of Asians also exist in East and Southeast Asia, and since many Asian Americans are immigrants from Asia, they are likely influenced by these images as well. Multinational corporations in Southeast Asia, for example, consider the female work force biologically suited for the most monotonous industrial labor because they claim the "Oriental girl" is "diligent" and has "nimble fingers" and a "slow-wit" (Ong 1987:151). In addition, American magazines and films have become increasingly available in many parts of Asia since World War II, and Asian popular magazines and electronic media depict models with Western facial types, especially when advertizing Western products. In fact, many of my Asian American woman informants possessed copies of such magazines, available in various Asian stores and in Chinatown. Some informants, like Jane, a twenty-year-old Korean American who underwent double-eyelid surgery at age sixteen and nasal bridge surgery at age eighteen, thumbed through Korean fashion magazines which she stored in her living room to show me photos of the Western and Korean models who she thought looked Caucasian, Eurasian, or had had double-eyelid and nasal bridge surgeries. She said these women had eyes that were too wide and noses that were too tall and straight to be on Asians. Though she was born and raised in the United States, she visits her relatives in Korea often. She explained that the influences the media had on her life in Korea and in the United States were, in some sense, similar: "When you turn on the TV [in Korea] you see people like Madonna and you see MTV and American movies and magazines. In any fashion magazine you don't really see a Korean-type woman; you see Cindy Crawford. My mother was telling me that when she was a kid, the ideal beauty was someone with a totally round, flat face. Kind of small and five feet tall. I guess things began to change in the 50s when Koreans started to have a lot of contact with the West." The environment within which Asian women develop a perspective on the value and meaning of their facial features is most likely not identical in Asia and the United States, where Asian women are a minority, but in Asia one can still be influenced by Western perceptions of Asians.

Some of the women in my study maintained that although racial inequality may exist in many forms, their decision to widen their eyes had little to do with racial inequality; they were attempting to look like other Asians with double eyelids, not like Caucasians. Nina, for example, described a beautiful woman as such: "Her face should not have very slender eyes like Chinese, Korean, or Japanese but not as round as Europeans. Maybe a Filipino, Thai, or other Southeast Asian faces are ideal. Basically I like an Asian's looks. . . . I think Asian eyes [not really slender ones] are sexy and have character." The rest of her description, however, makes it more difficult for one to believe that the Asian eyes she is describing actually belong on an Asian body: "The skin should not be too dark . . . and the frame should be a bit bigger than that of Asians." Southeast Asians, too, seek cosmetic surgery for double eyelids and nose bridges. One doctor showed me "before" and "after" photos of many Thai, Indonesian, and Vietnamese American women, who, he said, came to him for wider, more definite creases so that their eyes, which already have a double-eyelid, would look deeper-set.

In the present global economy, where the movement of people and cultural products is increasingly rapid and frequent and the knowledge of faraway places and trends is expanding, it is possible to imagine that cultural exchange happens in a multiplicity of directions, that often people construct images and practices that appear unconnected to any particular locality or culture (Appadurai 1990). One might perceive Asian American women in my study as constructing aesthetic images of themselves based on neither a Caucasian ideal nor a stereotypical Asian face. The difficulty with such constructions, however, is that they do not help Asian Americans to escape at least one stereotypical notion of Asians in the United States—that they are "foreign" and "exotic." Even when Asians are considered sexy, and attractive in the larger American society, they are usually seen as exotically sexy and attractive (Yang and Ragaz 1993:21). Since their beauty is almost always equated with the exotic and foreign, they are seen as members of an undifferentiated mass of people. Even though the women in my study are attempting to be seen as individuals, they are seen, in some sense, as less distinguishable from each other than white women are. As Lumi, a Japanese former model recently told *A. Magazine: The Asian American Quarterly*, "I've had bookers tell me I'm beautiful, but that they can't use me because I'm 'type.' All the agencies have their one Asian girl, and any more would be redundant" (Chen 1993:21).

The constraints many Asian Americans feel with regard to the shape of their eyes and nose are clearly of a different quality from almost every American's discontent with weight or signs of aging: it is also different from the dissatisfaction many women, white and nonwhite alike, feel about the smallness or largeness of their breasts. Because the features (eyes and nose) Asian Americans are most concerned about are conventional markers of their racial identity, a rejection of these markers entails, in some sense, a devaluation of not only oneself but also other Asian Americans. It requires having to imitate, if not admire, the characteristics of another group more culturally dominant than one's own (i.e., Anglo Americans) in order that one can at least try to distinguish oneself from one's own group. Jane, for instance, explains that looking like a Caucasian is almost essential for socioeconomic success: "Especially if you go into business, or whatever, you kind of have to have a Western facial type and you have to have like their features and stature—you know, be tall and stuff. So you can see that [the surgery] is an investment in your future."

Unlike those who may want to look younger or thinner in order to find a better job or a happier social life, the women in my study must take into consideration not only their own socioeconomic future, but also more immediately that of their offspring, who by virtue of heredity, inevitably share their features. Ellen, for instance, said that "looks are not everything. I want my daughter, Stacy, to know that what's inside is important too. Sometimes you can look beautiful because your nice personality and wisdom inside radiate outward, such as in the way you talk and behave." Still, she has been encouraging twelve-year-old Stacy to have double-eyelid surgery because she thinks "having less sleepy looking eyes would make a better impression on people and help her in the future with getting jobs." Ellen had undergone cosmetic surgery at the age of twenty on the advice of her mother and older sister and feels she has benefited.[4] Indeed, all three women in the study under thirty who have actually undergone cosmetic surgery did so on the advice of their mother and in their mother's presence at the clinic. Elena, in fact, received her double-eyelid surgery as a high school graduation present from her mother, who was concerned for her socioeconomic future. The mothers, in turn, are influenced not so much by a personal flaw of their own which drives them to mold and perfect their daughters as by a society that values the superficial characteristics of one race over another.

A few of the women's dating and courtship patterns were also affected by their negative feelings toward stereotypically Asian features. Jo, for example, who is married to a Caucasian man, said she has rarely dated Asian men and is not usually attracted to them, partly because they look too much like her: "I really am sorry to say that I am not attracted to Asian men. And it's not to say that I don't find them attractive on the whole. But I did date a Japanese guy once and I felt like I was holding my brother's hand [she laughs nervously]."

A MUTILATION OF THE BODY

Although none of the women in my study denied the fact of racial inequality, almost all insisted that the surgical alteration of their eyes and nose was a celebration of their bodies, reflecting their right as women and as minorities to do what they wished with their bodies. Many, such as Jane, also said the surgery was a rite of passage or a routine ceremony, since family members and peers underwent the surgery upon reaching eighteen. Although it is at least possible to perceive cosmetic surgery of the eyes and nose for many Asian Americans as a celebration of the individual and social bodies, as in a rite of passage, this is clearly not so. My research has shown that double-eyelid and nasal bridge procedures performed on Asian Americans do not hold, for either the participants or the larger society, cultural meanings that are benign and spontaneous. Rather, these surgeries are a product of society's racial ideologies, and for many of the women in my study, the surgeries are a calculated means for socioeconomic success. In fact, most describe the surgery as something to "get out of the way" before carrying on with the rest of their lives.

Unlike participants in a rite of passage, these Asian American women share little *communitas* (an important element of rites of passage) with each other or with the larger society. Arnold Van Gennup defined rites of passage as "rites which accompany every change of place, state, social position, and age" (quoted in Turner 1969:94). These rites create an almost egalitarian type of solidarity (communitas) between participants and between the participants and a larger social group. A body modification procedure which is an example of such a rite is the series of public head-scarification rituals for pubescent boys among the Kabre of Togo, West Africa (Brain 1979:178). The final scars they acquire make them full adult members of their group. Their scarification differs considerably from the cosmetic surgery procedures of Asian American women in my study in at least two of its aspects: (1) an egalitarian bond is formed between the participants (between and among those who are doing the scarring and those who are receiving it); and (2) both the event and the resulting feature (i.e., scars) signify the boy's incorporation into a larger social group (i.e., adult men), and therefore, both are unrelentingly made public.

The Asian American women who undergo double-eyelid and nasal bridge surgeries do not usually create bonds with each other or with their plastic surgeons. Their surgery, unlike the scarification rite of the Kabre, is a private event that usually occurs in the presence of the patient, the doctor, and the doctor's assistants only. Moreover, there is little personal connection between doctor and patient. Though a few of the Asian American women in my study were content with their surgery and with their doctors, most describe their experience on the operating table as one of fear and loneliness, and some described their doctors as impersonal, businesslike, and even tending toward profit-making. Annie, for instance, described the fear she felt being alone with the doctor and his assistants in the operating room, when her mother suddenly left the room because she could not bear to watch:

> They told me to put my thumbs under my hips so I didn't interfere with my hands. I received two anesthesia shots on my nose—this was the only part of the operation that hurt, but it hurt! I closed my eyes. I didn't want to look. I didn't want to see like the knives or anything. I could feel like the snapping of scissors and I was aware when they were putting that thing up my nose. My mom didn't really care. They told her to look at my nose. They were wondering if I wanted it sharper and stuff. She said, "Oh no. I don't want to look" and just ran away. She was sitting outside. I was really pissed.

Elena described her experience of surgery in a similar manner: "I had no time to be nervous. They drugged me with valium, I think. I was awake but drugged, conscious but numb. I remember being on the table. They [doctor and nurses] continued to keep up a conversation. I would wince sometimes because I could feel little pinches. He [the doctor] would say, "Okay, Pumpkin, Sweetheart, it will be over soon." . . . I didn't like it, being called Pumpkin and being touched by a stranger. . . . I wanted to say Shut up! to all three people." Clearly, the event of surgery did not provide an opportunity or the atmosphere for the women in my study to forge meaningful relationships with their doctors.

Asian American women who undergo cosmetic surgery also have a very limited chance of bonding with each other by sharing experiences of the surgery, because unlike participants in a Kabre puberty rite, these women do not usually publicize either their operation or their new features. All informed me that apart from me and their doctors, few people knew about their surgery since at the most they had told three close friends and/or family members about it. As Annie stated, "I don't mind if people found out [that I had a nose operation], but I won't go around telling them." Jane explained: "It's nothing to be ashamed of, not at all, but it's not something you brag about either. . . . To this day my boyfriend doesn't notice I had anything done. That makes me feel pretty good. It's just that you want to look good, but you don't want them [other people] to know how much effort goes into it." In fact, all the women in my study said they wanted a "better" look, but one that was not so drastically different from the original that it looked "unnatural." Even those who underwent revision surgeries to improve on their first operation said they were more at ease and felt more effective in social situations (with boyfriends, classmates, and employers) after their primary operation, mainly because they looked subtly "better," not because they looked too noticeably different from the way they used to look. Thus, it is not public awareness of these women's cosmetic surgery or the resulting features which win them social acceptance. Rather, the successful personal concealment of the operation and of any glaring traces of the operation (e.g., scars or an "unnatural" look) is paramount for acceptance. Clearly, the alteration of their features is not a rite of passage celebrating the incorporation of individual bodies into a larger social body; rather, it is a personal quest by marginal people seeking acceptance in a society where the dominant culture's ideals loom large and are constraining. The extent to which the Asian American women have internalized society's negative valuation of their natural features is best exemplified by the fact that these women feel more self-confident in social interactions as a result of this slight alteration of their eyelids—that is, with one minor alteration in their whole anatomy—which others may not even notice.

MEDICINE AND THE "DISEMBODIMENT" OF THE ASIAN AMERICAN FEMALE CONSUMER

Some sectors of the medical profession fail to recognize that Asian American women's decision to undergo cosmetic surgery of the eyelid and the nose is not so much triggered by a simple materialistic urge to feel better with one more status item that money can buy as much as it is an attempt to heal a specific doubt about oneself which society has unnecessarily brought on. For instance, one doctor in my study stated the following about double-eyelid surgery on Asian American women: "It's like when you wear certain shoes, certain clothes, or put certain makeup on, well—why do you wear those? Why this brand of clothes and not another? . . . You can label these things different ways, but I think that it [the double-eyelid surgery of Asian Americans] is just a desire to look better. You know, it's like driving a brand-new car down the street or having something bought from Nordstrom." By viewing cosmetic surgery and items bought from a department store as equally arbitrary, plastic surgeons, like economists, sometimes assume that the consumer (in this case, the cosmetic surgery client) is disembodied (O'Neill 1985:103). They view her as an abstract, nonhuman subject whose choice of items is not mediated by any historical circumstances, symbolic meaning, or political significance.

With "advances" in science and technology and the proliferation of media images, the number of different selves one can become appears arbitrary and infinite to many Americans, including the women in my study. Thus, many of them argue, as do some plastic surgeons (see Kaw 1993), that the variation in the width of the crease requested by Asian Americans (from six to ten millimeters) is indicative of a whole range of personal and idiosyncratic styles in double-eyelid operations. The idea is that the women are not conforming to any standard, that they are molding their own standards of beauty. However, they ignore that a primary goal in all double-eyelid operations, regardless of how high or how far across the eyelid the crease is cut, is to have a more open appearance of the eye, and the trend in all cases is to create a fold where there was none. These operations are an instance of the paradoxical "production of variety within standardization" in American consumer culture (Goldstein 1993:152). Thus, there is a double bind in undergoing a double-eyelid operation. On the one hand, the women are rebelling against the notion that one must be content with the physical features one is born with, that one cannot be creative in molding one's own idea of what is beautiful. On the other hand, they are conforming to Caucasian standards of beauty.

The women in the study seem to have an almost unconditional faith that science and technology will help them feel satisfied with their sense of self. And the plastic surgery industry, with its scientific advances and seemingly objective stance, makes double-eyelid surgery appear routine, necessary, and for the most part, harmless (Kaw 1993). The women in my study had read advertisements of cosmetic surgery clinics, many of them catering to their specific "needs." In my interviews with Nellee, who had once thought about having double-eyelid surgery, and Jo, who is thinking about it for the near future, I did not have to tell them that the operation entailed creating a crease on the upper eyelid through incision and sutures. They told me. Jo, for instance, said, "I know the technology and it's quite easy, so I am not really afraid of it messing up."

CONCLUSION: PROBLEM OF RESISTANCE IN A CULTURE BASED ON ENDLESS SELF-FASHIONING

My research has shown that Asian American women's decision to undergo cosmetic surgery for wider eyes and more prominent noses is very much influenced by society's racial stereotyping of Asian features. Many of the women in my study are aware of the racial stereotypes from which they suffer. However, all have internalized these negative images of themselves and of other Asians, and they judge the Asian body, including their own, with the critical eye of the oppressor. Moreover, almost all share the attitude of certain sectors of the media and medicine in regard to whether undergoing a surgical operation is, in the end, harmful or helpful to themselves and other Asian Americans; they say it is yet another exercise of their freedom of choice.

The American value of individualism has influenced many of the women to believe that the specific width and shape they choose for their eyelid folds and nose bridges indicate that they are molding their own standards of beauty. Many said they wanted a "natural" look that would be uniquely "in balance" with the rest of their features. However, even those such as Jane, who openly expressed the idea that she is conforming to a Western standard of beauty, emphasized that she is not oppressed but rather empowered by her surgical transformation: "Everything is conforming as I see it. It's just a matter of recognizing it. . . . Other people—well, they are also conforming to something else. Nothing anybody has ever done is original. And it's very unlikely that people would go out and be dressed in any way if they hadn't seen it somewhere. So I don't think it's valid to put a value judgment on [the type of surgery I did]. I'm definitely for self-improvement. So if you don't like a certain part of your body, there's no reason not to change it."

The constraints Asian American women in my study feel every day with regard to their natural features are a direct result of unequal race relationships in the United States. These women's apparent lack of concern for their racial oppression is symptomatic of a certain postmodern culture arising in the United States which has the effect of hiding structural inequalities from public view (Bordo 1990). In its attempt to celebrate differences and to shun overgeneralizations and totalizing discourses that apparently efface diversity among people in modern life, this postmodern culture actually obscures differences; that is, by viewing differences as all equally arbitrary, it effaces from public consciousness historically determined differences in power between groups of people. Thus, blue contact lenses for African American women, and double eyelids and nose bridges for Asian women are both seen as forms of empowerment and indistinguishable in form and function from perms for white women, corn rows on Bo Derek, and tans on Caucasians. All cosmetic changes are seen in the same way—as having no cultural meaning and no political significance. In this process, what is trivialized and obscured is the difficult and often frustrated struggle with which subordinate groups must assert their difference as something to be proud of in the face of dominant ideologies (Bordo 1990:666).

With the proliferation of scientific and technological industries, the many selves one can become appear infinite and random. Like the many transformations of the persona of Madonna throughout her career or the metamorphosis of Michael Jackson's face during his "Black and White" video, the alteration of bodies through plastic surgery has become for the American public simply another means of self-expression and self-determination. As Ellen said, "You can be born Chinese. But if you want to look like a more desirable one, and if surgery is available like it is now, then why not do it?" She said that instead of having to undergo the arduous task of placing thin strips of transparent plastic tape over the eyelids to create a temporary crease (a procedure which, she said, many Asians unhappy with single eyelids used to do), Asians now have the option to permanently transform the shape of their eyes.

Thus, instead of becoming a battleground for social and cultural resistance, the body has become a playground (Bordo 1990:667). Like Michael Jackson's lyrics in the song "Man in the Mirror" ("If you want to make the world a better place, then take a look at yourself and make a change"; Jackson 1987), it is ambiguous whether political change and social improvement are best orchestrated through changing society or through an "act of creative interpretation" (Bordo 1990) of the superficial details of one's appearance. The problem and dilemma of resistance in U.S. society are best epitomized in this excerpt of my interview with Jo, the twenty-eight-year-old law student who is thinking of having double-eyelid surgery:

> JO: In my undergraduate college, every Pearl Harbor Day I got these phone calls and people would say, "Happy Pearl Harbor Day," and they made noises like bombs and I'd find little toy soldiers at my dorm door. Back then, I kind of took it as a joke. But now, I think it was more malicious. . . . [So] I think the surgery is a lot more superficial. Affecting how society feels about a certain race is a lot more beneficial. And it goes a lot deeper and lasts a lot longer.
> INTERVIEWER: Looking into the future, do you think you will do both?
> JO: Yeah [nervous laughter]. I do. I do.

Jo recognizes that undergoing double-eyelid surgery, that is, confirming the undesirability of Asian eyes, is in contradiction to the work she would like to do as a teacher and legal practitioner. However, she said she cannot easily destroy the negative feelings she already possesses about the natural shape of her eyes.

IMPLICATIONS: ASIAN AMERICANS AND THE AMERICAN DREAM

The psychological burden of having constantly to measure up has been often overlooked in the image of Asian Americans as model minorities, as people who have achieved the American dream. The model minority myth assumes not only that all Asian Americans are financially well-to-do, but also that those Asian Americans who are from relatively well-to-do, non-working-class backgrounds (like many of the women in my study) are free from the everyday constraints of painful racial stereotypes (see Takaki 1989; Hurh and Kim 1989). As my research has shown, the cutting up of Asian Americans' faces through plastic surgery is a concrete example of how, in modern life, Asian Americans, like other people of color, can be influenced by the dominant culture to loathe themselves in such a manner as to begin mutilating and revising parts of their body.

Currently, the eyes and nose are those parts of the anatomy which Asian Americans most typically cut and alter since procedures for these are relatively simple with the available technology. However, a few of the women in my study said that if they could, they would also want to increase their stature, and in particular, to lengthen their legs; a few also suggested that when safer implants were found, they wanted to augment their breasts; still others wanted more prominent brow bridges and jawlines. On the one hand, it appears that through technology women can potentially carve an endless array of new body types, breaking the bounds of racial categories. On the other hand, these desired body types are constructed in the context of the dominant culture's beauty ideals. The search for the ideal body may have a tremendous impact, in terms of racial discrimination, on patterns of artificial genetic selection, such as occurs at sperm banks, egg donation centers, and in the everyday ritual of courtship.

Acknowledgments

I first thank the many women who generously gave their time and shared their thoughts in interviews with me. Without their contributions, this research project would not have been possible.

I continue to thank Cecilia de Mello, without whose encouragements I never would have even begun to formulate my research. I am also grateful to Nancy Scheper-Hughes, Aihwa Ong, Paul Rabinow, Lynn Kwiatkowski, and Steve McGraw, as well as the various anonymous reviewers, for their insightful comments on earlier versions of this chapter.

This chapter appeared, in slightly different form, in *Medical Anthropology* 7:1(March 1993). Reproduced by permission of the American Anthropological Association.

I thank Nicole Sault for her patience, continual advice, and careful readings of the present chapter. Also, I am grateful to John Kelly and Rena Lederman for their willingness to read and provide helpful comments.

Notes

[1]I have not yet found descriptions, in medical texts and newspaper articles, of the types of cosmetic surgery specifically requested by Latinos. However, one newspaper article (Ellison 1990) reports that an increasing number of Mexicans are purchasing a device by which they can attain a more Nordic and Anglo-Saxon "upturned" nose. It requires inserting plastic hooks in the nostrils.
[2]The shapes of the eye and nose of Asians are not meant in this chapter to be interpreted as categories which define a group of people called Asians. Categories of racial groups are arbitrarily defined by society. Likewise, the physical traits people in a racial group are recognized by are arbitrary (see Molnar 1983).

Also, I use the term *Asian American* to name collectively the women in this study who have undergone or are thinking about undergoing cosmetic surgery. Although I recognize their ethnic, generational, and geographical diversity, people of Asian ancestry in the United States share similar experiences in that they are subject to many of the same racial stereotypes (see Hurh and Kim 1989; Takaki 1989).

[3]Cosmetic surgery for double eyelids, nasal tip refinement, and nose bridges are not limited to Asians in the United States. Asians in East and Southeast Asia have requested such surgeries since the early 1950s, when U.S. military forces began long-term occupations of such countries as Korea and the Philippines. Some American doctors (such as Millard) were asked by Asians in these countries to perform the surgeries. See Harahap 1982; Kristof 1991; Millard 1964; Sayoc 1954.

[4]Ellen's mother, however, did not receive double-eyelid or nose bridge surgery. It appears that the trend of actually undergoing such surgeries began with Asian women who are now about forty to fifty years of age. Jane and Annie, sisters in their early twenties, said that though their mother who is about fifty had these surgeries, their grandmother did not. They also said that their grandmother encouraged them to have the operation, as did their mother.

None of the women in my study mentioned their father or other males in their household or social networks as verbally encouraging them to have the surgeries. However, many said they felt their resulting features would or did help them in their relationships with men, especially boyfriends (Asians and non-Asians alike). We did not discuss in detail their father's reaction to their surgery, but those who mentioned their father's reaction summed it up mainly as indifference.

References

American Society of Plastic and Reconstructive Surgeons (ASPRS). N.d. "Estimated Number of Cosmetic Surgery Procedures Performed by ASPRS Members in 1990." Pamphlet.

APPADURAI, ARJUN. 1990. "Disjuncture and Difference in the Global Cultural Economy." *Public Culture* 2(2): 1–24.

BLACKING, JOHN. 1977. *The Anthropology of the Body*. London: Academic Press.

BORDO, SUSAN. 1990. "Material Girl: The Effacements of Postmodern Culture." *Michigan Quarterly Review* 29:635–676.

BRAIN, ROBERT. 1979. *The Decorated Body*. New York: Harper and Row.

CHEN, JOANNE. 1993. "Before and After: For Asian Americans, the Issues Underlying Cosmetic Surgery Are Not Just Skin Deep." *A. Magazine: The Asian American Quarterly* 2(1): 15–18, 26–27.

DALY, MARY. 1978. *Gyn/ecology: The Metaethics of Radical Feminism*. Boston: Beacon Press.

DAVIS, KATHY. 1991. "Remaking the She-Devil: A Critical Look at Feminist Approaches to Beauty." *Hypatia* 6(2): 21–43.

DOWER, JOHN. 1986. *War without Mercy: Race and Power in the Pacific War*. New York: Pantheon.

ELLISON, KATHERINE. 1990. "Mexico Puts on a Foreign Face." *San Jose Mercury News*, December 16, p. 14a.

FLEMING, CHARLES, and MARY TALBOT. 1993. "The Two Faces of Michael Jackson." *Newsweek*, February 22, p. 57.

GILMAN, SANDER L. 1985. *Difference and Pathology: Stereotypes of Sexuality, Race and Madness*. Ithaca, N.Y.: Cornell University Press.

GOFFMAN, ERVING. 1979. *Gender Advertisement*. Cambridge: Harvard University Press.

GOLDSTEIN, JUDITH. 1993. "The Female Aesthetic Community." *Poetics Today* 14(1): 143–163.

HARAHAP, MARWALI. 1982. "Oriental Cosmetic Blepharoplasty." In *Cosmetic Surgery for Non-white Patients*, ed. Harold Pierce, pp. 79–97. New York: Grune and Stratton.

HURH, WON MOO, and KWANG CHUNG KIM. 1989. "The 'Success' Image of Asian Americans: Validity, and Its Practical and Theoretical Implications." *Ethnic and Racial Studies* 12(4):512–537.

IWATA, EDWARD. 1991. "Race without Face." *San Francisco Image Magazine*, May, pp. 51–55.

JACKSON, MICHAEL. 1987. "Man in the Mirror." On *Bad*. Epic Records, New York.

KAW, EUGENIA. 1993. "Medicalization of Racial Features: Asian American Women and Cosmetic Surgery." *Medical Anthropology Quarterly* 7(1):74–89.

KIM, ELAINE. 1986. "Asian-Americans and American Popular Culture." In *Dictionary of Asian-American History*, ed. Hyung-Chan Kim. New York: Greenwood Press.

KRISTOF, NICHOLAS. 1991. "More Chinese Look 'West.' " *San Francisco Examiner and Chronicle*, July 7.

LAKOFF, ROBIN T., and RAQUEL L. SCHERR. 1984. *Face Value: The Politics of Beauty*. Boston: Routledge and Kegan.

LEFLORE, IVENS C. 1982. "Face Lift, Chin Augmentation and Cosmetic Rhinoplasty in Blacks." In *Cosmetic Surgery in Non-White Patients*, ed. Harold Pierce. New York: Grune and Stratton.

LOCK, MARGARET, and NANCY SCHEPER-HUGHES. 1990. "A Critical-Interpretive Approach in Medical Anthropology: Rituals and Routines of Discipline and Dissent." In *Medical Anthropology: Contemporary Theory and Method*, ed. Thomas Johnson and Carolyn Sargent, pp. 47–72. New York: Praeger.

MCCURDY, JOHN A. 1990. *Cosmetic Surgery of the Asian Face*. New York: Thieme Medical Publishers.

MACGREGOR, FRANCES C. 1967. "Social and Cultural Components in the Motivations of Persons Seeking Plastic Surgery of the Nose." *Journal of Health and Social Behavior* 8(2):125–135.

MERRELL, KATHY H. 1994. "Saving Faces." *Allure*, January, pp. 66–68.

MILLARD, RALPH, JR. 1964. "The Original Eyelid and Its Revision." *American Journal of Ophthalmology* 57:546–649.

MOLNAR, STEPHEN. 1983. *Human Variation: Races, Types, and Ethnic Groups*. Englewood Cliffs, N.J.: Prentice-Hall.

NAKAO, ANNIE. 1993. "Faces of Beauty: Light Is Still Right." *San Francisco Examiner and Chronicle*, April 11, p. D-4.

O'NEILL, JOHN. 1985. *Five Bodies*. Ithaca, N.Y.: Cornell University Press.

ONG, AIHWA. 1987. *Spirits of Resistance and Capitalist Discipline: Factory Women in Malaysia*. Albany: State University of New York Press.

RAMSDELL, DANIEL. 1983. "Asia Askew: U.S. Best-sellers on Asia, 1931–1980." *Bulletin of Concerned Asian Scholars* 15(4):2–25.

ROSENTHAL, ELISABETH. 1991. "Ethnic Ideals: Rethinking Plastic Surgery." *New York Times*, September 25, p. B7.

SAYOC, B. T. 1954. "Plastic Construction of the Superior Palpebral Fold." *American Journal of Ophthalmology* 38:556–559.

———. 1974. "Surgery of the Oriental Eyelid." *Clinics in Plastic Surgery* 1(1):157–171.

SHEETS-JOHNSTONE, MAXINE, ed. 1992. *Giving the Body Its Due*. Albany: State University of New York Press.

TAJIMA, RENEE E. 1989. "Lotus Blossoms Don't Bleed: Images of Asian Women." In *Making Waves: An Anthology of Writings by and about Asian American Women*, ed. Diane Yeh-Mei Wong, pp. 308–317. Boston: Beacon Press.

TAKAKI, RONALD. 1989. *Strangers from a Different Shore*. Boston: Little, Brown.

TURNER, TERENCE. 1980. "The Social Skin." In *Not Work Alone*, ed. J. Cherfas and R. Lewin, pp. 112–114. London: Temple Smith.

TURNER, VICTOR. 1969. *The Ritual Process: Structure and Anti-Structure*. Chicago: Aldine.

WOLF, NAOMI. 1991. *The Beauty Myth: How Images of Beauty Are Used against Women*. New York: William Morrow.

YANG, JEFF, and ANGELO RAGAZ. 1993. "The Beauty Machine." *A. Magazine: The Asian American Quarterly* 2(1):20–21.

Michelle Fine and Pat Macpherson

Over Dinner: Feminism and Adolescent Female Bodies*

> *The experience of being woman can create an illusory unity, for it is not the experience of being woman but the meanings attached to gender, race, class, and age at various historical moments . . . that [are] of strategic significance.*
> —CHANDRA MOHANTY, "Feminist Encounters" (1987, 123)

When we invited four teenagers—Shermika, Damalleaux, Janet, and Sophie—for a series of dinners to talk with us about being young women in the 1990s, we could not see our own assumptions about female adolescence much more clearly than we saw theirs. By the end of the first dinner, we could, though, recognize how old we were, how dated the academic literatures were, how powerful feminism had been in shaping their lives and the meanings they made of them, and yet how inadequately their feminism dealt with key issues of identity and peer relations.

Only when we started to write could we see the inadequacies of our feminism to understand the issues of female adolescence they struggled to communicate. In this space of our incredulity, between our comprehension of their meanings and our *incomprehension* of "how they could call themselves feminist," we are now able to see the configuration of our own fantasies of feminism for female adolescents. The re-vision that is central to feminist process gets very tricky when applied to adolescence, because our own unsatisfactory pasts return as the "before" picture, demanding that the "after" picture of current adolescent females measure all the gains of the women's movement. Our longing is for psychic as well as political completion. Michael Payne (1991, 18) describes the fantasy of the Other: "What I desire—and therefore lack—is in the other culture, the other race, the other gender"—the other generation, in our case. In the case of these four young women, to our disbelief, the desired Other is "one of the guys."

We grew convinced that we needed to construct an essay about these young women's interpretations of the discourses of adolescence, femininity, and feminism in their peer cultures. Barbara Hudson explains the incompatibility of femininity and adolescence:

*Complete citations to all the articles referred to in this reading can be found in M. Fine (1992). *Disruptive Voices: The possibilities of feminist research.* Ann Arbor: University of Michigan Press.

femininity and adolescence as discourses [are] subversive of each other. All of our images of the adolescent—the restless, searching teen; the Hamlet figure; the sower of wild oats and tester of growing powers—these are masculine figures. . . . If adolescence is characterized by masculine constructs, then any attempt by girls to satisfy society's demands of them qua adolescents is bound to involve them in displaying notably a lack of maturity but also a lack of femininity. (1984, 35)

75

MICHELLE FINE AND
PAT MACPHERSON
Over Dinner:
Feminism and
Adolescent Female
Bodies

Adolescence for these four young women was about the adventures of males and the constraints on females, so their version of feminism unselfconsciously rejected femininity and embraced the benign version of masculinity that allowed them to be "one of the guys." They fantasized the safe place of adolescence to be among guys who overlook their (female) gender out of respect for their (unfeminine) independence, intelligence, and integrity. For them, femininity meant the taming of adolescent passions, outrage, and intelligence. Feminism was a flight from "other girls" as unworthy and untrustworthy. Their version of feminism was about equal access to being men.

When we scoured the literatures on adolescent females and their bodies, we concluded that the very construction of the topic is positioned largely from white, middle-class, nondisabled, heterosexual, adult women's perspectives. The concerns of white elite women are represented as *the* concerns of this age cohort. Eating disorders are defined within the contours of what *elite* women suffer (e.g., anorexia and bulimia) and less so what nonelite women experience (e.g., overeating, obesity, etc.). The sexual harassment literature is constructed from *our* age perspective—that unwanted sexual attention is and should be constituted as a crime—and not from the complicated perspectives of the young women involved. The disability literature is saturated with images produced by *nondisabled* researchers of self-pitying or embarrassed "victims" of biology and is rarely filled with voices of resistant, critical, and powerfully "flaunting" adolescents who refuse to wear prostheses, delight in the passions of their bodies and are outraged by the social and family discrimination they experience (Fine and Asch 1988; Frank 1988; Corbett 1989).

We found that women of all ages, according to this literature, are allegedly scripted to be "good women," and that they have, in compliance, smothered their passions, appetites, and outrage. When sexually harassed, they tell "his stories" (Brodkey and Fine 1988). To please the lingering internalized "him," they suffer in body image and indulge in eating disorders (Orbach 1986). And to satisfy social demands for "attractiveness," women with and without disabilities transform and mutilate their bodies (Bordo 1990).

We presumed initially that the three arenas of adolescence in which young women would most passionately struggle with gendered power would include eating, sexuality, and outrage. And so we turned to see what these literatures said and to unpack how race, class, disability, and sexuality played with each of these literatures. In brief, within these literatures, we saw a polarizing: (1) eating disorders appear to be a question studied among elite white women in their anticipated tensions of career vs. mother identities; (2) sexuality is examined disproportionately as problematic for girls who are African-American and underprivileged, with motherhood as their primary identity posed as "the problem"; and (3) finally, young women's political outrage simply does not exist as a category for feminist intellectual analysis. The literature on adolescent women had thoroughly extricated these categories of analysis from women's lives. So, in our text, we decided to rely instead upon the frames that these young women offered as they narrated their own lives and the interpretations we could generate through culture and class.

Our method was quite simple, feminist, and, ironically, anti–eating disorder. We invited the six of us to talk together over pizza and soda, while Sam—Michelle's four-year-old—circled the table. We talked for hours, on two nights two months apart, and together stretched to create conversations about common differences—about the spaces in which we could delight together as six women; the moments in which they bonded together as four young women who enjoy football, hit their boyfriends, and can't trust other girls (not ever!); and, too, the arenas in which the race, class, and cultural distances in the room stretched too far for these age-peers to weave any common sense of womanhood. Collectively, we created a context that Shermika and Sophie spontaneously considered "the space where I feel most safe." We were together, chatting, listening, hearing, laughing a lot, and being truly interested in understanding our connections and differences, contoured always along the fault lines of age, class, race and culture, bodies, experiences, and politics.

But we each delighted in this context differently. For Michelle and Pat, it was a space in which we could pose feminist intellectual questions from our generation—questions about sexuality, power, victimization, and politics—which they then turned on their heads. For Shermika (African-American, age fifteen), it was a place for public performance, to say outrageous things, admit embarrassing moments, "practice" ways of being female in public discourse, and see how we would react. For Damalleaux (African-American, age fourteen), it was a place to "not be shy," even though the room was integrated by race, a combination that had historically made her uncomfortable. For Sophie ("WASP," age seventeen), it was a "safe place" where, perhaps for the first time, she was not the only "out" feminist in a room full of peers. And for Janet (Korean-American, age seventeen), like other occasions in which she was the only Asian-American among whites and African-Americans, it was a time to test her assimilated "sense of belonging," always at the margins. In negotiating gender, race/ethnicity, and class as critical, feminist agents, these four women successfully betrayed a set of academic literatures written by so many of us only twenty years older. Our writings have been persistently committed to public representations of women's victimization and structural assaults and have consequently ignored, indeed misrepresented, *how well young women talk as subjects*, passionate about and relishing their capacities to move between nexus of power and powerlessness. That is to say, feminist scholars have forgotten to take notice of how firmly young women resist—alone and sometimes together.

The four young women began their conversation within this space of gendered resistance. Shermika complained, "Boys think girls cannot do *any*thing," to which Sophie added, "So we have to harass them." Shermika explained, "[Guys think] 'long as they're takin' care of 'em, [girls will] do anything they want. And if I'm in a relationship, I'm gonna take care of you just as much as you take care of me. You can't say 'I did this'—No: 'We did this.' . . . Guys think you're not nothin'—anything—without them." Janet sneered, "Ego."

77

MICHELLE FINE AND
PAT MACPHERSON
*Over Dinner:
Feminism and
Adolescent Female
Bodies*

Shermika recruited her friend into this conversation by saying, "Damalleaux *rule* her boyfriend [Shermika's brother]." Damalleaux announced her governing principle: "Boys—they try to take advantage of you. . . . As far as I'm concerned, I won't let a boy own me." Janet provided an example of the "emotionally messed up guys" she encounters: "I didn't want to take care of him. I didn't want to constantly explain things to him. . . . I want to coexist with them and not be like their mother. . . . It happened to me twice." And Sophie explained: "I'm really assertive with guys [who say sexist stuff]. If they have to be shot down I'll shoot them down. They have to know their place."

The four expressed their feminism here as resistance to male domination in their peer relations. They applied the same principle in discussing how they saw careers and marriage, when Michelle asked about men in their future plans. Shermika laid it out in material terms: "I imagine bein' in my *own* house in *my name*. And then get married. So my husband can get out of *my house*." Sophie chimed in, "Seriously," and Shermika nodded, "Yes, *very important*. So I won't end up one of them battered women we were talkin' about. I'm not going to have no man beatin' on me." Sophie offered her version: "You have to like be independent. You have to establish yourself as your own person before some guy takes you—I mean." Janet asserted her standard of independence: "I wouldn't follow a guy to college." Their feminism asserted women's independence from men's power to dominate and direct.

Class and cultural differences entered the conversations with their examples of domination and resistance. Shermika's example of guys materially "takin' care" of girls to establish dominance and Damalleaux's resistance to male "ownership" reflected the practice of gift giving as ownership, a norm of their local sexual politics (see Anderson 1990). Damalleaux explained that respect could interrupt this dominance structure: "How much respect a guy has for you—especially in front of his friends? . . . If a boy finds out you don't care how they treat you, and you don't have respect for your*self* . . . they won't have respect for you." Damalleaux turned to Shermika and said, "You try to teach me." Shermika's talk was full of lessons learned from her mother and examples of their closeness. "My mom and me like this. 'Cause she understands." Not talking "*leads* to problems. My mom tells me so much about life."

Sophie and Janet defined their resistance within their "professional class," peopled by "individuals," not relationships, who suffer from the dilemmas of "independence," typically explained in terms of psychology. Their isolation from their mothers and female friends enabled them to frame their stories alone, as one-on-one battles across the lines of gender and generations.

WAYS OF TALKING: ON CULTURES OF WOMENHOOD

Herein lies a cautionary tale for feminists who insist that underneath or beyond the differences among women there must be some shared identity—as if commonality were a metaphysical given, as if a shared viewpoint were not a difficult political achievement. . . . Western feminist theory has in effect . . . [demanded that] Afro-American, Asian-American or Latin-American women separate their "woman's voice" from their racial or ethnic voice without also

requiring white women to distinguish being a "woman" from being white.
This double standard implies that while on the one hand there is a seamless
web of whiteness and womanness, on the other hand, Blackness and woman-
ness, say, or Indianness and womanness, are discrete and separable elements
of identity. If . . . I believe that the woman in every woman is a woman just
like me, and if I also assume that there is no difference between being white
and being a woman, then seeing another woman "as a woman" will involve
me seeing her as fundamentally like the woman I am. In other words, the
womanness underneath the Black woman's skin is a white woman's, and deep
down inside the latina woman is an Anglo woman waiting to burst through
the obscuring cultural shroud. As Barbara Omolade has said, "Black women
are not white women with color."

—ELIZABETH SPELMAN, The Inessential Woman (1988, 13)

At this moment in social history, when the tensions of race, class, and gender couldn't be in more dramatic relief, social anxieties load onto the bodies of adolescent women (Fine 1991: Halson 1990). Struggles for social control attach to these unclaimed territories, evident in public debates over teen pregnancy, adolescent promiscuity, parental consent for contraception and abortion, date rapes, and stories of sexual harassment, as well as in women's personal narratives of starving themselves or binging and purging toward thinness. For each of these social "controversies" there is, however, a contest of wills, a set of negotiations. Young women are engaged with questions of "being female"; that is, who will control, and to what extent can they control, their own bodies?

Threaded through our conversations at the dining room table, culture and class helped to construct (at least) two distinct versions of womanhood. It became clear that the elite women, for instance, constructed an interior sense of womanhood out of oppositional relations with white men. They positioned white men as the power group White Men (H. Baker, pers. com., 1989). And they positioned themselves in an ongoing, critical, hierarchical struggle with these men. Sophie, for example, often defined her feminism in relation to white boys; instead of "reinforcing guys all the time, I BUST on guys. Because if you don't bust 'em they'll get ahead. You have to keep 'em in their place."

It was quite another thing to hear the sense of womanhood constructed horizontally—still in struggle—by African-American women, situated with or near African-American men. Given the assault on African-American men by the broader culture, it was clear that any announced sense of female superiority would be seen as "castrating" and unreconcilable with cross-gender alliances against racism (Giddings 1984; hooks 1984). So, the construction of African-American womanhood was far less dichotomized and oppositional toward men and far richer in a sense of connection to community.[1] In the context of being "deprived," then, of the traditional (oppositional to White Men) feminine socialization, women of color, like women with disabilities, may construct womenhoods less deeply repulsed by the traditional accoutrements of femininity, less oppositional to the cardboard White Male, and less assured that gender survives as the primary, or exclusive, category of social identity.

Among these four, then, we heard two quite distinct constructions of "being female." From the African-American women, both living in relatively impoverished circumstances, we heard a "womanhood" of fluid connections

79

MICHELLE FINE AND
PAT MACPHERSON
Over Dinner:
Feminism and
Adolescent Female
Bodies

among women within and across generations; maturity conceived of as an extension of self with others; a taken-for-granted integration of body and mind; a comfortable practice of using public talk as a place to "work out" concerns, constraints, and choices; and a nourishing, anchored sense of home and community. bell hooks describes "home" as the site of nurturance and identity, positive in its resistance to racist ideologies of African-American inferiority:

> Despite the brutal reality of racial apartheid, of domination, one's homeplace was the one site where one could freely confront the issue of humanization, where one could resist. Black women resisted by making homes where all black people could strive to be subjects, not objects, where we could be affirmed in our minds and our hearts despite poverty, hardship and deprivation, where we could restore to ourselves the dignity denied us on the outside in the public world. (hooks 1990)

As the words of Damalleaux and Shermika reveal to us, however, the drawback of this centeredness in community is in its fragility, its contingent sense of the future, terrors of what's "across the border," and the lack of resources or supports for planned upward mobility.

Indeed, when we discussed future plans, Shermika "joked" that she'd be a custodian or bag lady. She joked that she'd like to be dead, to see what the other world was like. She said she'd like to come back as a bird—"Not a pigeon, I hope," said Sophie. "Dove or peacock," Shermika decided, "something nobody be kickin' around all the time." Shermika finally confided—in an uncharacteristic whisper—that she'd like to be a lawyer, even the D.A. (district attorney). What Shermika can be, could be, would like to be, and will be constitutes the terrain of Shermika's and Damalleaux's dilemma. Shermika doesn't worry that education would defeminize her or that her parents expect more or different from her career than she does. She quite simply and realistically doubts she'll be able to get all the way to D.A.

Nevertheless, Damalleaux and Shermika, on the other hand, expressed the connections with and respect for mothers found in Gloria Joseph and Jill Lewis's African-American daughters: "A decisive 94.5% expressed respect for their mothers in terms of strength, honesty, ability to overcome difficulties, and ability to survive" (1981, 94). Shermika's many examples of respect for her mother and Damalleaux's mother calling her "my first girl" suggest "the centrality of mothers in their daughters' lives" (Joseph and Lewis 1981, 79). In their stories, active female sexuality and motherhood are everywhere "embodied," while "career" is a distant and indistinct dream—marginal, foreign, and threateningly isolated.

In contrast, from the two privileged women, both living in relatively elite circumstances, we heard a womanhood struggling for positive definition and safe boundaries; a sharp splitting of body and mind; maturity as a dividing of self from family and school to find individual identity; and an obsessive commitment to using privacy—in body, thought, and conversation—as the only way to "work out" one's problems. All nourished a highly individualized, privatized, and competitive sense of home and community as sites from which they would ultimately leave, unfettered, to launch "autonomous" lives as independent women. Materially and imaginatively these two women recognized an almost uninterruptable trajectory for future plans. Their womanhood was built on the sense of *self as exception*, "achievement" meritocratically determining how exceptional each individual can prove herself (away) from the group. Self-as-exception, for women, involves transcending gender. Rachel Hare-Mustin describes the illusion of gender-neutral choices:

> The liberal/humanist tradition of our epoch assumes that the meanings of our lives reflect individual experience and individual subjectivity. This tradition has idealized individual identity and self-fulfillment and shown a lack of concern about power. Liberalism masks male privilege and dominance by holding that every (undergendered) individual is free. The individual has been regarded as responsible for his or her fate and the basic social order has been regarded as equitable. Liberal humanism implies free choice when individuals are not free of coercion by the social order. (Hare-Mustin 1991, 3)

The invisibility of women's "coercion by the social order" came out most clearly in Janet's and Sophie's relationships with their working mothers. They did not analyze their mothers' lives for power.

Sophie said, "My mom doesn't like her job but she has to work so I can go to college." Janet and Sophie said they were afraid of becoming their mothers, unhappy and overworked in jobs they hate, their workloads doubled with domestic responsibilities. "I fear I might be like her. I want to be independent of her," white, middle-class women said of their mothers in the research of Joseph and Lewis (1981, 125). Janet and Sophie said they didn't talk much, or very honestly, to their mothers and didn't feel they could ever do enough to gain their mothers' approval. Janet said, "My mother [says] I really have to go to college . . . be a doctor or lawyer. . . . That's her main goal . . . job security . . . then she wants me to get married and have a nice family . . . preferably Catholic. . . . Mom's got my life mapped out." Ambition and career embody this mother-daughter relationship, in a sense, while the daughter's problems with sexuality and power and the mother *as woman* are absent in the relationship Janet describes.

When discussing who they'd tell if they had a problem, Shermika immediately said, "My mom," and Damalleaux said, "I tell Shermika almost everything before I tell my mother." Sophie and Janet agreed only in the negative. It wouldn't be their mothers: "Don't talk to my mom."

JANET: I can't tell my mother anything. If I told her something she would ground me for an entire century.

SOPHIE: Once you tell them one thing, they want to hear more, and they *pry*. I keep my home life and school—social—life so separate.

JANET: I'll be noncommittal or I won't tell her the truth. I'll just tell her what she wants to hear.

SOPHIE: I wish I could talk to my mom. It'd be great if I could.

SHERMIKA: It's the wrong thing to do [not talking], though. . . . It always *leads* to problems. My mom tells me so much about life.

Janet said her mother stares at her complexion [her acne] and says, "You're not going to get married, you're not going to have a boyfriend." "I get so mad at her," Janet says. She tells her mother either "I'm leaving, I'm leaving" or "Stop it! Stop it!" Later, when Pat asked whether self-respect was learned from the mother, Janet said her self-respect had "nothing to do with my mother. I used to hate myself, partly because of my mother. But not anymore. My mother's opinion just doesn't matter to me." Sophie said,

81

MICHELLE FINE AND
PAT MACPHERSON
*Over Dinner:
Feminism and
Adolescent Female
Bodies*

> My mother . . . nitpicks. . . . I'm sure it was like her mom [who] never approved anything about her. I get self-respect from my mom because she wants me to respect myself. . . . I don't think she respects herself enough. I respect her more than she respects herself. Her mother belittled her so much.

Later Sophie said, "I have the feeling that no matter what I do, it's not enough," Janet said her mother makes her and her sister feel like her mother's "racehorses":

> My mom *lives* through her kids. Two daughters: two *chances*. My sister wants to be an actress and my parents hate that [dykey] way she looks. . . . My mom; "You're just not *feminine* enough!" I'm just like, "Mom, grow up!" . . . She compares her daughters to everyone else's. [One example is] a straight-A student on top of all her chores. . . . I know there's things in her personality that are part of myself. . . . We're just like racehorses. . . . "My daughter has three wonderful children and a husband who makes a million dollars a year."

For Janet and Sophie, their mothers were supports to get over, central to the life these daughters wished to escape, and to revise, in their own futures. Within their liberal discourse of free choice, the inequalities of power determining their mothers' misery were invisible to them—and their own exceptional futures also unquestioned.

THE BODY: BOUNDARIES AND CONNECTIONS

Over our dinners, we created a democracy of feminist differences. That is, all four, as an age/gender cohort, introduced us to the female body in play with gendered politics. These young women consistently recast *our* prioritizing of sex at the center of feminist politics into *their* collective critique of gender politics. Using a language that analyzed dominance and power, they refused to separate sex from other power relations. Perhaps even more deeply Foucaultian than we assumed ourselves to be, they deconstructed our voyeurism with examples of sexuality as only one embodied site through which gendered politics operate. All four shared a distrust of men ("they think they have power"), but they also distrusted female solidarity ("they backstab you all the time"). Their examples overturned our notions of sisterhood by showing us that both young women and young men proficiently police the borders, and tenets, of masculinity and femininity among today's teens. They are often reminded of their bodies as a public site (gone right or wrong), commented on and monitored by others—male and female. But as often, they reminded us, they forcefully reclaim their bodies by talking back and by talking feminist. "It'd be harder not to talk," Sophie thinks. "It'd be harder to sit and swallow whatever people are saying."

Resonating with much of feminist literature, when these four young women spoke of their bodies, it was clear that they found themselves sitting centrally at the nexus of race, class, and gender politics. Gender determines that the young women are subject to external surveillance and responsible for internal body management, and it is their gender that makes them feel vulnerable to male sexual threat and assault. Culture and class determine how—that is, the norms of body and the codes of surveillance, management, threat, assault, and resistance available to them.

Susan Bordo (1990) writes about body management as a text for "the controlling" / "controlling the" middle class. Reflecting both elite material status and a pure, interior soul, this fetish of body management, operated by the "normalizing machinery of power," produces a desire to control flesh otherwise out of control, as it positions individuals within an elite class location. The tight, svelte body reflects material and moral comfort, while the loose, sagging body falls to the "lumpen." Bordo's cultural analysis of the representations and experiences of women's bodies, and women's revulsion at sagging fat, captures, and yet too narrowly homogenizes, what the four young women reported.

Each of the four, as Bordo would argue, was meticulously concerned with her body as the site for cataloging both her own and others' "list" of her inadequacies. Indeed, each body had become the space within which she would receive unsolicited advice about having "too many pimples," "being too chocolate," "looking chubby," "becoming too thin," "looking like a boy," or, in the case of a sister, dressing "very butch." The fetish to control, however, was experienced in ways deeply classed and raced. While the elite women were familiar with, if not obsessed by, eating disorders now fashionable among their status peers, the African-American women were quite literally bewildered at the image of a young woman binging on food and then purging. Therein lies a serious problem in white feminist literature: class and culture practices are coded exclusively as gender, reinforcing hegemonic definitions of (white) womanhood, while obscuring class/culture contours of the body.

For these women, the female body not only signified a site of interior management vis-à-vis male attention/neglect. It was also a site for gendered politics enacted through sexual violence. Celia Kitzinger (1988), in an analysis of how two thousand young women and men frame their personal experiences with "unfairness," found that 24 percent of interviewed girls spontaneously volunteered instances of body-centered unfairness, including sexual harassment, rape, and/or abuse. So, too, violence stories were offered by all four of the young women, each particular to her social context:

> When I got my first boyfriend [he] pressured me to have sex with him. That's why I didn't never go over his house. (Damalleaux)
> I feel safe nowhere. (Sophie)
> When he pulled a gun on me, I said, "This is over." (Shermika)
> I know it's unlikely, but I am terrified of someday being date raped. It's always been something I've been afraid of. (Janet)

For Janet, violence is imagined as possible because of the stories of her friends. For Sophie, violence is encountered as harassment on the street. For Damalleaux and Shermika, violence is encountered or threatened in relations with boyfriends.

*   *   *

MICHELLE: Is there any place where guys have more power than you?
DAMALLEAUX: In bed.

SHERMIKA: In the street. In the store, when he has all the money.
DAMALLEAUX: And all the guys can beat girls. But I don't think it's true.

83

MICHELLE FINE AND
PAT MACPHERSON
*Over Dinner:
Feminism and
Adolescent Female
Bodies*

MICHELLE: Are you ever afraid that the hitting will get bad?
SHERMIKA: Yeah, that's why I don't do so much hitting.
DAMALLEAUX: When I go out with a boy I hit him a lot to see if he's going to do anything. . . . You hit me once, I don't want anything to do with you.

* * *

SHERMIKA: Sometimes you can get raped with words, though. You feel so slimy. . . . The guy at the newspaper stand, I speak to him every morning. Then one day he said, "How old is you? I can't wait till you sixteen." And I told my mom, and she came [with me and told him off]. He lost respect. He didn't give me none. And that day I felt bad, what was I, bein' too loose? . . . You just can't help feelin' like that [slimy].

Liz Kelly (1988, 41) offers this definition of sexual violence:

> Sexual violence includes any physical, visual, verbal or sexual act that is experienced by the woman or girl, at the time or later, as a threat, invasion or assault, that has the effect of degrading or hurting her and/or takes away her ability to control intimate contact.

We found that the impression and/or experience of surviving male violence was indeed central. But its expression was, again, classed and raced. These fears and experiences were deeply traumatic to all the women, and yet the African-American women more frequently and more publicly, if uncomfortably, related them in the context of conversation. For the elite women, the assaults and fears were more privatized and so left relatively unanalyzed, unchallenged, and in critical ways "buried." For example, Janet's story of a friend's date rape contrasts radically with Shermika's stories of male violence and female resistance.

JANET: That happened to one of my friends.
SOPHIE: A date rape?
JANET: Sort of. . . . He'd been pressuring her for a long time, and she's just "no no no no." She's at this party, her [girl] friend says, "Why don't you just do it?" and she says, "Because I don't *want* to." . . . She was drunk, puking. She fell asleep, and the next thing she knows she wakes up and he's on top of her and she's not really happy about it but she didn't do anything about it so she just let it happen. And . . . she was upset about it, she was really angry about it, but there was nothing she could *do* about it? [Janet's voice rises to a kind of question mark.] It didn't really bother her, but after that she totally knew who her friends were . . .
SOPHIE: She could've done something about it.
JANET: I guess we didn't talk about how she really felt about it. She seemed really comfortable with it after it. She was upset for a while. After she—
SOPHIE: There's no way she was *comfortable* with it.
JANET: She's dealt with it in a way. She's gotten to the point where it doesn't really make her cry to talk about it.

Earlier in the conversation, Sophie complained that the popular crowd got drunk at parties and had one-night stands. Somewhat defensive, Janet said as an aside to Sophie, "Hey, *I've* done that." Janet's story of the rape included Janet's anger at the girl's girlfriend: "Her *friend* was the hostess of the party and gave her the condoms and told her to go do it." Betrayal by the girlfriend and the boyfriend, a rape Janet calls "sort of" a date rape, in a party situation Janet has been in many times, anger and helplessness, talking about it finally without tears: this worst-case scenario of women's sexuality and powerlessness is "dealt with" by *not* "talk[ing] about how she really felt about it." Janet's story was about the social and interior limits on one girl's control, before and after "sex" she didn't want.

In sharp contrast, Shermika offered a story of embodied resistance through public talk. Michelle asked, "Have you ever been in a relationship where you felt you were being forced to do what you didn't want to do?" Shermika's answer was immediate and emphatic, "Yeah, I quit 'em, I quit 'em." She followed with a story about what happened when she "quit" the boyfriend who was getting possessive:

SHERMIKA: I almost got killed. Some guy pulled a gun on me. . . . He put the gun to *my head*. I said, "You'd better kill me 'cause if you don't I'm gonna kill you." Then he dropped the gun. . . . I kicked him where it hurts . . . hard. He had to go to the hospital. I was scared . . .

JANET: What happened—have you ever seen him again?

SHERMIKA: I see him every day.

MICHELLE: Did you call the cops?

SHERMIKA: Yeah. . . . he had to stay in jail [two weeks] till I decided not to press charges. . . . Don't nobody around my way playin' like that with them guns . . .

Shermika's examples of male threat and violence all show her and her mother talking back, striking back, or disarming the man. The woman is embodied as her own best protector. Shermika followed up her first story (which stunned her audience into awed silence) with a second, another jealous boyfriend: "He told me if I went with anybody else he'd kill me. And he pulled a knife on me. . . . 'Stab me. Either way, you ain't gonna have me.' " Later she told a story about her mother:

My stepfather and my mother were fightin'—it's the only time they ever fought. And he stepped back and hit my momma with all his might. And he thought she was gonna give up. She stepped back and hit *him* with all *her* might—and he fell asleep. She knocked the mess outta him. He never hit her again.

And another about herself, with her mother as model: "A guy tried to beat me with a belt, and I grabbed it and let him see how it felt to get beat with that belt. My mom wouldn't even take that." The scars of actual and/or anticipated sexual violence were clear for each of the young women, and always culturally specific as encounter, resistance, and recounting.

As with the violence of gender, the violence of racism on the female body was painfully voiced by the three women of color. Fears of attending a white prep school "where they'll ignore me," stories of fleeing an integrated school after three weeks, and retrospective outbursts of anger at being "the only woman of color in my class!" showed a kind of agoraphobia that kept Shermika and Damalleaux in their wholly African-American communities, and, inversely, created in Janet deep assimilative wishes to disappear into the white suburbs. For Janet the "white church" in her elite suburban neighborhood—not the Korean church her parents attend—was the "safest place" she could imagine.

85

MICHELLE FINE AND
PAT MACPHERSON
*Over Dinner:
Feminism and
Adolescent Female
Bodies*

For Damalleaux and Shermika, the neighborhood and its school are clearly the only safe place. Damalleaux reported that she'd lasted three weeks at an integrated school: "It was OK, but I didn't feel right. I didn't know anybody. I don't like introducing myself to people, I'm too shy. . . . I came back to the neighborhood school."

Shermika was offered a scholarship to go to a fancy private school in a white suburb. When discussing what scares us about the future, Shermika admitted she fears "being neglected. Not fitting in. . . . One time I'm goin' in and nobody likes me." When Michelle asked if that was her fear about the prep school, Shermika said, "Not as far as the people. But I don't like traveling. And I'm not staying on the campus. . . . I ain't stayin' away from home, though." By the time of our second interview, Shermika had convinced her mother to delay her going to prep school, from mid-year until the next fall. Shermika said she feared she would not be able to keep her grades up in the new school. Shermika's reliance on nonstandard English meant she would have to manage a major cultural shift both academically and socially. Her only envy of Sophie and Janet's school was what she called its "socializing" function, which taught them "how to get along, socialize, fit in, knowin' the right thing to say and do." Shermika said that, when she has a job, she wants to stay in her neighborhood, "where it all happenin', [not] where you won't fit in." Racial identity, segregation, and racism combine to reinforce the boundaries of Shermika's and Damalleaux's lives and futures by defining where and who is "safe."

Shermika evidently decided our dinner table was a "safe" enough place to explore our own racial (and maybe racist) differences. Shermika asked Janet, "Are you Chinese?" and Janet said, "No, Korean," and launched into a story about Japanese racism, including the sale of "Sambo" dolls in Japan, and then a story about the four-thousand-year-old hatred of Koreans for the Japanese. Shermika responded, "Well I don't understand that. I mean, I'm supposed to hate somebody white because somebody I know was a slave?" Then Shermika put race and racism right on our dinner table:

SHERMIKA: I walk into a store and Chinese people be starin' at me. [Shermika was mistaking Korean for Chinese for the third time.]
JANET: My *mother* does that—I hate that, my *mother* does it. [Her mother runs a dry cleaner.] And I'm just like, "Mom, *stop* it."
DAMALLEAUX: I leave [the store].
JANET: How do you feel when you're the only minority in a room?
DAMALLEAUX: I don't care.
SHERMIKA: I make a joke out of it. I feel like a zebra.

Unlike Janet's experience, the assaultive nature of Shermika's and Damalleaux's encounters with the white world had given them little encouragement to isolate themselves among a white majority. Shermika said her "darkness" meant she "looked like a clown" when they put on make-up for her local TV interview about the scholarship program she's in; then her pride and excitement about the video of herself on TV was clouded by family jokes about her dark skin making her "invisible" to the camera. Shermika reported plenty of harassment about her dark skin from girlfriends and boyfriends, even those as dark as herself. *Chocolate!* was the common, hated term, and Shermika was troubled by its implied racial hierarchy and self-hatred. Atypically, she had no easy comeback for that one.

Race in Sophie's (WASP) experience is about being privileged and feeling harassed for her blonde and blue-eyed good looks. Janet, for instance, annoys Sophie by calling her the "Aryan Goddess." Sophie is harassed on public transportation on her daily commute, where she is in the minority as a white woman. (Janet, in contrast, drives from suburb to school.) Sophie became exasperated in our interview when she felt targeted for white racism and said she didn't "notice" race half as often as race identified her in public situations in which she is made to represent WASPhood or white womanhood.

Just as these women cocreated for us a shared, if negotiated, sense of body politics, they separated along culture lines in their expressed reliance on social connections and surveillance of bodily borders. The African-American women, for instance, detailed deeply textured and relational lives. They not only care for many, but many also care for them. They give much to others and receive much in turn, but they don't call it volunteer or charity work—simply "what I do." When they receive favors (from mothers and boyfriends), they feel neither "guilty" nor "obligated." Held in a complex web of reciprocal relations, they contribute, easily assured that "what goes around comes around." They echo the writings of Robinson and Ward:

> Nobles' conception of "the extended self" is seen in the value structure of many black families. Willie (1985) argues that many African American children are encouraged to employ their own personal achievements as a means to resist racism. The importance of hard work and communalism is viewed threefold: as a personal responsibility, as an intergenerational commitment to family, and as a tie to the larger collective. A resistant strategy of liberation, in keeping with African American traditional values, ties individual achievement to collective struggle. We maintain that in the service of personal and cultural liberation, African American adolescent girls must resist an individualism that sees the self as disconnected from others in the black community and, as it is culturally and psychologically dysfunctional, she must resist those who might advocate her isolation and separation from traditional African American cultural practices, values and beliefs. (Robinson and Ward 1991, 9)

The elite women, in contrast, deployed a language of bodily integrity, patrolled borders, social charity, obligation, and guilt. As for any favors of gifts or time from mothers and boyfriends, they felt a need to "pay back." Bearing often quite deeply hostile feelings toward their mothers, they nevertheless both feel obligated to repay her sacrifices by fulfilling her expectations, often a professional career in return for a gigantic tuition bill. As vigilantly, they monitor their social and bodily boundaries for what and how much comes in and leaves—food, drink, drugs, exercise, money, sacrifices, and gifts. And they give back to community in the form of "charity." They live their connections almost contractually.

87

MICHELLE FINE AND
PAT MACPHERSON
*Over Dinner:
Feminism and
Adolescent Female
Bodies*

Related to these contrasting forms of body-in-relation, these two groups performed quite differently within our public talk. That is, they parted sharply in terms of how they hibernated in privacy and how they revealed themselves through public talk. In numerous instances the white and Korean teens deferred to a cultured privacy in which "personal problems" were rarely aired, "personal grievances" were typically suffocated, "personal disagreements" were usually revealed "behind our backs." They often withheld juicy details of life, safe only in diaries or other private writings. Their bodies absorbed, carried, and embodied their "private troubles." These elite girls made it quite clear that their strategies for survival were interior, personal, and usually not shared. The costs of "privilege," as they revealed them, were in the internalizing, personalizing, and depoliticizing of gender dilemmas. Research makes evident these costs in anorexia, bulimia, depression, "talking behind each other's back," and even the "secrets" of rape or abuse survival stories. Socialized out of using public talk to practice varied forms of womanhood, while these women recognized collective gender power struggles, they retreated from women, and they embodied their resistance alone, through feminist individualism.

> The individualism from which modern feminism was born has much to answer for but much in which to take pride. Individualism has decisively repudiated previous notions of hierarchy and particularism to declare the possibility of freedom for all. In so doing, it transformed slavery from one unfree condition among many into freedom's antithesis—thereby insisting that the subordination of one person to any other is morally and politically unacceptable. But the gradual extension of individualism and the gradual abolition of the remaining forms of social and political bondage have come trailing after two dangerous notions: that individual freedom could—indeed must—be absolute, and that social role and personal identity must be coterminous.
>
> Following the principles of individualism, modern Western societies have determined that the persistence of slavery in any form violates the fundamental principle of a just society. But in grounding the justification in absolute individual right, they have unleashed the specter of a radical individualism that overrides the claims of society itself. To the extent that feminism, like antislavery, has espoused those individualistic principles, it has condemned itself to the dead ends toward which individualism is now plunging. (Fox-Genovese 1991, 240–41)

In contrast, the African-American women were publicly playful as well as nasty to each other and about others—"because we love each other." Shermika told wonderful, vivid, outrageous tales, in part to "test" what the others would do, including, we believe, testing whether she was being classified as exotic/sexualized/Other/specimen for the white women and the evening's analysis. Their school context made their bodies a matter of public talk, exposed.

SHERMIKA: I don't like my rear end. Guys are so ignorant. "Look at all that cake."
PAT: Maybe it's their problem.
SHERMIKA: No, it *is* my problem. Because you see my butt before you see me.

Public talk could be aggression as well:

DAMALLEAUX: I wouldn't talk to him [a stranger] and he got mad.
SHERMIKA: I hate when they constantly talk to you and they get closer and closer.

The African-American women used and experienced conversation, public disagreements, pleasures, and verbal badgerings as ways to "try on" varied ways to be women.

During the second evening, the four young women discovered and explored these differences through the metaphor of the "private" and "public" schools they attend.

JANET: I've got a question. At [your school, Shermika], are there kids who are like by themselves? Loners . . . who don't sit with anyone else? . . . who nobody wants to sit with?
SHERMIKA: Yeah, but they can't because there's somebody always messin' with 'em, tryin' to get 'em to do something. So if they wanted to be by themselves they couldn't.

* * *

JANET: At our school it's easy to get shut out when you're by yourself.
SOPHIE: You just kind of—disappear.

* * *

JANET: They don't say it [criticism or insult] in front of your face.
SOPHIE: You insult someone by not considering them. . . . You don't consider their existence . . .
SHERMIKA: Sometimes people need you to tell them you feel . . .
JANET: . . . for the most part when I'm mad at someone I don't say it to them.
SOPHIE: Only one on one. You don't say it to them in front of others unless you're joking. It's more private.
SHERMIKA: But if you say it *to* the person, you avoid fights. . . . If they hear you saying it behind they back, they wanna fight.

The four pursued this discovered difference between the private and the public school.

SHERMIKA: Ain't nothin private at my school. If someone got gonorrhea, everyone knows it.
SOPHIE: *Everything's* private at my school.
JANET: 'Cause nobody really cares about each other at our school . . .
SHERMIKA: In our school, when I found out I had cancer, I heard about it on the loudspeaker. And everybody come and offer me help. When you're havin' problems in our school, people talk. That's why they're more mature at my school—excuse me. Say somebody poor, need name-brand sneaks, they'll put they money together and give 'em some sneaks. And teachers do that too, if someone need food.
SOPHIE: We like to pretend that we're good to the neighborhood and socially conscious.

Over time, we came to see that the "facts" of these young women's lives were neither what we had invited them to reveal in our conversations, nor what they were giving us. Rather, we were gathering their interpretations of their lives, interpretations that were roaming within culture and class.

89

*MICHELLE FINE AND
PAT MACPHERSON
Over Dinner:
Feminism and
Adolescent Female
Bodies*

ON GOOD AND BAD GIRLS: PROSPECTS FOR FEMINISM

I consider myself a bad girl, but in a good sorta way.

—SHERMIKA

Feminist scholars as distinct as Valerie Walkerdine (1984), Carol Gilligan (1990), and Nancy Lesko (1988) have written about polarizations of good girls and bad ones—that is, those who resist, submit, or are split on the cultural script of femininity. Gilligan's recent essay "Joining the Resistance" (1990) argues that at the outset of adolescence, young women experience a severing of insider from outsider knowledge, such that "insider knowledge may be washed away." Gilligan and her colleagues have found that young women at early adolescence begin to submerge their interior knowledge, increasingly relying on "I don't know" to answer questions about self. They say "I don't know" at a rate amazingly greater the older they get—an average of twice at age seven, twenty-one times at age twelve, and sixty-seven times at age thirteen. Gilligan and colleagues conclude: "If girls' knowledge of reality is politically dangerous, it is both psychologically and politically dangerous for girls not to know . . . or to render themselves innocent by disconnecting from their bodies, their representations of experience and desire" (33).

Nancy Lesko (1988) has written a compelling ethnography of gendered adolescents' lives inside a Catholic high school, where she unpacks a "curriculum of the body" mediated by class distinctions. In this school, female delinquency was sexualized and embodied. The genders segregated in high school by class and created categories of behaviors to hang onto within these class groups. The rich and popular girls at her school paraded popular fashions, spoke in controlled voices, muted their opinions, and worked hard at being "nice." If they pushed the boundaries of wardrobe, it was always in the direction of fashion, not "promiscuity." The "burnouts," in contrast, were young women who fashioned their behaviors through smoking and directness. They rejected compulsions toward being "nice" and excelled at being "blunt." Refusing to bifurcate their personal opinions and their public stances, they challenged docility and earned reputations as "loose" and "hard" (like Leslie Roman's [1988] working class women, who displayed physicality and sexual embodiment). Social class, then, provided the contours within which a curriculum of the body had its meaning displayed, intensifying within gender oppositions and undermining possibilities for female solidarity.

Departing somewhat from Gilligan and Lesko, Walkerdine (1984) sees adolescence for young women as not a moment to *bury* the questioning female self, but a time in which young women must negotiate their multiple selves, through struggles of heterosexuality and critiques of gender, race, and class arrangements. In an analysis of popular texts read by adolescent women, Walkerdine finds that "heroines are never angry; most project anger onto others and suppress it in self, yielding the active production of passivity" (182). She asks readers to consider the notion that "good girls are not always good," and asks "[but] when and how is their badness lived?" Interested in the splitting of goodness and badness, we, like Walkerdine, asked these young women that question. When Shermika said, "I consider myself a bad girl, but in a good sorta way," she was positioning herself in our collectively made feminist context where good girls follow femininity rules, and bad girls don't. This good kind of bad girl plays by male rules of friendship, risk, danger, and initiative.

Within five minutes of our first meeting, the four girls discovered they all liked football—*playing* football—and they eagerly described the joys of running, catching the ball, tackling, and being tackled. Only Janet drew the line at being tackled, citing a "three-hundred-pound boy" in her neighborhood. As an explanation for their preferred identities as "one of the guys," they suggested that football exemplifies "masculine" values of gamesmanship. It is a game with rules and space for spontaneous physicality, with teamwork and individual aggression in rule-bound balance, and with maximum bodily access to others of both sexes, without fear about sexual reputation or reproductive consequences. When asked why they trust and like boys over girls, they cited boys' risk-taking as making them more fun, their ability to "be more honest" and not backstab and to "be more accepting": "You can tell when a guy's lyin'." "First of all they won't even notice what you're wearing and they won't bust on you." Shermika bragged that all of her boyfriends said they valued her most as a friend, not merely a girlfriend. The behavior, clothing, and values associated with such identification with boys and sports suggests both a flight from the femininity they collectively described as "wearing pink," "being prissy," "bein' Barbie," and "reinforcing guys all the time"—*and* an association of masculinity with fairness (vs. cattiness), honesty (vs. backstabbing), strength (vs. prissiness, a vulnerability whether feigned or real), initiative (vs. deference or reactionary comments), and integrity (vs. the self-doubt and conflicting loyalties dividing girls). The four's risk-taking behaviors—driving fast, sneaking out at night—reinforced identities as "one of the guys." Such are the Bad Girls.

But being "one of the guys" makes for a contradictory position of self versus "other girls." Sophie mocked the femininity of good girls at its worst when she said dismissively, "You should sit and wait in your little crystal palace" rather than "chase after guys." This constructed difference between self (the good kind of bad girl) and other girls (the bad kind of good girl) is an essential contradiction of identity that all four girls were struggling with. Valerie Hey, in her study of adolescent female friendships, calls this "deficit dumping": "all the 'bad' bits of femininity, social and sexual competitiveness, placed upon the 'other,'" that is, other girls (1987, 421). Sophie, like the girls in Hey's study, excepted her best friend along with herself from the generality of femininity: "It's different, though, with best friends. I mean like girls in general." Shermika, likewise, excepted Damalleaux when Michelle asked whether *no* other girls were to be trusted. "She a boy," Shermika countered, raising a puzzled laugh. But when Shermika's boyfriend likened her to a bodybuilder when she was running track, she felt ashamed to "feel like a boy . . . like a muscle man."

91

*MICHELLE FINE AND
PAT MACPHERSON
Over Dinner:
Feminism and
Adolescent Female
Bodies*

Sophie confessed ruefully, "I'm certainly no bad girl," and Janet taunted her, "Sophie has a little halo." Certainly Sophie's good grades, good works, politeness, friendliness, and trustworthiness were acceptably "good" to both adults and peers, even if the popular crowd had not approved or welcomed her. "I don't want that image," Sophie told Janet about the halo. Goody-goody-ism would be unacceptable to *all* peers. Good-*girlism*—Sophie's uncomfortable state—seems good for her conscience and adult approval but bad for approval by the popular set, whose upper-class drink- and drug-induced party flirtations and sexual liaisons Sophie disapproves of.

The meaning of Sophie's good girl image is, however, quite class-specific, as Mary Evans describes in her analysis of middle-class schooling, *A Good School*:

> as far as possible a 'good' girl did not have an appearance. What she had was a correct uniform, which gave the world the correct message about her—that is, that she is a well-behaved, sensible person who could be trusted not to wish to attract attention to herself by an unusual, let alone a fashionable, appearance. (1991, 30–31).

Signaling her acceptance of the career-class uniform, Sophie could not also signal her interest in boys. Indeed, she walked away from her body, except at an athletic court. "Other girls" dressed either "schleppy" (the androgynous or indifferent look) or "provocative." Sophie's neat, "sporty" look—tights and a lean body made her miniskirt look more athletic than hooker-inspired—seems designed to be comfortable and competent as one of the guys while ever so casually gesturing toward femininity (no dykey trousers). Her dress is designed to bridge the contradiction of middle-class education and femininity, as Evans describes it in her own schooling in the 1950s:

> To be a successful [prep] school girl involved, therefore, absorbing two specific (but conflicting) identities. First, that of the androgynous middleclass person who is academically successful in an academic world that is apparently gender blind. Second, that of the well-behaved middleclass woman who knows how to defer to and respect the authority of men. (1991, 23)

Over the course of history, feminism has altered these young women's terms of deference to men, their ability to name sexism and resist. But their feminism does not seem to have revised the categories of gender or body at all. What seems intact from the 1950s are their terms of respect for the authority of men as superior and normal forms of human being. What seems distinct in the 1990s is that these young women think they have a right to be young men too.

Damalleaux's example of her own good-girlism shares some of Sophie's dilemma of being a good student at the expense of peer popularity. But Damalleaux resolved this tension differently, as Signithia Fordham (1988) would argue is likely to happen among academically talented, low-income African-American students:

DAMALLEAUX: I used to be a straight-A girl and now I'm down to B's and C's. I used to be so good, it's a shame . . .

PAT: What changed?

DAMALLEAUX: I couldn't help it any more. . . . When I got straight A's they'd call me a nerd and things. But I'd be happy because my mother would give me anything I want for it. . . . Mom [would say to teasing brothers], "Leave my first girl alone!" . . . [Then] I got around the wrong people, I don't study so much . . .

PAT: Is it uncool to be a girl and get good grades?

DAMALLEAUX: Yes it is. . . . I'll do my work and they'll say "Smarty Pants! Smarty Pants!"

Janet gave an example of "acting stupid" with peers, which seemed to be her manner of flirtation. Sophie pointed out that Janet could afford to because everyone already knew she was smart. Sophie clearly felt more trapped by being smart and a good girl.

Girls can be good, bad or—best of all—they can be boys. This version of individualized resistance, or feminism, reflects a retreat from the collective politics of gender, and from other women, and an advance into the embattled scene of gender politics—alone, and against boys, in order to become one of them.

ON CLOSINGS, OR, THE END OF THE SECOND PIZZA

We heard these four women struggling between the discourses of feminism and adolescence. Perhaps *struggling* is even too strong a word. They hungered for a strong version of individualistic, "gender-free" adolescence and had rejected that which had been deemed traditionally feminine, aping instead that which had been deemed traditionally masculine. Delighted to swear, spit, tell off-color jokes, wear hats, and trash other girls, they were critical of individual boys, nasty about most girls, rarely challenging of the sex/gender system and ecstatic, for the most part, to be engaged as friends and lovers with young men. But we also heard their feminism in their collective refusal to comply with male demands, their wish for women friends to trust, their expectations for equality and search for respect, their deep ambivalence about being "independent of a man" and yet in partnership with one, and their strong yearnings to read, write, and talk more about women's experiences among women. They appreciated our creation of a context in which this was possible. "The women of Michelle's place," Shermika called us at the end of one evening, prizing our collectivity by re-using an African-American woman writer's novel title.

> The public terms of the discourse of femininity preclude the expression of deviant views of marriage, motherhood, and the public terms are the only ones to which girls have access. Part of the task of feminist work with girls is thus, I would suggest, giving girls terms in which to express their experiential knowledge, rather than having to fall back into the stereotyped expressions of normatively defined femininity in order to say anything at all about areas of life which vitally concern them. (Hudson 1984, 52)

Through critical and collaborative group interview, we evolved a form of conversation with these four young women that allowed us to engage in what we might consider collective consciousness work, as a form of feminist methodology. Our talks became an opportunity to "try on" ways of being women, struggling through power, gender, culture, and class.

With Donna Haraway's (1989) notion of "partial vision" firmly in mind, we realized that in our talk, no one of us told the whole truth. We all occluded the "truth" in cultured ways. The conversation was playful and filled with the mobile positionings of all of us women. While we each imported gender, race, class, culture, age, and bodies to our talk, we collectively created an ideological dressing room in which the six of us could undress a little, try things on, exchange, rehearse, trade, and critique. Among the six of us we were able to lift up what had become "personal stories," raise questions, try on other viewpoints, and re-see our stories as political narratives.

> As a critique of the excesses of individualism, feminism potentially contributes to a new conception of community—of the relation between the freedom of individuals and the needs of society. The realization of that potential lies not in the repudiation of difference but in a new understanding of its equitable social consequences. (Fox-Genovese 1991, 256)

We could recount together how alone and frightened we have each felt as we have walked, and are watched, down city streets; how our skin tightens when we hear men comment aloud on our bodies; how we smart inside with pain when we learn that other women define themselves as "good women" by contrasting themselves with our feminist politics; how we fetishize those body parts that have betrayed us with their imperfection. Within the safety of warm listening and caring, yet critical, talk, we attached each of these "secret" feelings to political spaces defined by culture, class, and gender contours of our daily lives. This method moved us, critically and collectively, from pain to passion to politics, prying open the ideologies of individualism, privacy, and loyalty that had sequestered our personal stories.

After our last dinner, stuffed and giggly, tired but still wanting just one more round of conversation, we—Pat and Michelle—realized that the four young women were getting ready to drive away. Together and without us. Before, Pat had driven Shermika and Damalleaux to Michelle's and back home. But now they were leaving us behind. Stunned, we looked at each other, feeling abandoned. We thought we were concerned about their safety. Four young women in a car could meet dangers just outside the borders of Michelle's block.

We turned to each other, realizing that even our abandonment was metaphoric, and political. These four young women were weaving the next generation of feminist politics, which meant, in part, leaving us. We comforted ourselves by recognizing that our conversations had perhaps enabled this work. No doubt, individual interviews with each of the four would have produced an essay chronicling the dangers of femininity—eating disorders, heterosexual traumas, perhaps some abuse or abortion stories; that is, deeply individualized, depoliticized, and atomized tales of "things that have happened to me as an adolescent female." What happened among us, instead, was that a set of connections was forged—between personal experiences and political structures, across cultures, classes, and politics, and within an invented space, cramped between the discourses of a rejected femininity, an individualized adolescence, and a collective feminism as resistance.

> Resistance is that struggle we can most easily grasp. Even the most subjected person has moments of rage and resentment so intense that they respond,

they act against. There is an inner uprising that leads to rebellion, however short-lived. It may be only momentary, but it takes place. That space within oneself where resistance is possible remains: It is different then to talk about becoming subjects. That process emerges as one comes to understand how structures of domination work in one's own life, as one develops critical thinking and critical consciousness, as one invents new alternative habits of being and resists from that marginal space of difference inwardly defined. (hooks 1990, 15)

In our finest post-pizza moment, we—Pat and Michelle—realized that as these women drove off, they were inventing their own feminist legacy, filled with passions, questions, differences, and pains. We were delighted that we had helped to challenge four young women's versions of individualistic feminism without solidarity by doing the consciousness work of our generation. We taught, and relearned, feminism as dialectical and historical discourse about experience and its interpretation, a collective reframing of private confessions. As we yelled, "Go straight home!" to their moving car, for a moment we felt like the world was in very good hands.

Notes

Many thanks to Elizabeth Sayre for her patient assistance.

[1]And, although not at the table, it is still another thing to construct a sense of womanhood by and for women whose disabilities socially and sexually "neuter" them, propelling them out of any presumed relation with men and depriving them of the many burdens of being female, including the privileges that come with those burdens, in experiences such as sexual harassment, motherhood, sexuality, having others rely on you, etc. Disabled women's identities are rarely positioned under, against, or with men's. As Kathryn Corbett, Adrienne Asch and Michelle Fine, Harilyn Rousso, and others have written (Asch & Fine 1988), it is no blessing for the culture to presume that because you are disabled, you are not female; not worth whistling at, not able to love an adult man or woman; not capable of raising a child; not beautiful enough to be employed in a public space.

Illness and Imagery:
Feminist Cognition, Socialization,
and Gender Identity

In 1980, the feminist poet Audre Lorde wrote in *The Cancer Journals:* "May these words serve as encouragement for other women to speak and to act out of our experiences with cancer and with other threats of death, for silence has never brought us anything of worth" (1980a, p. 10). With her encouragement, today I will explore a web of taboos and silences that surround breast cancer, a disease that affects so many of us that we can all expect a friend, if not ourselves, to experience it. Breast cancer currently affects one of every eleven women and is expected to affect one out of ten in the near future. Of those, some will inevitably be feminists. I am one of them.

It is a central tenet of feminism that women's invisible, private wounds often reflect social and political injustices. It is a commitment central to feminism to share burdens. And it is an axiom of feminism that the personal is political. It is in that spirit that I ask you to come with me in imagination where I hope nobody will ever go in fact, to a hospital bed on the morning after a mastectomy, where I found new expression for a recent theme of the *The Journal of Social Issues,* "Social Issues and Personal Life: The Search for Connections" (Clayton & Crosby, 1986).

Studies of women with breast cancer typically focus on women's responses to the disease. This chapter is a naturalistic ethnography which explores a stimulus designed to shape women's responses: the Reach to Recovery material presented to women after surgery. Crisis demands coping: Reach to Recovery is an effort to shape coping responses.

In its own words, "Reach to Recovery is one woman reaching out to share and support another in time of need. . . . Reach to Recovery works through carefully selected and trained volunteers who have fully adjusted to their surgery. . . . The volunteer visitor brings a kit containing a temporary breast form, manuals of information and appropriate literature for husbands, children, other loved ones, and friends. The visitor can provide information on types of permanent prostheses and lists of where they are available locally. . . . Reach to Recovery can provide information to women interested in breast reconstruction" (American Cancer Society, 1982b). Thus the first message of Reach to Recovery is that one's body has been mutilated and that steps must be taken to remedy its deficiency.

My Reach to Recovery volunteer brought a kit with exercise equipment, cosmetic disguise, and a collection of reading material, all for me to keep; and three samples of breast prostheses for me to examine. The exercise equipment consisted of a small rubber ball attached to a length of elastic cord and a length of nylon rope knotted at each end with two wooden tongue depressors to be inserted into the knots. The cosmetic disguise was a small pink nylon-covered, dacron-filled pillow, which proved more useful and safer for throwing exercises than the rubber ball intended for that purpose, which rebounded on its elastic cord painfully into my chest when I threw it.

Substitute breasts of various sorts outweighed everything else in the Reach to Recovery visitor's kit; a corresponding weight was found in the reading material. A crude quantitative analysis of the Reach to Recovery reading material offers a preview of the emphasis on the prosthetic.

One-page pamphlets or form letters:

- What is Reach to Recovery?
- After Mastectomy: The Woman on Her Own
- "An Ounce of Prevention:" Suggestions for Hand & Arm Care
- How to examine your breasts
- A letter to husbands
- A letter to daughters
- A letter to sons

And, at greater length:

- Exercises after Mastectomy: Patient Guide (8 pages)
- Helpful Hints and How To's (8 pages)
- After Mastectomy: A Patient Guide (10 pages)
- Prostheses List 1984–1986 (14 pages)
- Breast Reconstruction Following Mastectomy (20 pages)

Buried in this material is the fact that a mastectomy may bring disability and even occasionally death as a consequence of damage to lymphatic circulation, which may produce permanent arm swelling. Of a total of 67 pages of information, only one page addresses this issue. Surgery limits arm motion: exercises that promote recovery and help prevent arm swelling take up an additional eight pages. Thus only about 10% of this material is actually addressed to health considerations. What then is the nature of the "recovery" to which one is supposed to reach?

The principal focus of this material, the exclusive focus of three of the five multipage pamphlets, of 42 of a total of 67 pages of information, is on strategies for temporary or permanent substitutes for the missing breast. Thus on quantitative grounds alone, the woman who has just had a mastectomy is overwhelmed by the message that her body is now defective and that her first priority will be to seek an artificial, cosmetic remedy. Her kit provides her with an emergency solution—the small pink pillow that can be pinned into her clothing even before her bandages are removed. It is illusory comfort, like the promise of ice cream after a tonsillectomy to a child who wakes up to discover a throat too sore to swallow. But throats do heal, so the illusion and the consequent disillusion are short-lived. Reach to Recovery offers a woman a lifetime of disguise. What this kit does not provide is room to accept the loss of a breast, the wound, and the scar that healing will bring.

I came to surgery with a very different view of mastectomy, which I owe to Audre Lorde, whom I first discovered in April 1980, when *Savvy* carried her article "After Breast Cancer: I am a Warrior, not a Victim." She described her rejection of the physical pretense in the cosmetic emphasis of Reach to Recovery in words that transcended the experience she had just had and I never anticipated:

> Implying to a woman that, with the skillful application of a lambswool puff or an implantation of silicone gel, she can be the same as before surgery prevents her from dealing with herself as real, physically and emotionally. . . . We are expected to mourn the loss of a breast in secret, as if it were a guilty crime . . . [but] When Moshe Dayan stands before Parliament with an eye patch over his empty eye socket . . . he is viewed as a warrior with an honorable wound. . . . Well, we are warriors also. I have been to war, and so has every woman with breast cancer, the female scourge of our time. . . . "Nobody will know the difference," said the Reach to Recovery volunteer, with her lambswool puff. But it is that very difference which I wish to affirm, because I have lived it, and survived it and grown stronger through it. I wish to share that strength with other women. (1980b, pp. 68–69)

In 1980 it seemed so simple. Even in 1986 it did not seem so complex: Audre Lorde had spoken first and assured me a voice for my autonomy and my grief. As she did, I mourned my breast. It was the first breast to develop erotic feelings, the first breast to fill with milk, the first breast my firstborn child suckled, and the last breast my last child suckled. That breast carried a special aura into middle age: one summer afternoon our small red dog shepherded me into a hike with a leap and nip exquisitely and precisely placed at the very tip of my nipple. I also remembered the last time that breast was part of my body in lovemaking, just a handful of hours before surgery. As Audre Lorde had done, I intended to grieve, and to go on, with gratitude to her for going before me and making it easier.

I had rejoiced in Audre Lorde's rejection of a prosthesis and shared her horror at the reprimand her surgeon's nurse issued:

> "We really like you to wear [a prosthesis] when you come in. Otherwise it's bad for the morale of the office."
> I could scarcely believe my ears [wrote Lorde]. Every woman there had either had a mastectomy, or might have a mastectomy. Every woman there could have used the reassurance that having one breast did not mean life was over, nor did it mean she was condemned to using a placebo in order to feel good about herself and the way she looked. . . . I refuse to have my scars hidden or trivialized behind a puff of lambswool or silicone gel (1980b, p. 69).

If the need for defiance was regrettable, it was not incomprehensible: ground rules for public appearance occupy fashion pages in the daily newspaper. To flout them is to defy culture, and Lorde was clearly, intentionally doing precisely that. I looked forward to joining her in revolution. But it had not occurred to me until I found myself in a hospital bed with a lapful of Reach to Recovery material that it would be war 24 hours a day. A mastectomy, it seems, ushers in a lifetime of round-the-clock disguise: so I discovered after I found that I underestimated the power of a nonconscious ideology. Breast cancer is not a cosmetic disease, but it is embedded in a larger social and political context in which the cosmetic industry is itself a social and political phenomenon. Thus, if one rejects the a priori assumption that a missing breast demands an all-out coverup, one finds oneself at war with the very material that is meant to promote healing. This discussion follows the course of a naturalistic ethnography which I undertook involuntarily in my hospital bed, reading the Reach to Recovery material with the vulnerability that comes after surgery and the educated cynicism that comes from years of feminist analysis.

In 1964, driving down Jaffa Road in Jerusalem, pregnant with my second child, my breasts swelling and my brassiere confining, I reached under my shirt in the middle of traffic, unhooked it, removed it, and never expected to think about brassieres again. But on December 3, 1986, as a conscientious patient intending to learn all I could about mastectomy and the healing process following surgery, I read every word of the Reach to Recovery material, and the first lesson I learned was that I was expected to resume wearing a brassiere as part of my recovery: "Reach to Recovery suggests and encourages each woman to wear the bra in which she is most comfortable. When your doctor says you are ready, you should be fitted with the breast substitute—prosthesis—suited to you," instructs the cover page of the *Prostheses List, 1984–1986* (American Cancer Society, 1984).

That imperative is twofold if one has not worn a brassiere for 22 years: not only should you be fitted with a substitute breast—Audre Lorde had prepared me for that—but you should wear a brassiere. And nothing prepared me for that. If, for whatever reason—political principle or personal comfort—one has discarded a brassiere, both freedom and comfort come to an end with breast cancer: research has shown that discomfort in wearing a prosthesis is a commonly reported physical complaint following mastectomy (Meyerowitz, Chaiken, & Clark, 1988). Yet this instruction—no mention of the discomfort—is the message a woman gets on the first morning after surgery.

The invasion of the brassiere was just the beginning. The booklet *Helpful Hints and How To's* assured me that leisure and sleep bras "provide a solution for the woman who feels she needs to wear a breast form in bed. Women who do not want to wear a bra and form to bed, but still want contour on the side of the surgery might want to make a form similar to the temporary form in the Reach to Recovery kit and attach it inside the bodice of their sleepwear garment. Nylon netting can be gathered in a round shape and with some experimentation can also be attached inside a loose garment to simulate the contour of the natural unsupported breast" (American Cancer Society, 1982a, pp. 1–2).

It is not enough to deceive the public; not even enough to deceive one's mate—I assumed that "the woman who feels she needs to wear a breast form in bed" does not sleep alone. *Helpful Hints and How To's* encourages the woman who has had a mastectomy to deceive herself. A reader of Audre Lorde's *The

Cancer Journals (1980a) might assume that "making your own form" refers to the construction of a dressmaker's form adapted to one's altered body. But no: "form" takes on new meaning after breast cancer and is used as a presumably innocuous substitute for "substitute breast." The reader is warned that such a "form," if not weighted properly, will cause that side of the brassiere to ride up on the body (p. 5). The Reach to Recovery solution: "use the pocket of the temporary Reach to Recovery form as a pattern and fill it with birdseed, rice, barley, small plastic beads . . . drapery weights, fishing sinkers, gunshot or BB's" (p. 1).

My first reaction to this suggestion was the cognitive equivalent of wound shock. Surely this represented a merger of Frederick's of Hollywood, Ace Hardware, and the American Cancer Society. Yes, one possible first response to this suggestion is to assume that it is a bad joke and to fight off the assault on one's intelligence with better jokes.

But when the initial shock wears off, the imagination does not have to work very hard to call up the confining sensation of a brassiere, the discomfort compounded by one side riding up over wounded or scarred flesh, and the remedy proposed by Reach to Recovery and published with the seal of the American Cancer Society: a pouch of birdseed or gunshot, lying against the body where there was once the first touch of a boy's hand or a baby's mouth—or even a small dog's teeth. In 1980, I agreed immediately with Audre Lorde when she declared: "For not even the most skillful prosthesis in the world could undo that reality, or feel the way my breast had felt, and either I would love my body one-breasted now, or remain forever alien to myself" (1980a, p. 44). It seemed to me then, and still does, that hers was the most elemental of protests: do not add insult to injury. I had no way of guessing how outrageous these insults could be.

The pièce de resistance, most extensive and handsomest of the material put into my hands the day after surgery, is a 20-page pamphlet, nearly one-third of the total number of pages in my kit, on breast reconstruction, urging that the most effective treatment for breast surgery is more surgery. I thought I was prepared for this as well: breast reconstruction had been mentioned by every doctor I had seen from the time I was first told that I had cancer. Since no surgeon could restore the flesh that had swollen first with desire and then with milk, it seemed pointless to me until I inquired about the procedure itself. A mastectomy, I was told, is comparatively simply surgery—45 minutes or so. A reconstruction is more complex—it may involve several operations, the removal of muscle from the back to be inserted into the chest wall, and the subsequent insertion of a silicone implant. When I asked my oncologist why any woman would subject herself to that, he explained that it would avoid the inconvenience of a prosthesis that might slip out of place. Surely if one rejected the first premise, that would be that.

But I was wrong again. The war on cancer patients is being fought with as much or more determination as the war on cancer. The booklet on breast reconstruction goes beyond the helpful hints and how-to's which keep one's bra from riding up and "allow" one to wear one's favorite clothes. It redefines one's sexual identity at the very moment that identity is most vulnerable. This

booklet is written in question and answer format. It should be required reading as part of training in questionnaire construction and restricted to graduate
students. Instead, it is distributed to women on the morning after surgery.

Question: "Should every woman have a breast reconstruction after mastectomy?" Answer: "Every woman should know that breast reconstruction is possible and make her own decision. Some women seem to be able to adapt psychologically to the post-mastectomy physiological change. Others who opt for
breast reconstruction are usually the strongly motivated patients who are willing to undergo an additional operation" (pp. 5–6). As someone with a high
need for achievement, I read this material with the best of intentions, hoping to
make the most of my experience. I graduated from college with honors, had
managed other life transitions with some distinction, and meant to do the
same with cancer. I had always considered myself to be strongly motivated.
And so, as students of cognitive dissonance will understand, I turned to the
title page to find out who the responsible reference group was, so that I could
dissociate myself from it and retain my claim to strong motivation.

Like everything else about the cosmetic approach to breast cancer, that
seemed easy enough at first. Unlike every other item in my kit, this was not the
work of Reach to Recovery, but of the American Society of Plastic and Reconstructive Surgeons, Incorporated. Like the birdseed breast, it seemed at first to
be a bad joke. But if one is trying to make sense of a new experience, one seizes
upon whatever is offered; in an understimulating hospital room, one reads
whatever is available; and, although knowledge of the distorting effects of
questions and answers skewed in the direction of presumed social desirability,
like any other knowledge, provides some power, on the first day after surgery
one is simply not powerful enough to dismiss casually such statements as the
following:

> If you are like most women, your breasts have great psychological significance
> to you and you will feel more feminine and more secure socially and sexually
> with a reconstructed breast following mastectomy for cancer. (p. 6)

In other words, your sisterhood or your scar: if your breast has mattered to
you, and mine certainly had, you are told that you will want the benefit of
"surgical advances [which] have provided plastic and reconstructive surgeons
with techniques to create the appearance of breasts" (p. 4). If not, Aristotelian
logic leads the reader to believe, you are not like most women. And if so, you
have cancer, you are groggy from surgery, and you are all alone.

Here I distinguish between the 20,000 women who undergo breast reconstruction every year, according to this booklet, and the authors of the booklet.
Two Reach to Recovery volunteers came to my bedside, the first, like me a runner, as part of her scheduled round and the second, like me a cross-country
skier, at my surgeon's request. The first had run a 10K and the second had
skied the Korteloppet after surgery; that bonded us. Both had had "implants,"
as they termed them; that divided us. Which took priority, our commonalities
or our differences?

Virginia O'Leary offers a model for the reconciliation of our differences in
her Division 35 presidential remarks, "Musings on the Promise (and Pain) of
Feminism" (1987). She notes: "The very intensity of involvement that makes

women's connections with women so rewarding has the potential to evoke pain as well. . . . Trashing someone usually involves impugning her (feminist) motives." Since I have identified myself with feminist Audre Lorde and have agreed that the cosmetic response to breast cancer leads to self-alienation, does it follow that I am forced to deny the feminism implicit in my visitors' athletic efforts, or for that matter in their volunteer participation in a program of women helping women? Indeed not. If a hospital room is no place for a crash course in Total Womanhood, neither is it the place for retroactive consciousness raising. Breast cancer is a trauma; if a woman feels she is entitled to four silicone breasts after a mastectomy, I applaud her originality, and, as O'Leary does, I urge tolerance of the diversity of interpersonal styles, in sickness as well as in health. It is precisely the question of tolerance for diversity which was the issue in my hospital room.

101

NANCY DATAN
Illness and Imagery:
Feminist Cognition,
Socialization, and
Gender Identity

In the spirit of tolerance for diversity, I considered breast reconstruction. In the words of its advocates, the American Society of Plastic and Reconstructive Surgeons, Incorporated, a breast reconstruction

> will not only provide greater physical self-confidence, but will also enable you to wear a wide range of clothing. After reconstruction, you need not worry about "slipping" or displacement of the prosthesis which may occur with external devices. (p. 7)

However, it is acknowledged that even modern surgery will not bring you everything:

> The reconstructed breast will look reasonably normal when covered with an undergarment but will show scarring and subtle imperfections when you are nude (p. 9). . . . Breast reconstruction cannot restore normal sensation to a breast after mastectomy (p. 14). . . . Most women say it may take a while to get used to the reconstructed breast . . . there may be some tenderness and discomfort when you [sleep on your stomach] . . . when people hug you they may not be able to distinguish any difference in the feel of the breasts. In some cases, however, the contraction of your body tissues around the implant may cause the reconstructed breast to feel firmer than your other breast. (p. 15)

Furthermore,

> Complications can occur. . . . If an infection or heavy bleeding occurs around a breast implant, it sometimes has to be removed but it can usually be replaced after a period of several months. If the implant shifts to an undesirable location or feels hard due to the contraction of the tissue, an additional surgical procedure may be required to release it. (p. 9)

Finally,

> A small number of recurrences [of cancer] occur on the chest wall itself and breast reconstruction might delay but would not prevent detection of these. (p. 14)

Thus, in the words of a pamphlet intended to promote the process, breast reconstruction makes it easy to wear clothes, but not to go naked. The public self is affirmed, but it is at the expense of discomfort to the private self, who wants to hug or to sleep on her stomach. The surgery carries a risk of complications and further surgery and might delay detection of a recurrence of the cancer—and this procedure, it is claimed, provides "greater physical self-confidence" (p. 7).

My quarrel is not with the women who choose this procedure but with the surgeons who assert that physical self-confidence will be enhanced by this painful, potentially dangerous invasion of the body. It is one option. Another option is to live, as Audre Lorde inspired me to do, without any thought of disguise: this enables one to hug, to find erotic nerves reawakening even before the mastectomy incision is fully healed, and to sleep on one's stomach, all components of my physical self-confidence.

Now the time has come to get out of the hospital bed and to resume my identity as a feminist social scientist. What if this experience is not merely an illness, but a naturalistic experiment designed by Rhoda Unger as a test of my epistemology? In that case it is not my body which is in need of reconstruction—it is reality.

I begin by disputing a 1983 volume of *The Journal of Social Issues* (Janoff-Bulman & Frieze, 1983) which takes as its theme "Reactions to Victimization," among whom are numbered cancer victims. I read those words without a pause in 1983, not even the briefest of pauses to consider that Audre Lorde's 1980 article, which I remembered nearly verbatim, had been entitled, "After Breast Cancer: I am a Warrior, not a Victim." However, the word "victim" becomes far more salient when it refers to oneself. And, after a while, it becomes offensive. One is "stricken," "afflicted," maybe even "victimized" by cancer at first. But months later? Years? Have I earned tenure as a victim?

The term victim suggests passive acceptance, when responding adequately to cancer demands continuous active coping. Consider the distinction Bruno Bettelheim makes of the Holocaust: its victims are those who were buried; those who go on are survivors. Circumstances victimize; the individual coping response is part of the struggle for survival. Bettelheim states:

> [Holocaust] survivors are not alone in that they must learn to integrate an experience which, when not integrated, is either completely overwhelming, or forces one to deny in self-defense what it means to one personally in the present. . . . Engaging in denial and repression in order to save oneself the difficult task of integrating an experience into one's personality is of course by no means restricted to [Holocaust] survivors. . . . Survivors have every right to choose their very own way of trying to cope. The experience of being a concentration camp prisoner is so abominable, the trauma so horrendous, that one must respect every survivor's privilege to try to master it as best they know and can. . . . But to have come face to face with such mass murder, to have come so close to being one of its victims, is a relatively unique, psychologically and morally most difficult, experience. It follows that the survivor's new integration will be more difficult—and, one may hope, also more meaningful—than that of [those] spared subjection to an extreme experience (1979, pp. 24, 33, 34)

Denial or integration, the polarities of response to the Holocaust described by Bettelheim, parallel those found in Reach to Recovery and in Audre Lorde's response: oblivion or awareness. Oblivion is a form of death of the self. Yet awareness in an oblivious world is agony, as Wisconsin naturalist Aldo Leopold observed:

One of the penalties of an ecological education is that one lives alone in a world of wounds. Much of the damage inflicted on land is quite invisible to laypersons. Ecologists must either harden their shell and make believe that the consequences of science are none of their business, or be the doctor who sees the marks of death in a community that believes itself well and does not want to be told otherwise. (1953, p. 165)

103

NANCY DATAN
Illness and Imagery:
Feminist Cognition,
Socialization, and
Gender Identity

Substitute feminism for ecology and we see a spectrum of social ills which feminism has rendered visible. The woman who has been raped or might be, the mother seeking child care, or the woman seeking an abortion, all face issues that once were defined as personal and private and now are seen as public and political. Breast cancer too can be seen as more than a singular affliction, as feminists consider rape to be not an isolated personal trauma but an expression of a larger social context in which male sexuality, the patriarchal family, and aggression against women are blended. Similarly, breast cancer is not a solitary ordeal but an illness of the community, to which the community responds with an expression of communal values, which may certainly include repudiation, denial, and isolation.

These communal values are highlighted by issues in gender identity specific to particular illnesses (Meyerowitz et al., 1988). As journalist Martha Weinman Lear observes:

To be American, male, in one's fifties, a compulsive worker—as who of them is not—worried about cholesterol and unpaid bills, working under stress and watching old friends succumb, one by one, to that crisis of the heart . . . I do not suppose women can fully understand that fear. Not that particular one. We agonize instead over cancer; we take as a personal threat the lump in every friend's breast. (1980, p. 11)

Many researchers (Meyerowitz et al., 1988; Rosen and Bibring, 1968) have noted that heart attacks strike at masculine values: aggression, achievement, striving, and sexuality come to have new meanings. Rosen and Bibring (1968) suggest that heart attacks in young men accelerate issues of aging and dependency, since the immediate treatment demands enforced passivity. Breast cancer strikes at the core of femininity: as Rossi observes, "in contemporary Western societies the breast has become an erotic symbol," rather than a functional component of reproduction (1986, p. 120).

Recovery from a heart attack is measured by renewed participation in activities: for example, some survivors of heart attacks go on to run marathons. No such physical triumphs are celebrated by recovery from breast cancer, which is measured by the restoration of appearance. To put it another way, the implied identities regained by men and women recovering from these gender-specific illnesses are that of the midlife jock and the would-be perpetual cheerleader. Last year I ran my first marathon, at the age of 45. As Audre Lorde wrote after her Reach to Recovery volunteer had visited her: "I ached to talk to women about the experience I had just been through, and about what might be to come, and how were they doing it and how had they done it. But I needed to talk with women who shared at least some of my major concerns and beliefs and visions, who shared at least some of my language" (1980a, p. 42). I have never been a cheerleader, and I could not see trying out for the part with falsies. I want to run another marathon, and nothing at all in Reach to Recovery tells me about my prospects as a distance runner.

I propose that Reach to Recovery is, however inadvertently, an example of what sociologist Irving Rosow (1974) terms the socialization to old age, which he views as socialization to a normless, devalued status. As a heart attack accelerates passivity and dependency and other issues of aging for men, breast cancer accelerates the progress of women toward the double standard of aging (Bell, 1970; Sontag, 1972): not merely devalued, but devalued and dependent sooner, and desexualized as part of the devaluation. The image of women presented in Reach to Recovery material underscores the status of victim and trivializes the victimization. One is victimized not by a disease but by its cosmetic consequences: the threat of a desexualized body. The effectiveness of this process rests on the circumstances of socialization, which is facilitated by the ambiguity and anxiety that are abundant on surgical wards. The message, which does not stand up well under critical scrutiny, depends on the power of a nonconscious ideology.

Years ago, I was introduced to the power of a nonconscious ideology when I conducted a small experimental study of mothers' responses to an infant presented in pink or in blue clothing, designed as a modest test of the nature–nurture question (Will, Self, & Datan, 1976). On the one hand, proponents of the "nurture" perspective argue that differences in sex-role socialization reflect the imposition of gender roles which may or may not be appropriate for any given individual; thus mothers inflict social norms on their children before the children are able to express independent preferences. On the other hand, proponents of the "nature" perspective argue that these differences are the outcome of presocial, innate dispositional differences in female and male infants who present different cues to mothers; thus, by socializing sons and daughters differently, mothers are responding effectively and indeed with sensitivity to biologically based differences in individuals.

We tested this question by presenting a single five-month-old baby, whose dispositional cues would not vary across settings, dressed as a boy and as a girl, to mothers who were asked to interact "naturally" with the baby and were provided with a doll, a fish, and a train. If cultural norms shaped the mother's behavior, we anticipated differences in the treatment of the same baby depending on whether it was wearing pink clothing and identified as "Beth" or wearing blue clothing and identified as "Adam." If, on the other hand, the baby's needs determined the mother's response, we would expect no variation in the treatment of the baby.

It will not surprise this audience that mothers handed "Beth" the doll, held her close, touched her, comforted her if she expressed distress, and told us during debriefing that they "knew" she was a girl because she looked so feminine and soft, while "Adam" was given a train, less often cuddled or comforted if he expressed distress, and "looked strong" or "masculine." Mothers further asserted during debriefing that they did not believe in treating sons and daughters differently and did not treat their own sons and daughters differently in any way. Yet these mothers' behavior offers a glimpse at their children's future, which is less egalitarian than the mothers' declared attitudes: girls who will outperform boys on tests of verbal ability, boys who will show deficits in social skills as early as high school; women who will choose affiliation over achievement and pay for their choice with impoverished old age; men who will choose achievement over affiliation and pay for their choice by dying sooner.

105

NANCY DATAN
Illness and Imagery:
Feminist Cognition,
Socialization, and
Gender Identity

To conclude: It has been a task of feminist psychology to expose, explore, and ultimately reject the inequities that begin in the nursery and accumulate over the life course. This chapter has explored some inequities that are part of the social response to breast cancer. It can be seen as a special case of a recent theme of *The Journal of Social Issues:* "Social Issues and Personal Life: The Search for Connections." As I learned, women with breast cancer soon discover that they are in the middle of a minefield of taboos. Feminist epistemology proves invaluable as a mine detector and has been a tool for me in guiding this effort to transform victims into survivors. If socialization is viewed as the transmission of values from one generation to the next, it may be argued that feminists are failures in socialization, and this chapter can be seen as yet one more instance of a repudiation of culture, its nonconscious ideology, and its oppressions.

Cancer is a powerful stimulus word which, thanks to a growing number of survivors, has recently begun to shed first one taboo status, that of unspeakability, and then another, that of death sentence. Breast cancer partakes of a third taboo status: it represents an assault on a symbol of sexuality (Rossi, 1986). In a review of studies of psychological research on women's responses to breast cancer, Meyerowitz et al. (1988) note: "Unfortunately, at times there has also been a tendency for authors to draw conclusions that may be founded more in stereotypes of women and their needs than in sound data." A typical statement of this stereotyped concern is expressed by Derogatis, who asserts as a hypothesis that "the fundamental female role is seriously threatened by breast cancer" (quoted by Meyerowitz et al., 1988). But as Meyerowitz, Taylor, and others have shown, it is by no means clear that cancer itself poses such a universal threat (see Meyerowitz et al., 1988; Taylor, Lichtman, & Wood, 1984; Taylor, Wood, and Lichtman, 1983).

Yet the very material intended to promote recovery assumes that breast cancer is a threat to sexual identity and imposes this assumption on women just as they are most in need of reassurance. Cancer may go into remission, but breasts do not grow back; to accept the message of Reach to Recovery is to accept mutilation as a core feature of one's postsurgical identity, and thus to accept the status of victim. And for victims the most appropriate response is grief. Survivors, by contrast, command our respect—and speaking for myself, I have done my grieving and am ready for some applause.

References

American Cancer Society (1982a). *Reach to Recovery: Helpful hints and how to's.* (Available from the American Cancer Society, 777 Third Avenue, New York, NY 10017.)

American Cancer Society (1982b). *Reach to Recovery: What is reach to recovery?* (Available from the American Cancer Society, 777 Third Avenue, New York, NY 10017.)

American Cancer Society (November 1984). *Prostheses list: 1984–1986.* (Available from the American Cancer Society, 777 Third Avenue, New York, NY 10017.)

American Society of Plastic and Reconstructive Surgeons, Incorporated (January 1982). *Breast reconstruction following mastectomy.* (Available from American Society of Plastic and Reconstructive Surgeons, Incorporated, Patient Referral Service, 233 North Michigan Avenue, Suite 1900, Chicago, IL, 60601.)

BELL, J.P. (November–December 1970). The double standard. *Trans-Action,* pp. 23–27.

BETTELHEIM, B. (1979). *Surviving and other essays.* New York: Knopf.

CLAYTON, S.D., & CROSBY, F. (Eds.) (1986). Social issues and personal life: The search for connections. *Journal of Social Issues, 42* (2), 1–221.

JANOFF-BULMAN, R., & FRIEZE, I. H. (Eds.) (1983). Reactions to victimization. *Journal of Social Issues, 39* (2), 1–227.

LEAR, M.W. (1980). *Heartsounds,* New York: Simon & Schuster.

LEOPOLD, A. (1953). *Round river,* New York: Oxford University Press.

LORDE, A. (1980a). *The cancer journals,* 2nd ed. San Francisco: Spinsters Ink.

LORDE, A. (April 1980b). After breast cancer: I am a warrior, not a victim. *Savvy,* pp. 68–69.

MEYEROWITZ, B.E., CHAIKEN, S., & CLARK, L.K. (1988). Sex roles and culture: Social and personal reactions to breast cancer. In M. Fine & A. Asch (Eds.), *Women with disabilities: Essays in psychology, culture, and politics* (pp. 72–89). Philadelphia: Temple University Press.

O'LEARY, V. (Winter 1987). Musings on the promise (and pain) of feminism. *Psychology of Women,* pp. 1, 3.

ROSEN J.L., & BIBRING, G.L. (1968). Psychological reactions of hospitalized male patients to a heart attack: Age and social-class differences. In B.L. Neugarten (Ed.), *Middle age and aging.* Chicago: University of Chicago Press.

ROSOW, I. (1974). *Socialization to old age.* Berkeley: University of California Press.

ROSSI, A.S. (1986). Sex and gender in the aging society. In A. Pifer & L. Bronte (Eds.), *Our aging society* (pp. 111–139). New York: Norton.

SONTAG, S. (1972, October). The double standard of aging. *Saturday Review,* pp. 29–38.

TAYLOR, S.E., LICHTMAN, R.R., & WOOD, J.V. (1984). Attributions, beliefs about control, and adjustment to breast cancer. *Journal of Personality and Social Psychology, 46,* 489–502.

TAYLOR, S.E., WOOD, J.V., & LICHTMAN, R.R. (1983). It could be worse: Selective evaluation as a response to victimization. *Journal of Social Issues, 39,* 19–40.

WILL, J.A., SELF, P., & DATAN, N. (1976). Maternal behavior and perceived sex of infant. *American Journal of Orthopsychiatry, 46,* 135–139.

Ynestra King

The Other Body:
Reflections on Difference,
Disability, and Identity Politics

Disabled people rarely appear in popular culture. When they do, their disability must be a continuous preoccupation overshadowing all other areas of their character. Disabled people are disabled. That is what they "do." That is what they "are."

My own experience with a mobility impairment that is only minorly disfiguring is that one must either be a creature of the disability, or have transcended it entirely. For me, like most disabled people (and this of course depends on relative severity), neither extreme is true. It is an organic, literally embodied fact that will not change—like being a woman. While it may be possible to "do gender," one does not "do disability." But there is an organic base to both conditions that extends far into culture, and the meaning that "nature" has. Unlike being a woman, being disabled is not a socially constructed condition. It is a tragedy of nature, of a kind that will always exist. The very condition of disability provides a vantage point of a certain lived experience in the body, a lifetime of opportunity for the observation of reaction to bodily deviance, a testing ground for reactions to persons who are readily perceived as having something wrong or being different. It is fascinating, maddening, and disorienting. It defies categories of "sickness" and "health," "broken" and "whole." It is in between.

Meeting people has an overlay: I know what they notice first is that I am different. And there is the experience of the difference in another person's reaction who meets me sitting down (when the disability is not apparent), and standing up and walking (when the infirmity is obvious). It is especially noticeable when another individual is flirting and flattering, and has an abrupt change in affect when I stand up. I always make sure that I walk around in front of someone before I accept a date, just to save face for both of us. Once the other person perceives the disability, the switch on the sexual circuit breaker often pops off—the connection is broken. "Chemistry" is over. I have a lifetime of such experiences, and so does every other disabled woman I know.

White middle-class people—especially white men—in the so-called First World have the most negative reactions. And I always recognize studied politeness, the attempt to pretend that there's nothing to notice (this is the liberal response—Oh, you're black? I hadn't noticed). Then there's the do-gooder response, where the person falls all over her/himself, insisting on doing everything for you; later they hate you; it's a form of objectification. It conveys to you that that is all they see, rather like a man who can't quit talking with a woman about sex.

In the era of identity politics in feminism, disability has not only been an added cross to bear, but an added "identity" to take on—with politically correct positions, presumed instant alliances, caucuses to join, and closets to come out of. For example, I was once dragged across a room to meet someone. My friend, a very politically correct lesbian feminist, said, "She's disabled, too. I thought you'd like to meet her." Rather than argue—what would I say? "I'm not interested in other disabled people," or "This is my night off"? (The truth in that moment was like the truth of this experience in every other moment, complicated and difficult to explain)—I went along to find myself standing before someone strapped in a wheelchair she propels by blowing into a tube with a respirator permanently fastened to the back of the chair. To suggest that our relative experience of disability is something we could casually compare (as other people stand by!) demonstrates the crudity of perception about the complex nature of bodily experience.

My infirmity is partial leg paralysis. I can walk anywhere, climb stairs, drive a car, ride a horse, swim, hang-glide, fly a plane, hike in the wilderness, go to jail for my political convictions, travel alone, and operate heavy equipment. I can earn a living, shop, cook, eat as I please, dress myself, wash and iron my own clothes, clean my house. The woman in that wheelchair can do none of these fundamental things, much less the more exotic ones. On a more basic human level I can spontaneously get my clothes off if I decide to make love. Once in bed my lover and I can forget my disability. None of this is true of the woman in the wheelchair. There is no bodily human activity that does not have to be specially negotiated, none in which she is not absolutely "different." It would take a very long time, and a highly nuanced conversation, for us to be able to share experiences as if they were common. The experience of disability for the two of us was more different than my experience is from the daily experience of people who are not considered disabled. So much for disability solidarity.

With disability, one is somewhere on a continuum between total bodily dysfunction—or death—and complete physical wholeness. In some way, this probably applies to every living person. So when is it that we call a person "disabled"? When do they become "other"? There are "minor" disabilities that are nonetheless significant for a person's life. Color blindness is one example. But in our culture, color blindness is considered an inconvenience rather than a disability.

The ostracization, marginalization, and distorted response to disability are not simply issues of prejudice and denial of civil rights. They reflect attitudes toward bodily life, an unease in the human skin, an inability to cope with contingency, ambiguity, flux, finitude, and death.

109

YNESTRA KING
The Other Body:
Reflections on
Difference, Disability,
and Identity Politics

Visibly disabled people (like women) in this culture are the scapegoats for resentments of the limitations of organic life. I had polio when I was seven, finishing second grade. I had excelled in everything, and rarely missed school. I had one bad conduct notation—for stomping on the boys' blocks when they wouldn't let me play with them. Although I had leg braces and crutches when I was ready to start school the next year, I wanted desperately to go back and resume as much of the same life as I could. What I was not prepared for was the response of the school system. They insisted that I was now "handicapped" and should go into what they called "special education." This was a program aimed primarily at multiply disabled children, virtually all of whom were mentally retarded as well as physically disabled. It was in a separate wing of another school, and the children were completely segregated from the "normal" children in every aspect of the school day, including lunch and recreational activities. I was fortunate enough to have educated, articulate parents and an especially aggressive mother; she went to the school board and waged a tireless campaign to allow me to come back to my old school on a trial basis—the understanding being that the school could send me to special education if things "didn't work out" in the regular classroom.

And so began my career as an "exceptional" disabled person, not like the *other* "others." And I was glad. I didn't want to be associated with those others either. Apart from the objective limitations caused by the polio, the transformation in identity—the difference in worldly reception—was terrifying and embarrassing, and it went far beyond the necessary considerations my limitations required.

My experience as "other" is much greater and more painful as a disabled person than as a woman. Maybe the most telling dimension of this knowledge is my observation of the reactions of others over the years, of how deeply afraid people are of being outside the normative appearance (which is getting narrower as capitalism exaggerates patriarchy). It is no longer enough to be thin; one must have ubiquitous muscle definition, nothing loose, flabby, or ill defined, no fuzzy boundaries. And of course, there's the importance of control. Control over aging, bodily processes, weight, fertility, muscle tone, skin quality, and movement. Disabled women, regardless of how thin, are without full bodily control.

I see disabled women fight these normative standards in different ways, but never get free of negotiating and renegotiating them. I did it by constructing my life around other values and, to the extent possible, developing erotic attachments to people who had similar values, and for whom my compensations were more than adequate. But at one point, after two disastrous but steamy liaisons with a champion athlete and a dancer (during which my friends pointed out the obvious unkind truth and predicted painful endings), I discovered the worlds I had tried to protect myself from; the disastrous attraction to "others" to complete oneself. I have seen disabled women endure unspeakably horrible relationships because they were so flattered to have such a conventionally attractive individual in tow.

And then there's the weight issue. I got fat by refusing to pay attention to my body. Now that I'm slimming down again, my old vanities and insecurities are surfacing. The battle of dieting can be especially fraught for disabled women. It is more difficult because exercising is more difficult, as is traveling around to get the proper foods, and then preparing them. But the underlying rage at the system that makes you feel as if you *are* your body (female, infirm) and that everything else is window dressing—this also undermines the requisite discipline. A tempting response is to resort to an ideal of self as bodiless essence in which the body is completely incidental and irrelevant.

The wish that the body should be irrelevant has been one of my most fervent lifelong wishes. The knowledge that it isn't is my most intense lifelong experience.

I have seen other disabled women wear intentionally provocative clothes, like the woman in a wheelchair on my bus route to work. She can barely move. She has a pretty face, and tiny legs she could not possibly walk on. Yet she wears black lace stockings and spike high heels. The other bus occupants smile condescendingly, or pretend not to notice, or whisper in appalled disbelief that this woman could represent herself as having a sexual self. That she could "flaunt" her sexual being violates the code of acceptable appearance for a disabled woman. This woman's apparel is no more far out than that of many other women on our bus—but she refuses to fold up and be a good little asexual handicapped person.

The well-intentioned liberal new campaigns around "hire the handicapped" are oppressive in related ways. The Other does not only have to demonstrate her competence on insider terms; she must be better, by way of apologizing for being different and rewarding the insiders for letting her in. And the happy handicapped person, who has had faith placed in her/him, must vindicate "the race" because the politics of tokenism assumes that there are in fact other qualifications than doing the job.

This is especially prejudicial in a recession, where there are few social services, where it is "every man for himself." Disabled people inevitably have greater expenses since assistance must often be paid for privately. In the U.S., public construction of the disabled body is that one either is fully disabled and dysfunctional/unemployable (and therefore eligible for public welfare) or totally on one's own. There is no in-between—the possibility of a little assistance, or exceptions in certain areas. Disabled people on public assistance cannot work or they will lose their benefits. (In the U.S. ideology that shapes public attitudes and public policy, one is either fully dependent or fully autonomous.) But the reality of human and organic life is that everyone is different in some way; there is no such thing as a totally autonomous individual. Yet the mythology of autonomy perpetuates in terrible ways the oppression of the disabled. It also perpetuates misogyny—and the destruction of the planet.

It may be that this clear lack of autonomy—this reminder of mortal finitude and contingency and embeddedness of nature and the body—is at the root of the hatred of the disabled. On the continuum of autonomy and dependence, disabled people need help. To need help is to feel humiliated, to have failed. I think this "help" issue must be even harder for men than women. But any disabled person is always negotiating both the provisionality of autonomy and the rigidity of physical norms.

From the vantage point of disability, there are some objective and desirable aspects of autonomy. But they have to do with independence. The preferred protocol is that the attendant or friend perform the task that the disabled person needs done in the way the disabled person *asks it to be done*. Assistance from friends and family is a negotiated process, and often maddening. For that reason most disabled people prefer to live in situations where they can do all the basic functions themselves, with whatever special equipment or built-ins are required.

111

YNESTRA KING
*The Other Body:
Reflections on
Difference, Disability,
and Identity Politics*

It's a dreadful business, this needing help. And it's more dreadful in the U.S. than in any place in the world, because our heroes are dynamic overcomers of adversity, and there is an inevitable cultural contempt for weakness.

Autonomy is on a continuum toward dependency and death. And the idea that dependency could come at any time, that one could die at any time, or be dismembered or disfigured, and still have to live (maybe even *want to live*) is unbearable in a context that understands and values autonomy in the way we moderns do.

I don't want to depict this experience of unbearability as strictly cultural. The compromising of the human body before its natural time is tragic. It forces terrible hardship on the individual to whom it occurs. But the added overlay of oppression on the disabled is intimately related to the fear of death, and the acknowledgment of our embeddedness in organic nature. We are finite, contingent, dependent creatures by our very nature; we will all eventually die. We will all experience compromises to our physical integrity. The aspiration to human wholeness is an oppressive idealism. Socially, it is deeply infantilizing.

It promotes a simplistic view of the human person, a static notion of human life that prevents the maturity and social wisdom that might allow human beings to more fully apprehend the human condition. It marginalizes the "different," those perceived as hopelessly wedded to organic existence—women and the disabled. The New Age "human potential movement"—in the name of maximizing human growth—is one of the worst offenders in obscuring the kind of human growth I am suggesting.

I too believe that the potential for human growth and creativity is infinite—but it is not groundless. The common ground for the person—the human body—is a place of shifting sand that can fail us at any time. It can change shape and properties without warning; this is an essential truth of embodied existence.

Of all the ways of becoming "other" in our society, disability is the only one that can happen to anyone, in an instant, transforming that person's life and identity forever.

Alice Mayall and Diana E. H. Russell

Racism in Pornography

In pornography, all of the culture's racist myths become just another turn-on. Thus, Asian women are portrayed as pliant dolls; Latin women as sexually voracious yet utterly submissive; and black women as dangerous and contemptible sexual animals.

(DORCHEN LEIDHOLDT, 1981)

I visited seven pornography stores in the San Francisco Bay area to investigate the kinds of racist pornography being sold. I also wanted to find out which ethnic groups are most often portrayed in pornography, and in what manner. Once in the store, I looked at every accessible piece of pornography on every shelf. I noted all the titles and covers that displayed people of color.

I divided the pornography into the following categories: magazines, books, films, videos and, for one store, games and cards. I recorded the total number of items found in each category as well as the number containing people of color in each category.

Once I had identified the pornography as containing a person of color, I listed the title, a description of the cover picture, as well as the type of pornography it represented. My observations of magazines were limited to their covers because most of them were encased in plastic. I also selected eight pornography books about people of color and Jews in order to make more detailed analyses of their contents.

The salience of skin color is evident in most of the materials displayed in pornography stores. White women were featured in most pornography (92 percent of total) presumably because they fulfill the prevailing racist equation of beauty with whiteness and Caucasian features. People of color fall into the special interest category, other examples of which are rape, bondage and sado-masochism, anal sex, sex with children, large-breasted women and sex with animals. Some pornographic covers also focus on particular body parts or different methods of penetrating bodies.

TABLE 1. Pornographic Book Titles Using People of Color[a]

African-Americans
Animal Sex Among Black Women
Animals and Black Women
Bisexual Teacher
Bitch's Black Stud
Black Beauty
Black Bitch
Black Fashion Model
Black Ghetto Teens
Black Girl's Animal Love
Black Head Nurse
Black Lady's Lust for Girls
Black Leather Doll
Black Passion
Black Stepfather
Black Teacher
Black Woman's Hunger
Boy for Black Mama
By Sex Possessed
Candy's Black Lover
Dark Detective
Diner Doll
Demon Dictator
Gang Banged by Blacks
Garment Center Black Sex
The Heiress' Black Slave Boy
Her New White Master
Hot for Black Studs
Man-Hungry Black Bitch
Mother's Black Lovers
Seductive Black Bitch
Spread Black Thighs
Teacher's Black Passion
Young Intern's Surprise

Nazi-Jewish
Gestapo Bondage Brothel
Gestapo Lust Slave
Gestapo Sex Crimes
Gestapo Stud Farm
Gestapo Training School
Nazi Dungeon Slave
Nazi Sex Captives
Nazi Whip Mistress
Sadist's Prisoner
Sluts of S.S.
Swastika She Devil

Asian
Bawdy Tales of Wu Wu Wang
Bloody Encounters
Geisha's Girls
Geisha's Torment
Japanese Sadist's Dungeon
May Ling's Master
Oriental Sadist's Pet
Samurai Slave Girl
Teen Slaves of Saigon
Vietcong Rape Compound
Whips of Chinatown

Asian/Indian
The Talking Pussy

Arab
Bound Harem Girl
Harem Hell
Raped by Arab Terrorists
Sheik's Hand Maiden

[a]This is a complete list of the pornography book titles from six stores that portrayed people of color on their covers.

A large majority of the magazine covers that portrayed people of color in sexual poses ($n = 109$), but not engaged in sexual contact, used African-American women: 73 covers exhibited African-American women, 18 Asian/Asian-American women, and 4 Hispanic women. Of the covers displaying men of color, 9 were African-American transvestites or transsexuals, while 2 others were portrayed as 'normal', 3 were Asian transvestites and only one was Hispanic.

My analysis of book titles revealed the same disproportionate numbers of portrayals of African-Americans compared with other people of color. Anti-Semitic pornography is another special interest evident in the book titles examined, along with a smaller amount of anti-Arab pornography.

The breakdown of the ethnicity on the 131 cover pictures on which a person of color was displayed in a state of sexual contact is too complex to describe completely, since there are so many possible inter-ethnic and intra-ethnic permutations. The largest number of these covers portrayed African-American women with white men (28), followed by white women with African-American men (20), Asian women with white men (17), and Asian women with men of unknown ethnicity (12). Significantly, as judged by these covers, interest in intra-ethnic heterosexual relations was minimal.

When people of color are used in books, magazines or videos, the titles usually conveyed this information for consumers. For example, an average of 77 percent of the magazines on display in six different stores identified the ethnicity of the person in the title. This presumably means that skin color is very salient to most consumers. It comes as no surprise in a racist culture like the United States, that people of color are a specialty item in pornography. Some of the titles listed in Table 1 show how blatantly racist pornography can be.

In contrast with other women of color, several titles in Table 1 associate animals with African-American women. As Alice Walker (1980: 103) has pointed out, 'where white women are depicted in pornography as "objects," Black women are depicted as animals. Where white women are at least depicted as human bodies if not beings, Black women are depicted as shit.'

Asian women tend to be depicted as sweet young lotus blossoms or objects of bondage. The notorious December 1984 issue of *Penthouse* contained 'nine images of Asian women . . . bound tightly with ropes cutting into their ankles, wrists, labias and buttocks. Two of the images showed women bound and hanging from trees, heads lolling forward, apparently dead. . . . Throughout these murderous images are sprinkled "artsy" haiku quotes which exude dominance and subordination' (Farley, 1992). These appalling photos eroticizing the murder of Asian women provoked Nikki Craft, Melissa Farley and many other women to organize a 2-year feminist rampage against *Penthouse* in nine states resulting in more than 100 arrests (Farley, 1992).

Some of the book titles presented historical periods of abuse as if they were sexually stimulating, for example, the enslavement of African-Americans (*The Heiress' Black Slave Boy, Her New White Master*) and the genocide of Jews (*Gestapo Lust Slave, Nazi Sex Captives*).

The magazine titles are much the same as those used on books. A few examples of particularly racist titles include *Jungle Babies, Wet, Wild and Black, Black Mother Fucker, Geisha Twat, Hot Asian Asses, Oriental Pussy* and *Oriental Bondage*.

Dorchen Leidholdt (1981: 20) points out that 'pornography contains a racial hierarchy in which women are rated as prized objects or despised objects according to their color'. Nevertheless, Hugh Hefner ignorantly boasted 'that portraying women of color as sex objects to a predominantly white male readership is a radical development that shows *Playboy's* social conscience' (Leidholdt, 1981: 20).

The following section presents a content analysis of eight books that exemplify the racism and violence against women prevalent in such 'literature'.

Soul Slave (1981) is one of a series of 'Punishment Books' presenting violent sexual attacks as pleasurable for the participants. A 16-year-old African-American woman is portrayed in *Soul Slave* as the willing victim of her white master. The following passage is a typical example of the contents of this book:

> Rance Godwin leaned over and drove his fist right into my lower stomach. I jerked and sighed when he gave me that blow, and I listened to the words that he had to say to me, 'I told you to get naked, you nigger slut', he said. And I knew then that, no matter how much I loved the pain, I would have to get naked. (p. 22)

Soul Slave is filled with examples of this kind of masochism. The author implies that the woman's pain is special because it is inflicted on an African-American woman by a white man. The derogatory term 'nigger' is used approximately 245 times in the 180-page book. This word is frequently put in the mouth of the young woman to describe herself and other African-Americans, and she is always depicted as enjoying it. For example, 'Rance looked down at me and said, "Get naked, Nigger!" And these words were like the greatest poetry in the world to me' (p. 20).

A second book entitled *Black Head Nurse* (Dakin, 1977), is a compilation of sexual encounters between patients, nurses and doctors in a Harlem hospital. Interracial sex is presumed to constitute evidence that racial or sexual discrimination is not a problem. 'In this hospital there is no discrimination. . . . Black nurses, white doctors, black doctors, white patients. It's all the same when the great equalizer Sex comes into play' (Dakin, 1977: 34). Absurd as this statement is, it is widely believed that sexual unions nullify sexism and racism.

'It just blew their minds to see this white chick on her knees begging that black dude to give her a little' (Dakin, 1977: 142). One of the messages in this example is that it is extraordinary for a white woman to beg an African-American man for sex. On the other hand, African-American women are frequently portrayed in pornographic literature as begging white men for sex. For example, 'Sucking on this fancy white doctor's cock was certainly living the good life. No one could talk her out of that' (p. 178).

The stereotypically tough, powerful, African-American woman is played out in *Black Head Nurse*. 'Up in the Harlem hospitals black nurses rule' (p. 34). The most powerful African-American women are portrayed as physically aggressive dykes. For example, the sadistic head nurse is depicted as whipping her nurses and as seducing another young woman. *Black Head Nurse* also presents other stereotypes about African-American life, such as notions of sexually promiscuous African-American children.

Abuse: Black and Battered (1981) is described as a collection of 'true' case studies based on 'Dr. Lamb's' interviews with eight African-American women. Violent sexual attacks are vividly described in coarse and racist language in all of these stories.

The first woman portrayed in these fake case studies observed after her alcoholic African-American husband raped her, 'I thought he was letting me go, but you can bet no drunk nigger was gonna do that'. In the second case, the woman gives a lengthy, gory description of watching her African-American father raping her mother. He and his friends later rape her when she is 16 years old. Four other cases also depict young girls observing their fathers raping their mothers. As is typical in pornography, all the perpetrators of sexual violence in these 'case studies' escape punishment.

In *Black Ghetto Teens* (Marr, 1977), teenage African-American girls are depicted as thriving on 'stealing, lying, and fucking those rich white dudes who come to the city looking for some nice Black meat' (Marr, 1977: 4). An African-American woman in *Soul Food* (Berry, 1978) is raped by three white men. 'He got to his feet and grabbed the black girl by her hair. He forced his thick, white cock into her mouth' (Berry, 1978: 21). As the pornography industry keeps broadcasting to the world, the victim ends up enjoying the rape: 'She had gained some confidence from having sex [*sic*] with the three men'. The woman tells her rapists, ' "You really have taught me something", Pearl laughed . . . "It can be fun. My ex asked me to do things like this and I always told Bruce "no way".' Rape as a liberatory experience for women is a popular male fantasy in pornography.

In *Animal Sex Among Black Women* (Washington, 1983), the case-study fabrication is used again, even including a bibliography listing other pornography books about sex with animals. This particular book presents five stories of African-American women having voluntary or coerced sex with animals. In one fantasy, a go-go dancer is coerced by two African-American men into having sex with a dog. In another, an African-American woman finds comfort in sex with a German Shepherd after being dumped by a white man.

In the 160-page *Black Fashion Model* (Wilson, 1978), the word 'black' is used 155 times to describe people, 'white' 50 times and 'Negress' eight times. As usual, the African-American rape victims end up loving the abuse. For example, one victim's thoughts as she is forced to have oral sex with a man are described as follows: 'I must be the worst little nigger girl in the entire city. . . . Here I am sucking this man's cock like a tramp . . . and worst of all, I'm enjoying it.'

One blatantly anti-Semitic book, *Sluts of the S.S.* (1979), uses the torture of Jewish women as its source of excitement. Throughout the book there are rapes, killings, as well as non-violent sex. In the rapes by Nazis, Jewish women are referred to as 'Jewish dog', 'Jewish whore', 'Yiddish swine', 'Jewish slut', etc., while the Nazis refer to themselves as members of the master race. ' "Whore", he yelled. "You will love the cock of your master." '

There are especially violent scenes of Jewish women being kicked to death, raped anally, forced to eat human excrement and being killed by dogs. ' "Filthy Jewish slut", he barked. "Drink my Nazi piss, you little pig" ' (p. 106). And:

> She sucked off the cum and blood and shit from his dick as he pounded it into her throat. She gagged at the taste and at the force with which he was fucking her face. He let go with a stream of hot piss and nearly drowned her as he filled her mouth with his hot yellow piss stream choking her as she tried to swallow it. 'Human toilet', he sneered . . . (p. 107)

CONCLUSION

This study's main purpose was to document the way different ethnic groups are portrayed in pornography. No comparable studies have been undertaken, to our knowledge.

The content analysis of seven pornography books about African-Americans shows that they are depicted in a variety of derogatory and stereotypic ways—as animalistic, incapable of self-control, sexually depraved, impulsive, unclean, and so forth. This kind of pornography likely fosters racist-sexist stereotypes as well as racist-sexist behavior, including sexual abuse and sexual violence against African-American girls and women. Similarly, anti-Semitic pornography likely fosters anti-Semitic sexism as well as sexual violence against Jewish girls and women. Future studies should include books portraying a greater variety of people of color, as well as whites.

An important unanswered question is why the liberal and radical community, as well as people of color who are not part of this community, appear to be totally unconcerned about the racism in pornographic materials in contrast to their concern about other manifestations of racism, such as those in ads, literature, media, verbal statements, and so on. If it is due to ignorance, then bringing the virulent racism in pornography to people's attention, as we have done in this article, will hopefully shock them into action.

Unfortunately, we think there is a stronger explanation for this apathy about racist pornography. The combination of sex and racism appears to blunt people's response to pornographic racism just as the combination of sex and violence appears to dull concern about the consequences of portraying violence in pornography.

In the following passage, Dorchen Leidholdt (1981: 20) offers two other thoughtful explanations for the liberal left's indifference to racism in pornography:

> First, in liberal ideology there is an invisible boundary separating the public and political from the personal and sexual. Whereas liberals readily deplore inequality and injustice in the public sector, the private sphere—and sexual relationships in particular—are sacrosanct. Radical feminists' insistence that the personal is political and that public life grows out of private, sexual interactions has been ignored or denied. Second, some 'progressive' men have not simply ignored pornography's racism, they have incorporated it into their personal sexual repertoires.

Whatever the best explanations turn out to be, it is vital that people be made aware of the glaring contradiction in being concerned about the destructive effects of racism and outraged by all manifestations of it—except when it appears in pornography.

References

Abuse: Black and Battered (1981). New York: Star Distributors.

BERRY, RONALD (1978) *Soul Food*. Sutton House.

DAKIN, CRYSTAL (1977) *Black Head Nurse*. New York: Star Distributors.

FARLEY, MELISSA (1992) 'Fighting Femicide in the United States: The Rampage Against Penthouse', in Jill Radford and Diana E.H. Russell (eds) *Femicide: The Politics of Woman-Killing*. New York: Twayne.

LEIDHOLDT, DORCHEN (1981) 'Where Pornography Meets Fascism', *Women's International Newsletter* 15 March: 18–22.

MARR, MANUEL (1977) *Black Ghetto Teens*. New York: Star Distributors.

Sluts of the S.S. (1979). New York: Star Distributors.

Soul Slave (1981) New York: Star Distributors.

WALKER, ALICE (1980) 'Coming Apart', in L. Lederer (ed.) *Take Back the Night*. New York: William Morrow.

WASHINGTON, SPENCER (1983) *Animal Sex Among Black Women*. North Hollywood, CA: American Art Enterprises.

WILSON, JOHN (1978) *Black Fashion Model*. Publishers Consultants.

In Praise of Women's Bodies

How long has it been since you spent a few days in the intimate company of women: dressing and undressing, talking, showering, resting—the kind of casual togetherness that seems more common to locker rooms of men?

For me, high-school gym class came the closest. But that was during the repressive fifties, when even the most daring of us hid behind our towels, and others were so insecure about our bodies' adolescent changes (or the lack of them) that we went through group showers with our underwear on, or endured the damp discomfort of gym suits under our clothes so we never had to undress at all.

By the time we got to college, I suppose we must have been more grown-up and open. Nonetheless, sports for women, still "unfeminine," became anti-intellectual besides. Those were two good excuses to avoid most situations of casual nudity among women, and thus to go right on concealing the imperfect bodies on which we secretly thought our worldly worth depended.

So I found myself belatedly having a basic, human, comforting experience that should have been a commonplace in my life long ago. Thanks to a few days spent at an old-fashioned spa in the company of ninety or so other women, I discovered a simple, visceral consciousness-raising that was just as crucial as the verbal kind. Like many basic experiences women are encouraged to miss, it brought both strength (through self-acceptance) and anger (why didn't I know this before?).

It's a truism, for instance, that a few clothes are more shocking than none. But for women especially, bras, panties, bathing suits, and other stereotypical gear are visual reminders of a commercial, idealized feminine image that our real and diverse female bodies can't possibly fit. Without those visual references, however, each individual woman's body can be accepted on its own terms. We stop being comparatives. We begin to be unique.

Nobody commented on these events, of course. They just happened. The more hours and days we spent together, moving between locker room and exercise classes or pool and sauna, the less we resorted to the silky wisps or formidable elastic of our various underwear styles. Nudity was fine. Exercise leotards were also okay. They coated the body comfortably instead of chopping it up into horizontal strips. But gradually, skinny bikinis, queen-size slips, girdles, and other paraphernalia begin to disappear from our bodies and our lockers, like camouflage in a war we no longer had to fight.

"I've always loved fancy lingerie," said one woman, "but it's beginning to look weird to me."

"That's why my husband likes black garter belts," said a Rubenesque woman in a towel. "They look the *most* weird."

"Did you ever hear the story about Judy Holliday?" asked a woman peeling off a sweaty leotard. "When she went for a movie interview, the head of the studio started chasing her around the desk. So she just reached into her dress, pulled out her falsies, and handed them to him. 'Here,' she said, 'I think this is what you want.' "

"My God," said a big-breasted woman who, by *Playboy's* standards, should have been very happy. "If only I could do that!"

Gradually there was also less embarrassment about appendectomy scars, stretch marks, Cesarean incisions, and the like. Though I had always resented the anthropological double standard by which scars are supposed to be marks of courage and experience on a male body but ugliness on a female one, I began to realize that I had been assessing such wounds in masculine terms nonetheless. Dueling scars, war wounds, scars-as-violence, tribal scars as painful initiations—those images were part of the reason I had assumed such marks to be evidence of violence on men as well as on women.

But many of women's body scars have a very different context, and thus an emotional power all their own. Stretch marks and Cesarean incisions from giving birth are very different from accident, war, and fight scars. They evoke courage without violence, strength without cruelty, and even so, they're far more likely to be worn with diffidence than bragging. That gives them a moving, bittersweet power, like seeing a room where a very emotional event in our lives once took place.

There were other surgical scars that seemed awesome to me, too, but not as evocative as those from childbirth. How do women survive even the routine physical price of skin stretched to its limit? After one Cesarean birth, where do some women find the courage to attempt one or several more?

True, there are tribal societies that treat women who give birth like honorary male warriors, but that is paying too much honor to war. Childbirth is more admirable than conquest, more amazing than self-defense, and as courageous as either one. Yet one of the strongest, most thoughtful feminists I know still hides in one-piece bathing suits to conceal her two Cesarean scars. And one of the most hypocritical feminists I know (that is, one who loves feminism but dislikes women) had plastic surgery to remove the tiny scar that gave her face character.

Perhaps we'll only be fully at ease with ourselves when we can appreciate scars as symbols of experience, often experiences that other women share, and see our bodies as unique chapters in a shared story.

To do that, we need to be together unself-consciously. We need the regular sight of diverse reality to wear away the plastic-stereotypical-perfect image against which we've each been taught to measure our selves. The impossible goal of "what we should look like" has worn a groove in our brains. It will take the constant intimacy of many new images to blast it out.

So, from my belated beginnings, I write in praise of diverse women.

- A cheerful, seventyish woman with short white curls held back by an orange ribbon, wearing a satiny green leotard that hugs her gently protruding stomach like a second skin. From her, I learn the beauteous curve of a non-flat stomach. I also learn that a great-grandmother can touch her toes with more flexibility than I can, and leave me panting in aerobic-dance class.
- A small, sturdy young masseuse with strong hands who dreams of buying a portable massage table so that she can start a business of her own. "My boyfriend's grandmother has arthritis real bad," she explains, "but I massage her hands every day to stop the pain." She also has insomniac clients she massages into drug-free sleep, and clients with painful knots of tension she relaxes through direct pressure. We agree that, if everyone had one good massage a day, there would be fewer wars. From her, I learn there can be sisterly satisfaction, not subservience, in serving other women's bodies.
- Two women friends who speak only Spanish and whose arrival causes uncertainty among locker mates who speak no Spanish at all. From them, we soon learn that the language of bodies and gestures is universal.
- A perfectly egg-shaped woman who sits upright and serene in the nude sunbathing area every day. From her, I learn beyond doubt that only the female curves of breasts and stomach make the Buddha image believable.
- A beautiful, tall, slender young woman whose legs dangle from her torso, scarecrowlike, as she leaps in exercise class. Older, stouter women are much more graceful in their movements, and, God knows, more in time with the music. From her, I learn that beauty may be skin-deep, but natural rhythm is deeper.
- A fiftyish locker-room attendant, under five feet tall, who jogs five miles every morning, and explains, "My husband used to go with me but he had to stop, "the cold air froze his lungs." We are discussing the need for this spa to offer judo or some other self-defense class, and she agrees. Why? Because she was attacked in the parking lot by a six-foot-tall man with a cement block in his hand, yet she fought him off with self-defense tactics that included a hard blow to the groin. From her, I learn that a small woman can be to a big man what a bullet is to Jell-O.
- A new, no-nonsense athletic director who is trying hard to persuade traditional women clients that there's more to fitness than the tape measure and the scale. Since spa management is still convinced that men are interested in fitness and health, but women want beauty and pampering, she is relieved when I complain to management that men in the same spa get cardiovascular and muscle-flexibility tests while women have to request them and pay extra. From each other, we re-learn the activist value of pressure from both outside and inside any system.
- A tall, calm, dark-haired mother and her tall, calm, dark-haired daughter who talk together about their mutual profession of social work. Mostly

they seem companionable without needing to talk. A woman's body has given birth to a friend.

- A tough, witty criminal lawyer who wants to figure out how to use her legal talents to advance other women. In nudity, she relaxes enough to gift us with an epigram: "Most men want their wives to have a jobette."

- A no-nonsense young beautician who gives a pore-cleaning facial and a discourse on cosmetic surgery at the same time. "I've seen all kinds of scars—breast implants, chin tucks, face lifts, eyelid tucks. There was a woman in here who had such a bad eyelid job that she couldn't close her eyes." I wait to hear some resentment of rich women with little to do but revise their faces, but I am wrong. "Poor things," says the beautician, digging away expertly. "I wouldn't trade places for any amount of money." More silence. "I'm only planning to have a chin tuck myself."

- A few women who sit quietly in the steam room, each immersed in a cloud of vapor, her own muscle pains, and her own thoughts. Two newcomers arrive and get help from veterans of a day or two. "Start on the first bench—it gets hotter as you go up."

"Use this ice for your forehead."

"Don't stay more than five minutes the first time." Together, we make a small misty world of diverse sizes, shapes, and colors: a quiet place that cares about the welfare of strangers. The steam that surrounds us seems to communicate our thoughts.

"It's nice that you can come here by yourself or with a group of women," says a voice from the mist.

"And not feel like a nut," finishes another.

"I thought I'd be embarrassed," says a young voice. "I've never been with a bunch of women like . . . like *this* before."

Laughter comes from the steamy Buddha in the corner. "Honey," she says, "what you see is what you get."

When I return home, caffeine free, sugar free, and relatively healthy, I ask a few much younger women about their experiences of seeing women's bodies. I had assumed this generation would be more at ease than mine, but the spa's younger guests have shaken my faith. From random answers, I learn that although no one is wearing underwear into the shower anymore, this nonverbal form of consciousness-raising still isn't an accepted part of younger women's lives.

"There's no real place where we can be together like that," says a high-school student thoughtfully. "Sports aren't important, and I don't know anybody who goes to the gym or to a steam bath. It just doesn't happen."

Meanwhile, two editors have reminded me that an evening in a Turkish bath in Jerusalem turned out to be one of the high points of a feminist tour of Israel that *Ms.* magazine organized a few years ago. It created an unexpected bonding among strangers at the beginning of the tour—"instant sisterhood"—and a realization of the beauty of women's bodies on their own terms. The few women who had missed that evening felt they were one step behind the group's intimacy for the rest of the trip.

I had listened to this same story when the tour group came home, but I hadn't really heard it. Like other basic experiences, this one is better absorbed than described.

But now I know: I know that fat or thin, mature or not, our bodies wouldn't give us such unease if we learned their place in the rainbow spectrum of women. Even great beauties seem less distant, and even mastectomies seem less terrifying, when we stop imagining them and see them as they really are.

Changing the artificiality of media images would help, but that isn't enough. Like the children who were shown photographs of women and men doing nontraditional jobs—women welding, for instance, and men diapering babies—but reversed those roles in their memories within a few weeks, we only retain a complete image when we experience it completely. A one-dimensional remedy can't cure a three-dimensional wrong.

Now, like the teenage heroine in *Gypsy* who is aware of her body only after she becomes a stripper, too many of us experience female bodies, our own and others, in social settings and private bedrooms, only when they are most isolated, artificial, self-conscious, and on display for men or conventional judgment.

A little natural togetherness would show us the Family of Woman, where each of us is beautiful and no one is the same.

PART THREE

Making Meaning

This set of stories is probably the most varied in any section of the book. You may find yourself wondering what connects them to each other or, even, what the title of the section means. We chose these readings, not for their content area, but because we believe that they each represent an attempt to question what is purportedly known to be true in a variety of areas important to women. Such "certainties" may be conveyed to us by our culture, by the media, through procedures following a traumatic event, and, most often, in everyday interactions with others. Because these messages are rarely stated overtly, they enter our consciousness without our awareness. We may, therefore, accept them as our own beliefs and values without recognizing the harm these messages carry for ourselves and other women. It may be somewhat disturbing for you to reexamine your assumptions, but it is very important, because we cannot make changes in ourselves or the world without changing our perceptions about them.

Social and personal change does not, however, always have to be a solemn undertaking.

The reading by an unknown author on the rape of Mr. Smith and Gloria Steinem's classic piece about what would happen if men could menstruate are witty pieces that also make important points. Ask yourself, whose definitions are considered to be legitimate? "The 'Rape' of Mr. Smith" shows how history can be used against powerless individuals. What happens when you change the sex, ethnicity, or class of the protagonist of this piece? Does it still seem funny?

Steinem's piece makes us ask why people think feminists do not have a sense of humor. The humor derives from how she inverts customary justifications for the way women and men are treated in our society. Think about how easily rationalizations become reasons. Can you come up with some other arguments in other areas that would make women's biological characteristics socially desirable if they were possessed by men? What is more important—the biological distinction or the value we place on it? This piece illustrates how language is used to make meaning and who has the power to determine what these meanings are to be.

Maureen Dowd, a journalist, takes on another cultural icon—*Cosmopolitan*—in this recent *New York Times* piece. Do you agree with her statement that the Cosmo Girl is, after all, just a tarted-up Cinderella, always believing that happiness is just one makeover away? She tells us how editors of women's magazines characterize early feminists as "women" who wanted to be like men, whereas today's grown-up "girls" such as Madonna and Courtney Love want the freedom to be "girly" for their own pleasure. What is different about being a girl rather than a woman? What advantages or disadvantages are embedded in these terms?

In the reading by Phyllis Teitelbaum on the structure of standardized tests, we move away from a direct look at how assumptions and values are built into the words we use. Teitelbaum—who works for the Educational Testing Service—examines how sex biases influence the construction of a test that affects virtually all would-be college students. You probably took SAT exams not too long ago. You may have questioned your scores, but you probably did not question whether the procedures used to test you were "normal and right." What does Teitelbaum mean when she charges that standardized tests are androcentric in nature? Evaluate each of the following terms: objectivity, dualistic thinking, quantitative measurement, atomistic analysis, timing for speed, and the competitive atmosphere that surrounds such testing. Do you believe that women and men are socialized differently so that these aspects of standardized testing are more unfair to women than to men? Did your scores on the SAT affect your perception of yourself or change your plans about where to apply for college? Think about whether we could or should develop "gynocentric" tests. Would such tests be useful and fair?

Just as most people have taken standardized tests, most also engage in sex or at least think about doing so. Greta Cristina's article from *Ms* questions the fundamental meaning of this "given" too. It shows how asking one question can lead to still more. For example, first she asked how she could determine what a "proper" number of sexual partners is. Note how the meaning of the same objective number of partners changes depending on how one labels the sexually active woman. How is a woman's sense of identity changed by such labels? Cristina next asks how sex itself is defined. Is it defined by the act of penetration or by its meaning to the participants? It is important to note that these meanings also change when she changes the sex of her partners. Cristina's friends argue it is sex if it feels like it when you are doing it. Does this definition leave anything out? Think about how your reconstruction of consent and memories about important events may be altered by subsequent changes in a relationship.

Carol Jacklin, a feminist psychologist, shares some painful experiences in her personal life in her story. She also questions the meaning of sexual labels in terms of self-identification and identification by others. Why does she see being identified as heterosexual as offensive? What does she think about receiving social privileges for being a member of this category without wanting them? She also notes, however, that there are disadvantages for heterosexual feminists too. They are at greater risk for having inequitable personal relationships, which have an impact on their careers as well as their self-esteem. Jacklin believes that there are insights that women who have "lived with the enemy" can bring to feminism. What are these insights? Do you believe they can be acquired in ways other than through bitter personal experience?

Of course, personal trauma is relative. Michelle Fine's story is about Altamese Thomas—a young, poor, African American woman whom Fine meets as a volunteer rape counselor—who lives in a much more destructive social environment than most of us will ever encounter. Her perceptions about what to do after a rape clash strongly with Fine's middle-class beliefs about taking control in the face of injustice. Fine asks: Is taking control the same as coping? Consider Altamese Thomas's situational context. What will happen to her mother and babies if she testifies about the rape? Does she have any reason to believe that the authorities will believe or help her? Will knowledge about her personal problems help her or make her feel worse about herself? This story forces us to examine how ethnic and class differences in power and powerlessness alter the meaning of events usually discussed primarily in terms of gender.

Mitsuye Yamada (who teaches English in a community college) gives us another perspective about how racism affects women's perception of themselves. Her story may be particularly disquieting because, until recently, Asian Americans were considered to be a "model minority." This meant that they were invisible to members of the dominant culture who did not perceive them as feeling oppressed or angry. Asian American women were particularly influenced by the stereotype of passivity. Do you agree with Yamada when she states that they stayed within their role so well that they were not even aware themselves that resistance was necessary or possible? Some radical feminists have argued that this kind of colonization of the oppressed individual's mind is the worst form of cultural domination. How does this kind of internalization of norms influence the individual's perception of what sort of choices are available to them? Look at Yamada's story and that of Altamese Thomas in terms of how freedom may be constrained by both external and internal forces. How do such forces influence our sense of responsibility for our own lives?

We saved Kate Bornstein's story for the last one in this section because we believe it questions the most fundamental category of all—the idea that there are two separate, easily identifiable sexes. Bornstein has transformed herself from a heterosexual male IBM salesperson to a lesbian playwright and performance artist. Unlike most autobiographical accounts by transsexual individuals, however, she does not claim that she has changed from a man to a woman. Instead, she questions how we make this determination for ourselves and others. Do you agree with her statement that we do not often question established certainties and that there are penalties attached to doing so?

In speaking of her own childhood gender identity, Bornstein suggests that "it paid to lie" because she always felt that "she" was acting out what others assumed "he" was. What is the difference between being labeled for what one *is* rather than for what one *does*? (This question can also be applied to other labels discussed in earlier stories.) Bornstein uses her life story to question the idea that sex/gender is natural rather than being the product of cultural construction. Of course, this is her account, and other interpretations may be possible. However, why are her questions about the existence of gender so threatening? Ambiguous gender cues may be more problematic in everyday life than when they are encountered in the media. What do you think when you encounter someone for whom gender cues are ambiguous? Are cultural beliefs about the permanence and indivisibility of gender changing as more examples of gender ambiguity are found in public life?

These stories show how closely the individual, her community, and her cultural matrix are intertwined. For example, Bornstein informs us that when individuals make a sex change they are told by professionals to change their personal histories, so as to seem to have a consistent identity, and not to associate with other transsexuals. How does this advice influence the person's view of themselves as well as of the meaning of sex and gender? Yamada tells us, "We have been trained not to expect a response in ways that mattered. . . . our psychological mind set has already told us time and again that we are born into a ready made world into which we must fit ourselves, and that many of us do it very well." (p. 39). How do these stories fit into more general social psychological research on the self-fulfilling prophecy?

We hope that this section shows you that the most insidious way of keeping people powerless is to let them speak only about harmless and inconsequential subjects, or let them speak freely and not listen to them. We also hope it helps you to understand that women's perceptions frequently are based on the fact that they are indeed less likely to get what they need or want from the established social system. Finally, we hope that these stories help you to better understand an early feminist maxim—the personal is political!

"The Rape" of Mr. Smith

The law discriminates against rape victims in a manner which would not be tolerated by victims of any other crime. In the following example, a holdup victim is asked questions similar in form to those usually asked a victim of rape.

"Mr. Smith, you were held up at gunpoint on the corner of 16th & Locust?"

"Yes."

"Did you struggle with the robber?"

"No."

"Why not?"

"He was armed."

"Then you made a conscious decision to comply with his demands rather than to resist?"

"Yes."

"Did you scream? Cry out?"

"No. I was afraid."

"I see. Have you have been held up before?"

"No."

"Have you ever given money away?"

"Yes, of course—"

"And did you do so willingly?"

"What are you getting at?"

"Well, let's put it like this, Mr. Smith. You've given away money in the past—in fact, you have quite a reputation for philanthropy. How can we be sure that you weren't *contriving* to have your money taken from you by force?"

"Listen, if I wanted—"

"Never mind. What time did this holdup take place, Mr. Smith?"

"About 11 p.m."

"You were out on the streets at 11 p.m.? Doing what?"

"Just walking."

"Just walking? You know that it's dangerous being out on the street that late at night. Weren't you aware that you could have been held up?"

"I hadn't thought about it."

"What were you wearing at the time, Mr. Smith?"

"Let's see. A suit. Yes, a suit."

"An *expensive* suit?"

"Well—yes."

"In other words, Mr. Smith, you were walking around the streets late at night in a suit that practically *advertised* the fact that you might be a good target for some easy money, isn't that so? I mean, if we didn't know better, Mr. Smith, we might even think you were *asking* for this to happen, mightn't we?"

"Look, can't we talk about the past history of the guy who *did* this to me?"

"I'm afraid not, Mr. Smith. I don't think you would want to violate his rights, now, would you?"

Naturally, the line of questioning, the innuendo, is ludicrous—as well as inadmissible as any sort of cross-examination—unless we are talking about parallel questions in a rape case. The time of night, the victim's previous history of "giving away" that which was taken by force, the clothing—all of these are held against the victim. Society's posture on rape, and the manifestation of that posture in the courts, help account for the fact that so few rapes are reported.

Gloria Steinem

If Men Could Menstruate—

A white minority of the world has spent centuries conning us into thinking that a white skin makes people superior—even though the only thing it really does is make them more subject to ultraviolet rays and to wrinkles. Male human beings have built whole cultures around the idea that penis-envy is "natural" to women—though having such an unprotected organ might be said to make men vulnerable, and the power to give birth makes womb-envy at least as logical.

In short, the characteristics of the powerful, whatever they may be, are thought to be better than the characteristics of the powerless—and logic has nothing to do with it.

What would happen, for instance, if suddenly, magically, men could menstruate and women could not?

The answer is clear—menstruation would become an enviable, boast-worthy, masculine event:

Men would brag about how long and how much.

Boys would mark the onset of menses, that longed-for proof of manhood, with religious ritual and stag parties.

Congress would fund a National Institute of Dysmenorrhea to help stamp out monthly discomforts.

Sanitary supplies would be federally funded and free. (Of course, some men would still pay for the prestige of commercial brands such as John Wayne Tampons, Muhammad Ali's Rope-a-dope Pads, Joe Namath Jock Shields— "For Those Light Bachelor Days," and Robert "Baretta" Blake Maxi-Pads.)

Military men, right-wing politicians, and religious fundamentalists would cite menstruation ("*men*-struation") as proof that only men could serve in the Army ("you have to give blood to take blood"), occupy political office ("can women be aggressive without that steadfast cycle governed by the planet Mars?"), be priests and ministers ("how could a woman give her blood for our sins?"), or rabbis ("without the monthly loss of impurities, women remain unclean").

Male radicals, left-wing politicians, and mystics, however, would insist that women are equal, just different; and that any woman could enter their ranks if only she were willing to self-inflict a major wound every month ("you *must* give blood for the revolution"), recognize the preeminence of menstrual issues, or subordinate her selfness to all men in their Cycle of Enlightenment.

Street guys would brag ("I'm a three-pad man") or answer praise from a buddy ("Man, you lookin' *good!*") by giving fives and saying, "Yeah, man, I'm on the rag!"

TV shows would treat the subject at length. ("Happy Days": Richie and Potsie try to convince Fonzie that he is still "The Fonz," though he has missed two periods in a row.) So would newspapers. (SHARK SCARE THREATENS MENSTRUATING MEN. JUDGE CITES MONTHLY STRESS IN PARDONING RAPIST.) And movies. (Newman and Redford in "Blood Brothers"!)

Men would convince women that intercourse was *more* pleasurable at "that time of the month." Lesbians would be said to fear blood and therefore life itself—though probably only because they needed a good menstruating man.

Of course, male intellectuals would offer the most moral and logical arguments. How could a woman master any discipline that demanded a sense of time, space, mathematics, or measurement, for instance, without that in-built gift for measuring the cycles of the moon and planets—and thus for measuring anything at all? In the rarefied fields of philosophy and religion, could women compensate for missing the rhythm of the universe? Or for their lack of symbolic death-and-resurrection every month?

Liberal males in every field would try to be kind: the fact that "these people" have no gift for measuring life or connecting to the universe, the liberals would explain, should be punishment enough.

And how would women be trained to react? One can imagine traditional women agreeing to all these arguments with a staunch and smiling masochism. ("The ERA would force housewives to wound themselves every month": Phyllis Schlafly. "Your husband's blood is as sacred as that of Jesus— and so sexy, too!": Marabel Morgan.) Reformers and Queen Bees would try to imitate men, and *pretend* to have a monthly cycle. All feminists would explain endlessly that men, too, needed to be liberated from the false idea of Martian aggressiveness, just as women needed to escape the bonds of menses-envy. Radical feminists would add that the oppression of the nonmenstrual was the pattern for all other oppressions. ("Vampires were our first freedom fighters!") Cultural feminists would develop a bloodless imagery in art and literature. Socialist feminists would insist that only under capitalism would men be able to monopolize menstrual blood. . . . In fact, if men could menstruate, the power justifications could probably go on forever.

If we let them.

Cosmic Girl

I went to Cosmopolitan once, looking for freelance work. An editor gave me some red binders filled with story ideas. The ideas were oddly reversible.

You could choose "I Had an Affair With My Best Friend's Father" or "I Had an Affair With My Father's Best Friend."

You could choose "My Fling With My Gynecologist/Psychiatrist/Dentist" or "My Year of Celibacy."

Or: "I Am a Puerto Rican Cosmo Girl," "I Am a Black Cosmo Girl," "I Am a Handicapped Cosmo Girl."

Helen Gurley Brown always understood you stick with a winning formula.

The editor of one of the most successful magazines of all time had never won a prize for editorial content at the National Magazine Awards. But last week, she was honored for her commercial success, named to the editors' Hall of Fame.

She put the glass award on a table outside her office, underneath a picture of the young Christie Brinkley glistening in a gold bikini.

"I parted company with the feminists in the 70's when it was thought that you had to wear charcoal gray turtleneck sweaters and no makeup," said Ms. Brown, wearing Adolfo and jangly gold jewelry. "I was accused of hurting the cause because I was still talking about women as though they were sex objects. But to be a sex object is a wonderful thing, and you're to be pitied if you aren't one."

We are sitting in her office, exactly the lair you would imagine for the editor who has spent her life urging young women to unleash the inner tiger. There is a leopard rug, pink flowered wallpaper, makeup mirrors on the wall, a candle on the desk, Chanel perfume by the window and "Sammy Davis Jr.'s Greatest Hits" by the CD player.

Even at 73, Ms. Brown is relentlessly girlish. Her magazine, which also has a case of arrested development, has been running the same stories ("How Big Should the Big O Be?" and "Just a Good Friend or Is She After Your Man?")

since I was in college. And it's still the best-selling magazine on college campuses.

In September 1992, the cover blurb was "How to Hold a Man by Giving Him His Freedom." In May '93, it was "How to Hold a Man By Giving Him His Freedom." One bow to modernity: "Men Tell On-Line What Scares Them Silly About Commitment."

Hearst Corporation executives are easing Ms. Brown out, embarrassed by her downplaying of the AIDS threat for women and her pooh-poohing of sexual harassment, and replacing her with a younger editorial model. In this less-permissive era, Hearst fretted that the Cosmo Girl, fond of lingerie and married men, was as passé as the Playboy Bunny.

But they can't get rid of Ms. Brown so easily. The Cosmo Girl has permeated the culture. She is, after all, just a tarted-up Cinderella, always believing happiness is just one makeover away. At any newsstand you'll see her man-crazy, sex-obsessed image endlessly, tiresomely replicated, even for the teen set.

On the May cover of YM: "Go Get HIM! Guy-snagging Moves That Really Work," Mademoiselle: "Make Love With the Lights On!" Glamour: "29 Things That Can Spark Great Sex." Marie Claire: "Dare to Compare! The Sex Experience Survey." Shape: "The Science of Seduction."

"I used to have all the sex to myself," Ms. Brown sighs.

She stayed in amber so long that women circled back her way. Some go to elaborate lengths—breast implants, collagen shots, Wonderbras—to attract men. The sultry fabrics Ms. Brown always promoted—zebra, leopard, satin—are now common at the office.

In an interview with Geraldine Baum of The Los Angeles Times, Debbie Stoller, the editor of BUST, a popular new zine for "girls," complained that "Helen Girly Brown" is stuck in a Valley of the Dolls world.

But the young editor does homage to Ms. Brown, even if she doesn't know it. She says that the early feminists were "women" who wanted to be like men, while today grown-up "girls," like Madonna and Courtney Love, want the freedom to be "girly" for their own pleasure.

Ms. Brown says: "Even when we grow up, we are all girls. Girl is the feminine side, the playful side, the hopeful side."

Even when Ms. Brown leaves, don't expect the Cosmo Girl to grow up. She's too profitable just the way she is.

Phyllis Teitelbaum

Feminist Theory and Standardized Testing

"Tests." The very word makes people feel anxious. When the tests are standardized examinations used for admission to college, graduate schools, occupations, or professions, the anxiety level rises. Most people hate to be evaluated or graded, and the standardized format of admissions and professional tests can be particularly upsetting.

But are such examinations discriminatory? Are current standardized tests biased against women and members of minority groups? Although much research has been conducted on this question, no single conception of what it means for a test to be biased has yet emerged, and no clear answer to the question has been found.

In this essay, I will first discuss the question of sex bias in college admissions tests and summarize the consequences of the score differences between men and women on these tests. Next, I will briefly review three of the major approaches currently taken by test publishers in attempts to eliminate sex and racial/ethnic bias from their standardized tests. Finally, I will present a very different approach to the question of whether and how standardized tests may discriminate against women—an analysis of such tests from the perspective of feminist theory.

My goal in applying feminist theory to testing is not merely to present an academic analysis. Rather, it is to provide you, the reader, with an "Aha" experience—a sudden insight into the arbitrariness of the current structure of things and a realization that they could be structured differently. Consider these questions: Why isn't housework counted in the GNP? Why isn't the emotional work that women do in relationships considered "labor" (Jaggar 1984)? Why must science be done in hierarchically-structured laboratories? Why can't a woman do scientific experiments in her home the way she does knitting or macramé (NWSA 1984)? Encountering these ideas in feminist theory has given me the kind of "Aha" experiences that I hope my ideas will elicit in you with respect to testing.

135

SEX BIAS AND COLLEGE ADMISSIONS TESTS

The issue of sex bias in standardized tests has been brought into sharp focus by a nationwide debate about the differential validity of college admissions tests—the Scholastic Aptitude Test (SAT), the Preliminary Scholastic Aptitude Test/National Merit Scholarship Qualifying Test (PSAT/NMSQT), and the American College Testing Program Assessment Exam (ACT). Phyllis Rosser (1987, 1988) has reviewed the data in this debate. I will summarize her reports here.

According to Rosser (1987:1), on average, women consistently earn higher high school and college grades than men; yet, on average, women receive lower scores than men on all three college admissions examinations. The score difference is particularly large in math; in the SAT math section in 1986 the gap was 50 points on average on a 200–800 point scale. But even in the verbal section of the SAT, where women used to perform better than men, women in 1986 scored on average 11 points lower than men. So the total score difference on the SAT in 1986 was 61 points (50 plus 11). Because women get higher grades in college than men, Rosser (1987:3) argues that the SAT does not accurately predict women's first-year college grades. According to Rosser, "If the SAT predicted equally well for both sexes, girls would score about 20 points higher than the boys, not 61 points lower."

Score differences between women and men on the PSAT/NMSQT and on the ACT are similar to those on the SAT. Rosser (1987:5–16) points out the serious consequences of these score differences:

1. College admissions—Nearly all four-year colleges and universities use SAT or ACT scores in admissions decisions, and many use cut-off scores, particularly for admission to competitive programs (Rosser 1987:4). If women's first-year grades indicate that their test scores ought to be higher than men's, then women applicants are undoubtedly being unfairly rejected in favor of less qualified male applicants.
2. College scholarships—According to Rosser (1987:8), over 750 organizations, including the National Merit Scholarship Corporation, use SAT, PSAT/NMSQT, or ACT scores in selecting scholarship recipients. In 1985–1986, largely as a result of the PSAT/NMSQT score difference, National Merit Finalists were 64 percent male and only 36 percent female (Rosser 1987:11). The results in other scholarship programs are similar; women lose out on millions of dollars in college scholarships because of a score difference that may be invalid.
3. Entry into "gifted programs"—Rosser (1987:6–8) points out that many academic enrichment programs are offered to students who achieve high scores on the SAT, PSAT/NMSQT, or ACT. Women's lower scores result in their loss of these opportunities as well.
4. Effect on self-perceptions and college choices—There is evidence that students alter their academic self-perceptions and decide where to apply to college partly on the basis of their test scores. If the tests underpredict women's academic abilities, women may not apply to academically demanding colleges for which they are in fact qualified, and their academic self-perceptions may be set too low.

The three tests' publishers currently argue that the tests are not biased against women. The publishers have put forward several explanations for the score differences; these explanations suggest that the scores reflect true differences in women's and men's academic preparation and/or abilities. For example, some argue that women take easier courses in high school and college than men or that women receive higher grades than men because women try harder to please their teachers.

The debate over standardized college admissions tests is important for two reasons: (1) it questions whether these tests are equally valid predictors of academic success for women and for men; (2) it points out what is at stake for women if these tests are biased against them. It is not yet clear whether the score differences are due to bias and, if so, to what kind of bias. Nevertheless, the data Rosser presents on the negative consequences for women of the score differences underscore the importance of investigating whether and how standardized tests are biased against women.

SOME CURRENT APPROACHES TO ELIMINATING SEX AND RACIAL/ETHNIC BIAS IN STANDARDIZED TESTS

For over a decade before the debate about college admission tests, psychometricians and test publishers have been concerned about eliminating sex and racial/ethnic bias from standardized tests. Several approaches have been tried and currently coexist.

Judgmental systems are designed primarily to eliminate sexist and racist language from tests, to make certain that women and minorities are adequately represented in test content, and to evaluate whether some groups of test-takers have been deprived of the opportunity to learn the material in the tests (Tittle 1982). Implicit in these systems is a *content conception* of "bias"—bias is implicitly defined as the inclusion of sexist or racist content, the omission of women and minority groups, and/or the inclusion of material that some groups of test-takers have not had the opportunity to learn. In fact, there is no clear evidence that the test performance of women and minority group members is affected by the use of sexist or racist language. However, there is some anecdotal evidence that women and minority group members perform better on test material about women or minorities. In any case, for ethical and political reasons, many test publishers have established procedures for eliminating the "content" kind of sex and racial/ethnic bias. These judgmental procedures involve review of test questions by knowledgeable, trained people, often themselves women or members of minority groups, sometimes applying guidelines to identify unacceptable questions or point out inadequate representation. Test publishers who use these procedures agree that, simply on the face of it, tests should not reinforce sexism and racism, even if test performance is unaffected (Lockheed 1982). But much remains to be done in this area. For example, Selkow (1984:8–13) reports that, in the seventy-four psychological and educational tests that she studied, females were underrepresented, generally appeared in gender-stereotyped roles, and were shown in fewer different types of vocational and avocational roles than males. Moreover, many of these tests' publishers had no plans to revise the tests; and some asserted that if test-users made changes to reduce sex imbalance, such as changing names or pronouns, the tests would be invalid psychometrically because they would then be different from the versions given in validation studies.

Item bias and *differential item performance* methods of eliminating bias use a *performance conception* of bias. They determine statistically the particular test questions on which various subgroups perform poorly, compared to the majority group. Test publishers may then eliminate these questions from the test. Interestingly, judgmental and item bias/differential item performance methods do not typically identify the same test questions. For example, minority or female students may perform less well than the majority group on a question with innocuous language and content while all groups may perform equally well on a question that contains sexist language or racial stereotypes. Indeed, psychometricians have not yet been able to identify the characteristics of test questions that cause groups to perform differentially on them. Partly for this reason, item bias/differential item performance work is currently in flux. Test publishers have developed different statistics to define item bias. There is as yet no agreement on which statistic should be used to identify biased questions or on how the information should be used in test construction.

Differential validity is a type of test bias in which the test does not predict equally well for different subgroups. For example, Rosser (1987:1–3) uses this *prediction conception* of bias when she argues that college admissions tests are biased against women. Some studies of differential validity have produced contradictory results, even when studying the same test. Because of the importance of accurate prediction in making fair decisions based on test scores, research in this area is continuing.

I have no quarrel with any of these approaches. I myself am a professional test developer at Educational Testing Service (ETS), in charge of training ETS's test developers and editors to apply ETS's judgmental method. Eliminating sexist and racist language and content seems to me essential to produce a test that is fair on its face. And I am following the progress of item bias and differential validity studies with interest. From the practical perspective of the daily construction and utilization of tests, in the world as it is structured today, I believe that we need more work on these and other methods in order to create fairer, less biased tests.

STANDARDIZED TESTING AND ANDROCENTRIC KNOWLEDGE

Most work currently being done on test bias accepts the basic underlying assumptions of standardized testing as given. What would happen if we questioned those assumptions from the perspective of feminist theory? What emerges is a radically different conception of sex bias as something inherent in the assumptions that underlie the content and format of standardized tests.

Feminist theorists have pointed out that what we have been taught to accept as standard scholarship is actually "androcentric" (that is, dominated by or emphasizing masculine interests or point of view). For example, the field called "history" has actually been the history of men; the history of women was simply left out. Similarly, "knowledge" and "science" are not universal; as currently taught, they are an androcentric form of knowing and of doing science.

The androcentric form of knowledge and science accepted in the twentieth-century United States is based on the theory of knowledge called positivism, which includes the following assumptions: scientific explanation should be reductionistic and atomistic, building up a complex entity from its simplest components; one can and should be objective (value-neutral) in scientific research (Jaggar 1983:356); and reason and emotion can be sharply distinguished (Jaggar 1985:2). This form of androcentric knowledge tends to be dualistic and dichotomous, viewing the world in terms of linked opposites: reason-emotion, rational-irrational, subject-object, nurture-nature, mind-body, universal-particular, public-private, and male-female (Jaggar 1985:2). It tends to be quantitative, and it takes the natural sciences as a model for all other academic disciplines. It contains an individualistic conception of humans as separate, isolated individuals who attain knowledge in a solitary, rather than a social, manner (Jaggar 1983:355). In addition, it includes a linear clock-and-calendar sense of time, rather than a circular sense of time (Wilshire 1985), and time is considered very important.

Standardized tests seem clearly to be based on this model of knowledge. In format, they are, as much as psychometricians can make them, positivistic, scientific, objective, value-free, dualistic, quantitative, linear-time-oriented, atomistic, and individualistic. In content, standardized tests reflect the androcentric model of knowledge by excluding everything that does not fit its definition of "knowledge" and everything that cannot be tested in a positivistic format.

First, consider the *format* of standardized tests:

1. The tests are "standardized" in an attempt to make them *objective and value-free*. Psychometricians hope that, if all test-takers receive the same test questions under the same standardized conditions and choose among the same multiple-choice answers, subjectivity and values can be excluded. But can they be? Test questions are written by subjective, value-laden human beings; questions and answer choices reflect the question-writer's upbringing and values, despite the question-writer's attempts to eliminate them. Test-takers bring to the test very different sets of experiences and feelings, and their interpretations of questions will vary accordingly. There is no such thing as a "culture-free" test. Every test question must assume some "common knowledge," and such knowledge is "common" only within a particular subculture of the society.

2. Multiple-choice tests are *dualistic* in that they force a choice between possible answers: one is "right"; the others are "wrong." The model is dichotomous—either/or, with no gradations. But, depending on the question, a graduated model in which several answers are "partly right" may be more appropriate. If test-takers were allowed to explain why they chose a particular "wrong" answer, we might find that it was "right" in some sense, or partly right.

3. Standardized tests are relentlessly *quantitative*. Their goal is to measure a person's knowledge or skill and to sum it up in one number. (This quantification adds to the impression that standardized tests are "objective.")

The single score reflects an androcentric fascination with simple quantification and precision; though psychometricians frequently state that test scores are not precise, test scores are often taken as absolute by both the public and the institutions that use the scores in decision making.

4. Tests are usually timed; thus, measurement of speed, as well as knowledge or skill, often contributes to the final score. This *linear-time-orientation* rewards speed even in subject areas where speed is not important.

5. Standardized tests are *atomistic*. Some systems of planning test content break learning down into "educational objectives" that are as narrow and concrete as possible—for example: "Can write legibly at X words per minute" (Krathwohl 1971:21). Even when such reductionistic educational objectives are not used, tests are inherently atomistic because they try to measure particular knowledge or skills separately from all other knowledge and skills.

6. Standardized tests are *individualistic* and usually competitive. A single person's performance is measured and compared, either with others' performances or with some preset standard of mastery. The ideas of "merit," of ranking, and of comparison are inherent in the testing enterprise. If there were no need or wish to compare individuals, there would be no standardized tests.

But even more important than format is *content*:

1. Standardized tests are in general designed to *test "reason" only*—the kind of knowledge that is included in the androcentric definition of knowledge. Excluded are whole areas of human achievement that contribute to success in school and work but are considered either inappropriate for testing or "untestable" from a practical point of view. Such characteristics and skills as intuition, motivation, self-understanding, conscientiousness, creativity, cooperativeness, supportiveness of others, sensitivity, nurturance, ability to create a pleasant environment, and ability to communicate verbally and nonverbally are excluded from standardized tests. By accepting and reflecting the androcentric model of knowledge, standardized tests reinforce value judgments that consider this model of knowledge more valid and important than other ways of viewing the world. Content that is not tested is judged less valuable than that included on tests.

2. Test publishers attempt to *exclude emotion* from test content. Topics that are very controversial are avoided. Emotions that test-takers feel about the test itself are labeled "test anxiety" and considered a source of "error"; test-takers' "true scores" would be based only on reason, not emotion.

IMPLICATIONS OF THIS ANALYSIS

Is an androcentric, positivistic standardized test necessarily biased against women? The answer you will give depends on whether you believe that women test-takers have completely adopted the generally taught androcentric model of knowledge and that they are as adept in manipulating its concepts as are men. If you believe that women think the way men do, that they share men's "common knowledge," that they are as comfortable with dualistic, quantitative, timed, atomistic, competitive tests as men, and that the content excluded from the tests is no more salient to women than it is to men, then you will conclude that standardized tests are not sex-biased by virtue of their androcentric origins.

If, on the other hand, you believe as I do that women and men perceive the world differently, excel in different areas, and feel comfortable with different test formats, then you will conclude that an androcentric test is bound to be sex-biased. And you need not be a biological determinist to believe that such sex differences exist. It seems to me that the different life experiences that gender creates are sufficient explanation; growing up female is a different social and intellectual experience from growing up male (Farganis 1985:21).

As an example, focus on the testing of particular content only. Assume that, because of socialization or biology or both, women tend to excel in different areas than men. Consider, from your own reading and experience, what those different areas may be for each sex. Then construct a 2×2 table with "Tested" and "Not tested" along the top and with "Males tend to excel at" and "Females tend to excel at" down the left-hand side. Which cells are heavily loaded? Which cells are nearly empty? My table looks like this:

TABLE 1. Content Tested

	Tested	Not tested
Males tend to excel at	Many (eg., math, physics, chemistry)	Few (eg., aggression)
Females tend to excel at	Few (eg., reading)	Many (eg., sensitivity, supportiveness of others, oral communication, cooperativeness, creating a pleasant environment)

You may not agree with the specific examples I have chosen. Nevertheless, you may well find yourself agreeing that many things males in our society excel at *are* tested while many things females excel at are *not* tested. If true, this is probably a direct consequence of the androcentric format and the androcentric choice of content that shape standardized tests, and it demonstrates the sex bias inherent in tests based on an androcentric model of knowledge.

If the content and format of tests are androcentric, this might help to explain situations in which women perform worse than men on standardized tests. The task of taking a standardized test is probably harder for women than it is for men. Women who take an androcentric test may be analogous to people who learned English as a foreign language and who take a test of knowledge (economics, for example) written in English. The task of working in English probably makes the economics test harder for those who learned English as a foreign language than for the native speakers. Similarly, a woman who takes a standardized test must show mastery both of the test's subject matter and of the test's androcentric format and content, which are foreign to her. A man who takes that test has had to master the subject matter, but he probably finds the androcentric format and content familiar and congenial. Women raised in an androcentric school system must master two worlds of knowledge; men must master only one. If the man and the woman know the same amount of economics, the woman may nevertheless receive a lower score than the man because of the test's androcentric format and content. Thus, androcentric tests may not provide a fair comparison between women and men.

WHAT NOW?

It seems that the application of feminist theory leads to a sweeping condemnation of standardized tests as sex-biased. As a professional test developer, employed by a major test publisher, I find it odd to be joining testing's many critics. When I have read the attacks on testing by Ralph Nader's group (Nairn 1980), the National Teachers Association, David Owen (1985), and Phyllis Rosser (1987), my usual response has been, "Some of your criticisms may be valid, but what can you suggest that is better than our current testing methods?" Testing is easy to attack but hard to replace. I must ask myself, then, what would I put in the place of androcentric standardized tests?

One possibility would be to develop a "gynecocentric" (that is, dominated by or emphasizing feminine interests or point of view) method of testing and to include in tests the content areas currently excluded. This is a visionary, even utopian goal, but it is one worth thinking about because it may produce "Aha" experiences. Clearly, such tests would not be standardized, "objective," or competitive. Scoring, if it existed, would be holistic and qualitative, taking into account both reason and emotion on the part of both the test-taker and the scorer. Psychometrics as we now know it would not apply; no "metrics" (measurement) would be involved. But would we then have a "test" at all? Perhaps not. Perhaps a gynecocentric test is a contradiction in terms; gynecocentric methods might not provide tools that can be used for testing. Perhaps testing is intrinsically androcentric and cannot be transformed into a gynecocentric exercise.

On the other hand, it might be possible to reconceptualize testing in a gynecocentric mode, changing it into something like "unstandardized assessment" or "voluntarily requested group feedback." For example, an elementary school class wishes to know how well it has learned to interact and requests feedback from the teacher of interpersonal skills. She spends time observing the class at work and at play; then, with the class in a participatory circle, she discusses her observations and listens to class members' responses. In the workplace, instead of individual performance appraisals, there are voluntarily requested group evaluations. Colleges alter their admissions procedures to admit cooperating groups of students, rather than competing individuals. Alternatively, in a world that places less emphasis on competitive individualism than we do today, standardized tests as we currently know them might exist only for specific tasks and situations without pretending to measure general capacities (Alison Jaggar, personal communication).

For either a utopian gynecocentric form of testing to emerge or for a reduced use of conventional tests to occur, the individualistic, competitive basis of our society would have to change considerably. Testing is embedded in a culture of schooling and work that is solidly androcentric. To predict an individual's success in a college that teaches only positivistic knowledge to individuals, one needs a predictor that is at least partially individualistic and positivistic.

It seems like a cop-out to say that testing cannot change until knowledge, school, work, and society change. Certainly, tests influence knowledge somewhat when teachers and school systems "teach to the tests." And if tests began using a gynecocentric format and testing such skills as supportiveness and cooperation, tests might tend to increase the value society places on such a format and such skills. To this extent, changing standardized tests could be one way to start changing society. Nevertheless, because tests tend to reflect the social and educational system much more than they shape it, it seems likely that tests will change only after society does.

Note

I am very grateful to Alison Jaggar and the participants in her seminar, "Feminist Ways of Knowing," for their contributions to my thinking on gender issues.

References

DIAMOND, ESTHER E., and CAROL K. TITTLE. 1985. "Sex Equity in Testing." In *Handbook for Achieving Sex Equity through Education*, ed. Susan S. Klein. Baltimore: John Hopkins University Press.

FARGANIS, SONDRA. 1985. "Social Theory and Feminist Theory: The Need for Dialogue." Manuscript.

FLAUGHER, RONALD L. 1978. "The Many Definitions of Test Bias." *American Psychologist* 33:671–679.

JAGGAR, ALISON. 1977. "Political Philosophies of Women's Liberation." In *Feminism and Philosophy*, ed. Mary Vetterling-Braggin, Frederick A. Elliston, and Jane English. Totowa, N.J.: Littlefield, Adams.

———. 1983. *Feminist Politics and Human Nature*. Totowa, N.J.: Rowman and Allenheld.

———. 1984. "The Feminist Challenge to the Western Political Tradition." The Women's Studies Chair Inaugural Lecture, November 27, Douglass College, Rutgers University, New Brunswick, N.J.

———. 1985. "Feeling and Knowing: Emotion in Feminist Theory." Manuscript.

KRATHWOHL, DAVID R., and DAVID A. PAYNE. 1971. "Defining and Assessing Educational Objectives." In *Educational Measurement*, ed. Robert L. Thorndike. Washington, D.C.: American Council on Education.

LOCKHEED, MARLAINE. 1982. "Sex Bias in Aptitude and Achievement Tests Used in Higher Education." In *The Undergraduate Woman: Issues in Educational Equity*, ed. Pamela Perun. New York: Lexington Books.

NAIRN, ALLAN, and ASSOCIATES. 1980. *The Reign of ETS: The Corporation That Makes Up Minds*. Published by Ralph Nader, Washington, D.C.

NWSA [National Women's Studies Association]. 1984. Sixth Annual Conference and Convention, June 24–28, *"Feminist Science: A Meaningful Concept?"* panel, Ruth Hubbard, Marian Lowe, Rita Arditti, Anne Woodhull, and Evelynn Hammonds. Douglass College, Rutgers University, New Brunswick, N.J.

OWEN, DAVID, 1985. *None of the Above: Behind the Myth of Scholastic Aptitude*. Boston: Houghton Mifflin.

ROSSER, PHYLLIS. 1988. "Girls, Boys, and the SAT: Can We Even the Score?" *NEA Today* (special ed.) 6, no. 6 (January):48–53.

ROSSER, PHYLLIS, with the staff of the National Center for Fair and Open Testing. 1987. *Sex Bias in College Admissions Tests: Why Women Lose Out.* 2d ed. Cambridge, Mass.: National Center for Fair and Open Testing (FairTest).

SELKOW, PAULA. 1984. *Assessing Sex Bias in Testing: A Review of the Issues and Evaluations of 74 Psychological and Educational Tests.* Westport, Conn.: Greenwood Press.

TITTLE, CAROL K. 1982. "Use of Judgmental Methods in Item Bias Studies." In *Handbook of Methods for Detecting Test Bias*, ed. Ronald A. Berk. Baltimore: Johns Hopkins University Press.

WILSHIRE, DONNA. 1985. "Ideas presented for discussion" and "Topics for discussion." Manuscripts prepared for the "Feminist Ways of Knowing Seminar." Douglass College, Rutgers University, New Brunswick, N.J.

Are We Having Sex Yet?

When I first started having sex with other people, I used to like to count them. I wanted to keep track of how many there had been. It was a source of some kind of pride, or identity, to know how many people I'd had sex with in my lifetime. So, in my mind, Len was number one; Chris was number two; that slimy, little barbiturate addict whose name I can't remember was number three; Alan was number four; and so on. It got to the point where, when I'd start having sex with a new person for the first time, when he first entered my body (I was only having sex with men at the time), what would flash through my head wouldn't be "Oh, baby, baby, you feel so good inside me," or "What the hell am I doing with this creep?" or "This is boring." What flashed through my head was "Seven!"

Doing this had some interesting results. I'd look for patterns in the numbers. I had a theory for a while that every fourth lover turned out to be really great in bed, and I would ponder what the cosmic significance of this might be. Sometimes I'd try to determine what kind of person I was by how many people I'd had sex with. At 18, I'd had sex with ten different people. Did that make me normal, repressed, a total slut, a free-spirited bohemian, or what? Not that I compared my numbers with anyone else's—I didn't. It was my own exclusive structure, a game I played in the privacy of my own head.

Then the numbers started getting a little larger, as numbers tend to do, and keeping track became more difficult. I'd remember that the last one was 17 and so this one must be 18, but then I'd start having doubts about whether I'd been keeping score accurately or not. I'd lie awake at night thinking to myself, well, there was Brad, and there was that guy on my birthday, and there was David and . . . no wait, I forgot that guy I got drunk with at the social my first week at college . . . so that's seven, eight, nine . . . and by two in the morning I'd finally have it figured out. But there was always a nagging suspicion that maybe I'd missed someone, some dreadful, tacky little scumball that I was trying to forget about having invited inside my body. And as much as I maybe wanted to forget about the sleazy little scumball, I wanted more to get that number right.

145

It kept getting harder, though. I began to question what counted as sex and what didn't. There was that time with Gene, for instance. I was pissed off at my boyfriend, David, for cheating on me. Gene and I were friends. I went to see him that night to gripe about David. He was very sympathetic, of course, and he gave me a back rub, and we talked and touched and confided and hugged, and then we started kissing, and then we snuggled up a little closer, and then we started fondling each other, you know, and then all heck broke loose, and we rolled around on the bed groping and rubbing and grabbing and smooching and pushing and pressing and squeezing. He never did actually get it in. He wanted to, and I wanted to, too, but I had this thing about being faithful to my boyfriend. We never even got our clothes off. It was some night. One of the best, really. But for a long time I didn't count it as one of the times I'd had sex.

Later, months and years later, when I lay awake putting my list together, I'd start to wonder: Why doesn't Gene count? Does he not count because he never got inside? Or does he not count because I had to preserve my moral edge over David, my status as the patient, ever-faithful, cheated-on, martyred girlfriend, and if what I did with Gene counts, then I don't get to feel wounded and superior? Much later, I did end up fucking Gene and I felt a profound relief because, at last, he definitely had a number, and I knew for sure that he did in fact count.

Then I started having sex with women, and, boy, howdy, did *that* ever shoot holes in the system. I'd always made my list of sex partners by defining sex as penile-vaginal intercourse—you know, screwing. It's a pretty simple distinction, a straightforward binary system. Did it go in or didn't it? Yes or no? One or zero? On or off? Granted, it's a pretty arbitrary definition, but it's the customary one, with an ancient and respected tradition behind it, and when I was just screwing men, there was no compelling reason to question it.

But with women, well, first of all there's no penis, so right from the start the tracking system is defective. And then, there are so many ways women can have sex with each other, touching and licking and grinding and fingering and fisting—with dildos or vibrators or vegetables or whatever happens to be lying around the house, or with nothing at all except human bodies. Of course, that's true for sex between women and men as well. But between women, no one method has a centuries-old tradition of being the one that counts. Even when we do fuck each other there's no dick, so you don't get that feeling of This Is What's Important, We Are Now Having Sex, and all that other stuff is just foreplay or afterplay. So when I started having sex with women the binary system had to go.

Which meant, of course, that my list of how many people I'd had sex with was completely trashed. In order to maintain it I would have had to go back and reconstruct the whole thing and include all those people I'd necked with and gone down on and dry-humped and played touchy-feely games with. Even the question of who filled the all-important Number One slot would have to be reevaluated. By this time I'd kind of lost interest in my list, anyway. But the crucial question remained: What counts as having sex with someone?

It was important for me to know. You have to know what qualifies as sex, because when you have sex with someone your relationship changes. Right?

Right? It's not that sex itself has to change things all that much. But knowing you've had sex, being conscious of a sexual connection, standing around making polite conversation with someone while thinking to yourself, "I've had sex with this person," that's what changes things. Or so I believed. And if having sex with a friend can confuse or change the friendship, think how bizarre things can get when you're not sure whether you've had sex with them or not.

As I kept doing more kinds of sexual things, the line between *sex* and *not-sex* kept getting more indistinct. As I brought more into my sexual experience, things were showing up on the dividing line demanding my attention. It wasn't just that the territory I labeled *sex* was expanding. The line itself had swollen, dilated, been transformed into a vast gray region. It had become less like a border and more like a demilitarized zone.

Which is a strange place to live. Not a bad place, just strange. It feels like cognitive dissonance, only pleasant. It feels like waking up from a compelling and realistic bad dream. It feels like the way you feel when you realize that everything you know is wrong, and a bloody good thing too, because it was painful and stupid and it really screwed you up.

But, for me, living in a question naturally leads to searching for an answer. I can't simply shrug, throw up my hands, and say, "Damned if I know." So, even if it's incomplete or provisional, I do want to find some sort of definition.

I know when I'm *feeling* sexual. I'm feeling sexual if my pussy's wet, my nipples are hard, my palms are clammy, my brain is fogged, my skin is tingly and supersensitive, my butt muscles clench, my heartbeat speeds up, I have an orgasm (that's the real giveaway), and so on. But feeling sexual with someone isn't the same as having sex. Good Lord, if I called it sex every time I was attracted to someone who returned the favor, I'd be even more bewildered than I am now. Even *being* sexual with someone isn't the same as *having* sex with them.

I have friends who say, if you thought of it as sex when you were doing it, then it was. That's an interesting idea. It's certainly helped me construct a coherent sexual history without being a revisionist swine: redefining my past according to current definitions. But it just begs the question. It's fine to say that sex is whatever I think it is; but then what do I think it *is*?

Perhaps having sex with someone is the conscious, consensual, mutually acknowledged pursuit of shared sexual pleasure. Not a bad definition. If you are turning each other on and you say so and you keep doing it, then it's sex. It's broad enough to encompass a lot of sexual behavior beyond genital contact/orgasm; it's distinct enough *not* to include every instance of sexual awareness or arousal; and it contains the elements I feel are vital—acknowledgment, consent, reciprocity, and the pursuit of pleasure. But what about the situation where a person consents to sex without really enjoying it? Lots of people (myself included) have had sexual interactions that we didn't find satisfying or didn't really want and, unless they were forced on us against our will, I think most of us would still classify them as sex.

Maybe if *both* of you (or all of you) think of it as sex, then it's sex whether you're having fun or not. That clears up the problem of sex that's consented to but not wished for or enjoyed. Unfortunately, it begs the question again. Now you have to mesh different people's vague notions of what is and isn't sex and find the place where they overlap. Too messy.

How about sex as the conscious, consensual, mutually acknowledged pursuit of sexual pleasure of *at least one* of the people involved. That's better. It has all the key components, and it includes the situation where one person is doing it for a reason other than sexual pleasure—status, reassurance, money, the satisfaction and pleasure of someone they love, et cetera. But what if *neither* of you is enjoying it, if you're both doing it because you think the other one wants to? Ugh.

I'm having trouble here. Even the conventional standby—sex equals intercourse—has a serious flaw: it includes rape. If there's no consent, it ain't sex, but I feel that's about the only place in this whole quagmire where I have a grip. The longer I think about the subject, the more questions I come up with. At what point in an encounter does it *become* sexual? If an interaction that begins nonsexually turns into sex, was it sex all along? What about sex with someone who's asleep? Can you have a situation where one person is having sex and the other isn't? It seems that no matter what definition I come up with, I can think of some real-life experience that calls it into question.

For instance, a couple of years ago I attended (well, hosted) an all-girl sex party. There were only a few with whom I got seriously, physically nasty. The rest I kissed or hugged or talked dirty with or just smiled at, or watched while they did things with each other. If we'd been alone, I'd probably say that what I'd done with most of the women there didn't count as having sex. But the experience, which was hot and sweet and silly and very, very special, had been created by all of us, and although I only really got down with a few, I felt that I'd been sexual with all of the women there. Now, when I meet one of the women from that party, I always ask myself: Have we had sex?

I still don't have the answer.

Carol Nagy Jacklin

How My Heterosexuality Affects My Feminist Politics

Being asked to contribute to an issue of *Feminism & Psychology* as a 'heterosexual' was offensive. Why? Because of what it means to say 'I am heterosexual'. More specifically:

1. Saying 'I am heterosexual' implies that my sexual preference is an unchanging and essential personal attribute. It is, however, certainly not clear that one's sexual preference is either unchanging or an essential attribute. No one should be limited by this or any other label. Sexuality is complex. Our lives are complex, and growth (or at least change) is the only constant.
2. Because heterosexuality has been an established sexual preference, 'I am heterosexual' also says 'I am traditional'. At the very least it connotes that I do not have to struggle with society about my sexual preference. Moreover, I do not want to think of myself as a member of the establishment, even though I know I have many of the privileges and rewards of the establishment.

Heterosexual feminists live, work and may be in love relationships with the 'enemy'. That is, they will be in more close-up and entangled situations with members of the group—men—that have traditionally had power over women than are asexual feminists or lesbian feminists. Heterosexual women are at greater risk of having inequitable personal relations. The disadvantages are clear, the advantages somewhat less so.

I lived for 20 years in a non-equitable heterosexual relationship. During that time I moved from wanting a traditional relationship (and not being able to imagine an alternative!), through many stages, to wanting an intimate heterosexual relationship based on mutuality and equity. An example of my own traditionalism still haunts me. At one time (*c.* 1965), I thought I would not work when my first child was born. After being unemployed, outside the home, for six months, I realized I had to work or emotionally and intellectually die. I got a full-time job teaching psychology at a junior college. I always carefully described my partner as the 'breadwinner' and myself as the 'jam-win-ner'. I consciously did not want to be threatening to him (or the status quo) in any way. Yet the desire, the need and finally the demand for 'a little respect when you get home' (in Otis Redding via Aretha Franklin's words) became greater and greater.

Changes in the culture paralleled (and probably made possible) my own changes. The Aretha Franklin version of the song 'Respect' was important to many of us because it articulated and validated some of our deepest longings. It made it acceptable for a woman to ask directly for both respect and sex. Being able to ask for sex was an important example of being able to ask for what we wanted. (Sex and respect are still conjoined in ways I do not understand.) It was to that song that I and many other heterosexually partnered women I knew danced together, *not* with our partners.

The disadvantages of a non-equitable relationship are clear. Much of my energy was taken up by doing the traditional servicing for my partner. Even at the time I wondered what I would have been able to do if I had a 'wife'. There has recently been some measurement in monetary terms of what a 'wife' does contribute to a career. A study of Stanford graduates nine years after graduation found women *and* men whose spouses or partners do all or most of the household tasks made 13 per cent more money than their classmates. For both women and men, having a 'wife' at home is profitable even after accounting for the effects on earnings of occupation, hours of work and the presence of children (Strober et al., 1991).

Being the 'lesser' member of a pair (a belief I shared with my partner) took a toll on my self-esteem and on my career. I was unaware of how much of a toll until I was out of the relationship.

What could be the advantages of a non-egalitarian heterosexual relationship?

Firstly, my experience helps me to understand and help other women in similar situations. I know how difficult it was for me to see the inequity in that relationship and finally to leave it. It was difficult to see the inequity because of my own low self-esteem. In part, I felt that I didn't deserve, wasn't worthy of, more than what I had. In retrospect, I realize that a second difficulty I had in leaving the relationship was a fear of living alone. Yet the experience of living alone later felt like a gift. I learned that living alone was unrelated to being lonely. It was an experience that freed me from dependence on relationships.

Secondly, there were advantages of having been able to grow in spite of the relationship. I now know deeply that change and growth are possible in many areas of my own life and in others' lives. I do not suggest we groom girls for traditional relationships so they can grow out of them, but those of us who survived traditional relationships learned from them.

Thirdly, it was clearly pressure from the larger culture, and not pressure from my family of origin, that kept me from seeing the inequity in my relationship. This fact was one of the first clues I had in my professional work, in the area of socialization of gender roles, of the strength of the larger culture over the family.

Fourthly, I have always had women's friendship and support apart from my sexual relationship. These friendships have given me a perspective on that relationship. It may be that lesbians have the same perspective on their sexual

151

CAROL NAGY JACKLIN
*How My
Heterosexuality
Affects My Feminist
Politics*

relationship from friends or even from males. This is something that requires discussion. Perhaps we need an issue of *Feminism & Psychology* devoted to a dialogue between lesbian and heterosexual feminists.

Do heterosexual relationships have to be non-equitable? No. I am currently in an egalitarian heterosexual relationship. I know, moreover, of many equitable heterosexual relationships as well as inequitable lesbian relationships. But the asymmetry of power is more common in heterosexual relationships.

My 20-year unequal heterosexual relationship has been important to my feminist politics. For it made clear to me, emotionally and intellectually, how central issues of power are to intimate relationships and to other institutions. Power inequity continues to be the basis of many heterosexual relationships. The personal is the political. My experience of power inequity has helped me to understand how pervasive this inequity is in larger societal issues.

Acknowledgments

I would like to thank Barrie Thorne, Myra Strober, Richard Caputo, Beth Meyerowitz, Tollie Grimes, Catharine Stimpson and Mary Hayden for comments on earlier drafts of this paper.

Reference

STROBER, M., JACKSON, D. and CHAN, A. (1991) 'Determinants of Income among Stanford Graduates of the Class of 1981: A View after Nine Years', unpublished manuscript.

Michelle Fine

Coping with Rape: Critical Perspectives on Consciousness

Abstract

Traditional psychological prescriptions for coping with injustice rest on a variety of assumptions which ignore the lived experiences of most women, especially those who are poor or working class, whose lives are embedded in a network of relationships that need be considered in their coping. This article, through a dialogue between the author, a rape counselor, and a woman who has survived rape, provides an analysis of the class, race and gender biases woven into the Taking-Control-Yields-Coping formulations.

Prosecute? No, I just want to get home. While I'm pickin' some guy out of some line, who knows who's messin' around with my momma and my baby.

—ALTAMESE THOMAS,
24-year-old rape survivor
October 1981, Hospital Emergency Room

At 2:00 a.m. one October morning, Altamese Thomas was led out of a police car, entered the hospital in pain, smelling of alcohol. Altamese had been drinking with some friends in a poor, high crime, largely Black neighborhood in Philadelphia. She found herself in an alley, intoxicated, with pants down. She reports being gang-raped. The story unfolds, from intake nurse, the police and from Altamese herself.

I was awakened, in the small office for volunteer rape counselors, when the emergency room nurse telephoned me: "A Code-R just arrived." "Code-R" is the euphemism used to describe a woman who has been raped. I spent the remainder of the evening and some of the morning with Altamese. A twenty-four-year-old Black mother of three, two of her children have been placed by the state in foster care. From 2:00 a.m. until 7:00 a.m. we held hands as she smarted through two painful injections to ward off infection; traveled through the hospital in search of X-rays for a leg that felt (but wasn't) broken; waited for the Sex Offender Officers to arrive; watched Altamese refuse to speak with them; and returned to the X-ray room for a repeat performance—and we talked.

I introduced myself and explained my role. Interested primarily and impatiently in washing "the dirt off" and receiving necessary medical care, Altamese was unambivalent about her priorities. She did not want to prosecute, nor talk with social workers or counselors. She couldn't call upon her social supports. She just wanted to get home. For five hours, we talked. Our conversation systematically disrupted my belief that I understood anything much about the psychology of taking control in the face of injustice. Through my dialogue with Altamese, this article provides a critical analysis of the class, race and gender biases woven into the social psychological literature on coping with injustice.

THE PSYCHOLOGY OF TAKING CONTROL

When confronting life crises, injustices or tragedies, psychologists argue, people fare best by assuming control over their circumstances. Accepting responsibility for one's problems and/or solutions correlates with psychological and physical well being [1], across populations as diverse as rape survivors [2, 3], disabled adults [4], the institutionalized elderly [5, 6], unemployed men and women [7], school children with academic problems [8], even high school drop outs [9]. This article examines the assumptions which underlie present formulations of Taking-Control-Yields-Coping. Weaving relevant theory and research with excerpts from the dialogue between this rape survivor and the author, it will be argued that the prevailing coping-through-control ideologies are often limited by class, race and gender biases. Further, these models are disproportionately effective for only a small and privileged sector of society.

Psychologists have demonstrated that individuals cope most effectively with unjust or difficult circumstances by controlling their environments [10, 11]. This may involve attributing behavioral blame for the onset of bad events [12], or personal responsibility for initiating change [1]. Taking control may require participating in social programs and "getting help" [13, 14], and relying upon one's social supports [15-17].

The current Taking-Control arguments often assume that people *can* control the forces which victimize them, *should* utilize available social programs, and *will* benefit if they rely on social supports. What is not explicit is that these prescribed means of coping are likely to be ineffectual for most people [18, 19]. Persons of relatively low ascribed social power—by virtue of social class position, ethnicity, race, gender, disability or sexual preference—cannot control those forces which limit their opportunities [20]. But while it has been proposed that many then learn to be helpless [21], I maintain instead that they do assert control in ways ignored by psychologists. For many, taking control involves ignoring advice to solve one's problems individually and recognizing instead the need for collective, structural change [22]. Taking control may mean rejecting available social programs as inappropriate to one's needs [8, 23], or recognizing that one's social supports are too vulnerable to be relied upon [24]. Such acts of taking control have long been misclassified by psychologists as acts of relinquishing control.

ACCESS TO MEANS OF TAKING CONTROL:
A FUNCTION OF SOCIAL POWER

The control-yields-well-being proposition is empirically robust and admittedly compelling. As a psychologist interested in the social psychology of injustice, I study and support efforts which encourage people to take control of their lives. A review of this literature reveals, however, *individualistic* coping strategies, effective for persons of relatively high social power, promoted *as if* they were optimal and universal ways to cope. By establishing a hierarchy of appropriate ways to take control, this literature often 1) denies the complex circumstances many people confront, 2) *de facto* delegitimates those strategies for taking control employed by persons of relatively low social power, 3) encourages psychological and individualistic responses to injustice, which often reinforce existing power inequities [25], and 4) justifies prevailing social structures.

Advancing the position that people need to exert individual control over their lives presumes that all people are able to do so, that all people want to do so, and that to improve their life circumstances, people need to change themselves rather than social structures. Three fundamental problems with this formulation emerge.

First, if asserting individual control promotes psychological health it may be because individualism is socially reinforced in our society [26]. Positive reinforcement follows individualistic acts (e.g., "Pulling oneself up by the bootstraps") [22, 27] with social disapproval displayed for collective acts (e.g., in school these collective acts may be considered cheating; at work trouble making). The health that is associated with acts of individualistic control may therefore derive from social and ideological supports in our culture, not because individual control is inherently healthy.

Given that psychological well being stems in part from social rewards for individualism and internality, a second problem emerges with this model of coping. If unfair treatment occurs and control of that treatment is unlikely, a presumption of internality may be delusional! Externality may benefit persons whose life conditions are indeed beyond their control [28]. To nurture the much-encouraged illusion of internality in many circumstances would be unreasonable. In situations of low probability of success for redressing an injustice, attempts to redress injustice personally can breed helplessness.

It may be true that when persons of relatively high social power assert a single act of "taking control" (e.g., voice a grievance or file a complaint) they are likely to succeed. In contrast, the undocumented worker who is sexually harassed by her factory foreman might be foolish to file a grievance. "Bearing it" does not mean she has given up, but rather that she determined a solution by which she can be in control and employed. Establishing strategies to survive, when change is unlikely, needs to be recognized as acts of control.

A third problem with current control formulations is that they often decontextualize coping [29]. The presumption that psychologists can extract optimal ways to assume control over failure or adversity *across situations* reduces the complexities of the situations *ad absurdum* [18].

The strategies popular in the literature and undoubtedly effective in many cases, may benefit persons of relatively high social power (e.g., by attributing successes to stable internal factors and failures to unstable factors; taking responsibility for solutions; relying on social supports, or utilizing available social programs). As psychologists, however, we lack an understanding of how people who are systematically discriminated against and restricted to low power positions take control. We fail to understand how they determine what is controllable and what is not [30]. We dismiss control strategies that look like "giving up" but are in fact ways to survive. Even more serious, we avoid the study of those ways of taking control which systematically disrupt traditional power relations [31, 32]. Our literature legitimates existing power asymmetries.

There are two major consequences to these theoretical problems. First, control efforts enacted by low power persons are often misdiagnosed as giving up. Such attempts to take control tend to be misread as counter productive ("Why don't they do something about their work conditions if they are dissatisfied, rather than slowing down on productivity?"); distorted as self-effacing ("Even she blames herself for the rape."); diagnosed as masochistic ("She must enjoy the abuse, why else would she stay?"); classified as learned helplessness ("She always says—'I can't do anything about it.' "); or denigrated as psychological resistance ("I tried to offer help but he won't listen!") by laypersons and psychologists alike. These behaviors may indeed function as strategies of asserting control; if not resistance.

Second, the existing body of research on allegedly healthy ways of coping reproduces existing power inequities by prescribing *as optimal* those ways of coping which are effective for high power persons [33]. Social programs designed for low power persons are often organized toward coping strategies (such as individualism and reliance on social institutions) effective for high power persons. The models are deceptive for persons of low social power who depend on higher power persons, economically, socially, and/or psychologically, and have other low power persons (e.g., kin) highly dependent upon them. This precarious web of interdependencies creates conditions in which social institutions are likely to be unresponsive and individualism to be inappropriate. Many low power persons will not improve their own circumstances at expense to others, and most are unlikely to have access to standard tools of control (e.g., grievance procedures, money, or leverage with Congressional representatives). If they do, these tools are unlikely to promote the kinds of changes they need [34]. Consequently, when low power persons decide *not* to use the resources or programs offered them (e.g., "Because my mother is sick, and I have to take care of my children.") their disadvantaged circumstances may come to be viewed as deserved. The perception that they are *unwilling* to act on their own behalf provides evidence of helplessness, if not laziness. Their need to rely on high power persons is then confirmed. The power asymmetries built into these relationships are systematically justified [35].

Below, through a dialogue between the author and a woman who survived a rape, a dialogue situated in a hospital emergency room the evening of the rape, we analyze how persons of relatively low social power do assert control, and how easily a psychologist can misread these as efforts to give up.

No, I don't want to do nothin' but get over this . . . When I'm pickin' the guy out of some line, who knows who's messin' around with my momma, or my baby. Anyway nobody would believe me. [Can I wash now?]

3:00 AM   Altamese, the police will be here to speak with you. Are you interested in prosecuting? Do you want to take these guys to court?

3:30 AM   [Once the exam is over you can wash and brush your teeth. First we need to wait for the doctor for your exam.] Wouldn't your friends testify as witnesses?

Where I live, nobody's gonna testify. Not to the police. Anyway, I'm a Baptist and I know God is punishing him right now. He done bad enough and he's suffering.

You know, I don't remember things. When I was little lots of bad things happened to me, and I forget them. My memory's bad, I don't like to remember bad stuff. I just forget. When I was a young child, my momma told me about rape and robberies. I told her she was wrong. Those things happen in the movies, not here. When I saw such things on the streets I thought they was making a movie. Then one day a lady started bleeding, and I knew it was no movie.

4:00 AM   Maybe If we talked about the rape you would feel better.

4:30 AM   . . . Do you think maybe you would like to talk with a counselor, in a few days, about some of your feelings?

I've been to one of them. It just made it worse. I just kept thinking about my problems too much. You feel better when you're talking, but then you got to go back home and they're still there. No good just talking when things ain't no better.

Is there anyone you can talk to about this?

Not really. I can't tell my mother, not my brothers either. They would go out and kill the guys. My mother's boyfriend too. I don't want them going to jail 'cause of me.

She's the one who took away my kids. If they take my baby, I would kill myself. I ain't gonna get myself in trouble, all I got is my baby and she already thinks I'm a bad mother. But I love my babies and I try hard to take care of them.

[I just don't understand why men have to rape. Why do they have to take when they could just ask?]

Those teachers think I'm stupid. Sometimes they call on me and I don't answer. When you got problems, your mind is on the moon. He calls on you and you don't know what he's saying. They treat you like a dog and you act like a dog.

It ain't safe there. I live in the projects with my baby. I can't go back there now. It feels safer here . . . I hurt so much.

Sure. . . .

You said you sometimes meet with a social worker. Can you talk with your social worker?

How about one of your teachers at _____ college? Can you talk to them?

5:30 AM   Soon you will get to leave here and go home, where you'll feel safe.

7:00 AM   Can I call you next week just to see how you're doing?

ASSERTING RELATIONAL CONTROL

At first glance, one might say that Altamese abdicated control: She "gave up." Unwilling to prosecute, uninterested in utilizing her social supports, she relied on God for justice. Resistant to mental health, social service, educational and criminal justice assistance, she rejected available options. Her coping mechanisms might be said to include denial, repression, and paranoia. She doesn't trust her friends to testify, her family to listen, her social worker to be supportive, her teachers to understand or the police to assist. She has refused available mechanisms of control.

And yet through our dialogue it was obvious that each of her decisions embodies a significant assertion of control. Likely to be misclassified as helpless or paranoid, she asserted strategies for taking control which insure both her well-being and that of her kin. Altamese organized coping around relational concerns [24]. Worried about her mother, child and siblings, she rejected options offered to help her cope. She viewed my trust in the justice system as somewhat absurd; my commitment to talking about the rape to friends, social workers, teachers or family somewhat impulsive; my expectations of witnesses coming forth almost naive, and even my role as volunteer counselor somewhat unusual.

Altamese	Michelle
So, you're a nurse?	
	7:00 AM— Actually I volunteer here, talking with women who have been raped.
You mean you do this for fun?	
	I do it because I think it's important. Do you?
. . . I don't know how you can do it all the time.	

Most people are denied the means to assume control over fundamentally changing their lives. Although prevailing ideology argues otherwise [36], Altamese and the millions of women who are unemployed, poor, minority and/or disabled and responsible for a network of kin, have limited options [37]. Although pursuing college, she may perhaps qualify for a low pay job some day. Given unemployment statistics, her personal style, life circumstances and lack of qualifications, her chances are slim.

The standard means of taking control promoted by counselors, policy makers and researchers, tend to be individualistic and most effective for a privileged slice of society. Trusting social institutions, maximizing interpersonal supports, and engaging in self disclosure are strategies most appropriate for middle class and affluent individuals whose interests are served by those institutions, whose social supports can multiply available resources and contacts and for whom self-disclosure may in fact lead not only to personal change, but to structural change [28, 36].

Unable to trust existing institutions, for Altamese self-disclosure would have exposed wounds unlikely to be healed. Responsible for a network of kin, Altamese could not rely on but had to protect her social supports. Resisting social institutions, withholding information and preserving emotional invulnerability emerged as her strategies for maintaining control [27]. Expecting God to prosecute, loss of memory to insure coping and fantasy to anesthetize reality, Altamese is by no means helpless.

While her social and economic circumstances are such that Altamese cannot change the basic oppressive structures which affect her, the social and psychological strategies she employs are mechanisms of control—protection for self and others [38]. An abstract pursuit of justice was not possible given her social context, commitments and concerns. She organized the realities of her life so as to manage effectively the multiple forces which *are* out to get her and her kin. Like Gilligan's concept of women's relational morality, Altamese exhibited what may be considered relational coping.

With little attention paid to relational concerns and a systematic neglect of power relations, psychologists have prescribed ways to cope as if a consensus about their utility had been established; as if there were no alternatives; as if universals could be applied across contexts, and as if these strategies were uninfluenced by our position in social and economic hierarchies. As the creators of what Foucault calls power-knowledge [33] psychologists have an obligation to expose the dialectics of psychological control and structural control, as experienced by women and men across lines of social class, ethnicity and race, levels of physical ability and disability and sexual preferences. In the absence of such knowledge psychologists impose, as healthy and universal, what may be narrow and elitist strategies for taking control.

One particular strategy, examined below, involves the prescription that persons treated unjustly or confronted by tragedy utilize available social programs. If Altamese is any indication such social programs are likely to be severely underutilized so long as they are designed top-down *for* (and not by) the persons supposedly served.

COPING WITH OPTIONS

One way to take control over adversity, supported by much psychological research (including my own), is to do something to improve one's own life circumstances; to use available options. To battered women, it may be suggested that they leave their abusive homes; to the unemployed, that they enroll for skills retraining; to the underpaid, that they learn to be assertive; to rape victims, that they "ventilate" and prosecute. Social programs have proliferated to offer individuals these services. These programs are generally designed by relatively high power individuals for persons who have what are considered personal problems. Offered as *opportunities* to improve the quality of life experienced by low power persons, these programs generally aim to correct presumed deficits [35, 39, 40]. Some disabled persons have the *opportunity* to work in sheltered workshops, often earning less than minimum wages, trained for non-marketable skills [41]. Some battered women have the *opportunity* to be sheltered in facilities which exclude women with drug or alcohol addictions, are located in unsafe neighborhoods, and limit a maximum stay of two weeks, promising an alternative to violent homes [42]. Some Black high school dropouts have the *opportunity* to earn their Graduate Equivalency Diplomas, promising greater vocational mobility, despite the fact that Black adolescent unemployment figures range from 39 percent to 44 percent for high school graduates and dropouts, respectively [43].

Efforts to fix people and not change structures, many of these options reinforce the recipient's low power position [39]. It is therefore most interesting that when such persons dismiss these options as inappropriate, ineffective or as decoys for the "real issues," these persons are often derogated [9, 23]. Individuals who reject available options, such as disabled adults who picket the Jerry Lewis Telethon claiming it to be condescending and reinforcing of the worst stereotypes, are viewed as ungrateful, unappreciative and sometimes even deserving of their circumstances [35]. The same option that appears valuable to a high power person may be critiqued as a charade by low power persons.

To demonstrate: there exists substantial evidence that high power persons do see social options (e.g., an appeal, grievance procedure, opportunity to flee) as more potentially effective than low power persons do. Experimental and survey data document that in social contexts in which an option to injustice is available, victims are more likely than nonvictims to consider their circumstances unjust, but nonvictims are more likely to rate *the option as powerful to promote change* [44]. Victims see injustice; nonvictims see the potential for change. But, victims are *not* more likely than nonvictims to use an option to change their circumstances. Why would victims reject an opportunity to avenge injustice?

To investigate this question, victim and nonvictim responses to open-ended questions about injustice and appeals were reviewed [9]. Victims claim to be reluctant to appeal an injustice not because they do not recognize injustice, they do; not because they felt they deserved to be treated unfairly, they do not; not because they respect victimizers who commit injustice, they don't. Victims appear to be reluctant because they are in fact less likely to win an appeal, and usually have more to lose than nonvictims who would appeal. The appeal procedure in this study was designed as an *opportunity* for the victim to redress inequity, but actually offered her only a remote chance of success.

To appeal successfully, the victim or nonvictim had to convince at least one other member of a three person group that an inequity had occurred. If she appealed, a victim 1) would appear self serving, 2) could not be sure she would be supported in her appeal, 3) could, if she lost the appeal, get double confirmation that her treatment was justified, and 4) could indeed have much to lose by initiating an appeal.

In marked contrast, a nonvictim who appeals on behalf of the victim 1) would appear benevolent, 2) could be relatively sure of support from the victim, 3) could enjoy public praise for her benevolence, and 4) could gain psychologically and socially from the appeal. It is little wonder, then, that observers view options as more viable for victims than victims do themselves. It is perhaps in this role as observers that psychologists have encouraged victims' utilization of available programs and services. By not understanding how disempowering it may be to be offered an inappropriate option, while reminded that this-is-your-last-chance, even the most benevolent observer/helper can create secondary injury [45].

CONCLUSIONS

At fifteen life had taught me undeniably that surrender, in its place, was as honorable as resistance, especially if one had no choice.

—MAYA ANGELOU
I Know Why The Caged Bird Sings,
1969, Bantam Books, p. 212

As social scientists generate master strategies for taking control and promote them as universally applicable, the paradox of "therapeutic hegemony" emerges. Those individuals with the least control over the causes of their problems, much less the means for structural resolution, are prescribed psychological models for individual efficacy. As long as individual victims (or survivors) act alone to improve their circumstances, oppressive economic and social arrangements will persist. The effects of such acts of psychological control may ultimately be indistinguishable from the effects of surrender. Even acts of resistance, if initiated individualistically, ultimately buttress power differentials. Altamese's unwillingness to use the justice system, her non-reliance on kin, and her trust that God will provide or punish, do nothing for the women that these rapist(s) will attack next. Nor do they stem the wave of violence against women. What these behaviors accomplish is that they give Altamese a control strategy by which she can survive, with the remaining child, her mother, and her brothers, in a community where she can get some support. Unfortunately these behaviors also allow psychologists to continue to weave the fantasy that Altamese needs to be educated about options available to her and taught to be assertive about her needs. Psychologists can remain ever convinced that if *only* Altamese would learn to use it, the system would work to her advantage. . . .

EPILOGUE

And so as psychologists we are faced with a conceptual dilemma. Should we expand the definition of "taking control" to incorporate the lived experiences of women and men across class, race, and ethnic lines? Or, do we dispense with the concept of "taking control" totally, rejected as too narrow to be salvaged? I would argue the former. Taking control is undoubtedly a significant psychological experience; knowing that one can effect change in one's environment makes a difference. How individuals accomplish this, however, does vary by economic and social circumstance, gender and perhaps personal style. The phenomenology of individuals like Altamese needs be integrated into our conceptions of taking control in order for the concept to have meaning for those persons most likely to confront injustice, tragedy or other life crises. A feminist psychology needs to value relational coping and to contextualize, through the eyes of those women affected, the meaning of victimization and taking control. The continued assessment of "women's coping" as helplessness need be reframed.

AUTHOR'S NOTE

Encouraged by the editors of this series, I have included this note to describe methodological and ethical dilemmas faced in writing this article as a social psychologist. I also hope to persuade others, particularly clinicians interested in using this "method," to consider its inherent ethical dilemmas.

This manuscript, which reflects critical thinking about social psychological theory, was provoked by a discussion with a woman I have chosen to call Altamese. This conversation was between me, as a volunteer rape counselor (not as clinician—which I am not—nor as researcher) in an urban hospital and Altamese, an emergency room patient. The conversation took place because I work at the hospital in this capacity, not because I intended to do research on the topic of rape. The information reported does not, therefore, conform to the traditional standards of ethical practices of data collection.

The ethical dilemmas, as I see them, arise in a way not addressed by the 1983 Ethical Principles (APA): Altamese was not "informed" because at the time there was no research to be informed of; she was not "debriefed" because our only conversation took place in the course of my offering her support, not through the use of a pre-defined research instrument. Because of these factors, I remain somewhat ambivalent about the presentation of material in this article.

The problem is, simply, what to do with information gathered in a context in which research was not being conducted, in which the assumption is one of privacy, from which a publishable article evolves two years later? Three issues need to be examined: anonymity, informed consent, and assumptions about privacy.

Anonymity concerns appear to be the easiest to satisfy in both the present work and any other which utilizes a similar methodology. In the present work, names, demographics and life circumstances have been changed radically so that anonymity is well guarded. The details of the rape and reactions to it have been omitted so that no one could identify this woman—perhaps not even she herself. When information provided in any private setting is subsequently introduced in a manuscript, revealing data should be deleted, changed and/or "checked back" (if possible) for use.

Informed consent is more complicated. In this case, there was no presumption of "doing research." There would have been no reason, therefore, to request such consent. And two years later, with neither telephone nor forwarding address available, it is impossible to ascertain consent today. Of course, as someone suggested, it is possible that Altamese did sign a statement upon entering the emergency room which "OKed" the research use of relevant information, but one cannot assume this to be *INFORMED CONSENT*.

In thinking about informed consent it must be clear that 1) if a researcher is explicitly interested in gathering clinical information for research purposes all clients need to complete informed consent forms non-coercively (so that they have the option to receive services even if they do not agree to be involved in research); and 2) even if informed consent is provided, clients have the right to delete certain quotes or information from a manuscript if they feel revealed or betrayed by that section of the manuscript.

The third issue is for me the most complicated—what to do when information is provided in a context presumed to be private and confidential. Do researchers have a right to use this information for research/theoretical ends? I want to say a blanket "no" but again my own work leaves me wanting a more qualified response. A central consideration, here, is the issue of risk. In the present case, I can see no risk. Clearly, if Altamese were prosecuting these rapists, the potential risk would be enormous and publication out of the question.

This legal aspect of risk acknowledged, however, we still need to consider how we would feel if information we provided confidentially showed up in a journal article. The more explicit we can be with clients about the potential research purposes and the more we can involve clients in the importance of writing about this material (e.g., to make "public" what are experienced as "private" and "personal" problems), the less damage we will do to the trust levels between ourselves and our clients/informants; the better we will understand how clients/informants view violations of confidentiality and breaches of contracts, and presumably the better the information we will gather (perhaps too optimistic).

This article is about an encounter between two women and incorporates my impression of that encounter. I have elected to use the material, while trying to describe my ambivalent feelings about the encounter and about this article based on the encounter. In this note I have tried to reflect on the ethical dilemmas I have confronted and offer suggestions to individuals who may be interested in utilizing such a methodology systematically and intentionally:

1. Develop informed consent procedures so that all clients/potential informants are aware that information could be used for research purposes, providing services even if research consent is denied, and recognizing that introducing the topic of informed consent may systematically alter the nature of the relationship. The question needs to be asked: are there some counseling relationships in which counselors cannot simultaneously be collecting research-relevant information?
2. Beyond this safeguard, the potential risks to clients of using their information for research purposes need to be weighed, and discussed with clients.
3. Our responsibilities to people who provide us information need be respected. Researchers need to be particularly careful about abusing information provided when people assume the exchange to be private, confidential and safe.

Acknowledgments

Many people deserve thanks for the production of this manuscript. David Surrey was helpful in reviewing, and listening about this article. His theoretical contributions and support are most appreciated. Dell Hymes provided invaluable outside analytic insight. Rhoda Unger and two anonymous reviewers have been supportive and conceptually most helpful. Theresa Singleton typed through numerous versions of the paper, until we got it "right." Her patience and good will are appreciated. Altamese Thomas, a pseudonym, and the millions of women who have been raped, have taught me a lot about being a psychologist and being a woman.

References

1. P. Brickman, V. Rabinowitz, J. Karuza, D. Coates, E. Cohn, and L. Kidder, Models of Helping and Coping, *American Psychologist, 37*, pp. 368–384, 1982.
2. A. Burgess and L. Holstrom, Coping Behavior of the Rape Victim, *American Journal of Psychiatry, 133*, pp. 413–418, 1976.
3. R. Janoff-Bulman, Characterological versus Behavioral Self Blame: Inquiries into Depression and Rape, *Journal of Personality and Social Psychology, 37*, pp. 1798–1809, 1979.
4. R. Janoff-Bulman and C. Wortman, Attributions of Blame and Coping in the 'Real World': Severe Accident Victims React to Their Lot, *Journal of Personality and Social Psychology, 35*, pp. 351–363, 1977.
5. D. Schorr and J. Rodin, The Role of Perceived Control in Practitioner-Patient Relationships, in *Basic Processes in Helping Relationships*, T. Wills (ed.), Academic Press, New York, 1982.

6. R. Schutz, Effects of Control and Predictability on the Physical and Psychological Well Being of the Institutionalized Aged, *Journal of Personality and Social Psychology, 33*, pp. 563–573, 1976.

7. S. Cobb and S. Kasl, *Termination: The Consequences of Job Loss* (Publication #LR 77–224), Department of Health, Education and Welfare, Washington, D.C., 1977.

8. C. Dweck and B. Licht, Learned Helplessness and Intellectual Achievement, in *Human Helplessness,* J. Garber and M. Seligman (eds.), Academic Press, New York, 1980.

9. M. Fine, The Social Context and a Sense of Injustice: The Option to Challenge, *Representative Research in Social Psychology, 13*:1, pp. 15–33, 1983(a).

10. R. Janoff-Bulman and G. Marshall, Mortality, Well Being and Control: A Study of a Population of Institutionalized Aged, *Personality and Social Psychology Bulletin, 8*:4, pp. 691–698, 1982.

11. H. Lefcourt, Personality and Locus of Control, in *Human Helplessness,* J. Garber and M. Seligman (eds.), Academic Press, New York, 1980.

12. C. Peterson, S. Schwartz and M. Seligman, Self Blame and Depressive Symptoms, *Journal of Personality and Social Psychology, 41,* pp. 253–259, 1981.

13. B. DePaulo, Social Psychological Processes in Informal Help Seeking, in *Basic Processes in Helping Relationships,* T. Wills (ed.), Academic Press, New York, 1980.

14. M. Fine, When Nonvictims Derogate: Powerlessness in the Helping Professions, *Personality and Social Psychology Bulletin, 8*:4, pp. 637–643, 1982.

15. T. Antonucci and C. Depner, Social Support and Information Helping Relationships, in *Basic Processes in Helping Relationships,* T. Wills (ed.), Academic Press, New York, 1982.

16. C. Solano, P. Batten and E. Parish, Loneliness and Patterns of Self-Disclosure, *Journal of Personality and Social Psychology, 43*:3, pp. 524–531, 1982.

17. C. Swenson, Using Natural Helping Networks to Promote Competence, in *Promoting Competence in Clients,* A. N. Maluccio (ed.), Free Press, New York, 1981.

18. R. Silver and C. Wortman, Coping with Undesirable Life Events, in *Human Helplessness,* J. Garber and M. Seligman (eds.), Academic Press, New York, 1980.

19. R. Unger, Controlling Out the Obvious: Power, Status and Social Psychology, paper presented at American Psychological Association, Washington, D.C., 1982.

20. J. B. Miller, *Toward a New Psychology of Women,* Beacon Press, Boston, 1976.

21. M. Seligman, *Helplessness: On Depression, Development and Death,* W. H. Freeman, San Francisco, 1975.

22. W. Ryan, *Equality,* Pantheon Books, New York, 1981.

23. M. Fine, Perspectives on Inequity: Voices from Urban Schools, in *Applied Social Psychology Annual,* L. Brickman (ed.), *4,* Sage, Beverly Hills, 1983(b).

24. C. Gilligan, *In a Different Voice,* Harvard University Press, Cambridge, 1982.

25. E. Sampson, Cognitive Psychology as Ideology, *American Psychologist, 36*:7, pp. 730–743, 1981.

26. E. Cagan, Individualism, Collectivism, and Radical Educational Reform, *Harvard Educational Review, 48,* pp. 227–266, 1978.

27. J. Anyon, Intersections of Gender and Class: Accommodation and Resistance by Working Class and Affluent Females in Contradictory Sex-Role Ideologies, in *Gender, Class and Education,* L. Barton and S. Walker (eds.), Fatiner Press, England, 1982.

28. L. Furby, Individualist Bias in Studies of Locus of Control, in *Psychology in Social Context,* A. Buss (ed.), Irvington Publishers, New York, pp. 169–190, 1979.

29. A. Buss (ed.), *Psychology in Social Context,* Irvington Publishers, New York, 1979.

30. C. Wortman and J. Brehm, Responses to Uncontrollable Outcomes: An Integration of Reactance Theory and the Learned Helplessness Model, in *Advances in Experimental Social Psychology,* Vol. 8, L. Berkowitz (ed.), Academic Press, New York, 1975.

Mitsuye Yamada

Invisibility Is an Unnatural Disaster: Reflections of an Asian American Woman

Last year for the Asian segment of the Ethnic American Literature course I was teaching, I selected a new anthology entitled *Aweeeee!* compiled by a group of outspoken Asian American writers. During the discussion of the long but thought-provoking introduction to this anthology, one of my students blurted out that she was offended by its militant tone and that as a white person she was tired of always being blamed for the oppression of all the minorities. I noticed several of her classmates' eyes nodding in tacit agreement. A discussion of the "militant" voices in some of the other writings we had read in the course ensued. Surely, I pointed out, some of these other writings have been just as, if not more, militant as the words in this introduction? Had they been offended by those also but failed to express their feelings about them? To my surprise, they said they were not offended by any of the Black American, Chicano or American Indian writings, but were hard-pressed to explain why when I asked for an explanation. A little further discussion revealed that they "understood" the anger expressed by the Black and Chicanos and they "empathized" with the frustrations and sorrow expressed by the American Indian. But the Asian Americans??

Then finally, one student said it for all of them: "It made me angry. *Their* anger made *me* angry, because I didn't even know the Asian Americans felt oppressed. I didn't expect their anger."

At this time I was involved in an academic due process procedure begun as a result of a grievance I had filed the previous semester against the administrators at my college. I had filed a grievance for violation of my rights as a teacher who had worked in the district for almost eleven years. My student's remark "Their anger made me angry . . . I didn't expect their anger," explained for me the reactions of some of my own colleagues as well as the reactions of the administrators during those previous months. The grievance procedure was a time-consuming and emotionally draining process, but the basic principle was too important for me to ignore. That basic principle was that I, an individual teacher, do have certain rights which are given and my superiors can-

165

not, should not, violate them with impunity. When this was pointed out to them, however, they responded with shocked surprise that I, of all people, would take them to task for violation of what was clearly written policy in our college district. They all seemed to exclaim, "We don't understand this; this is so uncharacteristic of her; she seemed such a nice person, so polite, so obedient, so non-trouble-making." What was even more surprising was once they were forced to acknowledge that I was determined to start the due process action, they assumed I was not doing it on my own. One of the administrators suggested someone must have pushed me into this, undoubtedly some of "those feminists" on our campus, he said wryly.

In this age when women are clearly making themselves visible on all fronts, I, an Asian American woman, am still functioning as a "front for those feminists" and therefore invisible. The realization of this sinks in slowly. Asian Americans as a whole are finally coming to claim their own, demanding that they be included in the multicultural history of our country. I like to think, in spite of my administrator's myopia, that the most stereotyped minority of them all, the Asian American woman, is just now emerging to become part of that group. It took forever. Perhaps it is important to ask ourselves why it took so long. We should ask ourselves this question just when we think we are emerging as a viable minority in the fabric of our society. I should add to my student's words, "because I didn't even know they felt oppressed," that it took this long because we Asian American women have not admitted to ourselves that we *were* oppressed. We, the visible minority that is invisible.

I say this because until a few years ago I have been an Asian American woman working among non-Asians in an educational institution where most of the decision-makers were men*, an Asian American woman thriving under the smug illusion that I was *not* the stereotypic image of the Asian woman because I had a career teaching English in a community college. I did not think anything assertive was necessary to make my point. People who know me, I reasoned, the ones who count, know who I am and what I think. Thus, even when what I considered a veiled racist remark was made in a casual social setting. I would "let it go" because it was pointless to argue with people who didn't even know their remark was racist. I had supposed that I was practicing passive resistance while being stereotyped, but it was so passive no one noticed I was resisting; it was so much my expected role that it ultimately rendered me invisible.

My experience leads me to believe that contrary to what I thought, I had actually been contributing to my own stereotyping. Like the hero in Ralph Ellison's novel *The Invisible Man*, I had become invisible to white Americans, and it clung to me like a bad habit. Like most bad habits, this one crept up on me because I took it in minute doses like Mithradates' poison and my mind and body adapted so well to it I hardly noticed it was there.

For the past eleven years I have busied myself with the usual chores of an English teacher, a wife of a research chemist, and a mother of four rapidly growing children. I hadn't even done much to shatter this particular stereotype: the middle class woman happy to be bringing home the extra income and quietly fitting into the man's world of work. When the Asian American

---

*It is hoped this will change now that a black woman is Chancellor of our college district.

woman is lulled into believing that people perceive her as being different from other Asian women (the submissive, subservient, ready-to-please, easy-to-get-along-with Asian woman), she is kept comfortably content with the state of things. She becomes ineffectual in the milieu in which she moves. The seemingly apolitical middle class woman and the apolitical Asian woman constituted a double invisibility.

I had created an underground culture of survival for myself and had become in the eyes of others the person I was trying not to be. Because I was permitted to go to college, permitted to take a stab at a career or two along the way, given "free choice" to marry and have a family, given a "choice" to eventually do both, I had assumed I was more or less free, not realizing that those who are free make and take choices; they do not choose from options proffered by "those out there."

I, personally, had not "emerged" until I was almost fifty years old. Apparently through a long conditioning process, I had learned how *not* to be seen for what I am. A long history of ineffectual activities had been, I realize now, initiation rites toward my eventual invisibility. The training begins in childhood; and for women and minorities, whatever is started in childhood is continued throughout their adult lives. I first recognized just how invisible I was in my first real confrontation with my parents a few years after the outbreak of World War II.

During the early years of the war, my older brother, Mike, and I left the concentration camp in Idaho to work and study at the University of Cincinnati. My parents came to Cincinnati soon after my father's release from Internment Camp (these were POW camps to which many of the Issei* men, leaders in their communities, were sent by the FBI), and worked as domestics in the suburbs. I did not see them too often because by this time I had met and was much influenced by a pacifist who was out on a "furlough" from a conscientious objectors' camp in Trenton, North Dakota. When my parents learned about my "boy friend" they were appalled and frightened. After all, this was the period when everyone in the country was expected to be one-hundred percent behind the war effort, and the Nisei† boys who had volunteered for the Armed Forces were out there fighting and dying to prove how American we really were. However, during interminable arguments with my father and overheard arguments between my parents, I was devastated to learn they were not so much concerned about my having become a pacifist, but they were more concerned about the possibility of my marrying one. They were understandably frightened (my father's prison years of course were still fresh on his mind) about repercussions on the rest of the family. In an attempt to make my father understand me, I argued that even if I didn't marry him, I'd still be a pacifist; but my father reassured me that it was "all right" for me to be a pacifist because as a Japanese national and a "girl" *it didn't make any difference to anyone.* In frustration, I remember shouting, "But can't you see, *I'm* philosophically committed to the pacifist cause," but he dismissed this with "In my college days we used to call philosophy, foolosophy," and that was the end of that. When they were finally convinced I was not going to marry "my pacifist," the subject was dropped and we never discussed it again.

*Issei—Immigrant Japanese, living in the U.S.
†Nisei—Second generation Japanese, born in the U.S.

As if to confirm my father's assessment of the harmlessness of my opinions, my brother Mike, an American citizen, was suddenly expelled from the University of Cincinnati while I, "an enemy alien", was permitted to stay. We assumed that his stand as a pacifist, although he was classified a 4-F because of his health, contributed to his expulsion. We were told the Air Force was conducting sensitive wartime research on campus and requested his removal, but they apparently felt my presence on campus was not as threatening.

I left Cincinnati in 1945, hoping to leave behind this and other unpleasant memories gathered there during the war years, and plunged right into the politically active atmosphere at New York University where students, many of them returning veterans, were continuously promoting one cause or other by making speeches in Washington Square, passing out petitions, or staging demonstrations. On one occasion, I tagged along with a group of students who took a train to Albany to demonstrate on the steps of the State Capitol. I think I was the only Asian in this group of predominantly Jewish students from NYU. People who passed us were amused and shouted "Go home and grow up." I suppose Governor Dewey, who refused to see us, assumed we were a group of adolescents without a cause as most college students were considered to be during those days. It appears they weren't expecting any results from our demonstration. There were no newspersons, no security persons, no police. No one tried to stop us from doing what we were doing. We simply did "our thing" and went back to our studies until next time, and my father's words were again confirmed: it made no difference to anyone, being a young student demonstrator in peacetime, 1947.

Not only the young, but those who feel powerless over their own lives know what it is like not to make a difference on anyone or anything. The poor know it only too well, and we women have known it since we were little girls. The most insidious part of this conditioning process, I realize now, was that we have been trained not to expect a response in ways that mattered. We may be listened to and responded to with placating words and gestures, but our psychological mind set has already told us time and again that we were born into a ready made world into which we must fit ourselves and that many of us do it very well.

This mind set is the result of not believing that the political and social forces affecting our lives are determined by some person, or a group of persons, probably sitting behind a desk or around a conference table.

Just recently I read an article about "the remarkable track record of success" of the Nisei in the United States. One Nisei was quoted as saying he attributed our stamina and endurance to our ancestors whose characters had been shaped, he said, by their living in a country which has been constantly besieged by all manner of natural disasters, such as earthquakes and hurricanes. He said the Nisei has inherited a steely will, a will to endure and hence, to survive.

This evolutionary explanation disturbs me, because it equates the "act of God" (i.e., natural disasters) to the "act of man" (i.e., the war, the evacuation). The former is not within our power to alter, but the latter, I should think, is. By putting the "acts of God" on par with the acts of man, we shrug off personal responsibilities.

169

MITSUYE YAMADA
*Invisibility Is an
Unnatural Disaster:
Reflections of an
Asian American
Woman*

I have, for too long a period of time accepted the opinion of others (even though they were directly affecting my life) as if they were objective events totally out of my control. Because I separated such opinions from the persons who were making them, I accepted them the way I accepted natural disasters; and I endured them as inevitable. I have tried to cope with people whose points of view alarmed me in the same way that I had adjusted to natural phenomena, such as hurricanes, which plowed into my life from time to time. I would readjust my dismantled feelings in the same way that we repaired the broken shutters after the storm. The Japanese have an all-purpose expression in their language for this attitude of resigned acceptance: "Shikataganai." "It can't be helped." "There's nothing I can do about it." It is said with the shrug of the shoulders and tone of finality, perhaps not unlike the "those-were-my-orders" tone that was used at the Nuremberg trials. With all the sociological studies that have been made about the causes of the evacuations of the Japanese Americans during World War II, we should know by now that "they" knew that the West Coast Japanese Americans would go without too much protest, and of course, "they" were right, for most of us (with the exception of those notable few), resigned to our fate, albeit bewildered and not willingly. We were not perceived by our government as responsive Americans; we were objects that happened to be standing in the path of the storm.

Perhaps this kind of acceptance is a way of coping with the "real" world. One stands against the wind for a time, and then succumbs eventually because there is no point to being stubborn against all odds. The wind will not respond to entreaties anyway, one reasons; one should have sense enough to know that. I'm not ready to accept this evolutionary reasoning. It is too rigid for me; I would like to think that my new awareness is going to make me more visible than ever, and to allow me to make some changes in the "man made disaster" I live in at the present time. Part of being visible is refusing to separate the actors from their actions, and demanding that they be responsible for them.

By now, riding along with the minorities' and women's movements, I think we are making a wedge into the main body of American life, but people are still looking right through and around us, assuming we are simply tagging along. Asian American women still remain in the background and we are heard but not really listened to. Like Musak, they think we are piped into the airwaves by someone else. We must remember that one of the most insidious ways of keeping women and minorities powerless is to let them only talk about harmless and inconsequential subjects, or let them speak freely and not listen to them with serious intent.

We need to raise our voices a little more, even as they say to us "This is so uncharacteristic of you." To finally recognize our own invisibility is to finally be on the path toward visibility. Invisibility is not a natural state for anyone.

The Hard Part

The novel being dead, there is no point to writing made up stories. Look at the French who will not and the Americans who cannot. Look at me who ought not, if only because I exist entirely outside the usual human experience . . . outside and yet wholly relevant for I am the New Woman whose astonishing history is a poignant amalgam of vulgar dreams and knife-sharp realities (shall I ever be free of the dull lingering pain that is my peculiar glory, the price so joyously paid for being Myra Breckinridge, whom no man may possess except on her . . . my terms!).

—GORE VIDAL, *Myra Breckinridge*, 1974

The hard part was sorting it all out. The hard part was taking a good look at everyone else and the way they looked at the world, which was a lot different from the way *I* was looking at the world!

There are some transsexuals who agree with the way I look at the world, and quite a few who are really angry with me for writing this stuff. Every transsexual I know went through a gender transformation for different reasons, and there are as many truthful experiences of gender as there are people who think they have a gender.

I know I'm not a man—about that much I'm very clear, and I've come to the conclusion that I'm probably not a woman either, at least not according to a lot of people's rules on this sort of thing. The trouble is, we're living in a world that insists we be one or the other—a world that doesn't bother to tell us exactly what one or the other *is*.

When I was a kid, everyone else seemed to know they were boys or girls or men or women. That's something I've never known; not then,

170

not today. I never got to say to the grownups,
"Hold on there—just what is it about me that
makes you think I'm a little boy?" As a kid, I
just figured I was the crazy one; I was the one
who really had some serious defect.

All my life, my non-traditional gender identity had been my biggest secret, my deepest shame. It's not that I didn't want to talk about this with someone; it's just that I never saw anything in the culture that encouraged me to talk about my feeling that I was the wrong gender. When I was growing up, people who lived cross-gendered lives were pressured into hiding deep within the darkest closets they could find. Those who came out of their closets were either studied under a microscope, ridiculed in the tabloids, or made exotic in the porn books, so it paid to hide. It paid to lie. That was probably the most painful part of it: the lying to friends and family and lovers, the pretending to be someone I wasn't. Going through a gender change is not the easiest thing in the world to do, but I went through it because I was so tired of all the lies and secrets.

It was a strange kind of lie. It was a lie by ac-
tion—I was always acting out something that
everyone assumed I was. I wonder what it
would have been like if someone had come
along and in a quite friendly manner had
asked, "Well, young one, what do you think
you are: a boy or a girl?" What would it have
been like not to have been afraid of getting hit
because of some wrong answer? See, "sex
changes" never were an appropriate topic of
conversation—not at the dining table, not in
the locker room, not over a casual lunch in a
crowded restaurant.

Nowadays, I try to make it easier for people to ask questions. I tell people that I've never been hurt by an honest question, and that's true: it's a cruel opinion that hurts, not a question. But people still don't ask questions easily; maybe that has something to do with manners or etiquette. Folks seem to naturally back off from inquiring as to the nature of someone's—my—gender. It seems to need some special setting. Like in my living room, or on television, or from behind a podium at some university. It's "good manners" to say and ask nothing, and that's sad. But the children still ask.

Two days after my lover and I appeared on The
Donahue Show, the five-year-old child of our
next door neighbor came up to me and asked me,
"So, are you a boy or a girl?" We'd been living
next door to these folks for over two years.

"I'm a girl who used to be a boy," I
replied. She was delighted with that answer
and told me I'd looked very pretty on televi-
sion. I thanked her and we smiled at each other
and went about our days. I love it that kids
will just ask.

Adults don't ask. Adults are afraid to ask, "What *are* you?" so we ask "What do you *do*?" . . . in hopes of getting a clue to someone's identity—gender identity seems to be an unspeakable thing in our culture, just as names are considered unspeakable in some other cultures. By the same token, we hardly ever ask outright "What kind of sex do you like?" When it comes to work, we can ask. When it comes to sex and gender, we're supposed to observe discreetly and draw our own conclusions.

Instead of asking directly, adults look in roundabout ways for answers to their questions about me and my people. Like reading transsexual and transvestite pornography which, judging by much of its content, must be written by people who have never met one of us, but who have certainly fantasized about us.

> *There's this entire wonderful underground genre of erotica. You may have seen some of the titles, they're terrific, like* **He's Her Sister!** *(Get it?) or* **Transvestite Marriage** *or* **Transvestite Trap**. *My personal favorites were* **Captive in Lace**, *and* **They Made Him Love It!**

Reading those stories came in handy when I was doing phone sex for a living, because a lot of the men calling in wanted to be cross-dressed as women, or they wanted to know what it would be like to be a woman and have sex with another woman—guys want to know that sort of thing. They want to know, "what do lesbians *do* with one another." It's a sad question really: it shows how little thought they give to exactly what pleases a woman.

> *There's another whole group of people who really* **like** *gender ambiguity, it turns them on. I remember a group of sailors in the audience on* **The Geraldo Show**. *After it was announced who and what I was, they kept on looking at me, they kept on wanting something. I could feel their eyes traveling up and down my surgically-constructed, hormonally-enhanced woman's body. What's the pull? What is it about a sexually-blended, gender-bended body that lights those flames? I know it gets me going!*

For the most part, people cautiously observe and don't ask questions, and there are plenty of opportunities in today's world to look at people like me. The talk show ratings go way up during sweeps month when they trot out the transsexuals and the cross-dressers. Then there are the drag shows and the female impersonator spectacles—even though we began them for our own entertainment and enjoyment, their widespread popularity seems to grow and grow; you've probably got one of those shows in your city, or in a nearby town. Comedy skits, like "It's Pat" (a skit based on a person whose gender is not clear) on *Saturday Night Live* are real popular. I'll have more to say about that later.

If I look past the ghettos of the drag bars and standup joints, both popular music and cinema reflect my transsexual face back to me. Glance discreetly, if you will, at some of the brightest deities in our cultural heavens. At this writing, some friends of mine are truly interested in seeing if Michael Jackson (all his other issues aside) will actually become Diana Ross. I've heard bets being placed on the gender of some of Madonna's lovers in some of her videos. And what really made *The Crying Game* the smash hit that it was? It's interesting that we can ask questions about transgender issues when there's some distance between us and the person we're asking about—we just don't ask directly.

There's a lot of writing about gender now. I keep reading the magazine articles, the newspaper columns, and the text books, pre- and post-modern. I read, watch, and listen to all the ads and commercials. You can learn a lot about gender from those commercials. I've also been watching the talk shows, listening to the call-in programs, and browsing the electronic bulletin boards. When I was very young, growing up in the 50s, I read the medical texts, devoured the tabloids, and hoarded the pornography—because I was intensely interested in me and my people. I was scared, though, shaking scared, to see what I might actually find out. But I couldn't stop reading.

> *See, I was a lonely, frightened little fat kid who felt there was something deeply wrong with me because I didn't feel like I was the gender I'd been assigned. I felt there was something wrong with me, something sick and twisted inside me, something very very bad about me. And everything I read backed that up.*

The possibility missed by most of the texts prior to the last few years, and by virtually all the various popular media, is this: the culture may not simply be creating roles for naturally-gendered people, the culture may in fact be *creating* the gendered people. In other words, the culture may be creating gender. No one had ever hinted at that, and so, standing outside a "natural" gender, I thought I was some monster, and that it was all my fault.

In living along the borders of the gender frontier, I've come to see the gender system created by this culture as a particularly malevolent and divisive construct, made all the more dangerous by the seeming inability of the culture to *question* gender, its own creation. The studies conducted by the duly-appointed representatives of the culture were still done on the basis of observation, not conversation. I want this book to begin to reverse that trend. I want this book to be the conversation I always wanted as I was growing up, and never had the chance to have.

The time for discreet and distant observation of transgendered lives seems to be coming to an end. There's more and more evidence that transgendered folks are making a place for themselves in the culture. I'm writing this book, for example, and it's getting published because there's been a shift. Up until the last few years, all we'd be able to write *and get published* were our autobiographies, tales of women trapped in the bodies of men or men pining away in the bodies of women. Stories by and about brave people who'd lived their lives hiding deep within a false gender—and who, after much soul-searching, decided to change their gender, and spent the rest of their days hiding deep within *another* false gender. That's what we could get published about our-selves—the romantic stuff which set in stone our image as long-suffering, not the challenging stuff. And it always seemed that the people who would write *about* us either had some ax to grind or point to prove, or they'd been hurt and needed someone to blame it on. People like Janice Raymond, Catherine Millot, and Robert Stoller have ultimately perpetuated the myth that transgendered people are malevolent, mentally ill, or monsters. We got left holding the cultural bag. We ended up wearing the cultural hand-me-downs.

But there's another kind of trans(gressive)gender experience going on in this culture, and nowadays we're writing our own chronicles of these times. Our stories all tie together, our stories overlap; and you can hear lots about me in the stories of other transgendered people. My story weaves through Caroline Cossey's story. My story lies within the story of late historian Louis Sullivan. Christine Jorgensen and Renee Richards wrote chapters of my story in their autobiographies. Sandy Stone teaches her story, my story, our story in any number of her classes. Rachel Pollack paints it into her tarot cards. Christine Beatty belts it out in heavy metal and whispers it in her poetry. Melanie Phillips makes it available in on-line cyberspace. Leslie Feinberg travels back and forth across the country to make our story heard in the political arena. Loren Cameron captures it in his black-and-white stills. Kristienne Clarke brings us into her made-for-television films. David Harrison performs our story live on stage, Wednesdays through Sundays. We're all of us speaking in our own transgendered voice these days: editor and publisher JoAnn Roberts, essayist and fiction writer James Green, activist and writer Susan Stryker, publishers Dallas Denny and Davina Anne Gabriel, poet Rikki Ann Wilchins, poet and essayist Max Valerio, publisher Marissa Sheryl Lynn, playwright and composer Omewenne Grimstone, performance artist Celie Edwards—the list keeps growing. We're talking to each other in meeting rooms, through newsletters and journals, and on electronic bulletin boards. It's an exciting time, here at the beginning of a movement. It's a time when we've begun to put down the cultural baggage. We've begun sewing sequins onto our cultural hand-me-downs.

My voice on this subject is not representative of all transgendered people. But when a minority group has been silent for as long as we have, as disjointed as we have been, the tendency is for those in the majority to listen to the loud ones when they first speak up; and to believe that we speak for the entire group. More important than my point of view, than any single point of view however, is that people begin to question gender.

The voices of transgendered people are now being raised in concert with the voices of more and more people who are writing their work based on what we have to say. Suzanne Kessler, Wendy McKenna, Marjorie Garber, Jennie Livingston, Judith Butler, Wendy Chapkis, Anne Bolin, Walter Williams, Holly Devor, Pat Califia, and Shannon Bell are all asking great questions and making room for us to respond.

I've taken as much care as I could to encourage questions in this book, especially questions about my conclusions. I hope that soon after this book is published I'll have some more questions. Questions are the hard part.

Which Outlaws?

or, Who Was That Masked Man?

> *On the day of my birth, my grandparents gave me a television set. In 1948, this was a new and wonderful thing. It had a nine-inch screen embedded in a cherrywood case the size of my mother's large oven.*
>
> *My parents gave over an entire room to the television set. It was "the television room."*

I've tried to figure out which questions get to the core of transgender issues—the answer to the riddle of my oddly-gendered life would probably be found in the area we question the least, and there are many areas of gender we do not question. We talk casually, for example, about *trans*-gender without ever clearly stating, and rarely if ever asking, what one gender or the other really is. We're so sure of our ability to categorize people as either men or women that we neglect to ask ourselves some very basic questions: what is a man? and what is a woman? and why do we need to be one or the other?

> *If we ask by what criteria a person might classify someone as being either male or female, the answers appear to be so self-evident as to make the question trivial. But consider a list of items that differentiate females from males. There are none that always and without exception are true of only one gender.*
>
> —KESSLER AND MCKENNA,
> *Gender: An Ethnomethodological Approach*, 1976

TOUCHING ALL THE BASIS

Most folks would define a man by the presence of a penis or some form of a penis. Some would define a woman by the presence of a vagina or some form of a vagina. It's not that simple, though. I know several women in San Francisco who have penises. Many wonderful men in my life have vaginas. And there are quite a few people whose genitals fall somewhere between penises and vaginas. What are *they*?

Are you a man because you have an *XY* chromosome? A woman because you have *XX*? Unless you're an athlete who's been challenged in the area of gender representation, you probably haven't had a chromosome test to determine your gender. If you haven't had that test, then how do you know what gender you are, and how do you know what gender your romantic or sexual partner is? There are, in addition to the *XX* and *XY* pairs, some other commonly-occurring sets of gender chromosomes, including *XXY, XXX, YYY, XYY*, and *XO*. Does this mean there are more than two genders?

Let's keep looking. What makes a man—testosterone? What makes a woman—estrogen? If so, you could buy your gender over the counter at any pharmacy. But we're taught that there are these things called "male" and "female" hormones; and that testosterone dominates the gender hormone balance in the males of any species. Not really—female hyenas, for example, have naturally more testosterone than the males; the female clitoris resembles a very long penis—the females mount the males from the rear, and proceed to hump. While some female humans I know behave in much the same manner as the female hyena, the example demonstrates that the universal key to gender is not hormones.

Are you a woman because you can bear children? Because you bleed every month? Many women are born without this potential, and every woman ceases to possess that capability after menopause—do these women cease being women? Does a necessary hysterectomy equal a gender change?

Are you a man because you can father children? What if your sperm count is too low? What if you were exposed to nuclear radiation and were rendered sterile? Are you then a woman?

Are you a woman because your birth certificate says female? A man because your birth certificate says male? If so, how did *that* happen? A doctor looked down at your crotch at birth. A doctor decided, based on what was showing of your external genitals, that you would be one gender or another. You never had a say in that most irreversible of all pronouncements—and according to this culture as it stands today, you never *will* have a say. What if you had been born a hermaphrodite, with some combination of both genitals? A surgeon would have "fixed" you—without your consent, and possibly without the consent or even knowledge of your parents, depending on your race and economic status. You would have been fixed—fixed into a gender. It's a fairly common experience being born with different or anomalous genitals, but we don't allow hermaphrodites in modern Western medicine. We "fix" them.

But let's get back to that birth certificate. Are you female or male because of what the law says? Is law immutable? Aren't we legislating every day in order to change the laws of our state, our nation, our culture? Isn't that the name of the game when it comes to political progress? What about other laws—religious laws, for example. Religions may dictate right and proper behavior for men and women, but no religion actually lays out what is a man and what is a woman. They assume we know, that's how deep this cultural assumption runs.

I've been searching all my life for a rock-bottom definition of woman, an unquestionable sense of what is a man. I've found nothing except the fickle definitions of gender held up by groups and individuals for their own purposes.

Every day I watched it, that television told me what was a man and what was a woman.

And every day I watched it, that television told me what to buy in order to be a woman.

And everything I bought, I said to myself I am a real woman, and I never once admitted

*that I was transsexual. You could say I'm one
inevitability of a post-modern anti-spiritualist
acquisitive culture.*

177

KATE BORNSTEIN
Which Outlaws?

A QUESTION OF PRIORITIES

I haven't found any answers. I ask every day of my life what is a man and what is a woman, and those questions beg the next: why? Why do we have to be one or the other? Why do we have to be gendered creatures at all? What keeps the bi-polar gender system in place?

I started out thinking that a theory of gender would bridge the long-standing gap between the two major genders, male and female. I'm no longer trying to do that. Some people think I want a world without gender, something bland and colorless: that's so far from how I live! I love playing with genders, and I love watching other people play with all the shades and flavors that gender can come in. I just want to question what we've been holding on to for such an awfully long time. I want to question the existence of gender, and I want to enter that question firmly into the fabric of this culture.

> *I used to watch* **The Lone Ranger** *on television. I loved that show. This masked guy rides into town on a white horse, does all these great and heroic deeds, everyone falls in love with him and then he leaves. He never takes off his mask, no one ever sees his face. He leaves behind a silver bullet and the memory of someone who can do no wrong. No bad rumors, no feet of clay, no cellulite. What a life! There's a self-help book in there somewhere.* **Who Was That Masked Man? Learning to Overcome the Lone Ranger Syndrome.**

As I moved through the '50s and '60s, I bought into the fear and hatred that marks this culture's attitude toward the genderless and the nontraditionally gendered. People are genuinely afraid of being without a gender. I've been chewing on that fear nearly all my life like it was some old bone, and now I want to take that fear apart to see what makes it tick. Nothing in the culture has encouraged me to stay and confront that fear. Instead, the culture has kept pointing me toward one door or the other:

Girls or Boys

Men or Women

Ladies or Gentlemen

Cats or Chicks

Faggots or Dykes

I knew from age four on, that something was wrong with me being a guy, and I spent most of my life avoiding the issue of my transsexuality. I hid out in textbooks, pulp fiction, and drugs and alcohol. I numbed my mind with everything from peyote to Scientology. I buried my head in the sands of television, college, a lot of lovers, and three marriages. Because I was being raised as a male, I never got to experience what it meant to be raised female in this culture. All I had were my observations, and all I could observe and assimilate as a child were differences in clothing and manners. I remember building a catalogue of gestures, phrases, body language, and outfits in my head. I would practice all of these at night when my parents had gone to sleep. I'd wear a blanket as a dress, and I'd stand in front of my mirror being my latest crush at school—I was so ashamed of myself for that.

I was obsessed, and like most obsessed people, I was the last one to know it. The culture itself is obsessed with gender—and true to form, the culture as a whole will be the last to find out how obsessed it really has been.

WHY WE HAVEN'T ASKED QUESTIONS

I know there must have been other kids—boys and girls—going through the same remorse-filled hell that held me prisoner in front of my bedroom mirror, but we had no way of knowing that: there was no language for what we were doing. Instead, cardboard cut-out versions of us were creeping into the arts and media: in poetry, drama, dance, music, sculpture, paintings, television, cinema—in just about any art form you can think of there have been portrayals of people who are ambiguously or differently-gendered, all drawn by people who were not us, all spoken in voices that were not ours.

Dominant cultures tend to colonize and control minorities through stereotyping—it's no different with the trans-gender minority. Make us a joke and there's no risk of our anger, no fear we'll raise some unified voice in protest because we're not organized. But that's changing.

We never did fit into the cultural binary of male/female, man/woman, boy/girl. No, we are the clowns, the sex objects, or the mysteriously unattainable in any number of novels. We are the psychotics, the murderers, or the criminal geniuses who populate the movies. Audiences have rarely seen the real faces of the transgendered. They don't hear our voices, rarely read our words. For too many years, we transgendered people have been playing a hiding game, appearing in town one day, wearing a mask, and leaving when discovery was imminent. We would never tell anyone who we were, and so we were never really able to find one another. That's just now beginning to change.

See, when we walk into a restaurant and we see another transsexual person, we look the other way, we pretend we don't exist. There's no sly smile, no secret wink, signal, or handshake. Not yet. We still quake in solitude at

the prospect of recognition, even if that soli-
tude is in the company of our own kind.

Silence = Death
—A̲C̲T̲-U̲P̲ S̲L̲O̲G̲A̲N̲

SILENCE OF THE MEEK-AS-LAMBS

Simply saying "Come out, come out, wherever you are," is not going to bring the multitudes of transgendered people out into the open. Before saying that coming out is an option (and I believe it's an inevitable step, one we're all going to have to take at some time), it's necessary to get transgendered people talking with one another. The first step in coming out in the world is to come out to our own kind.

Before I dealt with my gender change, I had gold card membership in the dominant culture. To all appearances, I was a straight, white, able-bodied, middle-class male. I fought so hard against being transsexual because I heard all the teasing and jokes in the locker rooms. I saw people shudder or giggle when they'd talk about Renee Richards or Christine Jorgensen. I was all too aware of the disgust people were going through when *Playboy* published its interview with Wendy Carlos. I watched Caroline Cossey (Tula) get dragged through the mud of the press on two continents. The lesson was there time after time. Of course we were silent.

In the summer of 1969, I drove across Canada and the United States, living out of my Volkswagen station wagon that I'd named Mad John after my acting teacher. I was a hippie boy, hair down past my shoulders and dressed very colorfully: beads, headband, bellbottoms. I pulled into a state park in South Dakota to camp for the night. Some good ol' boys came up to my campsite and began the usual "Hey, girl" comments. I ignored them, and they eventually went away. Later that night, I woke up in my sleeping bag with a hand on my chest and a knife in front of my face. "Maybe we wanna fuck you, girl," is what this guy said. He brought the knife down to my face—I could feel how cold and sharp it was. "Maybe you oughta get outa here before we fuck you and beat the shit outa you." Then I was alone in the dark with only the sound of the wind in the trees. I packed up camp and left.

The following summer, I traveled across country again, this time in a VW mini-bus, but I stuck to more populated areas: I'd learned. Too many transgendered people don't get off that easy.

A less visible reason for the silence of the transgendered hinges on the fact that transsexuality in this culture is considered an illness, and an illness that can only be cured by silence.

Here's how this one works: we're taught that we are literally sick, that we have an illness that can be diagnosed and maybe cured. As a result of the medicalization of our condition, transsexuals must see therapists in order to receive the medical seal of approval required to proceed with any gender reassignment surgery. Now, once we get to the doctor, we're told we'll be cured if we become members of one gender or another. We're told not to divulge our transsexual status, except in select cases requiring intimacy. Isn't that amazing? Transsexuals presenting themselves for therapy in this culture are channeled through a system which labels them as having a disease (transsexuality) for which the therapy is to lie, hide, or otherwise remain silent.

> *I was told by several counselors and a number of transgendered peers that I would need to invent a past for myself as a little girl, that I'd have to make up incidents of my girl childhood; that I'd have to say things like "When I was a little girl. . . . " I never was a little girl; I'd lied all my life to be the boy, the man that I'd known myself **not** to be. Here I was, taking a giant step toward personal integrity by entering therapy with the truth and self-acknowledgment that I was a transsexual, and I was told, "Don't **tell** anyone you're transsexual."*

Transsexuality is the only condition for which the therapy is to lie. This therapeutic lie is one reason we haven't been saying too much about ourselves and our lives and our experience of gender; we're not allowed, in therapy, the right to think of ourselves as transsexual.

> *This was where a different kind of therapy might have helped me. Perhaps if I hadn't spent so much time thinking and talking about being a woman, and perhaps if the psychiatrist who examined me had spent less time focusing on those aspects of my life which could never be changed by surgery, I would have had more opportunity to think about myself as a transsexual. It was exposure to the press that forced me to talk about my transsexuality, and it was a painful way to have to learn to do so.*
>
> —CAROLINE COSSEY, My Story, 1992

Another reason for the silence of transsexuals is the mythology of the transgender subculture. Two or more transsexuals together, goes the myth, can be read more easily *as* transsexual—so they don't pass. I don't think that's it.

> *I think transsexuals keep away from each other because we threaten the hell out of one another.*

Each of us, transsexual and non-transsexual, develop a view of the world as we grow up—a view that validates our existence, gives us a reason for being, a justification for the nuttinesses that each of us might have. Most non-transsexuals have cultural norms on which to pin their world view, broadcast by magazines, television, cinema, electronic bulletin boards, and the continually growing list of communications environments.

Since transsexuals in this culture are neither fairly nor accurately represented in the media, nor championed by a community, we develop our world views in solitude. Alone, we figure out why we're in the world the way we are. The literature to date on the transgender experience does not help us to establish a truly transgender world view in concert with other transgender people, because virtually all the books and theories about gender and transsexuality to date have been written by non-transsexuals who, no matter how well-intentioned, are each trying to figure out how to make us fit into *their* world view. Transgendered people learn to explain gender to themselves from a very early age.

> *When I was ten or eleven years old, I used to play alone in the basement, way back in the corner where no one would come along to disturb me. There was an old chair there to which I attached all manner of wires and boxes and dials: it was my gender-change machine. I would sit in that chair and twist the dials, and—presto—I was off on an adventure in my mind as a little girl, usually some budding dykelet like Nancy Drew or Pippi Longstocking.*

Most transsexuals opt for the theory that there are men and women and no inbetween ground: the agreed-upon gender system. That's what I did—I just knew I had to be one or the other—so, in my world view, I saw myself as a mistake: some*thing* that needed to be fixed and then placed neatly into one of the categories.

> *There are some wonderfully subtle differences in the world views developed by individual transsexuals. Talk to a few transgendered people and see how beautifully textured the normally drab concept of gender can become.*

We bring our very personal explanations for our existence into contact with other transsexuals who have been spending *their* lives constructing their *own* reasons for existence. If, when we meet, our world views differ radically enough, we wind up threatening each other's basic understanding of the world—we threaten each other. So we'd rather not meet, we'd rather not talk. At this writing, that's starting to change. Transsexuals and other transgendered people are finally sitting down, taking stock, comparing notes—and it's the dominant culture that's coming up short. Some of us are beginning to actually like ourselves and each other for the blend we are. Many of us are beginning to express our discontent with a culture that wants us silent.

This Western culture of ours tends to sacrifice the full range of experience to a lower common denominator that's acceptable to more people; we end up with McDonald's instead of real food, Holiday Inns instead of homes, and **USA Today** *instead of news and cultural analysis. And we do that with the rest of our lives.*

Our spirits are full of possibilities, yet we tie ourselves down to socially-prescribed names and categories so we're acceptable to more people. We take on identities that no one has to think about, and that's probably how we become and why we remain men and women.

The first step in liberating ourselves from this meek-as-lambs culturally-imposed silence is for transgendered people to begin talking with each other, asking each other sincere questions, and listening intently.

MYTHS AND MYTH-CONCEPTIONS

A transgender subculture is at this writing developing, and it's subsequently giving rise to new folk tales and traditions of gender fluidity and ambiguity. For example:

» *We are the chosen people.*

This is the point of view of many groups, and is not the sole property of the transgendered. This point of view makes me nervous, and I usually disassociate myself from any group whose members proclaim some unique kinship to, or favored station with, some higher power.

» *We are normal men and women.*

Is there such a thing as a normal man or woman? I have this idea that there are only people who are fluidly-gendered, and that the norm is that most of these people continually struggle to maintain the illusion that they are one gender or another. So if someone goes through a gender change and then struggles to maintain a (new) rigid gender, I guess that does make them normal. That's the only way I can see the grounding to this myth.

» *We are better men or women than men born men or women born women, because we had to work at it.*

I don't know about this one—I think everyone has to work at being a man or a woman.

Transgendered people are probably more aware of doing the work, that's all. The concept of some nebulously "better" class of people is not an idea of love and inclusion, but an idea of oppression.

» *We have an incurable disease.*

No, we don't.

» *We are trapped in the wrong body.*

I understand that many people may explain their preoperative transgendered lives in this way, but I'll bet that it's more likely an unfortunate metaphor that conveniently conforms to cultural expectations, rather than an honest reflection of our transgendered feelings. As a people, we're short on metaphors, any metaphors, and when we find one that people understand, we stop looking. It's time for transgendered people to look for new metaphors—new ways of communicating our lives to people who are traditionally gendered.

» *We are the most put-upon of people.*

I think this statement is sadly arrogant, and an admission of social ignorance. I heard this myth from a preoperative white, middle-class, male-to-female transsexual who is a medical doctor. I guess she hadn't heard too much about teenage African-American mothers on crack, or some other more "put-upon" people. Transsexuals get a lot of grief from nearly every level of this hierarchical culture, it's true, but it's important to maintain some perspective.

» *That there is a transgender community.*

*Someone asked me if the transgendered community is like the lesbian/gay communities. I said no, because the lesbian/gay communities are based on who one relates to, whereas the transgendered experience is different: it's about identity—relating to oneself. It's more an inward thing. When you have people together with **those** issues, the group dynamic is inherently very different.*
—DAVID HARRISON, *in conversation with the author, 1993*

We're at the beginning stages of a transgender community, but, at this writing, there are still only small groups of people who live out different aspects of gender. I'm extremely interested in seeing what develops, taking into account Harrison's analogy of personal and group dynamics. Just now, pockets of resistance to social oppression are forming, most often in conjunction with various gay and lesbian communities.

I *have* found an underground of male-to-female gender outlaws which already has its own unspoken hierarchy, definable from whatever shoes you happen to be standing in—high heels or Reeboks.

> **Post-operative transsexuals** *(those transsexuals who've had genital surgery and live fully in the role of another gender) look down on:*
>
> **Pre-operative transsexuals** *(those who are living full or part time in another gender, but who've not yet had their genital surgery) who in turn look down on:*
>
> **Transgenders** *(people living in another gender identity, but who have little or no intention of having genital surgery) who can't abide:*
>
> **She-Males** *(a she-male friend of mine described herself as "tits, big hair, lots of make-up, and a dick") who snub the:*
>
> **Drag Queens** *(gay men who on occasion dress in varying parodies of women) who laugh about the:*
>
> **Out Transvestites** *(usually heterosexual men who dress as they think women dress, and who are out in the open about doing that) who pity the:*
>
> **Closet Cases** *(transvestites who hide their cross-dressing) who mock the post-op transsexuals.*

The female-to-male groups, as well as some working-class transgender clubs that I've been associated with, seem to be more inclusive in their membership and attendance requirements than the mostly middle-class, mostly white examples cited above, and they're also less hierarchical in both club procedure and ways of relating to one another. Very few groups exist, however, that encompass the full rainbow that is gender outlawism, and sadly, groups still divide along the lines of male-to-female and female-to-male gender outlaws.

> *We are all longing to go home to some place we have never been—a place, half-remembered, and half-envisioned we can only catch glimpses of from time to time. Community. Somewhere, there are people to whom we can speak with passion without having the words catch in our throats. Somewhere a circle of hands will open to receive us, eyes will light up as we enter, voices will celebrate with us whenever we come into our own power. Community*

means strength that joins our strength to do the work that needs to be done. Arms to hold us when we falter. A circle of healing. A circle of friends. Someplace where we can be free.

—STARHAWK,
Dreaming the Dark: Magic, Sex, and Politics, 1982

*I'd like to be a member of a community some day. One of the reasons I didn't go through with my gender change for such a long time was the certain knowledge that I would be an outsider. All the categories of transgender find a common ground in that they each break one or more of the rules of gender: what we have in common is that we are gender outlaws, every one of us. To attempt to divide us into rigid categories ("You're a transvestite, and **you're** a drag queen, and **you're** a she-male, and on and on and on) is like trying to apply the laws of solids to the state of fluids: it's our fluidity that keeps us in touch with each other. It's our fluidity and the principles that attend that constant state of flux that could create an innovative and inclusive transgender community.*

I really *would* like to be a member of a community, but until there's one that's based on the principle of constant change, the membership would involve more rules, and the rules that exist around the subject of gender are not rules I want to obey.

PART FOUR

Making a Living: Women, Work, and Achievement

A powerful mythology has influenced thinking about women, work, and achievement. Success, it says, is solely a matter of individual hard work and will power; if women have not achieved as much as men, it is because too many of them lack ambition, fail to set clear career goals in advance, or let other things (such as marriage and family) interfere with getting ahead. A variation on the theme is that perhaps in the past women have been discriminated against or otherwise prevented from reaching their full potential, but today, no barriers exist.

The diverse group of women who speak about their work here tell us different stories. Perhaps the most important thread that links them is the importance of social structures in the experience of work. No achiever stands alone; her or his success takes place in a social environment that helps or hinders—usually a complex mixture of both. And the social context of women and people of color has been very different from that of white men.

But these women are far from being passive victims of society. Active agency within so-cietal constraints is expressed in each of their lives. A good place to look is in their solutions to the "balancing act." How do these women provide the money their families need, as well as foster their own growth and development, while remaining primarily responsible for caring for others? How are they willing to change direction when their path is blocked?

Women's work lives have been characterized by discontinuity, movement in spurts from one goal to another, and serendipity, taking advantage of unexpected opportunities. When confronted by roadblocks, these women often "zig-zagged" their way around them. How do such zig-zag work lives compare with more straightforward "male" careers? Do you see any advantages to them?

When Marcelle Williams began interviewing Punjabi (South Indian) women in their homes, others—husbands, grown children—kept jumping in to speak for them. Their behavior reinforced the stereotypes of Indian women as passive and dependent, yet these women handle the "double day" of paid work and family work with great skill. Mrs. Singh found a job despite her inability to speak English and then began to "network" to help her relatives migrate to this country. How did she use covert influence strategies at work to make her job easier? How did she use her paid work to increase her power at home?

Virtually all women juggle paid work and family responsibilities, but how they do it is structured by their social class. In Shellee Colen's study of West Indian women working as housekeepers and "nannies" for wealthy white families, the built-in contradictions of these two kinds of work become sharply visible. Like African American slave women before them, these women are expected to nurture the children of their employers above their own families. But are they really part of the white family they work for? What social markers do their employers use to reinforce class and power differences? What do the West Indian women want most of all from their employers? Why are the two groups of husbands invisible in these accounts? Are there ways in which women can support each other across lines of class and color? Look for examples in the housekeepers' stories.

Rosario Ceballo describes herself as a woman of color brought up in a working-class, immigrant family. She wrote her case study of Mary, an African American social worker, as part of a graduate class in the psychology of women. It is easy to see how she was drawn to Mary, whose strength and resilience helped her to overcome racial and economic oppression. What relationships did Mary seek out to provide role modeling, financial support, and mentoring? How was she affected by the demands of women's traditional role as caretaker, and how did she sidestep that role later on? What did Mary contribute to and gain from the Civil Rights Movement and the Women's Movement? Why do you think she reacted to these two social movements differently?

The story of Nora, one of the participants in Lewis Terman's famous study of gifted children, reminds us of how women's intelligence has been seen as causing trouble for themselves and others. Carol Tomlinson-Keasey, a developmental psychologist, shows how Nora "muted" and "buffered" her intellect to fit the constraints set by her father, her husbands, and her era. How was she affected by demands to fill women's traditional roles as caretaker for others and sex object? In what places and people did she find sanctuary from these demands? Do you think Nora ever achieved her full potential? Is there evidence that young women today experience some of the same pressures—or are women's minds no longer a "dirty little secret?"

Janice Yoder, a white woman, a feminist with a Ph.D., and a visiting professor at a U.S. military academy, might seem to have had all the advantages of race, class, and education. As a social psychologist, she had sophisticated analytical tools to interpret her experiences. Yet faced with an extreme version of tokenism as one of a tiny minority of women at the academy, she quickly began to suffer the diminished self-esteem, withdrawal, and depression that are the hallmarks of oppression.

Yoder's experience shows us that even the strongest and most privileged woman can be adversely affected by social isolation, harassment, and a woman-hating environment. In this situation, was quitting her job a failure or a creative "zig-zag?" How does she use the concepts and language of psychology to gain some distance from her pain? Do you think that writing her own story in a psychological journal contributes to empowering herself and others?

Think back over the work experiences of the women in these accounts. For some, work is repetitive, boring, even dangerous. Others work long hours without medical benefits or opportunities for advancement. They may experience discrimination and harassment. Some earn less than minimum wage—and no one ever claims to be particularly well-paid!

Now imagine turning on your TV and seeing the glittering images of "career women" float by. Our last selection in this section is by Susan Douglas, a professor of media studies. With wit and humor, she describes media portrayals of working mothers. Her style will make you laugh, but her message is serious: the images of glamorous careers and no-sweat family life "burrow into you," making real women feel perpetually inadequate.

Yet Douglas refuses to see women as passive victims of the media. How do myth-busters such as Roseanne and Murphy Brown influence the women who view them? Do you agree with Douglas when she argues that we women are skeptical viewers who know a media lie when we see one? Douglas points out that, along with the glittering images, the media sometimes bring us a strong dose of truth—as when Anita Hill exploded the myth that the barriers to women's achievement are all in the past.

A common theme in all these stories is women's striving to achieve meaningful work lives despite societal constraints. By exercising power within the limits set for them, and by expanding those limits, they make their own definitions of work and accomplishment. Perhaps they are "making a living" in more ways than one.

Marcelle Williams

Ladies on the Line: Punjabi Cannery Workers in Central California*

"Well, those ladies on the lines, they have it pretty easy," Mr. Singh replied when I asked Mrs. Singh about her job as a cannery worker. Mrs. Singh's husband continued to answer for her: "And now that she has seniority, you know, she can sit around and drink tea or something like that." While I tried to talk to Mrs. Singh about her life and work at a nearby food-processing plant, she moved industriously around the kitchen, preparing snacks for her two little granddaughters and me. As a guest in their home, an old farmhouse that they had recently refurbished, I was ushered into the formal living room where I sat drinking tea with Mr. Singh, a married daughter who was visiting, and an un-married, teen-age daughter. Although the entire family was very gracious and hospitable, whenever I asked Mrs. Singh questions about herself, the other members present frequently answered instead.

This situation did not occur only with this family. In fact, it happened over and over again during my interviews with Punjabi Sikh women who work in the California canning industry. Even though I requested to speak directly with the women, they were often busy in the kitchen while their family members spoke for them.[1]

At first glance my interviews seem to support previous research which stereotypes Asian Indian women as restricted to the domestic sphere of home and hearth, passive and unable to speak for themselves. In a review of the few studies of South Asian immigrant women, Pratibha Parmar states that they usually are depicted as "limited to the kitchen, the children and the religious rituals, and . . . emotionally and economically dependent upon their hus-bands."

However, my interviews with Punjabi cannery workers contradict the commonly held view that Indian immigrant women are economically depen-dent on men and do not work outside of the home. At the very least, my study

*Complete citations to all the articles referred to in this reading can be found in Asian Women United of California (1989). *Making Waves*. Boston: Beacon Press.

documents that these women work hard *outside* as well as *inside* the home, in both the public and the private realms. Very rarely, whether at work or home, did they "sit around and drink tea." Moreover, a closer examination of my interviews shows that these women are extremely active and that their actions may speak more loudly than their apparent lack of words.

I intend to illustrate in this essay that the Punjabi women with whom I talked are anything but passive, and that they actively influence and interlink the public sphere of work and the private sphere of family. Indeed, they are often able to gain the upper hand by manipulating the stereotypic images of their supposed domesticity, passivity, and inarticulateness.[2]

THE SINGHS ARRIVE IN CALIFORNIA

In order to convey the idea that Punjabi women are active in both the workplace and the home and to show the extent to which the two realms overlap, this essay will focus on one particular woman, Mrs. Singh, her work, and her family. I met Mrs. Singh and her family during the spring of 1985, when I began interviewing Indian immigrant women who worked in the fruit and vegetable canneries of Stanislaus County in central California. Mrs. Singh knew of approximately one hundred Punjabi Sikhs who worked as seasonal laborers at a specific plant in Modesto run by Tri/Valley Growers, Inc. While I spoke with some of the women who worked at this cannery, and to women from other food processing plants, I will concentrate on Mrs. Singh since her experiences are representative, for the most part, of the larger group of Punjabi women. When her life history appears atypical, however, I will note this and provide illustrative material from other sources.

Mrs. Singh and her husband, like 30 to 40 percent of the 59,674 Asian Indians currently in California, belong to the Sikh religion, which predominates in the state of Punjab in India. Mr. Singh left the Jullundur district in the Punjab in 1971 and settled with his sister's family north of Sacramento, in the Marysville-Yuba City area, which has had a sizable Punjabi Sikh population since the early 1900s. Mrs. Singh, also born and raised in the Jullundur district where she married her husband in 1958 at the age of seventeen, followed him to America a year later with their four children.

Many scholars have traced the historical development of the Punjabi community in rural California and have commented on its inception as a bachelor group of agricultural laborers. Mr. Singh was able to immigrate because of his relationship to this earlier group through his sister. She could sponsor her brother because she had married a man whose father had entered California as a farm worker. In turn, after immigrating as Mr. Singh's wife, Mrs. Singh became a United States citizen as soon as possible so that she could sponsor the entry of her own brothers and sisters.

So, contrary to the studies of Asian Indian immigrant women that stress their dependent status and imply that they migrate only because of men, Mrs. Singh, like her sister-in-law and many other women before her, served as a vital link in the immigration cycle—men bringing over women relatives who then bring their own relatives. Unlike the usual portrayal of Asian Indian women, Mrs. Singh took an active role in migration strategies.[3]

In their search for land and new opportunities, the Singhs, like many of the Sikhs in northern California, moved southward into Stanislaus County. In 1973, Mr. and Mrs. Singh left his sister's ranch, where they had worked picking peaches and tending the orchard, and moved to Stanislaus County, which is located about sixty miles south of Sacramento near the middle of the Central Valley. They settled on the outskirts of Modesto, the largest city in the county, in the hopes of acquiring some orchard land of their own.

193

MARCELLE WILLIAMS
*Ladies on the Line:
Punjabi Cannery
Workers in Central
California*

Although there is no official estimate of the size of the Punjabi community, the 1980 census calculates a total Asian Indian population of only 1,150 out of 293,400 people in the county. This figure may be a gross underestimation, however. Based on the Sikh temples in the area and the estimated number of families they each serve, there appear to be almost a thousand Punjabi Sikhs alone. Asian Indians other than Punjabi Sikhs reside in the county—they are primarily from the northern states, but probably every state in India is represented, as well as there being some Indians from Fiji, England, and Africa. And among them there is a fairly well-defined residential and class division. The Punjabi Sikhs tend to live in the smaller towns and more rural areas, in Turlock, Ceres, Patterson, Hughson, Denair, and Delhi; and they tend to be working-class, waged workers who also own or lease a little land. In contrast, the other Asian Indians seem to reside more often within the city of Modesto and to work in business or are professionals.[4]

Soon after they settled in Stanislaus County, the Singhs sought gainful employment. As one of the state's top ten producing agricultural counties, the county has well over three hundred food processing, packing, and distributing companies. Mr. Singh, who had been a taxi driver in India, found a year-round job as a forklift driver for a large food processing plant. Mrs. Singh worked in the fields picking various crops, sometimes along with the children of the family.

Just months after the Singhs moved into the area, Mrs. Singh found a seasonal job as an assembly line worker for Tri/Valley Growers, Inc. Fortunately Mrs. Singh was at the right place at the right time: she began working at Tri/Valley Plant 7, the world's largest "supercannery," soon after the company opened it and began expanding its holdings in Stanislaus County.

Since then, Tri/Valley Growers, a cooperative association of several hundred farming operations, has grown until it is now the largest fruit and vegetable processor in the state. This development is unfortunate for cannery workers at other plants, though, because Tri/Valley's growth has been related to an industry "shakedown" and merger mania that have resulted in numerous plant closures and shutdowns.[5]

WORKING AT THE CANNERY

When asked how she got her job at Tri/Valley, Mrs. Singh said that she "just went down to the [plant] office, filled out an application, and that was it." Unlike most of the other cannery workers with whom I spoke, she did not hear about, or get her job, through word-of-mouth since she was among the first Punjabis hired. Another Punjabi woman who was hired at Tri/Valley explained:

Okay, you just talk to your friends and family about where they work, and you usually hear who is hiring. You know from talking to them if they [the companies] are any good to work for. You know, Tri/Valley is usually good to work for, and Del Monte is not so good. It used to be that if you knew the floorlady or the foreman, you could tell them that so-and-so, your brother, needs a job and he's a good worker, and he'd get on. I don't think it's like that anymore.

Through word-of-mouth communication, it is not uncommon for relatively large numbers of Indian immigrants, often related by kinship and friendship, to work together at the same plant. Of course, this kind of networking also occurs with groups other than Asian Indians and, as a result, many canneries have clusters of particular ethnic groups. One nut processing plant in Modesto, for example, has a majority of Assyrian immigrant employees; another plant has mostly Chicanos; a third has mostly "Okies." Most plants, though, like Tri/Valley's Plant 7, have a combination of several ethnic groups.

There are many Punjabi Sikhs employed by Tri/Valley Growers, but it is difficult to know the exact percentage because the company does not keep any kind of tally of their Indian immigrant employees. Based on my discussion with the workers there, I estimate that Punjabis make up about 2 percent of the work force. According to company records for 1984, over half of this labor force is Hispanic (51.26 percent), while the rest is comprised of almost 3 percent black, 5 percent "Asian" (many of whom are Southeast Asian refugees), and the remainder unspecified (presumably white).[6]

Although being 2 percent of the Tri/Valley work force may not seem numerically significant, it is socially significant in the daily lives of the Punjabi Sikhs who work there. They interact in a very close-knit social world composed of kith and kin with whom they work, at the height of the canning season, for up to ten hours a day, and with whom they may then visit afterwards. An Anglo cannery worker with whom I talked complained about the Punjabi worker's social habits:

Yeah, they're really very clannish. You know, they sit together during breaks, and they usually manage to work together on the lines or wherever. The women are really the worst about sticking to themselves and sitting in gangs. It really bugs me when you walk past them, and they start giggling and talking about you in their language, you know, Indian or whatever it is. I don't know, it sort of sounds like Spanish.

As this comment inadvertently recognizes, the social world of the Punjabi Sikh women—who make up a little more than half of all the Sikh cannery workers—may be even more closely knit because they often do not speak English fluently. Quite often the Punjabi women state explicitly that they do cannery work because English language skills are not crucial in most of the work. Mrs. Singh points out that when Tri/Valley hired her in the early 1970s, when their business was booming, the hiring personnel were not interested in whether or not she spoke English.

I just filled out the application, and they asked me some questions. I just said "yes" to everything that they asked me; I didn't even know what they were asking. A couple of times when I said "yes," they looked at me kind of funny, so I guess I should've said "no" then. They didn't care that I didn't know the language.[7]

195

MARCELLE WILLIAMS
Ladies on the Line:
Punjabi Cannery
Workers in Central
California

The Punjabi Sikh women who work at the canneries share more than a small social world and the inability to speak English fluently; they share other cultural characteristics as well. Like Mrs. Singh, most of them immigrated to California during the 1970s from either the Jullundur or Ludhiana districts of the Punjab, and since their arrival most of them have been involved in agribusiness as pickers, packers, cannery workers, and small-scale farmers. Most were hired by Tri/Valley or by other canneries during the 1970s, and consequently have ten or more years of seniority.

The vast majority of the Punjabi Sikh women who work in the cannery are middle-aged. This fact is due to immigration cycles and hiring patterns in the canning industry resulting from "boom and bust" trends since World War II. As Mrs. Singh's daughter emphasized, most of the cannery workers, including her mother, are in their forties and fifties because "only the first ladies that came over here, the very first like them, you know, they're the only ones that work there [at the cannery]. But like the children, they don't work there."

In addition to sharing similar backgrounds and characteristics, most of the Punjabi Sikh women share similar work at the canneries. Most of them work in the lower paying jobs on the assembly lines or conveyor belts in preparation and canning, two of the three departments—preparation, canning, and warehouse—at the cannery.

The preparation department is made up almost exclusively of women and consists of numerous conveyor belts that move the produce from the trucks, through a lye solution that peels it, and ultimately into machines that fill the cans. In the canning department the cans move through seamer and cook machines, which are tended by both women and men. After the cans have been filled, seamed, and cooked, they proceed to the warehouse area where almost only men work to pack, store, and later distribute the canned goods. In most of the departments, but especially in the preparation and canning departments, the work is subdivided into minute single tasks. Women on the lines, for example, grade the produce by standing alongside the belt and tossing away the unsuitable fruit, hour after hour, day after day.

Not only is work in the cannery monotonous, it is also usually uncomfortable and sometimes dangerous. The noise level is so high that it is practically impossible to carry on a conversation in many of the work areas, so workers have developed a sign language instead. The stench of the processed food is at times overpowering and causes the nausea that most line workers experience at one time or another. One woman working at a cannery summed it up: "I don't like the monotony of the belt. I hate standing all day. It's noisy; it gives me a headache. The line makes me dizzy, and sometimes I get sick." Also workers sometimes become ill because of the disorientation from working the "swing" (usually 2:00 to 10:00 P.M.) or the "graveyard" (usually 10:00 P.M. to 6:00 A.M.) shift.

Overall these conditions can be very harsh, especially during the peak part of the season—July to mid-September—when workers may put in as many as ten hours a day, with only two twelve-minute breaks and a half-hour lunch, six or seven days a week. In addition, conditions at the cannery can be dangerous. Mrs. Singh, along with most other cannery workers, recounted stories of various cannery accidents, such as the story of a woman's finger being severed by the machinery and then "canned" with the peaches.[8]

Despite the implementation of affirmative action policies, cannery work is still difficult for women because of the de facto sex segregation of the work that keeps women in the lower-paying, lower-bracket jobs in the preparation and canning departments, which are more seasonal, more monotonous, and more strictly supervised. Although there are not official distinctions made between "male" and "female" jobs or their pay scales, the job brackets—eight levels that are hierarchically ranked according to the job description and wages—are divided by sex. On the whole, men occupy the upper brackets, women the lower. As of 1984, after a decade of reform measures, women at Tri/Valley still made up 71.38 percent of the less-skilled, lower-paying, lower job brackets.

For the Punjabi women, this situation of sex discrimination is aggravated by racial or ethnic discrimination. Affirmative action measures have not changed the fact that cannery work is also ethnically segregated, with people of color occupying the lower job brackets. After working at the cannery for thirteen years, Mrs. Singh, like all of the other Punjabi women, is still a seasonal worker. She is a Bracket Five worker and, as of last year, was finally moved off the lines to a higher level job running a seamer machine. Out of all the Punjabi women working at Tri/Valley, there are only two who have been able to reach even lower-ranking supervisory positions.

Although Mrs. Singh did not complain about discrimination at the cannery, many other workers have. In another study, a Chicana testified: "Discrimination is blatant. If you're white, or know the bosses, you last maybe a week on the lines. If you're brown or a woman, you work for years and never get promoted."[9]

Given the harsh conditions at work and the discrimination that exacerbates them, why do Punjabi Sikh women continue to work in the canneries? Aside from the more obvious reasons, their previous experience in agribusiness, their language limitations, and a competitive labor market, the Punjabi women I spoke with insisted that they actively sought out cannery work because it suited their purposes: to provide more income for their families while fulfilling their domestic roles as wives and mothers.

With seasonal cannery work lasting four or five months and then unemployment benefits the remainder of the year, Punjabi women earn up to a third of the family's income and yet can also be around the house as much as possible. In a sense, they use to their own advantage the cannery management's notion that they are expendable, secondary workers, a reserve army of labor.

WORK AND THE FAMILY

The key to understanding why Punjabi women work is to know that they do not view work and the family as incompatible, dichotomized spheres. According to most Punjabi women, they gain prestige from participating in both spheres, and as it happens, these very spheres overlap anyway. As Mrs. Singh laughingly said, "My work is sort of my family, you know, with all my relatives and friends there; and, of course, my family is my work."

Nearly all the Punjabi women emphasize that they are wage workers for their families' economic benefit. I heard over and over again, "It is good for Indian ladies from good families to work here. You see, everybody works because the pay is good, and it's good for the families." Punjabi families encourage every able-bodied adult to help finance the family goal of purchasing a small plot of orchard land. The women in the families are able to aid in this endeavor by working at the canneries, and they often can secure cannery jobs for other family members too. For example, Mrs. Singh was able to refer both her brother and her husband to Tri/Valley where both took on seasonal work to supplement their year-round jobs.

It is interesting to note that the women claimed they worked at the cannery in order to contribute to the welfare of their families, thereby fulfilling their domestic obligations. Essentially, they are legitimizing their departure from traditional domesticity, by saying their entry into the workplace is for domestic reasons. While these women are undoubtedly working outside of their homes for economic reasons, they are also hoping, according to what I learned in my interviews, to change their traditional roles within the family. They use their stereotypic image of devoted domesticity to justify becoming wage earners, but at the same time actually gain more control and decision-making power within the household. Many Punjabi women told anecdotes about their increased power in the family. One woman said with great satisfaction, "Now my husband, he listens to me when I say something; when I want to buy something, I do; and when I want to go in the car, I go." Although the family as a whole usually makes the decisions about where a family member will work, Mrs. Singh showed that she could break precedent and decide herself when to quit a job:

> I worked at another plant once, and they gave me a "man's" job. It was cutting this turkey into three pieces; it [the belt] was too fast and [the work was] too hard. I was the only woman working there. I worked hard all day to show that I could do it, that I could do a "man's" job. But I quit the next day 'cause it was too hard. It was too much work, and I didn't like it.

Other Punjabi women told of using their stereotypic image as passive and inarticulate workers to avoid doing certain jobs at the cannery. For instance, since the Punjabi women cannery workers form a close-knit social group at work, they sometimes do not want to leave the lines where that group interacts the most. One woman explained: "I work very hard, but I don't want to move away from the lines, from the belt, you know, 'cause that's where my friends are. So, I don't act all gung ho when the floorlady comes by and says there's a spot for someone on the filler machines or something." Another woman who usually worked the seamer machines resisted the authority of the supervisors in this small but effective way: "When a floorlady I don't like brings over someone and tells me to train them, you know, on my machine, I act like I don't understand her. I speak Punjabi back to her and act like I don't understand English. That way I don't have to fool with them." Someone else related that sometimes when she doesn't want to do a particular job, clean-up for instance, she says, "Okay, okay," and then just stands around and chats with her friends. When the supervisor chides her, she acts as though she doesn't understand what the supervisor wants her to do and says, "No English."

These women indicated to me that they were satisfied with working at the cannery, which, after all, was better than doing farm work. They were happy at

197

MARCELLE WILLIAMS
*Ladies on the Line:
Punjabi Cannery
Workers in Central
California*

being able to contribute to their families' income and fulfill domestic duties, while simultaneously being able to change their families' expectations of them. In order to do this, the women often used the traditional stereotype of their being domestic to their advantage. In the workplace, they also sometimes manipulated the stereotypes about passivity and inarticulateness to do what they wanted versus what their supervisors told them to do. In talking about their work and family experiences, it was evident that they sometimes said little or, even more often, said what fit their stereotypic image as domestic, passive, and inarticulate women. However, these statements sometimes obscured what was really happening in their lives. The actions of the women, these Punjabi Sikh "ladies on the lines," may well speak more loudly than their words.

Shellee Colen

"With Respect and Feelings"

Voices of West Indian Child Care and Domestic Workers in New York City

I'm not looking for them to shower us down with money, with clothes, but with a little respect and feelings. You know because they want full respect from us and at the same time they want to treat us like nothing. . . . A lot of West Indians are very insulted, but we do it because we have no choice.

    —JOYCE MILLER,[1] *a thirty-one-year-old Jamaican woman in Brooklyn, discussed her*
           past experiences as a domestic and child care worker in the New York City area.

It was a situation I resented. They had hampers and stuff like that, but when they undressed, they took [off] their clothes, they just walked out of them and left them on the bathroom floor. And I'd had enough. One Monday morning, I walked in and I said I'm not picking up any clothes today. (Laughs) I decided that I'm not picking up any CLOTHES today. . . . One day I went on strike and she (the employer) said, "Well this is what the job requires and if you're going to hold the job, it's part. . . ." I didn't do it that day but the next day I [picked them up]. . . . Her argument is that she has always picked up after her husband and that's the way he is and she accepted him like that. Since she doesn't want to pick . . . up, I'm sure she hires somebody who will pick . . . up for her.

    —MONICA COOPER, *a twenty-seven-year-old former domestic worker from Jamaica,*
           talked about an interchange with her suburban employer.

[This article is for the West Indian women who generously gave of their limited time to share parts of their lives with me. For the thought and care they took in relating their experiences and for their patience with the whole process, I am deeply grateful. For creating this book and for her enthusiasm and editorial assistance, I want to express my gratitude to Johnnetta Cole. For her constant support and her editorial suggestions on an earlier draft of this article I thank Rayna Rapp. The article has benefitted from editorial suggestions by Annick Piant and from comments by Mindie Lazarus-Black, Helen Evers, Deborah D. Samuels, and Michael Landy made on an early draft of a related article. Copyright © 1985 Shellee Colen.]

Whether or not the employer in the second incident resembles the 1980s media image of the working woman, professional, in skirt and tie, briefcase in hand, rushing from her apartment in a gentrified New York neighborhood or that of the affluent "housewife" giving parting instructions over her shoulder about picking up the kids from school and preparing dinner as she runs to meet friends and "go shopping," most working women's experiences are very different from hers. Whatever the current media image of women who work, the world of women's work is generally low paid, dead end, and undervalued. Nowhere is this truer than private household domestic and child care work. Within a sexual division of labor that assigns child care and domestic work to all women, private household workers take over these responsibilities for some women for pay. Shunned by men, this work becomes multiply devalued as it is passed from one woman to another along class, racial, ethnic, and migration lines, within the cash nexus.[2]

In this article, ten West Indian women currently or previously employed as private household child care and domestic workers in the New York City area speak of their experiences as domestic workers, as migrants, and as mothers.[3] They tell of how and why they do domestic work, what relationships exist with their employers, and how they balance their own family and household responsibilities with wage work. At times their voices could be those of other domestic workers over the last hundred or more years.[4] Sometimes their voices resemble those of other recent women migrants to the United States who have found themselves in the service sector of the economy. At other times, they echo the experiences of other working mothers.

MIGRATION AND DOMESTIC WORK

I am their only source of support . . . I thought about how the children are getting big and I wasn't working for the greatest salary. And I was thinking that there would come a time when I could just barely support the kids. So I need to make more money. So I just thought about coming to America. Maybe I'll be able to do it there.

—JUDITH THOMAS, *a Vincentian mother of four,*
migrated in 1980 at twenty-nine years old.

Their responsibility for themselves, their children, or other kin motivates their migration. Though all but one (who had just completed high school) were employed prior to migration, some jobs were unsteady while others offered little chance for mobility. For most, wages were inadequate. They worked a range of jobs including primary school teaching, police work, clerical and administrative assistant work in government or the private sector, factory work, postal work, higglering (petty trading), and servicing the tourist industry. Most had not done domestic work before.

Like their relatives and friends before them,[5] these West Indian women migrate to "better themselves." In New York they seek "opportunity," in employment and in education, for themselves and their children.[6] They are drawn, as well, by the availability of basic consumer goods unaffordable at home and especially important to them as mothers.

In spite of economic pressures and the expectations to migrate to "better oneself," some women, like Janet Robinson and Dawn Adams, postpone migration in order to remain with their children. Janet Robinson waitressed, did factory work and six months of domestic work that paid "just a farthing," enough "to just get the baby milk and that's it." Refusing several previous offers because she wanted to "watch my daughter grow," in 1968, at thirty years old, she accepted an offer to go to New York to do domestic work and support her twelve-year-old daughter. Dawn Adams said she "always wanted to be there to bring up my daughters. I didn't really have any thought of migrating." But after several years of teaching, nurses' training, and four years on the police force, the lack of opportunities to advance, to make better use of her talents, and to better support her mother and daughters created pressure on her to migrate in 1981 at the age of thirty-two, reluctantly leaving her children and her mother.

While to be a good mother means to leave one's children and migrate, ironically, taking care of someone else's children is often their first job in New York, especially for those without permanent residence status, the green card. Legal entrance to and residence in the United States with permanent residence status is available primarily to those sponsored by close relatives or by employers at the time of migration. Only a few in this group had this option. Most entered with visitors' visas which they overstayed, becoming undocumented. To achieve their goals, including reunion with their children, they needed green cards. To get them, they turned to employer sponsorship in child care and domestic work, the main route for West Indian women (other than marriage to a permanent resident or a citizen, or sponsorship by certain closely related permanent residents or citizens). None knew of any West Indian woman (besides registered nurses, of whom there is a shortage in New York) who had been sponsored by an employer outside of domestic work.[7]

Learning to be "Maidish"

> This is not something I thought I would ever do for a living. If somebody had said to me "You're going to clean somebody else's house to make money," I'd say, "Come off it." I had an attitude about that but then after I really thought about it, I said if this is what I have to do, I'm going to make the best until the situation changes.

Monica Cooper spoke of her domestic work experience. She did general housekeeping and took care of two children for a suburban New Jersey family in which the husband owned a health care related business and the wife did not work outside the home. She describes her responsibilities:

> Everything. Meals, cooking, everything. Everything. And at that point [1976] I was making $80 a week [laughs] for 5 1/2 days, they call it. . . . [My] day off was Sunday and I had to be back by noon on Monday. . . . I decided to do it to get my sponsorship.

After three weeks on her first job here, Marguerite Andrews, a thirty-three-[year] old former school teacher supporting four children, spoke of her adjustment. Although she had an "understanding," "good" employer, becoming a domestic worker and moving from the relative autonomy and high status of teacher to a subordinate, if not subservient, position was difficult.

> I'm not yet really adjusted to it. . . . She's not bossy or anything like that. But within myself I figure I should be more, I can't explain. . . . I don't like to use the word "maidish," but I should put myself all out to do everything. But you know this will have to take some time.

At that same time, Marguerite Andrews related an incident that took place in St. Vincent when Marguerite herself employed a domestic worker. When one of Marguerite's sons left his dirty clothes in a trail on the floor instead of placing them in the hamper, her employee refused to pick them up and wash them. Marguerite's son ordered the worker to do so, saying that she was paid to clean up after him. Although Marguerite took to heart the domestic worker's criticism of her son's manners, at that time, she shared his definition of the job. When Marguerite told me the story, she noted how her perspective on domestic work had changed and said she hoped that she would never receive such treatment. Ironically, with a change in jobs to new employers who demanded greater subservience, she has since experienced similar encounters from the subordinate position which has broadened her understanding of hierarchy from below.

Marguerite left this last job in which she had hoped to initiate sponsorship proceedings because "it is not humanly possible to stick it." Like Marguerite, others assess whether they can tolerate a particular job for the two or more years of sponsorship. Judith Thomas similarly assessed a potential sponsor job and left amicably before the procedure was begun: "I knew that the sponsor wouldn't work out with her, I couldn't last that long." Her next employers sponsored her.

Living In and the Sponsor Job

Everyone described sponsor jobs as the "worst," especially those which are live-in. Sponsored jobs on a live-in basis greatly exacerbate problems structural to domestic work. Although some employers seek to avoid exploitation and some are unaware of the impact of their behavior on the worker, many take advantage of the sponsorship situation, the workers' vulnerability, and their lack of experience with codes of behavior here. Exploitation may involve long hours, abysmal pay, a heavy work load, and particular attitudes and behaviors exhibited toward the worker.

Joyce Miller worked at her live-in sponsor job from 1977 to 1981. The couple for whom she worked, on the edges of suburban New Jersey, owned a chain of clothing stores. The wife worked part-time in the business and devoted the rest of her time to shopping for antiques, decorating, attending cooking classes, entertaining, traveling, and participating in her children's school. Joyce worked sixteen hours or more a day, was on call twenty-four hours a day, seven days a week, caring for the large house and three children for $90 a week ($110 at the time she quit). When she took a day off to see her lawyer, that day was deducted from her salary.

> The working situation there [was] a lot of work. No breaks. I work sometimes till 11 o'clock at night . . . I get up early in the morning and I get up at night to tend the baby. I wash, I cook, I clean.

As Joyce began to get "enlightened" (her words) to her own exploitation, her employer became upset.

When Dawn Adams, who was at the time undocumented, quit a short-lived suburban job, her employers threatened to report her to the Immigration and Naturalization Service. Others told of similar intimidation that plays on undocumented West Indian women's sense of vulnerability. This itself is heightened by occurrences such as INS raids at the Port Authority bus terminal on Sunday nights and Monday mornings to "catch" undocumented domestic workers returning to suburban jobs from their day off.

Workers often felt trapped in sponsor jobs with no apparent end in sight. After four years in what was supposed to be her sponsor job, Monica Cooper got "restless and very depressed." She knew that her papers had passed the labor board but that her employers had said that they would not "bend over backwards" to help with her sponsorship.

> It started one week where I would just cry. Just cry period. And I was crying constantly for this week in question and Mrs. S., she would ask me what's the matter. Because I resented them but . . . I'd wipe my eyes and I'm smiling when they're around. But this week I couldn't do it anymore. I mean they'd go out and I'm there [alone] with the kids. It was like a total disadvantage. By the time I left there I was making $100 and I was with them for 4 1/2 years . . . And this week in question, I was just crying, and crying, crying. I couldn't tell her why I was crying. She said "Is it anything we did?" But . . . it was everything. By this time I could say it's all of you. But I told her no.

Soon after this tearful week, Monica Cooper retained a different lawyer, made new arrangements for her sponsorship (by a relative), and a few months later gave notice, quit, and found clerical work. In spite of the cost in money and time, some workers do quit unsatisfactory sponsor jobs and reinitiate the process with new employers.

Judith Thomas was sponsored by a woman who owned a cafe and whose husband worked in his family's textile business. She took care of their child and maintained their three-bedroom and three-bathroom apartment (though they hired someone else to do the "heavy" cleaning once a week). She remembered this experience:

> They just somehow figure because they're sponsoring you, they own you. And if they say jump, you should jump. And if they say sit, you should sit . . . when you start in at the beginning they tell you certain amount of . . . work and then as you go on they just keep on adding more and more. It was really a dedication. . . . I felt as if I wouldn't hold out. I couldn't make it. But then when I just think . . . that . . . I'd be better off staying here now and continuing, knowing that one day I'll get it all over with . . . And I think about my kids and just say regardless to what, I just have to do this. But I tell you it wasn't easy. There were some nights when I would just cry and cry and cry myself to sleep, and say, "God, how long it's going to be?"

With her green card, she has been firm about defining her job, pay, and working conditions in her current child care work for two lawyers. As she said, "I paid my dues when I wasn't legally here and I just believe that since I became legal, then every right of a legal person should be mine."

Isolation from kin, friends, and community is a painful consequence of many live-in jobs. Immersion into a foreign world aggravates the loneliness and demoralization of many new migrants. Janet Robinson said that her first employer was good, "But I was very homesick and lonely." Those in isolated suburban areas often fared the worst. Those in the city and especially those who got away on days off to their "own" community fared better. Marguerite Andrews squeezed just enough out of her paycheck to escape from her Park Avenue live-in job to a furnished room in Bedford-Stuyvesant every weekend. Joyce Miller found that the isolation of a black woman living in a white world had other consequences when people mistook her for a convict from the nearby prison when she did the shopping in town. When faced with a snowstorm on her day off, Monica Cooper paid several times her normal bus fare to "get out" of her suburban live-in job and come to New York. As she said, "There's no way on earth I'm going to have a day off and stay in there."

Speaking of a short-lived, Park Avenue, potential sponsor, live-in job, Marguerite Andrews asked,

> Is slavery really abolished? There is not much difference between working in this situation and slavery. The working hours are the same, the exploitation is the same. There is no human recognition. We eat the same food, live together in the same house, but we don't mingle. I am in it but not part of it.

While a (potential) sponsor live-in job may feel like "slavery," what it resembles most closely is a form of legally sanctioned indentured servitude in which the worker performs until the green card is granted.

Despite the exploitation, several women feel gratitude toward their employers for sponsoring them. As Joyce Miller said: "That's why I give and take a lot of things. . . . A lot of things I let her get away with because I feel indebted to her." Like several others, she has maintained relations with her former employers, especially to visit the children.

In discussing the role of immigrant workers in New York, Joyce Miller said "they just want cheap labor . . . West Indians, or foreigners or what they want to call it." She indicated many ways in which undocumented workers support the U.S. economy that include providing exploited labor, retaining immigration attorneys, and purchasing food, clothing, and household items to send home regularly to kin.

Monica Cooper pinpointed racism as a major influence on immigration policy and procedure, noting the differential treatment of different immigrant groups:

> I do feel the system is set up to make it harder for black people coming here. It's . . . to a larger extent . . . people coming in from the black countries or [some of the] Third World countries . . . that sense that they have special quotas.

While not citing several political and economic factors, she compared the treatment of Korean and Haitian immigrants:

> Look at the difference [between the treatment of the Haitians and the Koreans]. You don't have to know a lot about what's going on, current events, to be able to pick that out. Black people or people from the Third World . . . [West-

ern] hemisphere, have a harder time gaining acceptance in this country than people from the East. . . . Their papers take longer. You go through everything that says you better go home. If you can stick it out then you're the better one and you *know* that people stick it out.

In spite of "everything that says you better go home" West Indian women do "stick it out." Visions of their children and families, letters from home, support from kin and friends in New York, and the determination to meet their goals empower them to overcome obstacles in their paths. Most must travel to their home islands for the final interview, a medical examination, and the granting of the green card.[8] They visit their children and kin, and with green cards in hand, many begin their children's "papers." Legal status permits them to visit home, but worsening economic conditions, including rampant inflation, often preclude long visits or returning to live. Joyce Miller, who after several years of "doing domestic" is a bookkeeper in a Manhattan real estate office, said, "A lot of Caribbean people come here and they are surprised. . . . They are disappointed. . . . They thought the life is easier. I think it's harder here than back home. In a certain way if we could get work back home as though we get it here, we would never stay."

Some leave private household work soon after receiving their green cards. Most who remain find "better" jobs with higher salaries which they command with their legal status. Most who have been in live-in positions find their own accommodations. Some remain in domestic work while preparing for other employment through further education and leave when they find other work. Fewer remain in domestic work indefinitely with "good" employers, often in spite of further education, for a variety of reasons.[9] The majority who leave private households, work in the "pink-collar" women's jobs, especially in clerical or health care occupations.[10]

"If people only knew what we went through to be here. I try to tell them but they don't hear," lamented Shirley Green. Remembering her sponsorship experiences, Joyce Miller said,

> People don't understand how hard it is to get here. And we try to explain to them. It's terrible. And you think of all you go through. You go through all this paperwork and go through the lawyer and pay so much money and you get this blooming little piece of card, green paper. It's not even green. The day when I got I said, "This is IT?" They should have a better system than this.

RESPECT, THE ASYMMETRICAL RELATIONS OF "DOING DOMESTIC"

I work hard. I don't mind working hard. But I want to be treated with some human affection, like a human being . . . I don't get any respect. . . . Since I came here this woman has never shown me one iota of, not even, go down to the smallest unit you can think, of human affection as a human being.
> —MARGUERITE ANDREWS *discussed the treatment she received on a job.*

While sponsored and live-in work are "the worst," carrying special meanings for the worker, they are exacerbations of problems possibly structural to domestic work. Although employers exhibit a range of behaviors, even with "good employers" some problems emerge which might be considered structural to the working conditions.

Low wages, lack of benefits, lack of formal contracts, lack of job ladders, low status, limited unionization, and personalized relations situate this work at the low levels of capitalism's tertiary sector framed by the asymmetrical relations of class, race, and sex. Beyond the low pay for repetitive and exhausting work, many women have difficulties with the asymmetrical social relations of the work. Like other relations mediated by a wage, these social relations mirror the dominant/subordinate class relations of capitalism. But they do so through the additional filters of sex, race, and migration which shape them in particular ways.

Within the contemporary sexual division of labor, child care and domestic work are assigned to women as extensions of women's supposedly "natural" nurturing and caregiving. "Naturalizing" the work implies that it is unskilled and not really worth wages, trivializing it. Devalued when passed from men to women in the society at large and within the same households,[11] the work is further devalued when passed from one woman who chooses not to do it and can pay for it, to another woman who performs it in someone else's household for the wages she needs to maintain her own household. The devaluation lends particular character to the dominant/subordinate relations between employee and employer.

The asymmetrical relations are further shaped by assigning this work, and much personal service work, to racially or ethnically distinct groups (either immigrant or native born) in the context of a society suffused with ideologies about racial and ethnic superiority and inferiority. The assignment of private household, personal service work to those with low status, by virtue of gender, and racial and ethnic hierarchies, reinforces the hierarchies.[12]

Class, sex, race, and migration have shaped the asymmetrical social relations for much domestic and child care work in the United States, from the first African house slaves to the Irish immigrant "servants" of one hundred years ago and to contemporary Salvadoran, West Indian, and other workers.[13] The worker is thus categorized as "other" (as defined by the dominant white male society), increasing the separation between employer and employee as well as the potential for exploitation. Marguerite Andrews states that "The racial thing really gets me down. I'm treated this way because of race. The only difference between us [Marguerite and her employers] is race." While race may be a major difference, it does not exist apart from sex, class, and migration for West Indian women of color in creating "otherness" which reflects and reinforces the particular asymmetrical social relations of the work.

The location of domestic work in the private household further influences the social relations of the work. While the nature of housework and its status as "productive" labor has been greatly debated,[14] work located in the home is often not recognized as work and is therefore devalued. In part, this is due to an ideological construct which paralleled the movement of much productive activity out of the home into a separate workplace during the process of capitalist industrialization in the West. The ideology strictly separated the workplace and the home, linking them to a parallel ideological separation between the genders which segregated women in the home.[15] In addition, the location of this work in the private household isolates and atomizes the worker and impedes the unionization of domestic work.

In discussing the asymmetrical relations, every woman spoke most about the lack of respect shown to her by employers. What the worker experiences as lack of respect often appears to be efforts to depersonalize the very personal relations involved in the work and to dehumanize the worker in a variety of ways. On one hand are the personalized relations of the work, the worker's intimate knowledge of her employers, her responsibility for maintaining and managing the household to free its members for other activities, her possible residence in the household, and her nurturance, guidance, and care, both physical and affective, for the children. On the other hand are the wage relations of the work, and the depersonalizing, dehumanizing treatment of the worker.

> The treatment here is terrible. . . . I think the employers should treat people much better because they're cleaning up after them to make the environment clean. They're helping them out. If they can do the work themselves, they [should] stay at their house or do the work themselves. Don't treat people like that.

Joyce Miller pointed out the unacknowledged need for the employee. She spoke of how her twenty-four-hour responsibility for the children and household freed her employers but at the same time was taken for granted by them.

> She thought she had me there inevitably. She wanted me to be there forever. No one ever came there and stayed. Not because she's bad, but because of the work. The responsibility. It was a lot. She doesn't like to stay home. She had her baby [third child] and like in the space of two weeks she's gone. She's not there at day. She's not there at night.

The employer worked short part-time hours at her husband's business, "otherwise she got herself other activities. I mean hanging out with friends for the day . . . shopping. . . . They don't give me anything extra when they go on vacation [a few times a year]. Because I have the responsibility day and night." She added, "I'm not looking for them to shower us down with money, with clothes, but with a little respect and feelings. You know because they want full respect from us and at the same time they want to treat us like nothing."

At times, Joyce Miller felt taken for granted by the employers for whom she worked after getting her green card. They were a wealthy couple with an elegant co-op on the Upper East Side of Manhattan. The husband was a lawyer from a manufacturing family, while the wife, from a New York real estate family, was an aspiring magazine writer who was somewhat "spoiled" and very "untidy."

> The thing I hate, everytime I clean the house, you know that woman make a mess. She throw everything on the floor. She leave all the cabinets open, you bump your head everytime of the day. She leave all the drawers out. . . . I don't like things to be messed up. If I fix it, don't throw it down. If you use a thing, don't throw it on the floor. Put it in the hamper.

While picking up after people may be "part of the job," Janet Robinson, Dawn Adams, and others disliked finding a mess where they had just tidied up and felt frustrated when they entered the apartment they left spotless the evening before to "meet juice under the table, pieces of bread on the floor, and the child's toys everywhere."

"Like a Human Being"

The most important thing is to show the person that you know they are human too. Most important is how you treat them.
— BEVERLY POWELL *commented on employers' behavior toward the worker.*

The low esteem for housework and for those who perform it was noted by some women as the "worst part." As Beverly Powell said,

> When people look down on you for cleaning up their messes, then it starts hurting. The worst thing is when they look at you as stupid, maybe not stupid, but as a damn fool. You should treat people exactly as how you want to be treated. We can't all be doctors or lawyers, someone has to clean up the dirt. I am a hard worker. I want a little consideration. If I'm paid $1,000 for work but treated like dirt, it will pay the bills, but forget it.

Like other West Indian domestic workers, Monica Cooper took pride in her housekeeping but resented her employers' distancing and denial of her as a person.

> It was like because I am the employee, because of what I'm doing, somehow I was looked down on. I was a good housekeeper. Because that's how I am. Whatever it is I do, I love to do my best. And I did my best. . . . But . . . there is a blockage in between. It's like she and I are O.K., but if a friend comes by, you feel the difference: "Oh, now she's the housekeeper."

Whatever the relationship otherwise, it is depersonalized as it is presented beyond the household.

Clothing is one of the clearest forms of depersonalization. While for some women uniforms provide an inexpensive mode of dress that saved their own clothes for "after work," most who were asked to wear uniforms resented it. Judith Thomas "hardly ever wore the uniform because it was white" and therefore impractical for both child care and housework. She recounted a story which pinpoints a uniform's function. She accompanied her employer (a part-time grade school teacher whose husband was in business) to Miami to take care of the children. Judith said,

> She wanted me to wear the uniform. She was really prejudiced. She just wanted that the maid must be identified. . . . She used to go to the beach every day with the children. So going to the beach in the sand and sun and she would have the kids eat ice cream and all that sort of thing. You know what a white dress would look like at the beach? . . . I tell you one day when I look at myself, I was so dirty, . . . just like I came out from a garbage can . . . I felt real upset.

That day, noting the condition of her uniform, she asked to wear jeans and a top and the employer agreed. The day she did, the employer's brother

> came by the beach to have lunch with [the employer]. I really believe they had a talk about it, because in the evening, driving back from the beach, she said, "Well, Judith, I said you could wear something else to the beach other than the

uniform, and I think you will have to wear the uniform because they're very formal on this beach and they don't know who is guests from who isn't guests."

In the context of racial segregation, uniforms function to unmistakably identify people of color as service workers, the only roles which would justify their presence in otherwise all white settings.

Food and eating are other arenas of dehumanization and depersonalization. Some employers left food for the worker to prepare for the children but none for the worker herself, though she might work an eight- to twelve-hour shift. One worker was accused of consuming "too much" of a particular food, milk, which she never drank. When one woman on a live-in job ate some pork chops which had been in the refrigerator for several days while her wealthy corporate executive employers dined out, she was informed that several pork chops were "missing" and that she should "find" them. With her own money, the worker replaced what she ate, and no comment was made. In other instances, the food that is left for the women to eat is inadequate for the amount of physical labor they perform. Janet Robinson remembered an early experience in which she was left a lunch of cottage cheese, which seemed practically inedible to her West Indian palate. Her reaction resembles that of the Barbadian domestic in Paule Marshall's story who exclaims, "as if anybody can scrub floor on an egg and some cheese that don't have no taste to it."[16]

Joyce Miller spoke of the classic situation in which, as a live-in worker for a young, wealthy family, she ate separately from the other members of the household.

> I couldn't eat with them at the table. . . . I have to eat after they finish eating. . . . And then I eat in the kitchen. There are a lot of people who do that because they want us to know that we are not equal. That's my point of view. You are the housekeeper. I think the only reason why I was in their house is to clean. . . . Like olden days. . . . That's the part I hate. I hate that part because it's showing me a lot of things. You need things from me, but when it comes down to sitting at the table with you, you are going to show me separation there. I just don't like it.

She contrasted this experience with her former New Jersey job in which she was underpaid but always included at the table. She said that if she went to sit by herself, they said to her, "'No, no, no. You've got to come right here at the table.' . . . That was something she try to do all the time. That's one thing with her she was great about, I never felt left out."

While spatial segregation means that some women eat in the kitchen after others, some live-in workers are denied the privacy of their own rooms. Some share a room with children. Some with their own rooms regularly take in an agitated or sleepless child in the middle of the night.

Judith Thomas spoke of the depersonalization, trivialization, and lack of respect involved in being treated like a child on a live-in job.

> It was another hard thing that as a woman, a mother, responsible for home, with a husband, and to come here to New York City and have to be living with people. . . . It was definitely hard for me. You know at times they would talk to you as though you were just some little piece of a girl. It was really humiliating at times. . . . Most of the time they wouldn't see me as that [fully adult] person.

. . . A couple of times I really had to tell them that. I really had to say, "Well, I want to be treated as a full adult. You know, you all must remember that there was once I had a husband and kids and had the same responsibility as you all but because people go through different stages in life, here I am now in this situation. So, you know, don't forget that. You know, remember, I was once this responsible person. And don't treat me like a child or some little girl."

In contrast, women spoke of "good employers" who are "fair," who "understand," who "have genuine human affection" and who "treated me like a human being." Besides attempting to minimize the material exploitation and disrespect on the job, some employers helped out in medical and family crises and tried to assist in the worker's education or self-development. Dawn Adams' sponsor employers, a theatrical lighting designer and her photographer husband living in Greenwich Village, was "the best person to work for." She was "willing to help" Dawn attend college by offering to continue to pay her a full-time rate though Dawn would attend classes in the morning while the child, for whom Dawn was primarily responsible, attended nursery school. Another woman who worked for this employer concurred with Dawn. Janet Robinson spoke highly of several of her employers including her current ones, two lawyers. Beverly Powell likes her current employers, involved in theater, who pay her overtime and treat her well. Those whose employers are regularly absent from the home, especially for their own full-time employment, fare the best. However, rarely did anyone speak of any employer without ambivalence. Even when airing a complaint, many workers said something like "she has her good side. Regardless of everything else, I think she's O.K." The flip side is also true. As several women said, "Nobody's perfect." Joyce Miller was often "confused" by the very friendly relations with her sponsor employer who "told [her] everything," always included her in dining and most other activities, yet paid her poorly. The basic outlines of the job include the inherent contradictions of employer/employee relations, including lack of respect, in a personalized context.

"One of the Family": Manipulation, Trust, and Distrust

The highly personalized relations of domestic work, especially that which is live-in, produce such phrases as "like one of the family." As Monica Cooper said,

> They never treated me in a way that I felt like, even though I'm working for them, that I'm family. 'Cause when you're living that close to someone for 4 1/2 years, if there is no bond between you, then something has to be radically wrong. I felt that I was just used for whatever they needed.

Joyce Miller said,

> whenever they want you to give your all in their favor, or anyway to feel comfortable to do what they want you to do, they use the words "we are family." That's the one I hate. "You are one of the family." That's not true. That's a password as sorry . . . if you're one of the family, don't let me eat after you. . . . They say it to make you feel O.K., but at the same time, they're not doing the right thing.

The ideology of family is used to manipulate the worker. Often used to explain why members of the *same* family should sacrifice for one another, here it is used to encourage people who are *not* family members to perform tasks or to tolerate treatment that may be exploitive. The image of family is called up to soften the edges of wage labor in personalized situations.

The image of family is most pervasive in child care. Most of the women in this group were hired primarily to care for children, which they preferred to their secondary housework responsibilities. Janet Robinson said, "I love the kids" and was echoed by many others who take pleasure in their relationships with the children. They put a great deal of thought and caring into tending the children. When the child that she took care of misbehaved, Dawn Adams said,

> You know, it's not my child but I take care of her and I love her. I've been with her since she was three months old [she was then four years old]. And when she did it I was embarrassed myself.

Emotional vulnerability and exploitation are risks in child care situations, especially in conjunction with separation from one's own children. Some children received no parental discipline when they teased, hit, spit at, or were otherwise rude to the workers. When told that "Janet will clean it up," children learned to expect others to clean up after them. Several women mentioned that the parents were jealous of worker/child relationships. A jealous parent humiliated one worker by ordering her to her room when the employer's child sought comfort from the worker after being scolded by the parent. Relationships with the children often lead women to stay longer on jobs than they would otherwise; they sometimes return to visit children once they have left. The weekend after leaving a job, Beverly Powell lamented the end of a four-year relationship with the eight-year-old boy, who sometimes called her "mommy." While many women do keep in touch with the children, Beverly knew that the strained relations with the child's parents would prevent her from doing so.

> I loved the kids and the kids loved me. They trusted me. . . . They could go on vacation far away and leave me with the kids and they'd call in because I was responsible enough for them to have confidence that "she's going to make them do what they're supposed to do."

Monica Cooper spoke about a major element in child care employment, trust. Beverly Powell's employers, a middle manager in a large corporation and her husband, a partner in a small import business, entrusted their son to her sole care twenty-four hours a day for five days a week at their country house each summer while they worked in Manhattan. However, the same employers who entrust their children to the worker may distrust the worker in other matters. Some women reported that the "thing she [the employer] hates most is to see me sitting down" as if the employers feared that the worker was cheating them by sitting down for a break. Though entrusting her with the care of their children for four years including while they were vacationing in the Caribbean, Monica's employers' trust vanished when she gave two-weeks notice.

> Everything was O.K. For four years I was with them and they trusted me and . . . all of a sudden . . . they couldn't find this and they couldn't find that. . . .

Now that I'm leaving they're going to miss a [gold] chain [necklace] and they're going to miss a slip, and they're going to miss everything else.

BALANCING BABYSITTING AND BARRELS

The Responsibilities of Work and Family

> Some of them don't even talk to you. They just want to know how their kid is or how the housework is going. They never one day ask you how you're feeling or anything else. . . . They're into their own little world and their own little life and leave you out, block you out like you're just nothing. And I think that really hurts a lot. Especially when people leave five, six kids in the West Indies and come here to do housework.

Joyce Miller, above, was joined by several others who said, "They don't ask how I am." This lack of consideration and denial of the worker's human identity beyond her role as child care or domestic worker contrasts with the ideology of family, a worker's intimate involvement in the household, and being entrusted with the care of children. A failure to recognize and respect her personhood makes an impact on her life off the job as well as on it. West Indian women juggle paid child care and domestic work with "the rest of their lives" to care for their own children.

While all wage-working mothers balance work and family responsibilities with some difficulty in contemporary capitalist society, child care and household maintenance are stratified by class. The resources on which women have to draw engender different ways of handling their work and family duties. While both employer and employee may work to support their households, the wages, working conditions, and nature of kin and household responsibilities of these West Indian women mean that they have to juggle a different set of responsibilities in a different material and social context than their employers.

For example, the West Indian woman employed in domestic and child care work must stretch her wages to support herself, her children, and usually other kin as well, across town and across oceans. While wages range according to legal status, live-in or out, length of employment and individual employers, they are generally low, and do not include either medical benefits or overtime pay. Sometimes less, current gross salaries generally range between $175 and $225 a week for those with green cards. Although $300 a week was rumored to be the highest salary available in 1985, no one in this group even approached this amount. Only Judith Thomas has medical insurance paid by her employers. Several without insurance were paying off large medical bills.

With their wages, women support at least two households, in full or in part: their own in New York, and one or more composed of kin (possibly including their children) in their home country. New York housing takes the biggest bite out of their wages. Lawyers' fees, for those who hire them for their own or their children's green cards, are another major expense. Every woman sends remittances regularly. Dawn Adams was not unusual in remitting at least half of her earnings every other week to support her mother and two daughters, before her daughters joined her. Like others, she sent both money, for living expenses and her daughters' school expenses, and barrels, packages filled with food, clothing, and household goods, basic nonluxury items either unavailable or exorbitantly priced in the home country. Due to the high cost of basic items in Trinidad, Janet Robinson sends barrels every few months to her daughter and grandson. The last one contained almost $800 worth of goods including three gallons of cooking oil, forty pounds of rice, twenty pounds of detergent, flour, tea, cocoa, toothpaste, and other items. Remittances of money (including school fees for siblings and others) and goods may account for 20 to 75 percent of the domestic worker's income. Even after their children join them, West Indian women send remittances as other kin depend on them.

As Joyce Miller said, "We get paid less, they still take taxes, and at the same time we're buying the goods for the regular price. We don't get the price cheaper." Many reported working extra jobs at nights and on weekends to meet their financial responsibilities. Dawn Adams said, "You have to have your budget planned."

The lack of standardization, contracts, job security, or regular hours add to a worker's concern beyond the job. Beverly Powell was asked to change from her regular nine to six or seven, five-day shift, to take full twenty-four-hour responsibility for the eight-year-old boy from Sunday evening to Friday evening at the summer house while the parents worked in the city. She had to send her own daughter who joined her from Jamaica to live with Beverly's sister in Canada for the summer since Beverly could not be present to care for her. Her schedule became more irregular and unpredictable. For example, one Sunday morning she was requested to arrive several hours earlier than previously planned. This necessitated cancelling other plans and packing up to go immediately, though on arrival she found her employers lounging with afternoon drinks, as yet unready to depart. Many women spoke about the inconsiderateness of the unpredictably shifting schedules and the impact on their lives. Dawn Adams was regularly requested to remain late just as she prepared to leave, which often interfered with her "after work" plans. Several times her employers returned very late, which, for Dawn and other women, meant later and therefore longer and more dangerous subway rides home. As she said, "It seems as if it never bothered them [that] when they were in their house, I had to be on the streets." These schedule extensions left less time in which women could accomplish their own household and kin responsibilities, be with children, other kin, or friends, or just relax. As Beverly Powell said, "No matter how well paid I am, I want a little time to myself. . . . She doesn't even think of the child that I have. And then she talks about loyalty." As different women said: "They don't think that I have my family waiting for me." "They don't think about my child." "It's O.K. for them to ask me to stay extra time because they have their family together, but what about me?"

While child care arrangements across town were difficult, those across oceans were more so. These women with young children present paid a large part of their salaries to a local babysitter, often another West Indian, who took several children into her apartment. Many women reported a variety of problems that occur in this situation. Children left at home when a mother migrates are generally kept by kin, often a mother or sister, or friends. Although the mother provides as best she can, her children may feel emotionally or materially deprived, and the situation may be stressful for her, the children, and the caretakers.

This balancing is not without its emotional costs. The pain and loneliness of leaving children was central to these women's experiences. As Dawn Adams said, "What could be harder than me leaving my kids in St. Vincent and coming here to work, not seeing them. I don't see them for about two and a half years after that last night I slept in the house with them." When Beverly Powell described getting into bed at night and wondering if her daughter had been bathed and was asleep yet, she spoke for many women who reported crying themselves to sleep many nights, missing their children and wondering about their welfare. Joyce Miller was "so very, very lonely" for her son that she said, "I think I give them [her employer's children] more because I just think of them as my own. Just 'cause I was lonely, I gave them all I have." For other women, as well, employers' children became substitutes for their own. Being torn between affluent and poor material worlds is cause for more emotional balancing. The West Indian woman may work in a world of relative wealth in which she witnesses waste "that makes your heart bleed" and go home to another with her low wages where she confronts demands from a "third world" to send goods which she cannot afford.

Determination and Resistance

In answer to the question of what gets her through, Judith Thomas replied forcefully, "I think strong will. . . . I've always had . . . a determined mind." Drawing on their strength, determination, and networks of support, these West Indian women cope with and resist the exploitation they confront on the job. Their determination to achieve their goals for themselves and their children keeps them going. It is buoyed by letters from home saying "we're praying for you" and "if it wasn't for you, we couldn't make it."

They use strategies such as defining their own tasks and airing grievances on the job. Joyce Miller answered with "my name is Joyce" when addressed or referred to as "the maid" or "the girl." Dawn Adams, tired of risking another late night subway mugging, instructed her employers to hire a separate night-time babysitter. None of these strategies eliminates the structural problems of the work which unionization, though difficult in domestic work, would begin to address. When exploitation is intolerable, quitting is the last option.

The support, pleasure, and meaning that they derive from other parts of their lives nourishes and renews them. Women spoke of the importance of relationships with their kin and friends, education, religious beliefs, and participation in church and community activities. Their ties to children and parents are primary. They seek out and recreate networks of kin and friends to ease their adjustment, provide companionship, and share housing, information, and jobs and services. Many exchange child care and household maintenance services with a friend or relative in the same household or between households. The conversations Dawn Adams had with the other babysitters in the park are reminiscent of Paule Marshall's description of a former generation of Barbadian domestic workers talking around the table after work "to reaffirm self-worth" and "overcome the humiliations of the work day."[17] Religious beliefs and activities provide crucial meaning and support for many women. Monica Cooper, who like many others "prayed a lot," also "set up school" for herself each night with her employer's college texts. School experiences benefit others. Active participation in West Indian church and community groups in New York empower and give pleasure to many women. Their identities derive primarily from these sources and not from their work.[18]

Leaving domestic work for the pink-collar ghetto may not seem to offer much, but it holds promise for many domestic workers. When Dawn Adams' $25 raise was rescinded a few months after it was given, because her employer, though a "good person to work for," had difficulty paying it, she had had enough. She found a bank teller job with regular hours, wages, and raises, and began college study toward a business and management degree. Though she took an initial pay cut, the job provides medical and dental benefits for herself and her children, who arrived in New York five months later. Judith Thomas, who earned her certification as a nursing aide, began looking for a job with medical and dental benefits for herself and her daughters soon after their arrival. No longer "frustrated" doing housework "because of circumstance," Monica Cooper expresses the optimism of many as she prepares for a singing career and does temporary clerical work: "Now I'm doing what I want to do because that's what I choose to do. At this point in my life, I'm not settling and doing anything that I don't want to do." Few are able to avoid doing things they do not want to do, but many are pleased to leave the particular constraints and exploitation of domestic work. Their balancing act as wage-working mothers continues as they enter another world of women's work.

CONCLUSION

While much domestic work resembles activities women do in their own families for love, it is in fact embedded in capitalist wage relations. While it resembles other work for wages, private household domestic work is fraught with contradictions: between its status as wage labor and the very personalized relations involved, between the framework of the cash nexus and the intimacies of child care, between the worker's involvement in a household and the peculiar forms of exploitation, depersonalization, and dehumanization she may experience.

These West Indian women share experiences with other women as mothers, workers, and migrants. While they balance kin and work responsibilities, they do so within a strikingly stratified system of child care and household maintenance. Their domestic work experiences most resemble those of other private household workers. Their obstacles and aspirations resemble those of other female migrants. Yet the particular interaction of gender, race, class, migration, and history makes their lives distinct.

Notes

1. I have assigned pseudonyms to protect the privacy of the women whose experiences are recounted here.
2. This article is based on ongoing doctoral dissertation research. It shares much data and analysis with the forthcoming dissertation and with my article entitled "Just a Little Respect: West Indian Domestic Workers in New York City," in a collection on domestic workers in Latin America and the Caribbean edited by Elsa M. Chaney

and Mary Garcia Castro which is being published in Spanish and English under the tentative title of *El Trabajo de la Cuarta Parte: Servicio Domestico en América Latina y el Caribe.*

3. This article is based on four or more interviews of two to four hours each with ten West Indian (English-speaking Caribbean) women currently or previously employed in private household child care and domestic work. The interviews and numerous other conversations with the women are part of ongoing anthropological fieldwork. These ten women range from late twenties to late forties, with most in their early to mid-thirties. All are mothers whose children reside either with them in New York or with kin or friends in their home countries. Many of them related stories of friends or acquaintances which enabled me to get a broader sense of West Indian women's experiences. In addition, interviews with immigration lawyers, Department of Labor officials, and personnel from a variety of agencies and offices which offer services to the West Indian community provided other information for this article.

4. Where "domestic work" appears alone in the text, in reference to the current research, it should be understood to mean both child care and housekeeping within the private household. Child care was the primary job responsibility of most of the women, though many, especially those who were living in, were also responsible for domestic tasks. For immigration purposes, the official designation is domestic work of which child monitoring and housekeeping are two categories.

5. Each woman interviewed has kin or friends abroad who migrated before her to England, perhaps in the peak period of the 1950s and 1960s, or to Canada and the United States, where West Indian immigration has peaked since the early to middle 1960s. Migration has been ever present in the Caribbean experience, linked to Caribbean participation in an international capitalist system. From the forced migration of Africans into slavery to the most recent migrations for wage work, Caribbean people have migrated to work. The legacy of colonialism and the persistence of multinational-influenced dependency create conditions of underdevelopment and poverty. Women experience these as unemployment, underemployment, lack of educational opportunity, limited occupational mobility, and low standards of living which pressure them to migrate. Labor needs, immigration policies, and "opportunity" influence the destination. (See D. Marshall 1982 for an historical overview of Caribbean migration. See Prescod-Roberts and Steele 1980; Foner 1978; Davison 1962; and Philpott 1973 on migration to England. See Henry 1982 for an overview of migration to Canada, and Silvera 1983 on West Indian domestic workers in Canada. See Bryce-Laporte and Mortimer 1976; Mortimer and Bryce-Laporte 1981; Dominquez 1975; and Gordon 1979 on the recent migration to the United States.)

6. Many cite their own and their children's education as motivations to migrate. Sacrificing precious nights and weekends, all but the most recent migrants have furthered their education since migrating. Some are currently studying, and others plan to resume study, especially in business and health care fields. Planning for their children's college education, unaffordable in their home countries, is central to several women's plans.

7. Domestic work has become a fairly simple path to the green card through employer sponsorship. The Immigration and Naturalization Service and the Department of Labor have several requirements, including proof of a shortage of documented workers available to work for the "prevailing wage," currently (1985) just under $200 for a 44 1/2-hour week for live-in domestic workers. Most live in as requirements favor it. Legally workers are supposed to receive at least the minimum wage throughout the sponsorship and the prevailing wage at the time the green card is granted. Because no agency actually monitors compliance with guidelines for

wages and working conditions, the sponsorship situation may result in exploitation of new immigrant women.

8. Joyce Miller estimates that 15 percent of the women who return to their home islands for their final interview for their green cards find themselves in the cruel situation in which they are either detained up to several months or denied the card entirely because of improper processing of their papers or failure of their medical exam (often because of conditions such as high blood pressure).

9. Often these are older women who may confront age discrimination in the labor market. They may also have benefits through another family member.

10. Pink-collar jobs are those jobs within a sex-segregated labor market which are filled primarily by women and which are characterized by low wages, lack of unionization, little security, and few job ladders. Employed women tend to cluster in 20 out of 420 jobs as delineated by the Bureau of Labor Statistics, such as clerical, service, and sales work. (See Howe 1977 on pink-collar work).

11. See Howe 1977 on the devaluation of women's work.

12. See Spellman 1981 for a discussion of the interaction of race, gender, and somatophobia in relation to personal service work.

13. Other than rural "help" in which young women of the same class, race, and ethnicity were sent to work alongside the members of a neighboring household, sex, race, class, and migration are integral to the history of domestic work in the United States. (See Dudden 1983, Katzman 1978, Hamburger 1977, Glenn 1980, Dill 1979, Almquist 1979, Davis 1981, and others on this history.)

14. On housework, see Glazer-Malbin 1976, Gardiner 1975, Dalla Costa and James 1972, Howe 1977, Strasser 1982, and others.

15. The relegation of women to the home has another implication for the relationship between employer and employee. Though the child care and domestic workers in this group have been hired by a male and female couple, the bulk of the interaction is between the worker and the female employer who, while not performing the work herself, has been minimally assigned the management of those who do perform it.

16. P. Marshall 1983: 6.

17. P. Marshall 1983: 6.

18. This may derive from a "double consciousness" as well as from the "occupational multiplicity" of West Indians which Lowenthal discusses (Lowenthal 1972: 141).

References Cited

ALMQUIST, E. M. 1979. *Minorities, Gender, and Work.* Lexington, Mass.: Lexington Books.

BRYCE-LAPORTE, R. S., and D. M. MORTIMER, eds. 1976. *Caribbean Immigration to the United States.* RIIES Occasional Papers 1. Washington, D. C.: Research Institute on Immigration and Ethnic Studies, Smithsonian Institution, pp. 16–43.

DALLA COSTA, M., and S. JAMES. 1972. *The Power of Women and the Subversion of the Community.* Bristol, England: Falling Wall Press.

DAVIS, A. Y. 1981. *Women, Race, and Class.* New York: Vintage.

DAVISON, R. B. 1962. *West Indian Migrants: Social and Economic Facts of Migration from the West Indies.* London: Oxford University Press.

DILL, B. T. 1979. "Across the Boundaries of Race and Class: An Exploration of the Relationship between Work and Family Among Black Female Domestic Servants." Ph.D. dissertation, New York University.

DOMINQUEZ, V. R. 1975. *From Neighbor to Stranger: The Dilemma of Caribbean Peoples in the United States.* New Haven: Antilles Research Program, Yale University.

DUDDEN, F. E. 1983. *Serving Women: Household Service in Nineteenth Century America.* Middletown, Ct.: Wesleyan University.

FONER, N. 1978. *Jamaica Farewell: Jamaican Migrants in London.* Berkeley: University of California Press.

GARDINER, J. 1975. "Women's Domestic Labor." *New Left Review* 89: 47–71.

GLAZER-MALBIN, N. 1976. "Housework: A Review Essay." *Signs* 1: 905–934.

GLENN, E. N. 1980. "The Dialectics of Wage Work: Japanese-American Women and Domestic Service, 1905–1940." *Feminist Studies* 6(3): 432–471.

GORDON, M. H. 1979. "Identification and Adaptation: A Study of Two Groups of Jamaican Immigrants in New York City." Ph.D. dissertation, CUNY Graduate Faculty in Sociology.

HAMBURGER, R. 1977. "A Stranger in the House." *Southern Exposure* 5(1): 22–31.

HENRY, F. 1982. "A Note on Caribbean Migration to Canada." *Caribbean Review* 11(1): 38–41.

HOWE, L. K. 1977. *Pink Collar Workers: In the World of Women's Work.* New York: Avon.

KATZMAN, D. M. 1978. *Seven Days a Week: Women and Domestic Service in Industrializing America.* New York: Oxford University Press.

LOWENTHAL, D. 1972. *West Indian Societies.* London: Oxford University Press.

MARSHALL, D. I. 1982. "The History of Caribbean Migrations: The Case of the West Indies." *Caribbean Review* 11(1): 6–9, 52–53.

MARSHALL, P. 1983. "From the Poets in the Kitchen." In *Reena and Other Stories.* Old Westbury, N.Y.: Feminist Press, pp. 3–12.

MORTIMER, D. M., and R. S. BRYCE-LAPORTE, eds. 1981. *Female Immigrants to the United States: Caribbean, Latin American, and African Experiences.* RIIES Occasional Papers 2, Washington, D.C.: Research Institute on Immigration and Ethnic Studies, Smithsonian Institution.

PHILPOTT, S. B. 1973. *West Indian Migration: The Montserrat Case.* London: Athlone Press.

PRESCOD-ROBERTS, M., and N. STEELE. 1980. *Black Women: Bringing it All Back Home.* Bristol, England: Falling Wall Press.

SILVERA, M. 1983. *Silenced.* Toronto: Williams-Wallace Publishers.

SPELLMAN, E. Y. 1981. "Theories of Race and Gender: The Erasure of Black Women." *Quest: A Feminist Quarterly* 5(4): 36–62.

STRASSER, S. 1982. *Never Done: A History of American Housework.* New York: Pantheon.

Rosario Ceballo

A Word and a Kindness: The Journey of a Black Social Worker

Mary, my friend's great-aunt, is an elderly African-American woman I first met at a college graduation in 1986. I was taking pictures of a rally for South African divestment when Mary was pointed out to me. I was struck by the ease with which she settled in among the crowd of college students. Most of the other parents and family members of graduating students watched the event from a safe, neutral distance. But Mary joined the rally, chanting with determination and raising her fist to the air. I was immediately drawn by the spark for life I saw in her.

In the years that followed, I had several opportunities to get to know Mary better. I was delighted when she allowed me to do an oral history of her life for my graduate school class on the psychology of women. I interviewed Mary over a span of three days during winter 1992, when she was seventy-six. We talked in the living room of her home in Oxford, North Carolina, and she allowed me to tape record most of our conversations. I have sought Mary's approval on everything I have written about her life, and she has therefore read and commented on all drafts of this chapter.

Mary was the youngest of nine children born in the Jim Crow South in 1915. She was only three years old when she experienced the traumatic loss of her mother, who died of TB. Three of Mary's older siblings also died around this time, and as a result, Mary grew up as the only female child in a family with her father and five older brothers. Mary's father, William, remained committed to raising all of his children himself with only periodic help from relatives. Although he initially hired people to look after the children, he later relied on his sons to look after Mary. The result, as Mary remembered, is that she was often left alone for much of the day. "They [her brothers] had to take care of me. But I remember that they would go off during the day and leave me in the house by myself. And they wouldn't come back until it was time for Dad to get home. Then they'd show up. I don't think I ever told on them."

Mary described her father as a quiet, undemonstrative, distant man, somewhat inept at managing the household of children he had been left with. Although he did not receive a formal grammar school education, he was taught enough in a neighbor's home to pass the entrance exam to Shaw University in Raleigh, North Carolina. After college, he "read law," apprenticing with a white lawyer for seven years. Upon passing the bar, William moved his family from Oxford to Durham, North Carolina, where Mary was born. As a young child, Mary spent several summers back in Oxford, where she stayed with relatives from both her father's and her mother's family. In 1926 when Mary was 10 years old, William moved the family to Washington, D.C. Mary then lived in other people's homes or in apartments where she, her father, and an older brother shared one rented room. "You see, we lived in rooms. We never established a home or anything. We had a room in somebody's house. That was the way we grew up."

While in the eleventh grade, Mary developed rheumatic fever, and her education was consequently interrupted by a series of hospitalizations. As a complication of this early illness, Mary was afflicted by a reactive arthritis, a form of ankylosing spondylitis, in her right hip. This condition was treated surgically, but Mary has slightly dragged one foot ever since. Despite these medical difficulties, Mary graduated on schedule with her high school class in 1934. She spent the next four years caring for the house and children of her oldest brother, Bob, whose first wife had passed away. She cooked, cleaned, did the laundry, and provided child care. Mary remembers those Depression years as particularly bleak and dreary. Her experiences during those years likely influenced the steadfast determination with which she later sought her independence. At age twenty-three, Mary gathered the determination and financial resources to enroll in Howard University. By 1948, she had received a master's degree from the Smith College School for Social Work and launched a successful career in the field of social work.

Mary's life story is marked by an ongoing struggle to cope with personal misfortunes and institutionalized systems of racism and sexism. In this chapter, I will explore how Mary's sense of identity emerged from interwoven layers of membership in different social groups and incorporated her transition in social class status. I will underscore Mary's use of relationships and surrogate family systems as a source of resilience. Finally, I will outline and examine the development of Mary's awareness of systems of racial oppression, beginning with her virtual lack of contact with white people as a child, extending to her pioneering efforts as the only black social worker in all-white social service agencies, and culminating with her participation in the civil rights movement as a fifty-one-year old, single black woman. I will also address how Mary's involvement in the struggle for civil rights influenced her reactions to the women's movement.

IDENTITY: RACE, CLASS, AND GENDER

Black feminist scholars have recently emphasized the need to explore interconnections between gender, race, and social class when investigating black women's identities and experiences with oppression. In addressing Mary's identity, I therefore wish to heed Patricia Hill Collins's (1990) advice of not starting "with gender and then adding in other variables such as age, sexual

221

ROSARIO CEBALLO
*A Word and a
Kindness: The
Journey of a Black
Social Worker*

orientation, race, social class, and religion, [but rather thinking] of these systems as part of an interlocking matrix of relationships" (p. 20). Indeed, as an adolescent Mary struggled with understanding just this kind of complicated matrix in her own identity.

Mary straddled the painful and complicated boundary of simultaneously belonging to an educationally privileged group of blacks while living under conditions of economic hardship. Academic achievement was a greatly esteemed and prominent value in Mary's family, and Mary excelled in all of her scholastic pursuits. Yet despite her father's legal career, Mary's family always lived under conditions of economic hardship. "It was a very, very peculiar kind of situation," Mary explained. "My dad, he was a good lawyer . . . but he never made money." William never became a prominent, financially well established attorney, in part because of his inability to participate in the social networks of the black middle class. He was a loner who did not care for the social obligations that accompany business life. For example, he attended church regularly, but never used the opportunities offered by the church's social network to foster a business clientele.

The tenuous interconnections between Mary's membership in different social groups marked several painful life experiences. For instance, Mary described the incompatibility of her educational privilege and lower socioeconomic status when she lived in the status-conscious black community of Washington, D.C. She described herself as a "little ragged kid who never had any decent anything. And here I sat in this school with these fancy D.C. folks' kids. When I had to go into another grade, you had to say what your daddy did. And I had to put on this thing that my daddy was a lawyer, and here I was looking like a Rag-a-muffin."

Moreover, the socially segregated climate of the black community in Washington, D.C., was not solely based on economic and occupational status. Discrimination pervaded all institutions, including the school system, where it was based on personal attributes such as hair type and skin color. Mary recalled a particularly illustrative school experience with great detail.

> I remember one time, I sat next to Charlotte. Her father was a doctor. She was very pretty, and very fair, and so on. She and I got along fine. A new teacher came and the first thing she did was rearrange the class and put all of the kids, the socialites, in front. And all of us, the rest of us had to go in the back. This is absolutely true, I am not lying. This was based on color and clout. Color and status . . . Yes, I was the blackest, and the poorest [in that class that went on to Dunbar high school].

Thus, Mary's sense of identity developed in recognition of her complex membership in different social categories of race, gender, and social class. Her sense of herself as an adolescent incorporated the ambiguous nature of her family's social class—a father who worked as a lawyer, but maintained a working-class lifestyle, her privileged academic orientation, her experiences as the only female child in a family of men, and the "blackness" of her hair and skin color. By the same token, Mary experienced the interlocking force of several oppressive systems. She simultaneously encountered classism due to her family's limited resources, racism based on the color of her skin, and sexism due to her gender. Mary's burden in navigating race-, class-, and gender-based oppressions was not like carrying separate and distinct weights, for as Elizabeth Spelman (1988) explained, "How one form of oppression is experienced is influenced by and influences how another form is experienced" (p. 123). It becomes clear then that the form of discrimination Mary experienced in school was linked to her gender (by the feminine attributes valued in black girls) as well as her lower socioeconomic standing.

RELATIONSHIPS AND FAMILIES

A significant source of Mary's resilient functioning lies in her ability to foster and then make use of relationships and surrogate family systems. Her father was unable to create a cohesive family unit following his wife's death, and Mary quickly learned that she would have to rely on a foundation of relationships with people outside of her immediate family to gain strength and nurturance. Mary's relational coping strategy is consistent with the psychological literature on "resilient children" who function adaptively in the face of severe and enduring strain. Stable relationships with adults buffer these children from a host of adverse life circumstances (Rutter, 1979; Werner and Smith, 1982).

Mary sought and found early positive role models among the extended family she visited in Oxford, North Carolina, during her childhood summers. For example, she frequently found a way of escaping the church revivals, attended mostly by the older people in the community, and visiting with the younger relatives, her maternal aunts. These aunts were young black teachers in their teens and early twenties who became important role models for Mary. She recalled that during her last summer in Oxford, "Sally was nineteen. That [teaching] was her first job, and I thought that was so wonderful, that she was going to be a teacher at nineteen! . . . Lena, Beecher, and Sally. They were all teachers."

Further, Mary was able to use a network of relationships to facilitate her own emotional growth and introspection during a difficult time in her life. After graduating from high school, she was hospitalized again for several long periods. During these hospitalizations, she was in a body cast for several months at a time. She believes the time spent in the hospital cured her of her "dependency needs." I knew all of the residents," she explained, "and everybody in the hospital knew me by then. I got a lot of attention, a lot of strokes. . . . I think I cured my dependency problem. . . . I mean I had all these needs that hadn't really been met. All the feelings I had about not being well taken care of somehow were satisfied during this period."

Although the story of Mary's unconventional route to college is poignantly heartwarming, it also illustrates how her life was powerfully shaped by the ties she established with others and how her professional beliefs incorporated an understanding of the primary role relationships may occupy in one's life.

> Let me tell you about how I happened to go to school. I came down here [Oxford, North Carolina] that summer, and Beecher [a maternal aunt] always somehow, was kind of special. I was special to her. She said to me, "We should have kept you after your mother died. If we had kept you, you would be finishing college this year." And it was true. If I'd stayed, I would have gone to

223

ROSARIO CEBALLO
A Word and a
Kindness: The
Journey of a Black
Social Worker

college. So I went back to Washington, I told my brother, Buster, that I wanted to go to school. And he said, "okay," and he said that "it was way late, but I'll help you." And I went to Howard and applied, and they accepted me, and he paid my tuition all through. He was working at the post office. He sent me through school.

I said, "And that all came about . . ." and Mary finished, "because of what Beecher said. And you never know. This is one of the things in the helping profession. This is one of the things I've learned. You never know the effect you're going to have on people. You never know. Just a word, or a kindness, or something can mean a lot to a person in life. The whole pattern of my life was set from just this one comment that she made."

Mary found a significant mentor and role model at Howard University, where she majored in sociology. E. Franklin Frazier chaired the Department of Sociology at that time, and Mary, who proved herself to be conscientious and dedicated, became one of his favorite students. The importance of familial ties and relationships had a profound influence on the professional goals Mary pursued after Howard. During an earlier hospitalization, Mary became friends with Catherine, her doctor's daughter. Catherine was a young black woman who was finishing her studies at the New York School of Social Work. Mary's motivation to become a social worker evolved out of this friendship. Upon graduating from college in 1943, she enrolled in Howard's two-year certificate program in social work and did her first clinical placement in a family agency. In view of her search and desire for supportive family connections, "it seems natural in terms of working, you work in a family agency. . . . The first job I had was in a family agency. Basically, my whole professional experience was with families."

Mary identifies her search for close, familial relationships as a salient theme resonating throughout her life story. "Throughout all of this, lack of family, lack of stability, I gravitate to situations where I'm in a family." In 1945 there was a small group of black professionals living in Milwaukee, Wisconsin, where Mary accepted her first job. This small professional group provided a supportive network for incoming members like Mary. Mary lived with one of these professional black families for ten years until she moved to accept a prominent position in a Philadelphia agency. To this day, they remain a surrogate family for her.

This family cushioned Mary's transition in social class status. Her socioeconomic position changed greatly as she became a securely established member of the black professional class in Milwaukee. Like her father, Mary spurned a socially elite lifestyle. However, her new family modeled positive attributes among middle-class blacks that Mary could accept. "This black group that I was in was not based just on social things. It was based on professional things, civic responsibility . . . That, I could accept."

DEVELOPING RACIAL AWARENESS

As Mary found ways to overcome the impediments that life placed before her, her awareness regarding systems of racial oppression developed in a remarkable fashion. Having come of age in the Jim Crow South, Mary's childhood was virtually devoid of any contact with white people. Black families who were financially more secure, like Mary's, could avoid interacting with whites to a great extent. Her parent's relatives owned their own land in the rural county surrounding Oxford, North Carolina. Because their primary source of income was farming, they did not have to work closely with white people in Oxford's city proper. The adults would take vegetables and butter to Oxford to sell to white people, but "that's the only contact they had [with them]. . . . They didn't work for them. They weren't maids or cooks for them." The amount of contact Mary had with white people was also influenced by her gender. For example, Mary's brother, William, Jr., was allowed to earn money by delivering newspapers to the white students at Duke University in Durham, North Carolina. In these instances, her family's financial circumstances and her gender shielded Mary from experiencing the subservient roles blacks occupied in their interactions with whites.

Not only did Mary have few physical interactions with white people, but the extent to which white people entered her daily thoughts and consciousness was negligible. I asked Mary, "What did you think about white people? What were you told about white people? How did your father feel about white people?" Mary explained, "He [her father] didn't talk about them. Certainly didn't talk about the racial part of it. You know, it was very interesting in the South. Because you just avoided everything. Your parents, they didn't tell you anything. They didn't talk about it." It was not until Mary was nine years old and spent a year in Boston living with her older brother George and his wife, Isabella, that she interacted with white children on a regular basis. In Boston she played and went to school with both black and white children.

As a child, Mary's understanding of racism did not emerge from a context of white-black relationships, but rather from experiences with the internalized racism exhibited by black people among themselves. Mary experienced discrimination in school at the hands of her black teachers who valued wealthy, well-dressed, light-skinned black children above the rest. When I asked Mary what she thought about the discrimination she had experienced at school, she replied, "We thought that the teachers were prejudiced. You just accepted it. It was just the way things are. I don't remember having really strong feelings about it one way or another. . . . I don't think I thought anything, except that it wasn't right. . . . That's just the way it was done. It wasn't anything you questioned." At this point, Mary did not have the life experiences to understand the hideous connections between society's racism and the ways in which black people came to despise their own culture. Mary resigned herself to accepting discrimination as part of the way the world worked.

Through her late twenties, Mary's awareness of racism continued to lie dormant. With a social work certificate in hand, she accepted her first job at a family agency that sought a black social worker to work with its black clientele. Mary remained the agency's only black social worker for several years. Although as a therapist, Mary saw only black clients, the clients of the white therapists were always white. Despite this practice, the social work profession in general avoided cultural issues in theoretical philosophy and clinical practice. The prevailing attitudes seemed to coalesce around a doctrine of unadulterated color blindness.

Mary learned to embrace this color-blind philosophy that asserted that race and culture do not enter into the clinical equation. At the time, she did not think that cultural factors influenced her professional work. She remembered not believing that race and culture "made any difference at all." After acquiring a master's degree in social work, Mary returned to work at the same Milwaukee agency where the policy of assigning therapists to clients of the same race had been abolished. Mary wondered how white clients would respond to working with a black therapist, but she did not discuss her concerns with anyone. "I think what happened in our day is that we didn't handle it," she explained. "It was really always covert. It was never really out in the open and on the table, unless some client came in and said, 'I will not work with a _____,' and then changes had to be made. But if it ever happened, then that was the only time it was discussed."

The denial of the presence and importance of racial issues applied not only to her views about clinical practice but also to her conceptualization of society at large.

> I think we [black women] kidded ourselves. I think we sort of bought into this total picture, treated ourselves as if we were totally like the white community, and that's absolutely not true. . . . Maybe it was not until the agitation from the civil rights [movement], where we began to take a look. You really had been kidding yourself. It's different. Society is different. Blacks have had a different experience. The black experience is different. . . . You really do live in a segregated society. No matter what you think, how you change your hair, where you live, how much money you make, as far as you go.

THE CIVIL RIGHTS MOVEMENT

Mary's participation in the civil rights movement marks a dramatic and striking departure from her earlier ideas about the role of race and culture in our society. A new and deeper awareness coupled with a national movement of protest sparked Mary's desire to resist racial oppression. Her involvement in the movement sprang from a well of rising and unsuppressible anger.

> The whole anger, the whole thing just sort of caved in at me. . . . As far as my working relationships, they were good, and I didn't have serious problems. But suddenly, socially, the many feelings that I had harbored throughout my life about being black and how I was treated and how blacks were treated just sort of caved in on me. And I just had to get out and get involved.

The events that created a movement in Selma, Alabama, drew Mary back to the South to join the struggle for civil rights. Alabama's proportion of blacks on the voter registration rolls was one of the lowest in the nation. Student Non-Violent Coordinating Committee (SNCC) workers in Alabama made voter registration a top priority in 1963, and the Southern Christian Leadership Conference (SCLC) began a similar campaign in 1965. In Selma, Sheriff Jim Clark's repeated use of force against blacks attempting to register received national media coverage. Coverage of the obstacles faced by blacks trying to vote continued with Martin Luther King, Jr.,'s arrest, a march to the courthouse by over

225

ROSARIO CEBALLO
*A Word and a
Kindness: The
Journey of a Black
Social Worker*

one hundred black school teachers, and the arrest of over a thousand people, including five hundred protesting school children (Carson, 1981; Garrow, 1978; Williams, 1987).

The shooting of Jimmie Lee Jackson, a twenty-six-year-old black man, during a nighttime march stimulated renewed protest and SCLC's announcement of a fifty-mile march across the Edmund Pettus Bridge in Selma, along Route 80 to the Montgomery capitol. On Sunday, March 7, 1965, Alabama state troopers met 2000 marchers on the Edmund Pettus Bridge. Tear gas was fired onto the marchers as policemen on horseback charged into the crowds. The day was dubbed "Bloody Sunday." King announced that the march would begin again as planned two days later. Hundreds of people from all over the country went to Selma for this march (Carson, 1981; Garrow, 1978; Williams, 1987).

Following King's announcement of another march attempt, Mary spontaneously bought a plane ticket to Selma. "I really called the airport, got a reservation, and just took off without too much thought about anything. I just wanted to be on that bridge, across the bridge, that was important to me." The rage that inspired Mary to buy a plane ticket on the spur of the moment marked the beginning of her activities in the civil rights movement. Mary's heightened awareness of her anger at racial injustice released a sense of rage and urgency and a strenuous desire to change society. "I had all these feelings in me, and I never recognized them or had not permitted myself to recognize them. And suddenly I'm angry . . . [and have] the anger and the energy to begin to do something about it, to fight, and to declare some of it." The Justice Department strongly urged King to call off the march. But before turning the march around, King led 1500 people across the bridge to face a line of state troopers on March 9, 1965. After the "Turnaround Tuesday" march, Mary returned to work, but she was not deterred by King's decision to abort that march. (It was not until March 21, 1965, that thousands of people set out on the march that would ultimately reach the Montgomery capitol with 25,000 people as Congress debated the Voting Rights Act.)

The following summer, Mary decided to go on a trip to Jackson, Mississippi, sponsored by a group called "Wednesdays in Mississippi," a subgroup of the National Council of Negro Women established in 1964 (Fitzgerald, 1985). This group consisted of black and white women who worked closely with SNCC's freedom schools, held conferences to discuss the problems blacks were facing in Mississippi, and developed programs to address these concerns. Afterward, Mary decided to join SCLC and spend the rest of her summer vacation participating in civil rights activities in the South. "The idea was to spend the whole vacation in the South. I don't know what I thought I was doing. I guess I thought I was being helpful, but I think that basically it was just an expression of my own anger at all of it."

During her vacation, Mary worked in Jackson, Mississippi; Atlanta, Georgia; Greensboro, Eutaw, Selma, and Birmingham, Alabama. Her memories about this time eagerly rushed forward, her words spilling over each other with enthusiasm. She remembered staying in King's house and being "the only old person there. The rest of them were young people. There were kids from all over the country in this house." She was stunned and outraged by the severity of the poverty she saw among the blacks whom she encouraged to vote and attend church rallies. She also recalled several frightening encounters with state troopers in which she knew her life was in danger.

Many black women have described a process of self-affirmation as a result of their involvement in the civil rights movement. For example, Bernice Reagon explained it as having "a sense of power, in a place where you didn't feel you had any power . . . a sense of confronting things that terrified you . . . [leading to] a change in my concept of myself and how I stood" (Cluster, 1979, p. 29). Similarly, Mary's experiences in the movement gave her insight into the strength and force of her own potential and abilities as a black woman. In this context, she explained her determination in the midst of extreme danger. "At this point I was so angry that I didn't care. I was scared that I might get killed, but I was determined. . . . In other words, you gotta fight it. Unless you get there and fight it, you gotta be willing to die or else nothing will ever happen. That was the way I was feeling." Standing for a principle that she believed in completely and resolutely and accepting the consequences of her actions yielded a powerfully self-affirming and liberating force on Mary's sense of identity.

Mary's desire and expectations for social change were also fulfilled during this time. "This was change," she explained. "This was definitely change. When blacks were staying in the [white] motel in Jackson, Mississippi, and when blacks were registered, and when I was standing on the sidelines seeing voters register in a small, rural community of Alabama, that was change!" Mary's sense of herself and of society was transformed by the movement's quest to end the legacy of slavery, segregation, and other racial injustices. She is immensely proud of having played an active role at a time and a place where history was made.

Mary's emerging awareness of her anger and her participation in the struggle for civil rights may appear somewhat sudden, but they are understandable if viewed in the larger context of the time. Mary had previously accepted society's systems of institutionalized racism because there were no practical alternatives, not because she found these systems and their values to be morally justifiable. The civil rights movement opened a door for the possibility of concrete change. It provided an alternative, a vehicle for channeling the accumulation of lifelong anger and the hope that change could happen. Belief in the possibility of change tipped the odds in favor of participation and action. Moreover, the impetus to act was reinforced by the belief that implementing change could not be left up to the federal courts. Black people had to assert control over their own destiny and unequivocally demand their basic human rights. The key issue then, as Mary sees it, is captured in a phrase from a song that she often heard during the movement: "The only thing that we did wrong was to let this go on so long."

It seems surprising that Mary felt her activities in the civil rights movement did not affect her professional work in a family agency. She identified her involvement in the movement as being of an extremely personal nature that did not permeate other areas of her life and career. "It was really personal. It didn't have to do with my working experience." When she returned to Philadelphia, it was "business as usual." Nothing had changed "in terms of my job and profession." She did not even share her experiences with co-workers. Stewart and

227

ROSARIO CEBALLO
A Word and a
Kindness: The
Journey of a Black
Social Worker

Healy (1989) posited that the impact of historical events on women's individual development is dependent upon a woman's age and life stage. Perhaps Mary's experiences in the civil rights movement were not immediately integrated into her professional work because they occurred when Mary was an older adult with firmly established life patterns and commitments.

FEMINISM AND THE WOMEN'S MOVEMENT

I wondered if Mary's heightened awareness of racial oppression influenced her reaction to the women's movement. In contrast to her involvement with the civil rights movement, Mary's sense of connection to the women's movement is very faint. She acknowledged the similarities between the women's movement and the goals of blacks during the civil rights movement, but personally her heart was only drawn to one of these agendas. Her identification with the struggle of black people runs deeper than her association with the experiences of women as a whole.

Feminist scholars have offered a multitude of theories to explain black women's limited involvement in the women's movement. Hooks (1981) argued that as a result of their participation in the civil rights movement, black women came to value "race as the only relevant label of identification" (p. 1). She went on to explain, "When the women's movement raised the issue of sexist oppression, we argued that sexism was insignificant in light of the harsher, more brutal reality of racism. We were afraid to acknowledge that sexism could be just as oppressive as racism. We clung to the hope that liberation from racial oppression would be all that was necessary for us to be free" (p. 1). Historical accounts have also documented that black female leaders of the civil rights movement were generally united in their belief that sexism was of secondary importance to the discrimination and oppression faced by blacks (Giddings, 1984; Standley, 1990).

Indeed, black women had many reasons to be suspicious of the women's movement, which quickly concentrated on the concerns of white, middle-class women. However, as Giddings (1984) remarked, "Not only were the problems of the White suburban housewife (who may have had black domestic help) irrelevant to black women, they were also alien to them" (p. 299). This situation was aggravated by the fact that white women continued to compare their status within society to that of blacks. In addition, black women in the civil rights movement did not experience the same degree and form of sexism that white women did. Black women were not, for example, entirely shut out of leadership circles, as the experiences of women like Diane Nash, Ruby Doris [Smith] Robinson, and Ella Baker attest (Giddings, 1984). Black women were also suspicious of the women's movement because its rise coincided with the decline of the civil rights movement, and black women were keenly aware of the fact that it was not only white men but also white women who perpetuate racism (Giddings, 1984; Fitzgerald, 1985). Several explanations may therefore account for the tenuousness of Mary's connections to the women's movement.

Although it is true that Mary's sense of connection to the women's movement remains weak, her endorsement of feminism is steadfast. To claim that black women felt no ties to women's rights and other issues raised in the

229

ROSARIO CEBALLO
*A Word and a
Kindness: The
Journey of a Black
Social Worker*

women's movement is far too simplistic, especially following their experiences in the civil rights movement. Black women were consistently in the forefront of the civil rights struggle; they carried the momentum and provided the stamina for the movement's progress. Black women did not "reject feminism itself but only the bourgeois white feminism that was at the heart of the women's movement" (Fitzgerald, 1985, p. 5) at that time. Mary showed no hesitancy in identifying herself as a feminist. "I consider myself a feminist because I believe in women's rights, but it isn't the feminism that I think whites are talking about, because my stronger feelings are about the racial thing."

To a great extent, many areas of Mary's life are characterized by feminist goals and values. As a young woman, Mary was guided by a burning desire to establish her independence and acquire a professional career. In her master's thesis at Smith, she directly addressed gender issues in professional relationships. She studied the working relationship between psychiatrists (the majority of whom were male) and the predominantly female social workers who made up an enormously undervalued segment of hospitals' mental health teams. Mary never acquired the traditional female roles of wife and mother. Moreover, she never felt an imperative to be married. "I never had the feeling that I had to be married. My feeling is that it would have to be somebody that I would want." She firmly declared a lack of regret about her life decisions and identified ways in which feminism has shaped her thinking. For example, she explained that "the new feminism has absolved me from much anxiety about the single state."

CONCLUSION

Mary's life is marked by her strong-willed determination to overcome the personal and societal obstacles that fall along her path. The obstacles have been numerous and significant: the early death of her mother, her family's limited financial resources, discrimination in the Jim Crow South, the absence of family unity, and a series of health problems and hospitalizations. Mary did not simply persevere and cope with these obstacles, she resisted their limitations and excelled beyond the boundaries they imposed on her. She attained exceptional academic, professional, and personal success. However, black female experiences should not, as hooks (1981) cautions, be romanticized into the stereotypical image of the "strong" black woman. Strength alone does not allow us to circumvent the forces of systemic oppression, but Mary and other women like her have given me courage and inspiration for continued struggle. As a woman of color who was raised in a working-class, immigrant family and as someone starting a career in psychology, I am strongly drawn to Mary and the ways in which she has lived her life despite the many obstacles in her path.

Academics in many fields, including psychology, have traditionally framed the study of black families on a deficit model. The use of white, middle-class families as a standard and basis for comparison draws out and highlights areas of deficiency and neglect among blacks in the United States. Mary is not privileged by her race, gender, or original social class position. She is neither white nor middle class, and she was not raised within the bonds of a cohesive nuclear family. Yet it would be a grave mistake to characterize Mary's life as deficient when her life and accomplishments are in fact remarkable in their richness. Approaching Mary's life with a focus on strengths and resiliency offers one road toward understanding how people located in the margins of society struggle with, resist, and in many ways, surmount oppression.

Appreciating the complexity and significance of intersecting social locations in Mary's life experiences also requires a sufficiently broad feminist perspective. A focus relying solely on gender as an analytical technique would conceal rather than illuminate our understanding. For instance, Mary did not resonate to the feminism she felt white women were addressing in the 1960s. She instead sought a balance between her feminist allegiance and those loyalties based on race and culture. To have narrowly zoomed in on a single historical moment in Mary's life would have provided a static picture. Instead, I have tried to document how the degree and nature of her feminist and racial awareness varied and changed throughout her life course as they do for all of us.

References

CARSON, C. (1981). *In struggle: SNCC and the black awakening of the 1960s.* Cambridge, MA: Harvard University Press.

CLUSTER, D. (1979). *They should have served that cup of coffee.* Boston: South End Press.

COLLINS, P. H. (1990). Women's studies: Reform or transformation? *Sojourner: The Women's Forum, 10,* 18–20.

FITZGERALD, T. A. (1985). *The national council of Negro women and the feminist movement 1935–1975.* Washington, DC: Georgetown University Press.

GARROW, D. J. (1978). *Protest at Selma: Martin Luther King, Jr., and the voting rights act of 1965.* New Haven: Yale University Press.

GIDDINGS, P. (1984). *When and where I enter: The impact of black women on race and sex in America.* New York: Bantam Books.

HOOKS, B. (1981). *Ain't I a woman: Black women and feminism.* Boston: South End Press.

RUTTER, M. (1979). Protective factors in children's responses to stress and disadvantage. In M. W. Kent & J. E. Rolf (Eds.), *Primary prevention of psychopathology: Vol. 3.* Social competence in children (pp. 49–74). Hanover, NH: University Press of New England.

SPELMAN, E. V. (1988). *Inessential woman: Problems of exclusion in feminist thought.* Boston: Beacon Press.

STANDLEY, A. (1990). Women in the civil rights movement. Trailblazers and torchbearers, 1941–1965. In V. L. Crawford, J. A. Rouse, & M. Walker (Eds.), *Black Women in United States History* (pp. 1–11). New York: Carlson.

STEWART, A. J., & HEALY, J. M. (1989). Linking individual development and social changes. *American Psychologist, 44,* 30–42.

WERNER, E. E., & SMITH, R. S. (1982). *Vulnerable but invincible: A study of resilient children.* New York: McGraw-Hill.

WILLIAMS, J. (1987). *Eyes on the prize: America's civil rights years 1954–1965.* New York: Penguin Books.

Carol Tomlinson-Keasey

My Dirty Little Secret:
Women as Clandestine Intellectuals

Women constitute over half of the population, yet their lives as individuals have often been conducted in the shadows of their more prominent social roles as wives and mothers. Only recently have psychologists focused the light of their investigative powers on women's individual hopes, goals, desires, and fears (Giele, 1982; Gilligan, 1982; Grossman and Chester, 1990; Gustafson and Magnusson, 1991). Their work has brought into sharp relief the realization that women's lives may not follow the same developmental patterns as men's lives.

Earlier theories developed by Erikson (1950), Vaillant (1977), and Levinson (1978) all offered accounts of adult development (see Tomlinson-Keasey, in press). Erikson's theory, pathbreaking though it was, served more as a sketch of adult lives, briefly outlining the challenges adults face and their resolutions of those challenges. As a description of women's lives, its details were meager. Vaillant and Levinson presented longitudinal accounts of men's development, focusing heavily on the occupational forces that directed men's lives, but both recognized the inadequacy of their theories as descriptions of women's lives.

More recent writings concerning adult women suggest that intimacy is as central to women's lives as achievement is to men's lives (Gilligan, 1982). When women describe themselves, they often portray a relationship, depicting their identity in the connection of their role as mother, lover, wife. Rather than achievement, they discuss the care they give to relationships. Gilligan's (1982) small sample of successful women seldom mentioned their academic and professional distinctions. On the contrary, they often regarded their professional activities as jeopardizing their sense of themselves. In contrast, men's descriptions of themselves often radiated from a hub of individual achievement, great ideas, and distinctive activities. These differences occurred despite the fact that both the men and women were in the same college class and were similarly situated as to occupational goals and marital status. The women's portraits seem much softer, less clear, and their identity becomes fused with intimacy. The women tend to depict themselves by their connection with other people (Gilligan, 1982).

David McClelland at Harvard has spent his career examining achievement motivation and power among men and women. He concluded (a) that women are more concerned than men with both sides of an interdependent relationship; (b) women are interested in people, whereas men are interested in things; (c) men are analytic and manipulative, whereas women are more interested in the complex, the open, the less defined (McClelland, 1975, pp. 86–88). His studies, like Gilligan's vignettes, suggest that women's lives often are driven by forces that men do not find as compelling. A drive for intimacy appears and reappears in women's TAT stories, looking much like the drive for achievement that fills men's interviews.

Eccles (1985) tackled the difficult issue of gender differences in achievement. She suggested that the individual's expectations for success and the importance attached to various career options influence women's choices. Women, she noted, often have perfectly sound reasons for selecting a particular course of action. The point to be drawn from Eccles's remarks is that women, for whatever reason, march to a different drummer, one seemingly less captivated by career success.

Eli Ginzberg was jolted into an awareness of gender differences in adult development when he contacted men and women who had excelled as graduate students at Columbia between 1944 and 1951. The questionnaire he drafted was duly returned by both sexes, but the women objected strenuously to the omission of salient aspects of their lives. After redrafting his questionnaire, Ginzberg reported the different paths that women took in their adult lives (Ginzberg, 1966; Ginzberg and Yohalem, 1966).

These snapshots of some of the major longitudinal studies of adult development remind us forcefully that descriptions and predictions of male achievements, personality, and intellectual interests cannot be applied indiscriminately to women. To alter male models to fit women or to discover alternative life paths that women follow, detailed, long-term studies of women's lives must be undertaken (Heilbrun, 1988). Only in such descriptions, in which women are encouraged to give voice to the salient aspects of their lives, will the patterns of women's lives emerge.

Given the differences in the life paths of men and women, it is easy to echo the following sentiments of Gilligan: "Among the most pressing items on the agenda for research on adult development are studies that would delineate *in women's own terms* the experience of their adult life. . . . As we have listened for centuries to the voices of men and the theories of development that their experience informs, so we have begun more recently to notice not only the silence of women but the difficulty in hearing what they say when they speak" (Gilligan, 1982, p. 112).

In the present chapter, as in this volume generally, Gilligan's charge is taken seriously. Through case studies, we can listen as women explain the forces that shape their lives. Nora Sol's[1] life, which is detailed in the present chapter, is sprinkled liberally with relationships, with vague career aspirations, and with choice points to analyze. In addition, as a subject in the Terman Genetic Studies of Genius, Nora was identified as a gifted child. Her life story holds particular interest because it allows us to see how one woman attempted to balance her substantial intellectual gifts with the many role demands made on women.

CAROL TOMLINSON-
KEASEY
*My Dirty Little
Secret: Women as
Clandestine
Intellectuals*

Lewis Terman first came to know Nora in 1922 as an eleven-year-old who was identified as a gifted subject for his study. From that point until his death in 1956, Terman followed Nora and over 1,500 other gifted boys and girls as they traversed adolescence, left their families, and established their own homes. Terman maintained contact with his subjects as adults through twelve questionnaires between 1936 and 1992. In addition, the study files contain holiday greetings, personal letters, and occasionally, notes from subjects' visits to Stanford. Terman maintained an active interest in each subject's life, offering encouragement and advice on particular problems when it was solicited. Nora's file was selected for this chapter initially because it was one of the most complete. In addition, the standard questionnaires were supplemented by long letters from both Nora and her father describing the various twists and turns in Nora's life.

Nora describes her intellect as her "dirty little secret," a secret layered in veils of different opaque qualities. She says, as if admitting to some major character flaw, "I am an intellectual." For eighty years, she has muted and buffered her intellect in ways to fit society's constraints as interpreted to her through her family of origin, her extended family, and her three husbands. Despite the opaque veils that screen her intellect from public view, she nurtured an active, private, dedicated intellectual life. As we watch her life unfold, we need to ask how she came upon this strategy of hiding her intellect when necessary, yet letting it peek through the veils periodically, in safe and accepted situations.

Family of Origin

Nora's family of origin was a swirling maelstrom of friction, chaos, hostility, and lack of nurturance. Her father, an autocratic taskmaster, listed his occupation as adventurer, explorer, and writer. Her mother was diagnosed as paranoid schizophrenic soon after her parents' marriage. By the time Nora, the oldest child, was four, her mother moved to a state hospital. During the family's occasional visits, Nora's mother often did not recognize her and occasionally denied that Nora was her daughter. Once, after visiting her mother and being rejected in the most palpable ways, Nora retired to her room and cried for three days. Recounting this period many years later, she said, "I was nine and the reality of my situation struck home for the first time. I would never have a mother, I had never had a mother that I knew and the tragedy and permanence of that situation drove me to my bedroom in tears." Nora's tears were linked to the profound understanding that reality is slippery, that her mother lived in a world of illusion and delusion and wasn't aware of it, and that both she and her mother experienced a cruel reality.

Nora's relationship with her father was a constant battle. She says from her vantage point as an octogenarian, "I was a bad girl until I was fifteen." Although her father's disciplinary measures seldom included any corporal punishment, Nora lived with a variety of strictures, both moral and real, that reinforced her notion that she could do nothing right. She remembers a favorite housekeeper saying "Why don't you learn to manage your father?" She admits that such management was "not in my repertoire, it wasn't in my nature. My nature was to go head to head against him."

Nora's father detailed their stormy relationship in the questionnaires he returned to the Terman study. He described Nora as "willful, headstrong, a lawyer, a liar," commenting that her moral instruction had been constant and that he had disciplined Nora frequently: "She is a problem, morally—on the verge of being sent to a convent. . . . We, two educated, thoughtful, painstaking adults, are in despair. . . . She lies, steals, and bears false witness, is slovenly, lazy, unclean, yet vain. In the category of her sins, few could truthfully be omitted, she having, it seems, about all the vices and few or none of the virtues appertaining to civilized life." His threat to send Nora to a convent was realized in 1924, when Nora was twelve. After two years at convents, her father described her behavior as much improved: "The periods of calm have lengthened. In these intermissions, she shows distinctly human traits. In especial, she seems to have developed a conscience. . . . She's a very good girl, patient with her brothers and even with her father; conscientious, rather honorable, even sweet, and damnably pretty."

Nora viewed these years in the convent in very different terms. They offered her peace, a seclusion, a sanctuary from the craziness of her family of origin. The life was structured, the demands were reasonable and easy to fulfill, she was no longer a "bad girl." She was accepted for who she was and she was able to satisfy some of her intellectual needs. Although her description of these two years was beatific, twelve-year-olds who are sent to convents must feel some rejection. Nora acknowledged that of course she had felt rejected, "but at home I had already been rejected. My actions, my person were always rejected. At the convent, I was accepted."

Nora's relationships with her two brothers, from whom she might have received some nurturance, were rocky and tenuous. The family's financial situation precluded any privileges, or much in the way of material possessions. Rather than binding the children together, the deprivation they experienced prompted them to fight over every detail of existence. The relationships with her brothers did not improve after these difficult childhood years. Her brothers snitched on Nora when she read a forbidden book. They chronicled every misadventure to her stern father, who responded with harsh punishments.

Nora's father offered only negative comments about her superior intelligence, a tested IQ of 150. When asked about indications of intelligence, he commented that she used her intelligence for excuses, alibis, and scheming to outwit and avoid the consequences of her misdeeds. In a long letter to Terman, he glorified a son's intellectual capabilities and minimized Nora's. It is noteworthy that the boy was not a subject in Terman's study.

By fifteen, Nora had skipped two grades, had read widely, wrote well, and was an important writer for the school paper. At every phase of her life, Nora described reading voraciously, but as a child, she often had to conceal her reading material. "I had my history book and I would conceal an acceptable writer like Dickens in the history book, but inside of that I had something by Jim Tulley. At home, there were layers of concealment, always."

One of Nora's first chances to follow her intellectual bent went awry during her senior year in high school. The family's financial situation worsened and the parade of housekeepers who had raised Nora stopped. Nora was given the primary responsibility for managing the home, a responsibility that she admits she performed perfunctorily. She says she always got into trouble because she would be reading instead of doing her chores. In the inner life she fashioned for herself, Nora read two to three books a week. As she says, "My problems paled in comparison to poor Eliza's in *Uncle Tom's Cabin*." A conference with Nora's teachers indicated that Nora was in line for a scholarship to UCLA, but they questioned the wisdom of awarding the scholarship. Nora had so many household responsibilities that the teachers were afraid she might not be able to spend the required time on her studies.

235

*CAROL TOMLINSON-
KEASEY
My Dirty Little
Secret: Women as
Clandestine
Intellectuals*

Nora's memory of her senior year at Hollywood High is one of a painfully shy girl who was poorly dressed and hence retreated to the solace of her books. In one of the many twists in her life, she had dozens of elegant hand-me-down gowns from an aunt in San Francisco. These designer gowns, however, went unappreciated because Nora had nowhere to wear them and no clothes that were suitable for high school.

In a letter to Terman, Nora's father commented on her beauty. A picture in the file suggests that his assessment was quite objective. Hollywood apparently noticed and she was offered a job as an extra. She took the job because it allowed her to remain at home, meet the needs of the family, and yet earn some money. When asked about her beauty as a teenager, Nora demurred: "I was little and I was cute. I learned to act little and cute. Everyone treated me as little and cute. I had an exterior life and an interior life and they did not fit with each other at all." Although these comments are particularly relevant to Nora's life, the society typically attended to a young woman's physical attributes and social skills, rather than encouraging or appreciating the intellectual qualities characteristic of the Terman women.

Nora's childhood seemed singularly devoid of nurturing adult relationships. She retreated to her books, found peace from her chaotic home, and began her double life as a closet intellectual. Her father, a writer himself, never saw or explored Nora's interests in books or writing. Her intellect was seen more as a diabolical plot to make his life difficult. He wanted her to follow his moral strictures, perform her chores with enthusiasm, and not disrupt the household. The thought that he might develop Nora's intellectual resources never occurred to him, yet he raged to Terman that his son's intellectual talents had been overlooked.

San Francisco: Nora's First Intellectual Forays

Nora credits her aunt with saving her life when she was nineteen. The family had left Los Angeles for a summer in Yosemite. When they were ready to return, the aunt invited Nora to stay with her instead of returning to Hollywood. Nora describes this as a turning point in her life because had she returned to Hollywood, she would have continued in the brainless roles assigned to most Hollywood extras. In one of her positions as an extra, she overheard a director and a producer commenting on how pretty she was. They added, however, that her legs were hopeless. Looking back from the vantage point of six more decades of living, Nora comments that they were right. With her aunt, she moved onto a different path, one on which she began to use her intellect, not her beauty.

Despite the Depression, Nora landed a job in San Francisco with a library circulating service. The inner life she had developed, focused on books to shut out her hostile, rejecting home environment, served her well when she applied for the job. Although still in her twenties, she was extraordinarily well read and her enthusiasm for books bubbled forth. Little wonder that she attracted the attention of a sales representative. He was thirty-six, almost fifteen years her senior, and had a high school education. She described him as handsome, charming, and unmarried. In one of the few goals that she recalls setting during her life, she decided that she would be his wife.

Although Nora and her husband had a beautiful daughter, she realized quickly that the marriage was a mistake as her husband had few intellectual interests. Within months of the marriage, she saw him and his life as vapid. Her response was to busy herself with the care of her daughter and retreat to her books, reading as many as twenty books a month. When her daughter was five, Nora talked with Terman about her marital difficulties and decided to dissolve the marriage. Although women rarely divorced, and as a divorcee with a young child, she was taking significant financial risks, she felt it was the only solution. In her talk with Terman she indicated that she longed for intellectual companionship. Some of the courage for her decision to divorce undoubtedly came from her success in a variety of jobs in San Francisco. She had been promoted quickly through the librarian ranks and had jurisdiction over the collections for seven libraries. She had her own radio program in San Francisco for which she reviewed books and wrote short scripts. In 1936, she indicated on her questionnaire that she had a horrible suspicion that she would end up as a writer. In 1939, she commented that her radio work blended her penchant for writing and her dramatic skills.

Nora's years in San Francisco brought her intellectual interests to the fore. She felt compelled to divorce her husband who could not appreciate her intellect. Her intelligence was given voice in her library work, in her review of books, and in the dramatic scripts that she wrote. As a young adult in San Francisco, Nora had the chance to express her intellect and to be valued for those skills. But the depth of her intellectual interests remained hidden. She joined a group designed to let women voice their feelings, needs, and desires in a safe setting. She says, "My dirty little secret was not that I was having an affair, had had an abortion, had given up my child, or was a lesbian; it was that I was an intellectual. I could not even tell this group of women, all of whom were baring their private lives and feelings. My secret was so traumatic and so deeply personal and private, that I couldn't bring myself to tell anyone."

Monterey—An Intellectual Community

After Nora left her husband in 1940, she visited a friend in Carmel; stayed for the Bach festival; and found herself drawn into the artistic, intellectual, Bohemian community of Monterey. She met a marine biologist, thirteen years her senior, who had an abiding interest in enjoying life. Hap introduced Nora to postimpressionist art, classical music, scientific research, current writing genres, and John Steinbeck. The impact was profound. She described a moment, sitting in a restaurant with Hap, discussing art, surrounded by baroque music,

237

*CAROL TOMLINSON-
KEASEY
My Dirty Little
Secret: Women as
Clandestine
Intellectuals*

in which she burst into tears because of the intense pleasure of discovering music by Monteverdi and poetry by Robinson Jeffers. Among the artists and writers, ideas were traded like currency, and she was entitled to have ideas and express them. Further, the unconventional atmosphere and the Cannery Row high jinks that flowed from that atmosphere made Nora feel safe in expressing her ideas more openly. She moved in with Hap and became part of a group that included John Steinbeck. She also began a very successful column for a local Monterey paper.

Hap had allowed, by virtue of his stature and interests, Nora's intellect to peek out from the veils of her childhood. She felt comfortable and accepted by the community. However, Hap did not personally encourage her intellectual growth except by introducing her to the community. He wanted "domesticity, dinner at six and a complete woman." Still, Nora's personal growth in this setting was obvious. She embraced a variety of avant-garde causes, including racial tolerance, and brought "vigorous leadership and dynamic conviction" to her work for these causes. She had fun, engineering a meeting between Henry Miller and a woman by suspending the woman from a barn beam. She wrote, achieving considerable notoriety and success through her own column in a local newspaper. She found other intellectual outlets—a glossary she completed for a marine biology text received special mention in one of the reviews. She edited a doctoral thesis. The freedom of the community allowed her to explore and develop.

Some of the spark went out of Nora's life when her daughter was diagnosed with a brain tumor. While she cared for her daughter, her relationship with Hap deteriorated. The moment her daughter died, Nora left Monterey and began a new relationship. What she took from Monterey was a heightened sense of awareness of her writing talents and an appreciation for an environment that encourages people to play with ideas.

Israel—Fulfilling Intellectual Promise

Nora had met her third husband at Stanford. He was on sabbatical and was planning to return to Palestine in a few months. In a momentous decision, she left Monterey and accompanied him to Palestine. She described the tumult of the moment: "I had supported several Zionist causes and there was tremendous fervency among the Jewish community about the formation of Israel. I was allowed entry into Palestine as a journalist and sailed aboard a converted liberty ship. The international tensions surrounding Israel turned the cruise into a mystery thriller, with everyone suspecting his neighbors of being spies, intelligence men, and secret agents." Palestine became Israel and Nora put her newly developed writing and analytical talents to use. As bureau chief for *Israel Speaks,* English editor for *Ktavim,* and editor and writer for *Wizo in Israel,* she produced thousands of words—"some sociological and economic analysis, some lighter commentary." In addition, she began helping others polish their writing. "The international community of scientists gathered in Israel were delighted to have me help them edit manuscripts, make sure the English was correct, and then make the manuscript easier to read and more interesting." She conducted seminars in scientific writing, prepared a manuscript on the topic, and had another child. In Israel, as much as any time in her life, she found fulfillment for her intellectual skills. She carved the time for her editing and writing out of a busy schedule as wife and mother and succeeded at all four tasks. Still, her own writing took a back seat to the editing she did for others.

In 1956, when Nora was forty-five, she and her husband returned to California. Although she continued her scientific editing, the pace was reduced. She again turned to her own work. Despite years of research on ideas for at least two books, her work never culminated in a final manuscript. She wrote in 1972 that she could have been quite a good scholar and researcher. She had come to admire the academic life and the scholarly and intellectual freedom it allowed. As an octogenarian, Nora is dynamic, sometimes fiery, and definitely passionate when speaking about issues dear to her heart. Certainly the spark that is described in the Terman files, sometimes called "strong will" or "stubbornness" by her father, is very much alive in her retirement years. She still reads voraciously and broadly, reporting during an interview on recent articles she had read concerning women's issues, the situation in the Middle East, social history, chaos theory, and DNA. Her life remains full and although Nora recognizes the complexity of her life and its various strengths and weaknesses, she evaluates the totality as unequivocally positive.

WOMEN'S PATHS

Drawing meaning from Nora's life requires that we examine the directions and events of her life in terms of theories and viewpoints about women's adult development. Five aspects of her life emerge that can be framed in more general terms: (a) the importance of relationships, (b) the force of serendipity, (c) discontinuity, (d) personal attributes that altered her life, and (e) the intentional minimizing of her intellectual skills.

Relationships, Intimacy, and Commitment

Rethinking Nora's life, we can try to cast it in the various molds provided by Levinson (1978), Vaillant (1977), Gilligan (1982), and Ginzberg (1966) to describe adult development. Despite her striking writing skills and her literary bent, Nora's career never ruled her life. In fact, Nora expresses reluctance to pursue writing, partly because her father's writing success had been sporadic and the family was often financially strapped. Hence, any model of adult development that concentrates on career goals and eclipses personal development seems inappropriate as a vehicle to examine Nora's life.

Instead, her life seems better captured by the series of relationships she had and a few specific, yet notably discontinuous, decisions. In this sense, Gilligan's views of the importance of relationships in women's lives provide a more appropriate lens for viewing Nora's life. Had she remained with her first husband, her intellectual life might well have remained stunted and secretive. By aligning herself with Hap and becoming involved in the intellectual community in Monterey, she began to establish her intellectual credentials. Notice, though, that her entrée was via her beauty, which facilitated her relationship with Hap and her position with John Steinbeck.

CAROL TOMLINSON-
KEASEY
*My Dirty Little
Secret: Women as
Clandestine
Intellectuals*

Relationships were important throughout Nora's life, and many of the significant changes in her life were tied to changes in her commitments. In what she regarded as a major redirection of her life, she moved to San Francisco and stayed with an aunt who was a psychologist. Here Nora reaped her first rewards from the reading that had been her refuge as a preadolescent and adolescent. Nora's father had often punished her for reading, feeling that it detracted from her chores. The move to San Francisco opened up avenues of expression and lines of intellectual inquiry that were new for Nora.

Although Nora's aunt was willing to continue to serve as a surrogate mother in San Francisco, Nora took the first opportunity to leave her family of origin. She certainly was not unique in using marriage as a vehicle to lessen the influence of her family. As in many such marriages, however, Nora was so anxious to leave a difficult situation that she was less than thorough in evaluating the situation she was entering. After her marriage, Nora realized very quickly that she could not exist simply as an attractive adjunct to her husband; she needed intellectual stimulation and an avenue for expressing her intellectual interests. Little wonder that she quickly outgrew her first husband.

The move to Monterey and her relationship with Hap allowed Nora's intellectual spirit to develop. The intellectual freedom in the fun, Bohemian atmosphere of Carmel encouraged Nora to experiment with her own modes of self-expression. For the first time, she began to feel comfortable committing ideas to paper and devoting her energy to causes she endorsed. Although she blossomed intellectually, her relationship with Hap lacked the commitment she needed.

When her daughter died, she made another surprising move, following her third husband to Israel. For the first time, she found a relationship that met her needs for intimacy and provided an environment where she could achieve intellectual satisfaction. Her successes as a wife, a mother, a writer, and an editor in the environment provided by this relationship were noteworthy.

Goals, Improvisation, and Serendipity

Three strategies for dealing with life can be plotted along a continuum: At one end we have the model of setting goals and moving down life's path in a thoughtful, planned way. At the other, we have serendipitous events in control, with the player being pulled helplessly along. In between, we have persons who do not set individual goals, but who assess their life situation and improvise to establish a life path that meets their needs.

Although many men lay out their lives in some detail as young adults, describing specific goals to be attained in three-to-five year phases, women are much less likely to set such goals (Gilligan, 1982; Locke, Shaw, Saari, and Latham, 1981). Each of Nora's primary life changes foreshadowed a different level of intellectual expression. Were these moves orchestrated to allow her intelligence to emerge or to facilitate career opportunities? She says that except for her decision to go to Israel, she often felt like a leaf drifting down a stream. Indeed, some of her decisions, like the one to leave her home in Hollywood and live with her aunt, were made on a whim. The decision to leave her first husband was, however, a thoughtful one, reached after several years of marital difficulty. Her move to Monterey was another fortuitous event. The friend that she went to visit could just as easily have lived in Santa Barbara or Berkeley.

Such serendipity frequently surrounded the career opportunities pursued by the Terman women (Tomlinson-Keasey, 1990). Because they put their husband's and children's needs ahead of their own, the work histories of these women seemed to defy planning. Economic exigencies, divorces, and a world war conspired to pull women who planned to be homemakers into the work force. The crisis atmosphere that often surrounded their job seeking meant that career planning was minimal.

Bateson (1989) described a career strategy she labeled "improvisation." Perhaps this intermediate characterization more accurately defines Nora's life. In each of her surroundings, Nora improvised a way to find personal satisfaction. The different status that evolved from her relationships with Hap and her third husband provided specific kinds of writing opportunities and she wisely capitalized on those opportunities. Like many of the capable women in the Terman study, Nora achieved a balance between the social roles dictated by the culture and her intellectual desires, and she did it with little education and minimal encouragement.

Discontinuity

Nora's life path has several sharp turns, but each one presaged a noticeable improvement in her life situation. With only an occasional course beyond high school, she became a valued editor to scientists in an academic community. Although she never achieved the goal of writing her own manuscripts, the success she achieved is a tribute to her persistence and intellect.

The discontinuities that we see in Nora's life have been chronicled in other women's lives (Bateson, 1989; Block, 1971; Gilligan, Lyons, and Hanmer, 1990). Divorce, the most obvious discontinuity in Nora's life, may represent a woman's move from stagnation to new challenge and growth (Bateson, 1989).

Gilligan et al. (1990) described a discontinuity in women's lives that results from more negative influences. In their view, adolescence poses problems of connection for girls coming of age in Western culture and defines a critical life disjunction for women. In support of such a major developmental discontinuity, one can cite the added stress women feel during adolescence (Rutter, 1986), the increase in depression (Gjerde, 1993), and the decline in self-image (American Association of University Women [AAUW], 1992). Jack Block (1971) in his careful evaluation of lives found a similar discontinuity in the lives of adolescent females. "The most striking phenomenon is a multifaceted move toward greater interpersonal deviousness" (p. 71). Still, one can argue that this developmental discontinuity results from the culture's changing messages to adolescent women. The discontinuities referred to by Bateson and seen in Nora's life are more typically the result of geographical relocation, career moves, or changes in relationships that alter adults' life paths.

Personal Attributes

Personal attributes warrant mention in almost every model of adult achievement (Terman and Oden, 1947; Vaillant, 1977). Personal attributes differentiating women who achieve from those who are less successful inevitably involve assessments of self-confidence and the willingness to take risks (Hennig and Jardim, 1977; Sanford and Donovan, 1984). Like many Terman women, Nora reported a lack of self-confidence, a reticence or hesitancy about approaching career tasks. However, a look at her life and the decisions she made suggests that she was willing to take risks when it was necessary. Not many young women in the Terman cohort divorced while they had a young child. Fewer would have left one man to marry another and travel to Israel. The risk taking that we see in Nora appears in other women who have achieved amidst an unsupportive culture (Hennig and Jardim, 1977).

The development of confidence in her ability posed a problem for Nora and for the majority of the women in the Terman cohort (Tomlinson-Keasey, 1990). Other, more recent studies of women found similar results, "a lack of self-esteem, an inability to feel powerful or in control of one's life, a vulnerability to depression, a tendency to see oneself as less talented, less able than one really is" (Rivers, Barnett, and Baruch, 1979, p. 134). This lack of self-esteem is not limited to a few women nor is it confined to a particular period of our history or a particular age group (Sanford and Donovan, 1984). Contemporary women experience doubts about their abilities and their acceptance in a variety of career positions (AAUW, 1992; Arnold, 1993; Inglehart, Brown, and Malanchuk, 1993).

What can we learn from those women who display an easy confidence in their abilities? Successful women often point specifically to adolescence as a time when they clarified and strengthened their identities (Hennig and Jardim, 1977). During adolescence, these women waged a determined struggle against the restricted, confining feminine role others might have carved for them. Instead, with the support of their father, they continued their strong achievement orientation in atypical fields.

Minimizing Cognitive Skills

Throughout her childhood, Nora hid her intellectual predilections. Yet they were such a vital part of her person that she was forced to nurture these skills in clandestine ways. The entire society loses whenever gifted women hide their intellectual skills, are put in situations where they cannot develop or use those skills, or are discouraged by a masculine culture from trying to succeed in an "atypical" profession. Of interest in Nora's life is the fact that she was able to give fuller voice to her intellectual skills in successive environments.

Gifted and talented women continue to mask their intellects (Hollinger and Fleming, 1988). Longitudinal research reveals a consistent pattern of lowering aspiration levels and declining achievements among adolescent women who are gifted (Arnold, 1993; Kerr, 1985). The stereotypes of genius that still pervade the society perhaps contribute to the negative view of gifted women. One of the earliest stereotypes equated high levels of intelligence with emotional and social maladjustment (Lombroso, 1895). From the 1840s to the 1950s, the notion that precocious triumph would be followed by tragic collapse was prominent, even in academic circles (Sears, 1979). Although the force of some of these stereotypes has been dissipated, it is interesting that college students still believe that gifted females suffer socially (Solano, 1987). Society, the young woman, and young men often view a high level of achievement in a woman as inconsistent with femininity (Fox, 1977), and achievement in junior high and high school can be an invitation to social rejection (Hollinger and Fleming, 1984, 1985). Given the importance of relationships to women, it is little wonder that Nora, her peers, and contemporary adolescents have hidden their intellectual interests.

Although all of the Terman women did not hide their intellectual skills, it is clear that many were unable to develop those skills. In the Depression of the 1930s, many women, even those with college educations, encountered severely limited career opportunities. The Depression meant that women who were married, and thus guaranteed a means of support, were often denied jobs, even in traditionally feminine areas such as nursing and teaching. U.S. society thus funneled women into the role of homemakers.

Much has changed in the society since the Terman women were in college. However, Swiatek and Benbow (1991) reported that families still feel that educational opportunities are more important for gifted men than they are for gifted women. In their study, gifted boys who had been accelerated in school attended colleges with a median rank of twenty-third in the country. The gifted girls who had been accelerated attended colleges with a median rank of 180. Among gifted students who were not accelerated, median rank for the boys' colleges was 46; for the girls' colleges, 299.

A description of the life paths of adult women must confront the complexity of lives in which relationships, intimacy, and commitment are a primary responsibility. It must allow for discontinuity in the flow of women's lives and recognize that serendipity and improvisation are substitutes for goal setting when the woman's life path is not clear. A description of women's development must assess personal attributes that differ from those of men and that have an impact on career directions and further development.

Given the above, an acceptable model for women's development can hardly resemble the stair steps of progressive occupational attainment offered by Levinson (1978) and Vaillant (1977). A possible alternative is a circle radiating outward from the woman to include relationships, career involvement, and family responsibilities. During different periods of adult life, time commitments, activity, and responsibilities in each of these sectors might vary, and each sector might have a developmental progression of its own compared to the developmental phase of another aspect of life.

FACILITATING WOMEN'S DEVELOPMENT

In examining women's lives, it is instructive to ask how Nora's situation could have been altered to actualize her intellectual skills. Empowering women, removing obstacles to their success, recognizing the critical importance of relationships to their lives, and allowing for discontinuous events would help women who would like to contribute their skills to the society.

Empowerment

Personal empowerment may be uniquely important to the facilitation of intellectual growth for young women simply because it counters the pervasive cultural messages about the importance of physical appearance. Having a father who makes it clear that you are appreciated for qualities that go beyond the su-

243

*CAROL TOMLINSON-
KEASEY
My Dirty Little
Secret: Women as
Clandestine
Intellectuals*

perficial and physical may be particularly salutary for women's intellectual development. Nora's father not only ignored the talent and predilections that should have been obvious to a writer, he disparaged them. Nora's teachers in high school described her promise and mentioned her for a scholarship, but decided against taking a chance on her. Nora's aunt was the only person who attempted to help by enticing Nora away from the Hollywood scene. Beyond that, Nora seems to have made her own way.

Women in the Terman era who pursued intellectual interests often had particular encouragement from their fathers. In fact, in Hennig and Jardim's study (1977) of managerial women in the 1950s, the women CEOs were always first born, typically the only child, and reported close, empowering relationships with their fathers. The fathers encouraged their daughters in a variety of venues. Further, the daughters were allowed to see and experience many facets of the father's life.

One can speculate about the mechanisms behind the father's particular influence. Were daughters of such fathers particularly likely to pursue a career and actualize their intellectual potential because their fathers demystified particular career paths? This is certainly a possibility. One pharmacist's daughter reports serving as a cashier for her father at an early age. She pursued a career in biology. An attorney's daughter remembers many visits to the courthouse and courtrooms as a child. She felt comfortable becoming an attorney. The daughter of a famed scientist grew up with scientific visitors from around the globe. She became a researcher of note in her own right. Even Nora knew about writers from her father. When a father demystifies a career, he shows his daughter that successful individuals in the occupation possess a range of talents and abilities. In doing so, he makes the career more approachable.

Perhaps the father's effect is more diffuse and should be seen as providing an opportunity for self-growth. Being encouraged by their father may help daughters define themselves and their abilities accurately. Such empowerment may also help daughters pursue both "typical" and "atypical" professions.

Both of these mechanisms could operate in a woman's life to mediate and explain a father's influence. Certainly, Nora had no nurturing, no encouragement, no empowerment, and no sense that her intellect was valuable. Still, even in her life, the occupation of writer was demystified, and Nora's familiarity with that career could well have directed her interests.

Other individuals or institutions might provide women with similar empowerment. Brothers, grandfathers, uncles, and husbands all empowered some of the Terman women. Here, too, Nora drew a blank. She was estranged from her brothers early in life. Female role models, when they exist, can demystify careers, but they are not as convincing when it comes to certifying the acceptability of developing your own intellect. Nora experienced little mothering. Only her aunt helped by offering her refuge. As I understand Nora's life story, this help turned out to be critical to Nora's intellectual development.

Recognizing the Importance of Relationships, Commitment, and Intimacy to Women's Lives

Recognizing the importance of relationships, commitment, and intimacy to women's lives as a way of facilitating women's development will require major restructuring of our society (O'Farrell and Harlan, 1984; Schroeder,

1989). The women of the Terman sample had much to offer society, and like Nora, they contributed in ways that fit with their circumstances. But listen carefully to their voices and you will hear that they did not find the structure of the world amenable to their skills. Here is Nora's comment when asked about her flaws: "I procrastinate, probably because of some basic uncertainty which leads to super-sensitivity and inferiority feelings." Simply recognizing women's hesitancies and their need for reassurance would keep many competent women from becoming discouraged. Nora suggested that her most appealing traits were her "fierce energy and her friendliness." Like many women, her social skills and her commitment to relationships could be turned into a positive force in career development and intellectual achievement. Nora noted that she refused to enter the career contests that depended on "aggressiveness and manipulation." Perhaps Nora's words allude to the differences in the way men and women contemplate and pursue their lives.

A curriculum that allows women to learn in a less competitive, more cooperative environment produces women who as high school students are more likely to pursue science (Dresselhaus, 1992). At the college level, Dresselhaus urged universities to make women feel welcome in physics, chemistry, engineering, and other disciplines. Women benefit from peer group and networking programs that provide them with information, guidance, and reassurance that they can succeed.

Organizers of professional training and career development programs need to recognize that if women are to participate in, enjoy, and succeed in their chosen field, ways have to be found to allow family goals to be met (Baruch, Biener, and Barnett, 1987). Although women in career positions initially brought attention to family concerns, men have relished the opportunity to deal with their own family-based stresses. Continued societal attention to family leave policies and flexibility in career strategies will encourage women to bring their talents to scientific and professional arenas.

Removing Societal Obstacles

The obstacles that Nora had to overcome are seldom mentioned in adult models of development. For women, many of these obstacles are cultural and invisible. Several times Nora was told that she could not be taken seriously, she was too cute. Her beauty also provided an entrée to relationships and social settings in which her intellect could then be expressed.

The intractability of the male orientation in particular fields remains. Even successful women report feeling excluded from office networks in areas like law and architecture (Milwid, 1982). In 1986, the National Research Council concluded that women's occupational choices and preferences did not account for the continued occupational segregation by sex; such barriers resulted instead from personnel practices that made advancement difficult and from stereotypes about women's proper roles and traits (Reskin and Hartmann, 1986).

Permitting Discontinuity

Instead of an orderly stepwise progression in a career, McGuigan (1980) envisioned women's adult development as "a braid of threads in which colors ap-

245

CAROL TOMLINSON-
KEASEY
*My Dirty Little
Secret: Women as
Clandestine
Intellectuals*

pear, disappear, and reappear" (p. xii). Such a model captures some of the discontinuity in women's lives that Bateson described. Allowing women with major discontinuities in their lives to compete in fields that currently have continuous career paths will require more flexible and inclusive policies than have previously existed. Medical school, for example, now offers women the opportunity to share postgraduate training. It takes these women longer to complete their studies, but it allows them to retain a family life. Governments, businesses, and other major institutions must adjust their programs to make it easier for women to follow a flexible life course that intermingles work, education, and family commitments (Giele, 1982).

CONCLUSIONS

Nora's intellectual growth radiated from the relationships she developed. Her first husband was uneducated and lived a life devoid of intellectual stimulation. Her second husband was a scientist who embraced all aspects of life and played in an intellectual community. Nora's third husband was a world-renowned researcher whose entire life revolved around intellectual questions. Nora's life and the intellectual opportunities open to her were delimited by these relationships. Could she have developed independent opportunities and pursued a goal as a writer or researcher? Perhaps, but few of the Terman women did (Terman and Oden, 1947, 1959). Instead they learned to create their opportunities out of the situations and relationships that defined their lives.

Serendipity, improvisation, and lack of goal setting were hallmarks of Nora's life and the Terman women generally. Ill-defined goals still characterize career aspirations of adult women. Very few women develop personal career goals and pursue them in a single-minded way. Their focus on relationships precludes the pursuit of clearly defined goals. Instead, women wait for serendipitous events that provide an opportunity for them to use their skills or else improvise in the situations available to them.

Nora hid her intellectual proclivities for years. Was this characteristic of intelligent women in her cohort and do we see similar behaviors today? Certainly, the women in Nora's cohort were schooled in the importance of relationships. Becoming a wife was the most frequent life goal mentioned when these women were in their mid-twenties. In accomplishing this goal, these bright women were often coy, were careful not to intimidate, and were eager to please. If this meant that they did not flaunt their intellect, it was probably a sensible decision.

The achievements of gifted women are constrained by their culture, their opportunities, their relationships, and the complexity of the lives they lead. This was true of Nora and was generally true of the women in the Terman sample. It remains true, to a lesser degree, of contemporary women. Could Nora have written a book that would have competed with some of John Steinbeck's works? Could she have pursued a research project that would have yielded answers to unsolved questions? She certainly had the cognitive ability. And the success she enjoyed with a high school education was impressive. What she lacked was education, encouragement, empowerment, and opportunities to develop those skills in ways that were compatible with a stable relationship and the family she desired.

Acknowledgments

This chapter derives from information originally collected by Lewis M. Terman and maintained in the archives at Stanford University. Hence, I owe a special debt to Robert Sears, Albert Hastorf, and Eleanor Walker of Stanford University for helping me gain access to the data. In addition, I must thank "Nora" who opened her life to scrutiny to help us better understand women's lives.

Notes

1. Names have been changed to protect privacy.

References

American Association of University Women. (1992). *How schools shortchange girls: A study of major findings on girls in education.* Washington, DC: AAUW Education Foundation.

ARNOLD, K. D. (1993). Academically talented women in the 1980s: The Illinois Valedictorian project. In K. D. Hulbert and D. T. Schuster (Eds.), *Women's lives through time: Educated American women of the twentieth century* (pp. 425–440). San Francisco: Jossey-Bass.

BARUCH, G. K., BIENER, L. & BARNETT, R. C. (1987). Women and gender in research on work and family stress. *American Psychologist, 42,* 130–136.

BATESON, M. C. (1989). *Composing a life.* New York: Plume.

BLOCK, J. (1971). *Lives through time.* Berkeley: Bancroft.

DRESSELHAUS, M. S. (1992, November 15). Setting Barbie straight is a start. *Davis Enterprise,* p. A-9.

ECCLES, J. S. (1985). Why doesn't Jane run? Sex differences in educational and occupational patterns. In F. D. Horowitz & M. O'Brien (Eds.), *The gifted and talented: Developmental perspectives* (pp. 251–295). Washington, DC: American Psychological Association.

ERIKSON, E. (1950). *Childhood and Society.* New York: Norton.

FOX, L. H. (1977). Sex differences: Implications for program planning for the academically gifted. In J. C. Stanley, W. C. George, & C. H. Solano (Eds.), *The gifted and the creative: A fifty year perspective* (pp. 113–138). Baltimore: Johns Hopkins University Press.

GIELE, J. Z. (1982). Women in adulthood: Unanswered questions. In J. Z. Giele (Ed.), *Women in the middle years* (pp. 1–35). New York: Wiley.

GILLIGAN, C. (1982). Adult development and women's development: Arrangements for a marriage. In J. Z. Giele (Ed.), *Women in the middle years* (pp. 89–114). New York: Wiley.

GILLIGAN, C., LYONS, N. P., & HANMER, T. J. (1990). *Making connections.* Cambridge, MA: Harvard University Press.

GINZBERG, E. (1966). *Life styles of educated women.* New York: Columbia University Press.

GINZBERG, E., & YOHALEM, A. M. (1966). *Educated American women: Self-portraits.* New York: Columbia University Press.

GJERDE, P. (1993). Depressive symptoms in young adults: A developmental perspective on gender differences. In D. Funder, R. D. Parke, C. Tomlinson-Keasey, & K.

247

*CAROL TOMLINSON-
KEASEY
My Dirty Little
Secret: Women as
Clandestine
Intellectuals*

Widaman (Eds.), *Studying lives through time: Approaches to personality and development* (pp. 255–288). Washington, DC: American Psychological Association.

GROSSMAN, H. Y., & CHESTER, N. L. (1990). *The experience and meaning of work in women's lives.* Hillsdale, NJ: Lawrence Erlbaum.

GUSTAFSON, S. R., & MAGNUSSON, D. (1991). *Female life careers: A pattern approach.* Hillsdale, NJ: Lawrence Erlbaum.

HEILBRUN, C. (1988). *Writing a woman's life.* New York: Norton.

HENNIG, M., & JARDIM, A. (1977). *The managerial woman.* Garden City, NY: Anchor.

HOLLINGER, C. L., & FLEMING, E. S. (1984). Internal barriers to the realization of potential: Correlates and interrelationships among gifted and talented female adolescents. *Gifted Child Quarterly, 28,* 135–139.

———. (1985). Social orientations and the social self-esteem of gifted and talented female adolescents. *Journal of Youth and Adolescence, 14,* 389–399.

———. (1988). Gifted and talented young women: Antecedents and correlates of life satisfaction. *Gifted Child Quarterly, 32,* 254–259.

INGLEHART, M., BROWN, D. R., & MALANCHUK, O. (1993). University of Michigan medical school graduates of the 1980s: The professional development of women physicians. In K. D. Hulbert & D. T. Schuster (Eds.), *Women's lives through time: Educated American women of the twentieth century* (pp. 374–392). San Francisco: Jossey-Bass.

KERR, B. A. (1985). *Smart girls, gifted women.* Columbus, OH: Ohio Psychological.

LEVINSON, D. J. (1978). *Seasons of a man's life.* New York: Knopf.

LOCKE, E. A., SHAW, K. A., SAARI, L. M., & LATHAM, G. P. (1981). Goal setting and task performance: 1969–1980. *Psychological Bulletin, 90,* 125–152.

LOMBROSO, C. (1895). *The man of genius.* London: Scribner.

McCLELLAND, D. (1975). *Power: The inner experience.* New York: Irvington.

McGuigan, D. G. (1980). Exploring women's lives: An introduction. In D. G. McGuigan (Ed.), *Women's lives: New theory, research and policy* (pp. i–xii). Ann Arbor: University of Michigan, Center for Continuing Education of Women.

MILWID, M. E. (1982). *Women in male dominated professions: A study of bankers, architects, and lawyers.* Unpublished doctoral dissertation, Wright Institute, Berkeley.

O'FARRELL, B., & HARLAN, S. L. (1984). Job integration strategies: Today's programs and tomorrow's needs. In B. F. Reskin (Ed.), *Sex segregation in the workplace: Trends, explanations, remedies.* (pp. 267–291). Washington, DC: National Academy Press.

RESKIN, B., & HARTMANN, H. (1986). *Women's work, men's work: Sex segregation on the job.* Washington, DC: National Academy Press.

RIVERS, C., BARNETT, R., & BARUCH, G. (1979). *Beyond sugar and spice: How women grow, learn and thrive.* New York: G. P. Putnam.

RUTTER, M. (1986). The developmental psychopathology of depression: Issues and perspectives. In M. Rutter, C. Izzard, & P. Read (Eds.), *Depression in young people: Developmental and clinical perspectives* (pp. 3–32). New York: Guilford.

SANFORD, L. T., & DONOVAN, M. E. (1984). *Women & self-esteem.* New York: Doubleday.

SCHROEDER, P. (1989). Toward a national family policy. *American Psychologist, 44,* 1410–1413.

SEARS, P. (1979). The Terman genetic studies of genius. In A. Passow (Ed.), *The seventy-eighth yearbook of the National Society for the Study of Education* (pp. 75–96). Chicago: University of Chicago Press.

SOLANO, C. H. (1987). Stereotypes of social isolation and early burnout in the gifted: Do they still exist? *Journal of Youth and Adolescence, 16,* 527–539.

SWIATEK, M. A., & BENBOW, C. P. (1991). Ten year longitudinal follow-up of ability matched accelerated and unaccelerated gifted students. *Journal of Educational Psychology, 83,* 528–538.

TERMAN, L. M., & ODEN, M. H. (1947). *Genetic studies of genius: Vol. 4. The gifted child grows up.* Stanford: Stanford University Press.

————. (1959). *Genetic studies of genius: Vol. 5. The gifted group at mid-life.* Stanford: Stanford University Press.

TOMLINSON–KEASEY, C. (1990). The working lives of Terman's gifted women. In H. W. Grossman & N. L. Chester (Eds.), *The experience and meaning of work in women's lives* (pp. 213–240). Hillsdale, NJ: Lawrence Erlbaum.

————. (in press). Tracing the lives of gifted women. In R. Jenkins-Friedman & F. D. Horowitz (Eds.), *Life-span research on gifted and talented children and youth.* Washington, DC: American Psychological Association.

VAILLANT, G. E. (1977). *Adaptation to life.* Boston: Little, Brown.

Janice D. Yoder

An Academic Woman as a Token:
A Case Study

With recent statistics continuing to document sex discrimination in academe (Stapp & Fulcher, 1983), case histories (Allport, 1942) remain an important source of information about the struggles that engage academic women. The following case history describes my experience as one of the first female civilian faculty members at a United States military academy. It is written with the following goals in mind: (a) to describe tokenism and its effects on an individual (rather than on a group) in order to illustrate its personal effects, (b) to develop hypotheses for future research, and (c) to consider some coping and change strategies to overcome the situational constraints and personal trauma of being a token. These goals seem particularly appropriate for this issue of the *Journal of Social Issues.*

TOKENISM AND ITS SOCIAL CONTEXT

Tokenism as an area of research became popular with the publication of Kanter's (1977) book, which defines tokenism as membership in a proportionally underrepresented subgroup (less than 15% of the entire group). Laws (1975), who has focused on tokenism in academia, adds richness to this definition by describing its social context. For Laws, academic women are double-deviants, first as women in a patriarchal society and secondly as seekers of accomplishments and rewards usually sought by men.

In fact, some recent research suggests that proportional underrepresentation has different consequences for women and men, and that the negative effects described by Kanter apply only to token women (Yoder & Sinnett, in press). Being underrepresented does not seem to handicap men's career devel-

The author would like to thank Cathy Burack, Seena Kohl, and Win Rogers for their assistance in revising the present paper, and Ed Hollander and Carolyn Wood Sheriff for their support at the 1980 meetings of the American Psychological Association.

opment. The present paper will regard tokenism only within the the context of broader societal sex role stereotypes; that is, as it relates to societal inequities for women (Richards, 1980).

Prior research on token women in business (Kanter, 1977) and the military (Yoder, Adams, & Prince, 1983) reveals three consequences of tokenism: visibility, contrast, and assimilation. Visibility arises from the salience of differences between token and dominant group members. For example, the female cadets at the academy stand out even as they march by in parades. Because of their visibility, tokens experience performance pressures, and dominants often come to resent the apparent ease with which token women get recognition. The latter may result in fears among dominant group members that women possess a "competitive edge."

Contrast refers to differences between men and women that lead to dominants' uncertainties about how to deal with tokens and the consequent isolation of tokens. Kanter (1977) describes how influential men in corporations may take their jokes and social banter from the boardroom to bars and other exclusionary places, isolating women from these informal social networks.

The uncertainties produced by contrasted differences may be resolved to some degree by encapsulating token women into stereotypic sex roles (Yoder & Adams, 1984). Kanter (1977) describes how token women come to be regarded as sex objects, mothers, pets, or iron maidens—roles that are degrading and incompatible with the fulfillment of their professional responsibilities.

BECOMING A TOKEN

In the summer of 1980 I joined the faculty of the academy as a distinguished visiting professor (VP). There were approximately 545 faculty members; of these, 97% were military officers, primarily academy graduates (56%). The overwhelming majority were men. There were 14 female military officers, and only two of the 11 civilian VPs were women—the first ever hired.

When I was interviewed for the position, my gender was important. With the newly coeducational format (female cadets were first admitted to military academies in 1976; see Durning, 1978; Stiehm, 1981; Vitters & Kinzer, 1977), the military was experiencing a gap in the number of female officers qualified to teach. Until a pool of female graduates becomes available for appointment, civilian women are regarded as a stopgap solution. An earlier longitudinal study of the integration of female cadets into the academy argued for the availability of female role models in both academic and military/tactical capacities (Adams, 1979, 1980). I was hired partly to serve that purpose.

During graduate school I had been associated with a longitudinal research project on the integration of cadet women. The opportunity for continuing and expanding my role in this research by giving me firsthand experiences with cadets' lives was of great interest. To help me further pursue this research, my position was formally described as half-time researcher/half-time teacher. One line of research I was pursuing at this time dealt with the situational consequences of tokenism for female cadets (Yoder et al., 1983). Needless to say, as a 27-year-old, single, civilian, female VP, I came to understand tokenism as both a researcher and an individual.

My life at the academy was lonely. I lived in the bachelor officers' quarters, one block from the building in which I taught. As a military base, the academy's facilities are excellent and comprehensive. One can buy a pizza, go to a movie, and get a beer all without leaving the base. One does not simply work at the academy; one lives there.

I am giving these details to show the extremes of my case. I differed from my colleagues by my civilian attire, my age, my gender, and my professional role as a researcher. The fact that I was different followed me from work to home, since these cannot be separated within the confines of a military post. I believe these exaggerated circumstances, while potentially restricting the generalizability of this case report, show the effects of tokenism more clearly than is possible in other academic settings where pressures exist in more subtle forms.

The primary resource for the present paper is a journal I kept throughout my six months at the academy. Obviously, my work on the integration of cadet women into the academy is also relevant to my case and the ideas I will present here. Finally, I kept piles of military materials—everything from the student newspaper to the historian's report, manuals, and memos, and I will refer to these where appropriate.

THE LIFE OF A TOKEN

Visibility did not produce performance pressures for me because I was not to be formally evaluated at any time during my two-year contract, and I was a VP with an admirable, albeit new, doctoral degree in the midst of a faculty mostly with master's degrees (56%). The problem of my visibility centered on perceptions of my specialness and the supposed privileges this would engender.

There was a lot of pressure for me to blend in and for me not to exploit my visibility by using my "competitive edge" over my colleagues. For example, the assignment of office space was not a simple matter. Except for the upper echelons, officers shared large rooms divided into semiprivate offices. My office was a cubicle off one of these large rooms—its small size was compensated for by a door and solid walls that assured privacy. As an added bonus, the cubicle housed a computer terminal that I used incessantly. As the semester began, I was asked to keep my door open to diminish one of the ostensible benefits of my privileged space: its privacy. Remarks about my "personal computer" encouraged me to do most of my computing at night away from the watchful eyes of my less-fortunate colleagues.

My specialness presented problems for several reasons: I had a half-time teaching load to give me time for research (in which few others engaged), many of the observations that were part of my research were conducted outside the office in the field, and I was isolated from the departmental "team."

The faculty of the academy represented success stories of military careers punctuated by a trip to graduate school and a three-year prestigious appointment to the academy. Competition and social comparisons, especially on officers' evaluations, were intense. As a civilian, I was exempt from these evaluations. Furthermore, the one salient measure of an officer's efforts was the amount of time he or she spent in the office. Shortly after my arrival, sign-out sheets were posted to keep track of officers missing during regular hours. When I spent a day in the field or stayed home to write, the perception soon developed that I was goofing off.

The primary duties of my colleagues were to teach and advise cadets. Courses were taught by teams that covered the same materials at the same time, in preparation for the same exams. The interdependency of teaching faculty encouraged "team spirit."

My differences as a civilian, a researcher, and a woman created uncertainties among my colleagues and threatened to disrupt the team. During our departmental presemester workshop, I frequently was isolated from group discussions on the grounds that I had different, and apparently irrelevant, goals. At these meetings, one subgroup dubbed itself the "Wolf Gang," used "we eat sheep!" as their motto, and howled when called upon to make group presentations. The departmental theme song chosen was "Macho Man," hardly appropriate for an academic department that included two female officers and myself. The gossip about my sexuality ranged from lesbian to heterosexually promiscuous.

This was the catch-22 of my role: Because I was different, I could not be a good team member; but, not being part of the team helped make me different and increased my isolation. I began to withdraw, reluctantly attending only mandatory events, which contributed further to my isolation.

My favorite "war stories" illustrate incidents of assimilation and role encapsulation. Specifically, I was assigned to one of two female roles: "wife" or "feminist/libber." In the former role, I was invited to a luncheon for the wives of the VPs. I learned to wear my name tag to help combat this misidentification, especially after a reception where I was presented to everyone in the reception line as the wife of the graying male VP (he wore his name tag) standing next to me. Before each introduction, I stated my name and position to deaf ears, a vigorous handshake, and a "Hello, Mrs. _____."

While this was mildly amusing, the effects of my second label as "feminist/libber" were not. I acquired this label by objecting to my invitation as the wife of a VP, departmental invitations open to "wives and girlfriends," being expected to bring three dishes to a pot luck dinner that I, not my wife, would cook, and sexist exam questions for our team-taught introductory psychology course: "Your new girlfriend has a habit that drives you insane. . . ." This last series of objections resulted in a suggestion book for exam questions where I could quietly record the same notes without disrupting faculty meetings. I watched as my colleagues began to get restless when I raised my hand, rolled their eyes as I spoke, and concluded by ignoring or defending. I became totally ineffectual, yet unwilling to keep quiet and thus implicitly condone these actions. My role as a deviate became predictable, unwelcome, and ignored.

Each of these processes (visibility, contrast, and role encapsulation) contributed to a downward spiral in my relations to my colleagues, especially to my department head. The ultimate result was a reevaluation of my position for the spring semester. Without discussing it with me, I was assigned a full teaching load comparable to those of my nonresearching colleagues.

This was the turning point of my short-lived adventure. Until this time, my attitudes fluctuated from acquiescence to moments of rebelliousness. I engaged in a heated discussion with the department head about my difficulties at the presemester departmental session. I insisted on going to the convention of the American Psychological Association to present a paper despite the appearance that I was being granted further privilege. It was at these meetings, among similar colleagues and mentors, that I realized that without the promise of research time my stay at the academy would not be fruitful professionally. I decided to terminate my two-year contract after completing only six months. I returned to the academy, armed with new-found self-confidence and determination, submitted my resignation, and began to search for another job.

UNDERSTANDING TOKENISM

I choose to share these particular anecdotes because they portray some of the frustrations and anxieties that come with the real-life role of a token operating in an extremely unfavorable environment. At times, they are amusing and I look forward to a time when I can humor grandchildren with my "war stories." No one event alone seems overly traumatic (see Frye, 1983). However, when you squeeze these events into six months and add the pressures of a move and a new job, separation from friends and my future husband, and my confinement to a military base, the interpersonal toll stands more clearly. Generally, these are the types of pressures that confront tokens. We ask them to go in and do a job to prove that they can do the job. The token becomes the test case, a test case doomed to suffer and often to fail. Let us hypothesize about the psychological and behavioral effects of tokenism.

Psychological Effects

I believe being a token has some measurable effect on the self-esteem of tokens. As I read my journal, I can relive the rapid decline in my self-image. On the first night, my tone was hopeful—I was filled with the adventure I was about to begin. A mere three months later I wrote the following:

> What does happen to the deviate? The deviate can convert, but short of a sex-change operation, a time machine to age me, and a personality overhaul, conversion seems out of the question for me. Be isolated? That originally was all right with me, but that surely does not make me a team member. What can I do? Yet, the failure is placed squarely on my shoulders. "What's wrong with you?" "Why can't you get along?" These questions haunt me, undermining my self-image to a point where I am reduced to crying at home alone at night . . . I feel impotent. I can't sleep, but I am never clear-headed and fully awake. I have an eye infection. Daily problems have become insurmountable difficulties. I am bored, yet I rush home to be alone. I can't work. I can't go out and have fun . . . I have become bad in my eyes; the attributions of blame have been internalized.

I engaged in a personal example of "blaming the victim" (Ryan, 1976; 1981) similar to what other researchers have found for victims of rape and sexual harassment (e.g., Janoff-Bulman, 1979; Jensen & Gutek, 1982). Like a disproportionate number of other women at the academy who left their positions early (including one of the officers in my department), I felt guilty for jeopardizing the opportunities of other women. One suggestion for future researchers is to document this turning inward and the accompanying loss of self-esteem, self-efficacy, and life satisfaction. Some of this anxiety was expressed in an eye infection; it seemed that even my body began to revolt. For fully one-half of the female cadets under the stress of basic training, anxiety is expressed physiologically in the disruption of their menstrual cycles (Vitters & Kinzer, 1977).

Behavioral Effects

My behavioral reactions fell along a continuum of withdrawal—from initially isolating myself in my apartment to eventually deciding to leave. A similar pattern is found among token women in both the military and corporate worlds. Withdrawal and attrition have important social consequences, in addition to their effects on the individual. In a movement toward social equality, tokens stand as test cases and their failures may be heralded as confirmation of the idea that they were unsuited for the position.

One approach to explaining withdrawal is person-centered, focusing on individuals as the sources of their own behavior. In contrast, situation-centered explanations focus on current environmental contingencies (Kanter, 1977; Riger & Gilligan, 1980). Women and men differ because of differences in opportunities, power, numbers, societal norms, and so on. In my particular case, a person-centered explanation for my "failure" would focus on me—my inability to blend in, my feminist values, and my emphasis on research. A situation-centered perspective, on the other hand, stresses external pressures: visibility, contrast, and assimilation that come about through the interaction of tokens and dominants. Combine these with sex-role stereotypes, and the token woman faces an aversive situation. It is not some defect in the token that causes some to withdraw; rather, it is the antagonistic and grudging *situation* that could cause anyone, male or female, to withdraw.

If the withdrawal of the token is largely the result of situational adversities, then the finding that women "fail" is a self-fulfilling prophecy (Merton, 1968). Women fail because the situation is devised, whether intentionally or inadvertently, to assure their failure. What needs to be changed is the negative situation and the individual's reaction to it. Research directed toward effective ways to change situations in order to increase the likelihood of success for both women and men is paramount.

BRINGING ABOUT CHANGE

If women are to succeed in roles that presently enlist token numbers, we must supplement effective affirmative action that facilitates *entry* into jobs with conditions that can help in *retention* and *promotion*. This is important not only for the particular individuals involved, but also because their lack of success can be used to threaten whatever standards of affirmative action currently exist (Macaulay, 1981). I have no doubt that my resignation jeopardized the opportunities of other civilian women at the academy, as I was not replaced. My work with female cadets shows that they too carry this burden. As one woman said, "anything one girl did reflected on every single girl here" (Yoder, Adams, Grove, & Priest, 1985).

Although I believe situational changes are most effective and compatible with my feminist ideology, the realities are such that tokenism often must be endured and overcome by at least one generation. For this reason, I here propose ideas for future work that concentrates on individual tokens, groups of tokens, and the situation.

Individual Tokens

When we focus on the individual, we should explore two interrelated aspects: (a) the effects of tokenism on the individual and (b) individuals' strategies for coping with and overcoming tokenism. My experiences make clear the impact of tokenism on myself: as my stress and frustration levels rose, my self-esteem plummeted. These individual consequences are well documented in other case histories (e.g., Datan, 1980; DeSole & Hoffmann, 1981; Nielsen, 1979; Weisstein, 1977). Analyses designed to explore the impact of tokenism on individuals should collect both personal (e.g., demographic, attitudinal, and personality measures) and situational (e.g., visibility, marginal peer acceptance, and role encapsulation) information in order to understand the interaction of both these sets of variables (Kulka & Colten, 1982; Sherif, 1979).

The effective coping strategies of successful, satisfied women need to be understood, and training individuals in the use of these strategies needs to be devised, implemented, and tested. Hall's (1972) descriptive study illustrates a useful starting point. Through a survey of college-educated women, Hall found that the most satisfied women used a coping strategy he labeled "structural role redefinition." This strategy involves changing externally imposed expectations: for example, negotiating an alternative set of role expectations within one's employer or family.

Tokens as a Group

Frequently women are exhorted to bond together to overcome tokenism (e.g., Kaufman, 1978). Women need to be made aware of their shared problems; effective networking is one way to accomplish this. Networks may help women validate themselves as individuals and thereby reduce the decline in self-esteem associated with tokenism. With my low self-esteem and without support, I could not break out of the downward spiral that ensued at the academy. Only leaving helped me do this. But for those who remain in the situation, effective networks may be a means by which they can cope with and change their situation.

Bonding does not occur spontaneously. In fact, tokenism itself may inhibit bonding in competitive settings (e.g., White, 1970). For example, we found that cadet women at the academy failed to sponsor incoming female cadets because the upperclass women were too burdened by their own tokenism and its consequences (Yoder et al., 1985). One of the last things these women wanted was to emphasize their gender by associating with other women.

I felt a similar discouragement with the two female military colleagues and the wives in my department at the academy. Wives did not associate with their husbands' female coworkers in much the same way Kanter (1977) describes. As for my colleagues, on one occasion the three of us sat together at a departmental meeting. This elicited comments about an exclusive "women's club" and that we were "plotting" something. Needless to say, we restricted our future interactions to less visible, nonwork settings.

Another way women are discouraged from bonding is by gossip about their sexuality. For example, a group of women bowlers at the academy was branded as lesbian. This was "validated" by their frequent hugs when one of them scored a strike. This vicious gossip seems to surround women as mentors and also in women's centers on many college campuses.

In sum, support groups may not be formed because of the situational constraints of tokenism. Institutional recognition of such groups may be limited and needs to be actively fostered over time. Additionally, women must be careful to structure support groups effectively. If a group simply touts the successes of a few superwomen, it may come to support the status quo by providing examples of success that encourage others to look inward for the source of their failures (an example of "blaming the victim"). On the other hand, the adoption of structural role redefinition by a group makes it a potential asset beyond the strivings of a lone individual with this perspective. This type of support group should be the ideal.

Situational Factors

Action research also is called for regarding situational factors: first, explore the situation and its impact, and then design, implement, and test situational changes to understand their effectiveness in bringing about desired change (see Larwood & Lockheed, 1979). However, there may be strong institutional resistance. Laws (1975) states: "Tokenism is the means by which the dominant group advertises a promise of mobility" so long as tokens do "not change the system they enter" (pp. 51–52). Tokens serve two functions for the institution: (a) they demonstrate to others that someone was good enough to make it, thereby encouraging other potential tokens to try harder (Yoder, 1983a); and (b) the presence of token group members assures the external world that the institution follows nondiscriminatory hiring practices (Laws, 1975). The effect of both of these is to reinforce the existent social structure and its apparent meritocracy (Denmark, 1980).

I believe Laws is right—dominants do not want tokens to change the system. Yet without change, tokenism and its negative effects will persist. For example, after an initial barrage of too much research directed at the first women cadets, which served to emphasize their visibility (Adams, 1979; Durning, 1978), the academy now no longer sponsors any systematic study of the current female cadets, despite persistently high attrition rates. An unstructured exit interview of most women graduates is the only remaining vestige of a once-active research program. "The woman problem is solved," I have been told. But then, why are women still referred to as "problems"?

In recognition of institutional resistance to change, research is needed not only to show the negative effects of tokenism, but also to develop realistic alternatives. These programs must include situational modifications shown to be conducive to positive organizational change. For example, our research suggests that an atmosphere of intense competition heightens the negative effects of tokenism (Yoder et al., 1984). One way to reduce this, the jigsaw technique used by Aronson and his colleagues (1978), has proven effective in newly racially integrated classrooms. Here, cooperation is necessary for the group's success, thereby making isolation and role encapsulation of tokens counterproductive.

Individual competition, however, is the hallmark of our academic system (Bowles & Gintis, 1976); changing it would be a formidable task. A more modest improvement would be to reassess standards of evaluation. At the academy, cadets are judged by criteria standardized on men. This is particularly problematic in areas involving physical prowess, an important component of each cadet's success (Rice, Yoder, Adams, Priest, & Prince, 1984). It is these biased standards that may frustrate tokens, lead to their withdrawal, and at the same time justify the current situation as being apparently nondiscriminatory (Yoder, 1983b). Women's groups can challenge these standards by calling into question the legitimacy of traditional criteria.

CONCLUSIONS

The case history method adds to the resources of feminist researchers by providing descriptive information, sharing the richness of individuals' accounts and reactions, and encouraging situational attributions (Jones & Nisbett, 1972).

People bring about change by altering both situations and their own perceptions. To do this, women's networks and feminist psychotherapists must help individuals adopt satisfying strategies, such as structural role redefinition, for working toward institutional change. Social psychologists and sociologists need to analyze existing social situations with an eye toward improvement. Kanter's (1977) and Laws's (1975) analyses are good examples. Policy-makers need to be aware of the impact of standards of evaluation, individual competition, techniques for physical training, and so on. New policies need to be devised to produce the positive qualities of all participants. Finally, social scientists need to conduct program evaluations to ensure that changes are working as projected. This system of change and feedback needs to involve all levels so that the downward spiral can be broken and progress initiated. To do this, change agents (women's networking groups, psychotherapists, social psychologists, sociologists, and policymakers) must effectively coordinate their efforts.

References

ADAMS, J. (1979). *Report of the admission of women to the U.S. military academy (Project Athena III)*. West Point, NY: United States Military Academy.

ADAMS, J. (1980). *Report of the admission of women to the U.S. military academy (Project Athena IV)*. West Point, NY: United States Military Academy.

ALLPORT, G. W. (1942). *The use of personal documents in psychological science*. New York: Social Science Research Council.

ARONSON, E., BLANEY, N., STEPHAN, C., SIKES, J., & SNAPP, M. (1978). *The jigsaw classroom.* Beverly Hills, CA: Sage.

BOWLES, S., & GINTIS, H. (1976). *Schooling in capitalist America.* New York: Basic Books, 1976.

DATAN, R. (1980). Days of our lives. *The Journal of Mind and Behavior, 1,* 63–71.

DENMARK, F. L. (1980). Psyche: From rocking the cradle to rocking the boat. *American Psychologist, 35,* 1057–1065.

DeSole, G., & HOFFMAN, L. (Eds.) (1981). *Rocking the boat: Academic women and academic process.* New York: Modern Language Association of America.

DURNING, K. P. (1978). *Women at the naval academy: The first year of interaction* (Report No. 78-12). San Diego, CA: Navy Personnel Research and Development Center.

FRYE, M. (1983). *The politics of reality: Essays in feminist theory.* Trumansburg, NY: Crossing Press.

HALL, D. T. (1972). A model of coping with role conflict: The role behavior of college educated women. *Administrative Science Quarterly, 17,* 471–486.

JANOFF-BULMAN, R. (1979). Characterological versus behavioral self-blame: Inquiries into depression and rape. *Journal of Personality and Social Psychology, 37,* 1798–1809.

JENSEN, I. W., & GUTEK, B. A. (1982). Attributions and assignment of responsibility in sexual harassment. *Journal of Social Issues, 38,* 121–136.

JONES, E. E., & NISBETT, R. E. (1972). The actor and the observer: Divergent perceptions of the causes of behavior. In E. E. Jones, D. Kanouse, H. H. Kelley, R. E. Nisbett, S. Valins, & B. Weiner (Eds.), *Attribution: The causes of behavior* (pp. 79–94). Morristown, NJ: General Learning Press.

KANTER, R. M. (1977). *Men and women of the corporation.* New York: Basic Books.

KAUFMAN, D. R. (1978). Associational ties in academe: Some male and female differences. *Sex Roles, 4,* 9–21.

KULKA, R. A., & COLTEN, M. E. (1982). Secondary analysis of a longitudinal study of educated women: A social psychological perspective. *Journal of Social Issues, 38,* 73–87.

LARWOOD, L., & LOCKHEED, M. (1979). Women as managers: Toward second generation research. *Sex Roles, 5,* 659–666.

LAWS, J. L. (1975). The psychology of tokenism: An analysis. *Sex Roles, 1,* 209–223.

MACAULEY, J. (1981). The failure of affirmative action for women: One university's experience. In G. DeSole & L. Hoffmann (Eds.), *Rocking the boat* (pp. 98–116). New York: Modern Language Association of America.

MERTON, R. K. (1968). *Social theory and social structure.* (rev. ed.) New York: Free Press.

NIELSEN, L. L. (1979). Sexism and self-healing in the university. *Harvard Education Review, 49,* 467–476.

RICE, R. W., YODER, J. D., ADAMS, J., PRIEST, R. F., & PRINCE, H. T. (1984). Leadership ratings for male and female military cadets. *Sex Roles, 10,* 885–902.

RICHARDS, J. R. (1980). *The skeptical feminist: A philosophical enquiry.* Boston: Routledge & Kegan Paul.

RIGER, S., & GALLIGAN, P. (1980). Women in management: An exploration of competing paradigms. *American Psychologist, 35,* 902–910.

RYAN, W. (1976). *Blaming the victim.* New York: Vintage.

RYAN, W. (1981). *Equality.* New York: Vintage.

SHERIF, C. W. (1979). What every intelligent person should know about psychology and women. In E. Snyder (Ed.), *The study of women: Enlarging perspectives of social reality* (pp. 143–188). New York: Harper & Row.

STAPP, J., & FULCHER, R. (1983). The employment of APA members: 1982. *American Psychologist, 38,* 1298–1320.

STIEHM, J. H. (1981). *Bring me men and women.* Berkeley, CA: University of California Press.

VITTERS, A. G., & KINZER, N. S. (1977). *Report of the admission of women to the U.S. military academy (Project Athena).* West Point, NY: United States Military Academy.

WEISSTEIN, N. (1977). "How can a little girl like you teach a great big class of men?" the chairman said, and the other adventures of a woman in science. In S. Ruddick & P. Daniels (Eds.). *Working it out.* New York: Pantheon.

WHITE, M. S. (1970). Psychological and social barriers to women in science. *Science, 170,* 413–416.

YODER, J. D. (1983a). *Queen bees or tokens? Person- versus situation-centered approaches to mentors.* Paper presented at the meetings of the Association for Women in Psychology. Seattle, WA.

YODER, J. D. (1983b). Another look at women in the United States Army: A comment on Woelfel's article. *Sex Roles, 9,* 285–288.

YODER, J. D., & ADAMS, J. (1984). Women entering nontraditional roles: When work demands and sex-roles conflict. *International Journal of Women's Studies, 7,* 260–272.

YODER, J. D., & SINNETT, L. M. (in press). Is it all in the numbers? A case study of tokenism. *Psychology of Women Quarterly.*

YODER, J. D., Adams, J., & Prince, H. T. (1983). The price of a token. *Journal of Political and Military Sociology, 11,* 325–337.

YODER, J. D., ADAMS, J., GROVE, S., & PRIEST, R. F. (1985). To teach is to learn: Overcoming tokenism with mentors. *Psychology of Women Quarterly, 9,* 119–131.

Susan J. Douglas

Where the Girls Are: Growing up Female with the Mass Media*

In the early months of my daughter's life, I watched more TV than usual, but with a more jaundiced eye. Yet even my old standbys let me down. On *L. A. Law,* Ann Kelsey and Stuart Markowitz, who had been trying unsuccessfully to have a baby, adopted an infant girl. The only difference this baby seemed to make in their lives was that they struggled to find the right mobiles and nanny. In one episode, Ann had to bring the baby to work, and the baby lay in her bassinet while Ann took a deposition. Although the point of the scene was to show how the baby's crying ruined the deposition, I was still completely incredulous. Where were Ann's eye bags? How could she have the presence of mind to do anything, let alone concentrate on legal work, if she had an infant who'd disrupted her sleep several times the night before? Why were there no unsightly milk splotches on the padded shoulders of her $700 outfit? When we saw Ann and Stuart at home with the baby, we didn't see them struggling to complete a brief phone conversation or yelling at each other about whose turn it was to walk the baby around the house until it stopped screaming. No, they were ecstatically rocking a quietly cooing baby who apparently never cried, defecated, or threw up, and who didn't have the poor taste to wreak havoc with her parents' schedules, let alone their previously contented relationship.

Motherhood had virtually no impact on this woman's life or work, while those of us sitting at home in our sputum-covered bathrobes and ratty slippers were wondering how we were going to survive the next day at work on no sleep. This baby, like most media babies, was a trouble-free, ecstasy-producing, attractive little acquisition; if you "get" one, it will make you feel real good, look great in a rocking chair, and make you fall in love with your spouse all over again. Now, while babies are, at times, an indescribable joy, caring for them makes you feel like you've been tortured in an especially sadistic sleep-

---

*Complete citations to all the articles referred to in this reading can be found in Susan J. Douglas (1994, 1995). *Where the Girls Are: Growing up Female with the Mass Media*. Times Books.

deprivation experiment. The feel-good images are a complete lie, and you know it. But they burrow into you, forcing you to castigate yourself for not being serene enough, organized enough, or spontaneous enough as a mother.

At the same time that this little fantasy world was beaming out from dramatic television, the concept of the "mommy track" was getting bandied about in the news media, promoted by huge cover stories in the newsmagazines and major stories on TV. According to this proposal, mothers should be on a separate—and unequal—career track that gives them more flexible hours in exchange for no promotions, no challenging assignments, less autonomy, and no raises.

Talk about getting the bends! On the one hand, we had the TV supermoms, size-six women with perfectly applied makeup who could do anything and apparently didn't need any sleep. On the other hand, we got a recognition that motherhood might be just a tad demanding, but acknowledged only in the age-old blame-the-victim solution of the mommy track. Between these two extremes were millions of us, the real mothers of America, with no place to stand. We were either supposed to act as if children don't hamper our ability to be overachieving workaholics and we can do everything we did before plus raise a baby or two or acquiesce to second-class citizenship, acknowledging that being a mother is so debilitating that we're only capable of having dead-end, place-holding jobs while men, including fathers, and women without kids step on our backs to get the next promotion. Either way, the real-life mother is humiliated, especially if she has a job, as opposed to a "career," in which the whole notion of advancement or a "track" is patently absurd. Meanwhile, there is no recognition that fatherhood might be exhausting too, and that new fathers are also operating under a completely different set of circumstances. In the supermom fantasies of TV and the mommy track proposals of corporate America, what remains enshrined is our country's craven, hypercompetitive yuppie work ethic. Babies and parents are supposed to work around these increasingly preposterous norms of what constitutes adequate job performance.

These contradictions surrounding motherhood and children differ from what our mothers confronted, but they have their roots firmly and deeply in the 1950s. For even now, no matter what you do, you can't ever be good enough as a mother. If you don't work, you're a bad mom, and if you do work, you're a bad mom. Then there's all the advice that comes at us from *Working Mother, Parents, Newsweek,* the nightly news, *20/20,* and *Oprah.* Let your baby cry herself to sleep; never let your baby cry. Don't be too rigid, but don't be too permissive. Don't ever spank your child; an occasional swat on the butt is good for a kid. Encourage your child to learn, but don't push her to learn. Be her friend; never be her friend. Rein her in; cut her some slack. The tightrope walks are endless. Once again we find ourselves under surveillance, not only as sex objects, or as workers, but as mothers. And on all sides of us are voices with megaphones, yelling completely opposite things to us as we figure out whether we have time to do a wash or will simply have to turn the kid's underwear inside out tomorrow.

And here, again, we feel the pull between sisterhood and competitive individualism. At 4:00 A.M., when it seemed like everyone in the world except my daughter and I was asleep, I felt myself part of that transhistorical and transcultural group called mothers, the ones who get up, no matter what, listening to the soft snorings of others, while tending to the needs of a child. Now this may sound overly romantic and sentimental, but I didn't expect to feel such a powerful bond with other women across space and time. And I still feel it, whenever I see a mother struggling to get the grocery shopping done with a couple of kids squirming and crying in the cart, or watch her trying to free herself from the frantic grip of a wailing toddler because Mom is late for work and, like it or not, has to leave the day-care center. At any playground, mothers who are complete strangers can enter effortlessly into conversation about kids and child rearing.[7] We smile knowingly at each other in shopping malls, parks, fast-food joints, and toy stores. We connect.

Yet we are divided against each other too. Motherhood, like everything else women do, has been turned into a competition over who's more patient, enterprising, inventive, decisive, hardworking, firm, and loving. Working moms are supposed to overcompensate for their time away from home and the kids by baking cakes in the shape of a triceratops and building marionettes for the weekend puppet show. Out of the media archetype of the supermom came the most revolting application of bureaucratic, human potential double-speak ever to accost mothers: quality time. Stay-at-home moms were hardly exempt from this. The competition across the street with her briefcase and high heels had to institute "quality time" segments in her household, and if you didn't too, your child would lag behind and grow up to hate you. This, at least, was how the news media framed motherhood, with its endless stories about "moms vs. moms."[8] At the same time, we're all supposed to conspire together in yet another grand masquerade that hides those moments when, out of frustration, exhaustion, and desperation, we say truly hateful and juvenile things to our children ("If you don't go to sleep, you'll *never* get to watch Barney again"), refuse to give them what they want or need, and fantasize, most of all, about sending them to Saturn.

This is why Roseanne Barr, now Arnold, became the top female sitcom star in America in the early 1990s. Despite the incredibly hostile treatment she has gotten in the press—because she's four things TV women are not supposed to be, working-class, loudmouthed, overweight, and a feminist—Roseanne became a success because her mission was simple and welcome: to take the schmaltz and hypocrisy out of media images of motherhood. Her famous line from her stand-up routine—"If the kids are alive at five, hey, I've done my job"—spoke to millions of women who love their children more than anything in the world but who also find motherhood wearing, boring, and, at times, infuriating. She spoke to women who had seen through June Cleaver and Donna Reed years ago, and were struggling to see through the supermom image now. Roseanne also took aim at the class biases around media images of motherhood: that good mothers looked like those svelte, smiling, beauty queen moms in Gerber ads or the moms in white muslin on the beach pitching Calvin Klein perfume. Most moms are not corporate attorneys, Roseanne insisted, nor do they fit into a size six, carry a briefcase, or smile most of the time. They are waitresses, or work in factories, or in tiny office cubicles, or in other dead-end jobs, and they don't have $700 suits or nannies. But the other much more upscale but defiant media mom, Murphy Brown, also gave all the traditional stereotypes about motherhood the raspberries and continued, even after the birth of her child, to be as insensitive, narcissistic, and bossy as before.

In many ways, the media environment that surrounds us is very similar to the one that surrounded our mothers. It is crammed with impossible expectations and oozes with guilt that sticks to every nook and cranny of our psyches. It is dominated by images of upper-middle-class moms, both real and fictional, who "have it all" with little sacrifice, counterposed by upper-middle-class women who have fled the fast track for the comforts of domesticity. These either/or images are our new impossible choices for the 1990s. And we also have, as a holdover from *The Rifleman, Bachelor Father,* and *My Three Sons,* the conceit that the best moms are really dads. This reversal got new life breathed into it by *Kramer vs. Kramer,* in which the selfish bitch wife up and left the cutest, most lovable boy in America to "find herself" while her previously neglectful husband turned into the Albert Schweitzer of dads. The movie never let us see how devoted she had been as a mom—and virtually a single mom, at that—for all those years Dad lived at the office, nor did we see what had provoked her to take the dramatic action she did. In the custody hearing, women viewers were supposed to root for Dustin Hoffman and repudiate Meryl Streep.[9] The "best moms are dads" motif spread through the prime-time schedule like measles, giving us *My Two Dads* and *Full House,* in which Mom is conveniently six feet under and a couple of cool dads move in together to raise the kids.[10]

But *Roseanne* and *Murphy Brown* dramatize the most important difference separating us from our mothers: our stance toward the various mass media. At the same time that media executives tamed the high-spirited Madeline Hayes in *Moonlighting,* or gave us *The Equalizer,* a former CIA agent who rescued terminally helpless and perennially stalked female victims in distress, they also brought us *China Beach, Kate & Allie, Designing Women, Cagney & Lacey, Sisters, Sirens,* and *Dr. Quinn, Medicine Woman.* They didn't do this out of altruism; they did it because we're still a big market and, as they are learning, an increasingly jaundiced, pissed-off market that wants to see women on their own, women being brave, women having adventures, and women with mouths on them. Yet this is not enough. Some of us would like to see a lot more women with lines on their faces and a little mileage on them, too.

Women are hardly immune to the svelte images, guilt trips, and all the other normative messages that come at us courtesy of America's media moguls. But we are not putty in their hands either. Our interactions with sitcoms, the news, women's magazines, popular music, and movies are dynamic, a contested push and pull, in which they have most of the power but not all of it. While we can't assume that every woman who saw *Fatal Attraction* or *Pretty Woman* moaned "oh, pleeze" and cursed a lot throughout, neither can we assume that they just got down on their knees at the end and offered to lick their boyfriends' or husbands' boots. And don't think, for a minute, that only upper-middle-class women with Ph.D.'s who study semiotics and discourse analysis can debunk a misogynistic piece of crap like *9 1/2 Weeks.* Some women, of course, are still slaves to the media, buying into liposuction, Ultra Slim-Fast, and the notion that all career women are vipers. But many other women, of all ages, classes, and ethnic backgrounds, have become, as a result of the last twenty years, skeptical viewers who know a lie when they see one.

This is why media women—celebrities as well as public figures—who have deliberately gone against the grain, who have attacked persistent stereotypes about women, have gained notoriety. . . .

The woman we owe the most to . . . is Anita Hill, who claimed her voice and her past with a dignity many of us found remarkable and thrilling. For testifying against the dumbest and possibly most reactionary and mean-spirited man ever to sit on the Supreme Court, she was labeled a liar, a hysteric, a scorned woman, a hallucinator. For many of us, watching the Republican men go after her like slavering pit bulls, while the Democratic men covered their little weenies and ducked for cover, exposed the lies embedded in *Charlie's Angels* and elsewhere, that there was no such thing as patriarchy, but if there was, it was beneficent and would protect women.

Although the Thomas-Hill hearings were very real, they resonated powerfully with all the accrued media images of women as victims, women needing to keep their mouths shut, women needing to stay in their place, women needing to be deferential, compliant, ever smiling. The sight of this poised, accomplished, well-spoken woman sitting alone, across from the firing squad of complacent, self-satisfied white men, who after all this time still didn't get it, hit a nerve. While Thomas whined about a high-tech lynching, women saw a high-tech gang rape. Here we watched our daily, private, often internal conflicts acted out before our eyes, in public. The drama we witnessed was the intersection between decades of media stereotypes about women and one woman's shameful treatment by men because of those stereotypes. We knew how she felt—on some level we had been there and were still there—trapped by prejudice, expectations, and norms not of our making. So we knew why she came forward, why she fought, and why she wanted it all to go away. For the same media that had told her, as a woman, to shut up and smile had also told her, as an American, to speak out against injustice and discrimination. Anita Hill dramatized exactly the conflicts each of us has struggled with since we were little girls.

In the aftermath of the Thomas-Hill hearings, the notion of men "not getting it," and especially of the mainstream media not getting it, has coexisted with *Vanity Fair* covers of Sharon Stone half dressed, busty bimbos advertising beer, the ongoing trashing of sisterhood in movies like *Single White Female* and *The Hand That Rocks the Cradle,* and enough douche commercials to choke Moby Dick. It may be the effects of the lobotomy, but Pat Robertson feels he can still declare that feminism "encourages women to leave their husbands, kill their children [and] practice witchcraft."[13] It is still a man's world and a man's media, but there are also cracks and veins for us to mine, as there were thirty years ago. And here we are, same as it ever was, on an ideological yo-yo not unlike the one that raised and lowered our mothers and their hopes, now raising, now lowering, our own.

PART FIVE

Making Connections

Our lives are lived in a web of connections with others. Traditional personality theories have often ignored this web, emphasizing the development of an autonomous, self-reliant adult. Feminist theories, in contrast, emphasize the development of a woman's identity in relation to others.

The connectedness of women—their engagement in relationships that further their own development and others'—is explored in this group of stories. We look first at women's relationships with their children, and then at feminist attempts to create new kinds of families. We next explore how women cross boundaries of class and color in forming friendships and helping relationships. Finally, we look at the dark side of connections—those that result in violence and harm to girls and women.

Anna Quindlen and Mary Gordon are both well-known authors (Quindlen is a *New York Times* columnist and Gordon a novelist.) Each is a mother to both sons and daughters, and each writes about nurturing her children's development. From their essays, we can learn how complicated it is to help a child become a sensitive, strong adult—and how very different the issues are for girls and boys. Why did Gordon feel more apprehensive about bringing up her son than her daughter? In what ways is her children's behavior inconsistent with gender stereotypes? How does Gordon reconcile her feminist beliefs with the task of raising a boy who will fit into a gendered society? Quindlen focuses on her daughter. What does she see as the special challenges in bringing up daughters? How does her own experience as an "outspoken, insatiably curious" child sensitize her to her daughter's needs and the obstacles she will encounter?

Their children's uniqueness and individuality shine through in both Gordon's and Quindlen's descriptions—yet both mothers are concerned about the harmful effects of gender stereotypes and roles on the children's character. Do you think they are right to be concerned? Is gender role learning becoming a mere relic of the past? If not, how can children be helped to resist it?

While most women are encouraged—even pressured—to devote their energies to raising children, some are denied that choice. Minnie Bruce Pratt, a poet, writes about her own loss and that of another lesbian mother, Sharon Bottoms, whose children were taken from them by court order solely because they were lesbians. How are Pratt's love for and connection with her children expressed in her essay? What were the costs to her, her family, and society of preventing her from caring for her children? How do patriarchal social structures ensure that "heterosexuality as an institution and female subservience as a tradition" will be perpetuated?

Despite the pressures to conformity, women and men continue to experiment with creating nonpatriarchal family structures, in the hope that they can meet the human need for connection without perpetuating restrictive roles. Mary Crawford describes her own "experiment": Can a woman and man choose to live apart, make her work equally important to his, and share parenting without wrecking their marriage and family? Lindsy Van Gelder's engaging "Gay Gothic" tells of a family that's "just like the Brady Bunch" except that it is composed of a gay couple, a lesbian couple, and the child they co-parent. In these accounts, both the women and the men struggle with the pressures of their "deviant" choices. What fears and doubts does each sex express? What personal rewards do they find? How do larger social norms and legal structures make their creative life plans harder to follow? Do you think that these "brave new families" are worth the pain and effort they involve?

Friendships and helping relationships are important forms of connection. Patricia J. Williams, who describes herself as an "over-thirty black professional with an attitude," writes about her friendship with a white woman. The Cinderella myth seems to be a strong influence on her friend, but it is not one that Williams can accept for herself. What alternative myths are expressed in Williams' dreams and in the stories her mother told her?

How do these incompatible myths affect the way each woman feels about being attractive to men, and the importance she puts on weight, clothes, makeup, and acting "charming"?

When the white woman jokes that maybe Williams needs therapy, she replies seriously that "we black women have bigger, better problems than any other women alive." Yet, according to Julia A. Boyd, an African-American feminist psychotherapist, black women may avoid therapy—a relationship where their helper is likely to be white. She explores how differences of ethnicity and culture affect the relationship between therapist and client.

Boyd points out that women of color become "bicultural" as a survival strategy. How is biculturalism expressed in Williams' story and in Boyd's? If white women are less likely to be bicultural than women of color, how can they bridge their differences? Boyd suggests that a feminist therapist working with a woman of a different cultural background needs to become a student again. Does this apply to friendship, too? How can mutual trust be fostered in friendship and in a helping relationship? What are the similarities and differences in establishing connections within these two kinds of relationship?

Abuses of power are a part of many relationships. Because relationships are seen as personal and private, these negative aspects, and their connection to larger social patterns, may remain invisible. Vicki Crompton writes about her daughter Jenny's murder, and how it made her aware of the prevalence and widespread social acceptance of male violence. How did her daughter's friends and the community deny the coercion Jenny was subjected to? What steps did Vicki Crompton take to name and speak out against dating violence after her daughter's death?

June Larkin and Katherine Popaleni connect courtship violence and sexual harassment. Do you think that these and other forms of violence against women form a continuum, as they suggest? Why are adolescent girls especially vulnerable to abuse by their dating partners and classmates? What is the relationship between the acts of diminishment, intimidation, and force described by Larkin and Popaleni, and Jenny Crompton's experience?

Returning to the theme of connectedness, ask yourself whether connections among women are a source of empowerment in both Vicki Crompton's story and Larkin and Popaleni's research. What different kinds of connections are described, and how do they enable women to support each other in challenging male violence?

Raising Sons

We were one of a minority of couples—one in ten, is it? one in a hundred?—who were hoping for a girl. The delivery room nurses, knowing my passionate wish, let out a joyous shout when they saw that the baby was a daughter. It took her 22 hours to be born, a difficult birth; she wanted to come into the world chin up, and she's kept it that way for 13 years. Anna looked at us, and at the world, with a gimlet eye; as soon as she could focus, she understood her job description: separating the sheep from the goats.

She so delighted us that three years later, we decided to try again. This time, I was older, and decided on an amniocentesis. We opted to know the gender of the fetus before it was born; we thought it was absurd that the lab technician should know more about our child-to-be than we did. The six weeks waiting for the results of an amnio are among the longest days in anyone's life, and when the doctor called, saying he had good news, I was elated. "Everything's fine," he said. "It's perfectly healthy. And it's a boy!"

"Oh, my God," I said. "What am I supposed to do with one of them?"

"They're very cute," the doctor said.

"Yes, but I don't know what to do with them."

He told me I'd figure it out.

I'd lived an unusually female-centered life. I am an only child, and my father died when I was seven. My mother and I then moved in with my grandmother and my aunt. I went to an all-girls' high school and a women's college. I wasn't a tomboy, and I wasn't someone who had a lot of male friends. The important relationships in my life were with women friends and male lovers—for most of my life it was in that order. Now I was (and still am) married when I learned the news that I was to have a son, so I was going to be bringing one of *them* up alongside one of *them*. You would think I needn't have been so alarmed. But I was.

I was in my early twenties in the first years of the women's movement; I came of age as a feminist. It would be pleasant if one could become a feminist without a consciousness of the injustices and abuses perpetrated on women by men. But it didn't happen to me. For those of us feminists who are heterosexual, it has been a struggle to reconcile our rage against male culture with our feelings for the men with whom we enter into what is perhaps the most intimate of human relations. The most intimate, that is, except that of giving birth.

It's one thing to be angry at a grown-up male, even unjustly sometimes, for acting according to type, or representing the values of a gender with a history of oppressing, but what about a kid? What about one who lived inside your body for nine months, who is sustained by the milk in your breasts? This is the kind of thing I was afraid of? Would I take my generalized anger against male privilege out on this little child who was dependent upon me for his survival, physical to be sure, but mental as well?

And what would I do with him? I didn't like sports; I wasn't interested in soldiers, or cowboys, or cops, or cars. What would we talk about? If I brought him up to be interested in what I was interested in—so we could have a good time hanging out—would I be depriving him of his rightful place in the world of men, a world he had no choice but to inhabit?

In retrospect, I realize that I was thinking about what men did all day in ways that were grotesquely stereotyped. I didn't imagine that my daughter and I were going to spend the day talking about cooking or hairdos; why did I think my son would come into the world equipped with a football helmet and a six-pack?

I had a lot to learn. Of course, the body is a great teacher. If my mind told me, occasionally, that the creature inside me was "the other," my heart leapt with joy every time I felt him move inside me. The slow grinding of his head against my belly, the undulant curve of his midnight swims wiped out the very hint of separateness. Then he was born: an easy birth, three hours. And he was David. He wasn't *him.*

From the beginning, he was less fierce than his sister; he always seemed to have more of those qualities Carol Gilligan says girls have than his sister did. He was much more interested in pleasing, in cooperating; she was interested in what was right. She could block out the world to achieve mastery of a task. I once saw her literally step over a weeping classmate in nursery school in order to get to the shelf where the books were kept. He could be distracted from his pursuits by the presence of other people, particularly if he felt they weren't happy.

Everyone told me that boys were more physically active than girls and created more domestic havoc. I was poised, but it wasn't true in my son's case. He has had, from the beginning of his life, a remarkably contemplative nature, an ability to sit quietly musing, looking, thinking; at 16 months, he crawled away from all of us at a dark beach picnic. In a panic I shone a a flashlight into the black night and saw him sitting quietly—transferring sand from one hand to another.

From the moment he noticed other people, he's had a tendency—anguishing for a mother to observe—to suffer when other people are suffering, to intuit their suffering, to turn himself into a pretzel—telling jokes, giving them toys—in order to make them happier. When he was in kindergarten, there was a child in his class who'd been born addicted, who'd had a difficult life, moving, often several times a month, from one welfare hotel to another. Each morning, he began his day sitting on David's lap, and David rocked him for a few minutes until he was ready to join the other children at their play. He always went out of his way to include difficult or isolated children. Anna, however, has never had any tolerance for bad behavior, no inclination for charity playdates. David's guilt (which he, but not Anna, took in with his mother's milk) often leads him to invite people he doesn't like, and then feel trapped by their presence. Anna knows her limits, and states them clearly. When she was a kindergartner we went (God help us all) to Disney World. There, the characters walk around, and children get their autographs. Mickey, Donald, and Goofy were mobbed. But no one was around Chip and Dale. I said to my daughter, "Why don't you ask Chip and Dale for their autographs. They must feel sad that no one's asking them."

"I didn't tell that guy to be Chip," she said. "It's his choice and his problem."

My daughter could hear the unexpurgated Grimm's stories, delighting Bruno Bettelheim's heart, and not turn a hair at the most bloodthirsty myths (Beowulf was a favorite with her), but we quickly learned that David was very troubled by cruelty or violence in stories or on the screen. *Raiders of the Lost Ark* did him in at age eight. A friend of mine had invited him over to watch it, and David came back, pale and distraught. "He invited me to see another Indiana Jones movie tomorrow," David said. "Tell him you won't let me go. Tell him you think it's too violent." When my friend walked in the house the next day, David said, "She won't let me see it. I just begged her to let me see it but she said she thinks it's too upsetting." He knew what he didn't like; but he felt it unmanly to admit that he was frightened by something. So he came up with a public strategy, one that he could be confident would be a hit: bend the truth and blame Mom. Whereas Anna is Joe Friday's ideal respondent—just the facts, ma'am—David's not above a little creative storytelling to grease the world's wheels, to make people happier, to spare their feelings, to make himself well liked.

You often hear mothers of boys and girls say that their boys are more fragile than their girls, and in the case of my family, it seems to hold. But thinking of your son as fragile can lead a feminist to the pitfall that my daughter insists is my chief one: overprotecting the son. Because many of us tend to characterize the world of men as predatory, aggressive, ruthlessly competitive, we fear for our sons more than mothers who see the world of men as more benign. We may worry that, growing up in homes that stress feminist virtues, they have been underprepared for the cold, tough world that is still run on the whole by men who haven't been very susceptible to the feminist message. In addition, many feminists who have managed to be competent simultaneously in the traditionally female world of domestic life and the traditionally male world of moneymaking, and who see that most men can't even conceptualize what we think of as routine, can fall into the trap of thinking that men are the weaker sex, perennial boys we have to do end runs around in order to keep the world spinning. And since even feminists sometimes undervalue domestic work, it's easier for me to remember that I want Anna to go to law school than that I want David to learn to cook.

Do I ask less of him because I think, as a male, he's capable of less? Or do I get off on serving a son in a way I don't a daughter? There is, I have found, a romance of a surprising potency between mother and son, one that male writers have told us about—from Lawrence, to Proust, to Philip Roth. But we've heard about it from the son's point of view. I never expect to be loved again with the uncomplicated sweetness with which David loved me when he was small. I always felt that Anna and I were shoulder to shoulder in the world, but I knew she saw me clearly, warts and all. For David, I was the most beautiful, the most charming, the best cook, the most brilliant writer in the history of the world. He would look through catalogs and tell me which clothes he was going to buy for me when he grew up. I basked in this adoration—who wouldn't—and worried what I'd do when it stopped. This year, I got a clue that the romance was ending. "You know," he said, "my friend Tommy's mother is very beautiful. I think she's a lot younger than you." He asked me if I knew how much gray there was in my hair and if I'd ever considered dyeing it. A few months ago he said, "My friend Johnny says he thinks you have a big butt, and I couldn't tell him he was wrong." This is the year he discovered basketball. Ten months ago, I coaxed him to join a team because a friend of mine was coaxing her son as well. Suddenly, he discovered he was very good at it. He practiced obsessively. He spent his money on basketball cards, hats, and posters. He watched games on TV that were broadcast from cities I'd never even heard of. What was worse, he asked me to watch with him. My husband couldn't be pulled in—but I couldn't say no to my son. Also, I had to admit that it was something of a relief to me to see him involved in a traditionally male activity that wasn't horribly aggressive, that seemed like it was fun, that might be able to teach him the good side of competitiveness, and those things that women are said to lack because we didn't play team sports.

There I was, watching basketball. The very person who'd always made fun of people who talked sports and accused women interested in sports of trying to please their fathers. As a teenager, I'd invented something called "sportspeak," a skill I tried to pass on to younger women. "Sportspeak" was based on the theory that any woman could learn three sentences and convince any man that she knew a lot about sports by inserting them, in well-chosen places, into his monologue. You could do fine by saying: "Well, at this point in the season, it's hard to tell"; "Of course, it all depends on what happens in the clutch"; and "Sometimes they start slow and pick up speed, but sometimes they just run out of gas." Suddenly, this year, I discovered buried in my heart a passionate, undiscovered Knicks fan. I found a new role model, Knicks coach Pat Riley. He had so many things I wanted: great hair, Armani clothes, blind obedience from those around him. When the Bulls beat the Knicks this year, I was inconsolable. But wait, it wasn't just me. It was me and my son.

The trouble came when he wanted me to actually play basketball with him. I told him I wasn't very good. He said he'd coach me. After a few minutes, he turned to me in near despair. "Mom," he said, "are you going to hold that ball like a baby, or are you going to hold it like a ball? Because if you're going to hold it like a baby, I'm going to grab it out of your hands." I told him I'd try to hold it like a ball. It wasn't good enough. "Mom," he said, "you're just not aggressive enough. You have to really want to get that ball away from me." I told him that our relationship had been based on my not being aggressive with him, and, rather than wanting to take things away from him, I always wanted him to have things. "Mom," he said, "don't think of me as your son. Think of me as your opponent."

For a few months, everything was basketball. He didn't want to go to museums with me anymore. Going to museums had been one of our favorite things to do; talented at drawing and painting himself, he was excellent at describing how he thought paintings had been constructed. But one day on our way to the Metropolitan Museum of Art, he asked if we couldn't just go for an ice cream instead. "I think I'm not into art anymore," he said. I took a deep breath and asked if he wanted hot fudge. A few months later, he said, "Why don't you take me to the museum anymore? You know art's one of my favorite things." We went to the museum and spent 20 minutes in front of a Hopper lighthouse, talking about the shadings of the sky. He's still obsessed with basketball. But there are other things, things that came to him partly as a result of knowing me. But maybe he needed to know he could get away from me, that he could move in a world I wasn't in charge of, that he could share a world with me, but on his terms.

As I was writing this, an incident happened that expressed for me the complexities of being a feminist mother of a son. We were all swimming in a lake—Anna and David had settled on the raft. I was off on my "long swim," a situation that puts me in a Zen-like state of calm. From far away, I could see my children on the raft. Then I saw a boy about Anna's age push her off the raft. She must know him, I said to myself, he must remember her from the day camp she went to when she was five. Then I saw the same boy wrestling with David, saw him push David off the raft, saw David get back onto the raft, only to be pushed into the water again. When I got to shore, I asked Anna what had happened. "That jerk pushed me in, and David got upset, and he told the guy he couldn't do that to his sister. So he tried to push David in. It happened twice. David was just too small for the kid; he didn't have a chance. I thought it was really nice of him to stand up for me."

I, too, was moved. But after a minute, I didn't want to buy into the idea that a woman needs a man to stand up for her. "Why didn't you do it yourself?" I asked.

"Why would I waste my time on that moron?" she said. It didn't seem to mean much to her.

But I could see that David was seething. He swam away from us, and headed toward the raft. I watched with trepidation as he treaded water near the raft and then swam back to us.

"What was all that about?" I asked.

"Well, I went out there. I said hi, how you doing to the guy, like I was trying to make friends. Then I gave him the finger and swam away."

He was very happy with himself.

It isn't just Huck and Jim on the raft now—if it ever was. Our boys have to contend with boys who are surrounded by people who give them enough rope to hang all of us and then excuse their behavior with a shrug, remarking that "boys will be boys." But what boys will be what boys? And what men will these boys become? As feminist mothers of sons, we have a stake in the world of men. We can't afford wholesale male-bashing, nor can we afford to see the male as the permanently unreconstructable gender. Nor can we pretend that things are all right as they are. We have hints that our sons are different from us, but it may be impossible to tease out what is DNA and what is environment. The task of setting limits while allowing a child to be her or himself is the central one for all parents, but a feminist mothering a son may find the limit/freedom tightrope a particularly vexing one to walk. We must love them as they are, often without knowing what it is that's made them that way.

Our best bet, I think, is to remember there's no perfect solution, to enjoy them, ourselves, and our relationship with them in all its paradoxical complexity, to keep our sense of humor, to provide them with excellent role models. Mel Brooks, maybe. Or Groucho Marx. Or perhaps Odysseus. Because it is a new journey we are making with our boys, one that they will eventually have to make without us. The routes are unmarked, the dangers misnamed, or named insufficiently. The vista we've dreamed of is still on the horizon, past the shoals, the whirlwinds, the distracting sirens' song.

Birthday Girl

In the summer of '68 I was expelled from convent school. Actually, the more ladylike term "asked to leave" was used, but the result was the same. No renegade, I was devastated by the disgrace, but I came to realize that the nuns made the right call.

Outspoken, insatiably curious, inclined to go where I was not allowed and to test the limits of authority, I was not cut out for the place. Of course, it is indisputable that those same qualities serve me well in the job I hold today. What passes for a good girl makes for a very poor columnist.

Tomorrow is Maria's fifth birthday, and she, too, is outspoken, adventurous, curious, sure of herself, so pleased to be in her own skin that she sometimes seems to wriggle with the sheer joy of it. The other night I told her that I was very annoyed at her for something she'd done. "I don't care," she said. She didn't even sound defiant. She sounded matter-of-fact.

I admire her enormously, an odd thing to say about someone who is just a shade taller than a yardstick. But she is my daughter, and so my admiration is not entirely uncomplicated.

"Mothers grapple with the harrowing task of reconciling their overriding desire to keep their daughters safe with their desire to keep them strong and free in a world that insists on women's inferiority and subordination," write Elizabeth Debold, Marie Wilson and Idelisse Malave in a new book entitled "Mother Daughter Revolution." Their premise is that women can help their daughters resist the old familiar good-girl ways.

I suspect that doing this may be one of the most difficult tasks of my mothering career. Maria's father says that the sheer tensile strength of her personality makes submission most unlikely. But he doesn't know what I know about growing up female.

Even now so much works against us, and not just the broad-stroke bigotries. Not long ago I was talking to a class of third graders. The boys sounded off as often as car alarms, and I called on them to keep them under control. Most of the girls had already learned that it was important to be quiet and well

275

behaved. I rewarded this by ignoring them. I didn't notice what I was doing until it was over.

Maria is smart. She will notice things like that. She will notice someday that even the words we use for girls like her are dismissive: bossy, feisty, opinionated. These are words never used for men, pejorative diminutives for what are otherwise signal character traits, words that imply being something a woman should not.

We want things to be easy for our children, and we know from sad experience that the world can be unkind to girls who do not please, who speak out, who go their own way. But we know from experience, too, that the role of the good girl can be a hollow one, with nothing at the center except other people's expectations where your character might have been.

I want all three of our children to be good people, sensitive, empathetic. When I wish those things for the two boys it feels like a welcome change from the macho ethic. When I wish them for Maria, it sometimes feels a little too close for comfort to the cult of the nice girl, who puts the needs of others before her own. When she says "I don't care," I feel fragmented: the mother who knows it would be easier if she were easily led, the former girl who saw herself in the fun-house mirror of the opinions of others, and the woman, who cheers "Atta girl!"

Maria and I are much alike; I joke that she represents the first known case of inherited personality. To love her requires me to love myself. To raise her right requires me to value the qualities that once got me in trouble, to teach her not to mute them to suit the world. But neither do I want to raise her to denigrate or deny the things we have long associated with women—the terrain of the emotions, the connection to others.

I would like to help make her a person who could look around the panoply of personality traits in the characters of both men and women, and choose—herself. Her true self, not some lipsticked version of it. That may be hard for her. And it may sometimes be hard for me to help. But, oh, Maria, 5 years old, full to the brim with a confidence I envy and sometimes wonder if I once had, you are worth it. Happy birthday, little woman. Stay strong.

One Good Mother to Another

In the *New York Times* photo, a young blonde woman sits staring, stunned. She holds up a large picture of her cherubic smiling little boy. At first this looks like a moment with which everyone sympathizes: a mother publicly grieving her child killed in a tragic accident or lost in a nightmare kidnapping. But in this photo, something jars slightly. There is no father next to the mother; her companion is a woman. The caption reads: "A Virginia court's decision to remove a child from his mother because of her lesbianism is stirring controversy. Sharon Bottoms, left, lost custody of her two-year-old son, Tyler Doustou, to her mother." At that moment, perhaps the reader's sympathy wanes or turns to animosity.

But I know her look. I've sat in that desolate place. I've had my children taken from my arms, and I've felt that my children were almost dead to me because I could not hold them or touch them.

I had two boys whom I saw emerge, bloody and beautiful, from my body. I nursed them at my breast. I bathed their perfect tiny bodies and changed their diapers. I spoonfed them babyfood spinach. I taught them how to tie their shoes. I rocked them through ear aches and bad dreams. I drove them to their first day in kindergarten.

Then, suddenly, when they were five and six, when I fell in love with another woman and left my marriage to live as a lesbian, the world looked at me and saw an unfit mother. Suddenly, my husband had legal grounds to take my children away from me and never let me see them again.

Like Bottoms, I was also a "somewhat immature and undisciplined, though loving, mother"—after all, we were both mothers at twenty-one, barely out of girlhood. Like Bottoms, I was an "irregular job holder"—finishing a Ph.D. in English literature. When I applied for teaching positions, the male interviewers would inquire, "How will you arrange child care? Are you planning to have more children? What will your husband do if we hire you?" And they never did.

But the standard for my being a "good mother" was not my parenting ability or financial stability. After all, my husband, a father at twenty-three and an unemployed graduate student, was no more mature in his role than I was in mine. No, I was considered a fit mother as long as I was married and loyal to the man who was my husband. As soon as I asserted my independence, as soon as I began a life in which I claimed the human right to form intimate social and sexual relations with whomever I chose, specifically with other women, I was seen to be a perverted, unnatural woman by my husband, my mother, the people of the town I lived in, and the legal system.

The letter from my husband's lawyer said he was seeking custody because of my "unorthodox ideas about the place of the father in the home"—my heresy consisted of disagreeing with the idea that men were superior to, and should govern, women.

Though more than fifteen years passed between my agony at losing my children and that of Sharon Bottoms, the issues remain the same. This is true despite the fact that I lost custody of my boys to my ex-husband, their biological father, while Sharon has, at least for now, lost her boy to her mother, the child's biological grandmother, who sued for custody. The reason for denying us our children was the same: simply because we were in lesbian relationships.

In the words of Judge Parsons, who ruled in Henrico County Circuit Court against Sharon: "The mother's conduct is illegal and immoral and renders her unfit to parent." Illegal because in Virginia (and more than twenty other states and the District of Columbia), sodomy—the "crime against nature" of lesbians and gay men—is still prohibited. And the 1987 U.S. Supreme Court, in *Bowers v. Hardwick,* actually stated in its majority opinion that it was maintaining the illegality of sodomy because that particular set of justices considered this kind of sex immoral, based on "traditional values."

Sharon Bottoms, as a lesbian in a committed relationship with another woman, is perceived as less fit to parent than her mother, whose live-in boyfriend for seventeen years was a man who, according to Sharon, sexually abused her twice a week during her teen years. Under the law and in the eyes of many people, Sharon's mother is more fit because she endorses heterosexuality as an institution and female subservience as a tradition, and presumably will pass these values along to her grandson. This arrangement is seen as being in the child's "best interests."

But should we not ask what kind of damage will be done to a boy if his sense of self depends on dominating another person? Should we not inquire about the immorality of teaching a child that love can only occur with state-sanctioned approval?

Much was made in the courtroom of the fact that Sharon's child calls her lover and partner "Dada." In most two-partner lesbian families, the children call one woman Mama or Mom or Mother, and the other woman some different maternal variation, or perhaps by her given name; often, these women lose custody of their children anyway. Certainly, Sharon could have been challenged for custody no matter what her child called April, Sharon's partner. But the word "Dada" evokes a truth about lesbian parenting that opponents violently condemn: Two women can raise children in a home together and challenge the very idea that gender roles, or gender expression, are irrevocably matched to biological gender.

Opponents of lesbian/gay parenting often present the "damage" to the child as a danger of him or her "becoming" gay. But this is only part of a larger fear that no matter what sexuality the child develops, the child might learn that rigid gender roles are not required. The child might learn the joy of possibility that comes when biological gender does not have to match socially mandated gender in jobs or thoughts or love.

Psychiatric specialists testified for Sharon by outlining studies that showed no noticeable difference between children reared in lesbian households and those reared in heterosexual ones. Nevertheless, Judge Parsons concurred with Sharon's mother that the child would be "mentally and physically harmed" by the lesbian relationship; he stated there was a strong possibility the boy would carry "an intolerable burden" for "the rest of his life."

Sharon can see her child on Mondays and Tuesdays but not in her own home, and not in the presence of her lover. By my divorce settlement ("And lucky to get it!" my lawyer said), I was forbidden to have the boys in my home if I shared the house with *any* person; I could take them out of their home state only if we went to be with my mother, whom my husband had threatened to call as a character witness for *him*.

To see my boys, sometimes I drove roundtrip on three-day weekends, fourteen hours nonstop there, fourteen hours nonstop back. The youngest boy wrote in his school journal how he wished he could be with me more; the oldest boy talked to me late at night, on long distance phone calls, about his depression, about how sometimes he just wanted to die.

I loved them, I called them, I saw them as much as I had time and money to do. We got through their baby years, pre-adolescence, and teens. When I finally asked the oldest, "What effect do you think my being a lesbian had on you?" he answered: "None. I think my personality was most shaped by not having you with me as a mother all those years, by having you taken away from me."

It is ironic that Sharon Bottoms's case was tried in Virginia, a state that enforced its law against racial intermarriage as late as 1967, until in *Loving v. Virginia* the U.S. Supreme Court finally declared unconstitutional all such laws. The determined political struggle of the African-American community, in the courts and in civil-rights battles in the streets, abolished a law that codified the prejudices of white Southerners.

When I fought for custody of my children in Fayetteville, North Carolina, as I struggled to live as a self-reliant woman, not dependent, not submissive, the tide of women's liberation was rising through the South. Women were beginning to challenge an economic system that uses the threat of competition between the sexes as a way to limit working people's wages, benefits, and job conditions.

Now, with cases like that of Sharon Bottoms, the gay and lesbian community is fighting to end other inhuman limits on how all of us can live and love. And now we have allies, like Sharon's ex-husband, Dennis Doustou, who asked to testify for her and who says, "Tyler means the world to her."

In 1976, when I went to a lawyer for help in my struggle for my children, he said to me, "This country is not ready for someone like you." Can we say now, in 1993, that we are ready for someone like Sharon Bottoms, just an ordinary woman, a part-time grocery clerk trying to raise a child on not enough money, but with the love and support of another woman who cares about both of them?

Let us declare, finally, that we are ready for this ordinary extraordinary woman who is saying to us, with her life, that to guarantee her right to be a lesbian and a mother is to take one more step toward liberation for *all* of us.

Mary Crawford

Two Careers, Three Kids, and Her 2,000-Mile Commute

A year ago I left Roger and the baby in our big old house in Iowa. Roger was busy getting ready for the semester's teaching; I was off to my new job as assistant professor of psychology at a Pennsylvania state college. Teenagers Mary Ellen and Mark, 15 and 14, earned boarding school scholarships and headed north to Minnesota. We're a tristate nuclear family, and it's a peculiar life.

I was raised in a world where married women stayed home. In all my growing-up years I remember my mother spending a night away from her children twice: when she and my father took their first vacation in 10 years and when she went to her father's funeral.

For at least some families, the world has changed since then. Still, my new life seems to make people uneasy; they don't know what sexual label to pin on me. I can't be "married," or I'd be in my husband's house where I belong. I'm not "divorced and available," but am I planning to be? After all, I am "separated." I don't think their interest has much to do with me personally; it's just that a woman's sexual availability is crucial to evaluating her as a person.

But for us, there is little ambiguity: we are still a family. The seeds of our separation were in our marriage contract:

> We value the importance and integrity of our separate careers and believe that insofar as our careers contribute to our individual self-fulfillment they will strengthen our relationship. We do not consider one partner's career to be more important than the other's.

We'd finished graduate school together and solved the job problem by sharing a psychology professorship in a tiny Iowa college. For four years we'd done everything together; team-teaching classes, being mentors to our students, encouraging each other's research. We'd made time for another child, and took turns caring for him.

Eventually, the advantages of the arrangement became its disadvantages. We tired of being each other's closest colleagues. We needed to develop individual approaches to our work, without constant comparisons with each other.

We each needed to pursue private career interests, and our rural isolation made branching out difficult. Paradoxically, we'd come to share too much. A little distance was in order.

Unfortunately, our unique experience didn't fit the mold of a résumé. Academic hiring committees saw only that we'd each been working part-time in a college that was both small and obscure. After two years and a number of fruitless applications, we finally agreed that whoever got an offer first would leave the other. We would allow two years for Partner B to find a job within commuting distance of Partner A. If none materialized, Partner A would return to the old shared professorship.

My worst conflicts centered around two-year-old Ben, the littlest child. The rest of us had agreed to the plan. But Ben was too small to have a voice in the decision, or anticipate the changes in his life. I never thought of taking him with me. He would be happiest in his own house, with his father's loving care.

And I had long dreamed of living alone. I was married at 18, a mother at 20, and had fantasized a life with time to work and space to breathe. I wondered who I would be without the people whose existence bracketed my life. Would I be sloppy or neat, would I run five miles every day at dawn or work and study late into the night? Would I eat junk food or serve splendid little dinners for one on the best china? Would it be miraculously easy to study without the nuisance of a family? I could not imagine what I would do with such perfect freedom.

When freedom came, it threw my world off center. I grieved for my family most terribly, especially Ben. His natural birth had been one of the great joys of my life, and the physical bond with him the strongest I have known. I thought longingly, sensuously, of his dimpled hands, sturdy legs, and innocent round belly. I wept easily, needing proof of my being. A mean-spirited word from a student or a curt remark from a colleague would do it. In a supermarket parking lot, I saw a father slap a two-year-old, and I fled to my car weak with despair.

Slowly the feelings stabilized; my sense of self began to return. And the self I discovered was very much like the person I have always been. Without my family's demands on my time I didn't magically turn into a marathon runner or a gourmet cook. Relieved of the necessity to set a good example, I remained reasonably neat and continued to eat my green beans. I accomplished the same amount of work I always had, discovering that weekends at the office are no fun. After years of feeling that the "real me" was being suppressed, I was amazed to find I'd been there all along, in the bosom of my family. I will never again be able to resent them with the old enthusiasm.

My pleasures now come from my work, my solitude, and my friends. I teach my favorite course, Psychology of Women, with a new understanding of what it means to be self-sufficient and new depth of feeling for the importance of family networks in defining our lives. I took up my research and writing again; and though I missed Roger's affirmation of my ideas, I turned to my colleagues and began to build the working relationships with other psychologists that I had missed so much in Iowa.

And I decided to enjoy my freedom—lots of dinners at the local French restaurant, all the first-run films, lazy Sundays with the *Times*. Perhaps the most exquisite pleasure—anyone who has shared living space with a family will understand—is to come home after a long day's work to a cup of tea, the mail, and the six-o'clock news in the utter peace of an apartment that is just as orderly as it was at breakfast time.

Still, there are problems. Roger and I have a feast-or-famine sex life—once a month I fly home to Iowa for three days. The distortions in our relationship are both funny and stressful. If we quarrel, we must explode-sulk-and-apologize in minutes. We haven't time for the luxury of fully developed bad moods. If we climb into bed weary, wanting just to sleep together spoon-fashion, we feel faintly guilty. This isn't what we've been fantasizing for the last month.

And then there's my relationship with Ben. On my first weekend home, I plunge into my role as Mommy. It seems to me that he is shamelessly overindulged. Nobody—even two years old and stubborn—needs three stories, six songs, four drinks of water, and a back rub before bed. I try to straighten him out, Roger and I exchange numerous sharp words, Ben cries and clings to Daddy. I realize I no longer know what it's like dealing with Ben's day-to-day needs. With a shock I see I'm behaving like the stereotype of a male absentee parent; proposing quick "cures" for his behavior and "taking charge" with demands that his live-in parent knows are unrealistic.

I realize that I am the "second parent" now, less intimately involved and less knowledgeable than Roger. Of all the changes in our lives, it is the hardest to accept. I learn to watch while Roger eases Ben through his two-year-old's struggle for autonomy, never forcing a confrontation, always respecting Ben's need to control his small world. I learn to respect Roger's need to parent in his own way.

It's easier being a parent to the teenagers. Boarding school was a great idea. They're finally in a school where the work is a challenge. They blossom. And I find myself more objective about their turmoils at a distance.

When Mark gets detention for failing to turn in assignments, I am able to see the problem as his, not mine. I point out in a friendly but detached way that if he wants to keep his scholarship he'll have to complete his assignments. If he wants advice on time-budgeting, he's welcome to write and ask. He doesn't ask, and he doesn't get detention again, either.

I can't pretend I never feel guilt. Guilt, that cradle-to-grave woman's home companion, is very much a part of my solitary life. I no sooner leave home than Ben gets sick, with chicken pox followed by complications. For a month Roger juggles his job and a child who's in pain. I am wild with worry. Selfishly I fear that Ben will connect his illness with my leaving and begin to hate me.

Late one night Roger phones and breaks down in tears of weariness and frustration. He doesn't blame me or ask me to come home. But *I know I ought to be there.* I pour it all out to a therapist friend. "Even if you were there, you couldn't 'make it all better' for Ben," she says. Her statement seems too easy an answer, but for some reason it stays in my thoughts. Exactly why does Ben "need" me? He has excellent medical care and is not in real danger. I know his father loves him as dearly as I, is at least as nurturing, and twice as patient. Do I really believe in some magical power, given to mothers, to ease the pain and make life trouble free? Perhaps it's not Ben's need I'm feeling, but my own: to be needed, and childishly, to be omnipotent.

Even now, with domestic matters under control, the guilt sometimes returns. If I were a genius, I tell myself, it would be okay. If I were the next Marie Curie or Margaret Mead, if Harvard wanted me to supervise a new research team . . . but I'm not that special, there's no justification for *my* selfishness.

There is some fundamental conflict here about *deserving* to work. And I dare say it to myself at last: *I am entitled to do work that I care about. Its value to me is at least as important as its value to the world.*

I meet many people who need to believe our experiment in living won't work. "You'll be divorced within a year" is a prediction I hear often, accompanied by a story of a couple who tried some bizarre long-distance relationship that ended in failure for the marriage. One person prophesies that Roger won't find another job within our two-year limit; the crunch will come if I refuse to give up mine. At first I'm wounded by my friends' cynicism. Don't they realize we care about each other and our marriage? I gradually see that their pessimism is too quick and too pervasive to be based on a realistic appraisal of the situation. It reflects their own needs for predictability and stability. Our experiment forces them to confront their own conflicts about risk-taking.

Our experiment *is* risky. We are beginning to stabilize; we can live this way a while longer and still be a family. But we do not do it lightly. We do it only because we need so much to have both halves of the human experience—love and work.

Gay Gothic

It's late afternoon in Santa Fe, and the last rays of the desert sun are coming through the kitchen windows. The adults are cooking dinner: lemon chicken and spaghetti alla puttanesca. The baby, Sarah, who has just learned to crawl, is exploring the kitchen cabinets closest to the floor. She pulls out all the wooden spoons, the whisks, a bag of onions. Then, with a big baby grin, she hauls out a turkey baster and waves it in the air. The four adults—Sarah's mother Nancy, her father Doug, Nancy's lover Amy, and Doug's lover Bjorn—all crack up.

The joke, of course, is that Sarah herself is the product of artificial insemination—not with an actual turkey baster, but with a technology that uses similar principles. Sarah is also part of what has been frequently described as a new "baby boom" within the lesbian community. (According to one estimate, there were at least 500 such babies born last year in San Francisco alone.) Until very recently, most lesbian mothers had their children in previous, heterosexual relationships. But Amy and Nancy—who are both 40—are typical of a generation of women who grew up with the feminist and gay movements. Just as straight feminists have questioned the old rules that say that intercourse always has to lead to babies, lesbians are rebelling against the idea that babies always have to come from intercourse.

Some lesbian mothers are emphatic about *not* wanting a father in the picture. But those who do want the sperm donor to be at all involved in the child's upbringing are likely to choose a man who is also gay (although the AIDS epidemic has tragically reduced the pool of risk-free candidates). Friendships frequently flourish across gender lines in the gay community, of course, but a gay donor is also a practical decision, since a gay father would have no advantage over a lesbian mother in the event of a future custody fight. The resulting Gay Gothic tableau—gay mom and pop, "forming a family," just like the Brady Bunch—flies in the face of the right-wing stereotype that gays "recruit" children since they "can't reproduce." (Not that homophobes haven't also opposed the efforts of gays to marry, adopt, and otherwise reap the benefits of the family.)

But gay families *are* different, starting with the number of coparents who may be on the scene. Amy says she's going to have a T-shirt made for Sarah to wear in the next Gay Pride Day parade with the message: "I'm proud of my gay mommies and daddies." Doug also likes to joke about the ways in which they really do fit the gay stereotype: "Thank God Amy likes baseball, because I *hate* sports. What *I* want to introduce Sarah to is the ballet."

Gay families are also made up of people who are painfully used to having no blessings from church or state for their relationships—and have therefore become adept at inventing their own ways to affirm them. Doug says he likes the fact that he and Nancy are making it up as they go along: "It's not like we're divorced people with some ancient history of bitterness with each other." In some ways, he and Nancy—and their mates—seem to regard each other as in-laws, connected by the happy coincidence that they're all part of Sarah's extended family, and therefore of each other's. Instead of two people meeting, falling in love, and having a baby, four people met, had a baby, and then became friends.

Amy and Nancy live in Brooklyn. Nancy, who has a runner's thin body and a high-cheekboned face that might remind you of Jeanne Moreau, worked as a civil servant before Sarah was born. Amy—an elfin Texan who was once a professional rock musician—now works as a secretary and is hoping to start her own gourmet-food business soon.

By the time they became lovers more than five years ago, Nancy had already begun to think about having a child. Amy, on the other hand, "had never wanted kids. But I love Nancy, and I certainly wasn't going to say, don't do it. I just wasn't saying, 'Whoopee, let's do it!'" It was only after Nancy became pregnant that Amy's misgivings disappeared. (At that point, according to Nancy, "she threw herself into it, like a project. She must have read every book in existence about childbearing and child-rearing.")

Nancy had decided early on that she didn't want to use a sperm bank. Her reasons were emotional rather than practical, since she wasn't then looking for a man to help raise the child. As far as she was concerned, the donor could drop his sperm into a test tube and then drop off the face of the earth—as long as she knew who he was. Given the possible complications, why was that so important? Nancy has a hard time explaining, except to say that she was vaguely bothered by having to tell a child that its father was an unknown quantity. She also frankly preferred good-looking genes. Friends warned her that she was being too conventional, but Nancy decided to follow her instincts.

One candidate in particular had long been in the back of her mind—an old boyfriend with whom she *might* have had a child. Nancy had had her first lesbian affair in high school, but between that time and her mid-twenties, "I got scared. In college and graduate school, I fell in love with women, but I went out with men." Nancy wrote a letter to Alan, who now lived in Vancouver but with whom she had remained friends.

I'd like to ask you something that rides close to the heart. For a long time I've wanted to have a child, and after much thought, I wonder if you'd consider being the father. It may be too complicated, [but] I figured the only way to find that out is to write you this letter. I would want to retain custody absolutely, and you might wish to protect yourself for a number of reasons. You would have no financial obligations or even have to acknowledge paternity. If you would like, you could still see the child, etc. Golly, it's harder to write about this than I had imagined.

Alan turned her down—ever so gently, explaining that he expected to marry and have a family someday, and that was where he felt his responsibilities should lie. Nancy was devastated; she realized that she had been so focused on her own decision to proceed that she hadn't even considered what she would do if he said no. She waited seven months before she approached anyone else.

Over the course of the next year and a half, Nancy asked at least eight men to father her child. The proposals followed a fascinating pattern that Nancy had never anticipated: first the men would feel flattered at the honor, and then they would back off—possibly aghast at the expendability that lay just beneath the honor. Another old boyfriend beamed at Nancy's request over dinner, and promised to call as soon as he had discussed the project with his therapist. When she didn't hear from him after several weeks, Nancy called him; his roommate said he couldn't come to the phone, but would call her right back. He never did.

There were similar reactions when she gave up on old beaux and began approaching friends of friends, both straight and gay. "One guy got to the point over dinner where we were even discussing private versus public schools," she recalls. "He didn't call me back either." One gay man was definitely interested—but his lover had AIDS. Most men just refused, ultimately leading Amy and Nancy and their friends to wonder if men are as freaked out at being relegated to the status of sperm donors as women are at being classified as sex objects.

While Nancy grew increasingly desperate, Amy found herself becoming furious on her lover's behalf: "Here there are guys all over the country, knocking women up and leaving them with unwanted children, but when Nancy *wants* a baby, all of a sudden it's like, oh man, this is too heavy, such a big responsibility, and they're all turning into Dustin Hoffman."

Nancy was about to give up and go to a sperm bank when she and Amy happened to attend a women's tennis match one night with their friend Marta and her lover Kate. While Navratilova and Shriver trounced their doubles opponents, Nancy poured out her story. "Gee," was Marta's reaction, "you ought to call my husband—I think he's already thinking about having a child."

It was news to Nancy that Marta even *had* a husband. Marta was born in Czechoslovakia, and as a lesbian, she was officially an undesirable alien in the United States. At the time that she was trying to find a way to stay in New York, she explained, her friend Doug—whose lover Bjorn is Norwegian and had to cope with similar worries—offered to marry her and make her a citizen. "The fact that he was willing to do that for Marta gave us a very good feeling about him from the start," Amy says now. Marta meanwhile got so excited at the idea of helping Nancy and Doug that she went to a pay phone on the spot and called him. Within a week, all of them were having dinner together.

Doug and Bjorn had been a couple for 10 years, and had spent the last several thinking about children. Doug says that there's nothing especially odd about that: "I think it's what happens to a lot of forty-year-olds who are in a stable relationship." If they hadn't met Nancy and Amy, he adds, he and Bjorn probably would have adopted or tried to find a woman to mother a biological child. (Bjorn had once donated sperm to a friend whose husband was sterile, but she failed to conceive.)

Doug is a successful entrepreneur and real estate investor who has achieved the enviable position of not having to work to support himself. The men now spend much of their time renovating new property, and they're very much "settled down" into comfortable middle age. Bjorn (who worked on a cruise ship before he met Doug and has always lived all over the world) acknowledges that "although I've always wanted children, my lifestyle held me back when I was younger. Even a few years ago, I wouldn't have been responsive to having Sarah in our lives. But now I see her as in some way *extending* my life together with Doug."

Although a man who wanted to play an active parenting role hadn't been part of the original calculations—much less *two* men—Amy remembers feeling an instant rapport when all four met. "I just knew. *This is it.* We had been aware that we needed someone who had been around enough to not be afraid to do it, but who would also be respectful of our position. And we wanted people who were enough like us that we could talk easily and work things out. These guys were our age, they had similar backgrounds and outlooks to ours, *plus* they really wanted to have a child."

Nancy and Doug had several more meetings. The two men were in the process of moving their primary residence from New York to New Mexico and were also about to go to Norway for several months. Both of the prospective biological parents felt under pressure to make a very fast decision, since Nancy was due to ovulate. Doug remembers "discussing our values while we subtly checked out each other's bone structure." Each would then run home and discuss details of their "date" with their respective lovers. Nancy soon decided Doug was definitely Mr. Goodbaster.

The potential parents signed no contracts. Nor (since Doug and Bjorn were monogamous) did Nancy ask Doug to take a test for the AIDS antibody. "I can see now that maybe it would have been wise to get some things in writing," Nancy says. "But then I was obsessed. Here I had finally met the right guy— and he was on his way to Oslo." Nancy ovulated literally the day before Doug was to leave town. The two showed up at Nancy's gynecologist's office; Doug masturbated into a jar, while Nancy waited on a table in another room. "I remember that when he was finished, the nurse was going to just send him on his way—which just seemed so cold! I asked her to have him come around first and stick his head in the door to say hi. I just wanted to tell him thank you."

Nancy conceived, right on schedule.

Living in New York with a network of supportive friends, Amy and Nancy spent the next few months much as would any other couple who were expecting a baby (although as Amy once joked when Nancy asked her to open a bottle of champagne, "Just because you're the pregnant one doesn't mean that I'm the boy"). Nancy's gynecologist was a lesbian who, with a gay male friend as father, had given birth the year before. The obstetrician was a supportive straight woman who had no problem with Amy's desire to be present at the birth. They went through Lamaze childbirth classes together, where they were the only female couple in the class, but no one batted an eyelash. They waited through the amniocentesis and were delighted to hear that Clove, as they had been calling the fetus, was a girl. They thought about names, and they read Dr. Spock. Their friends gave them a baby shower. (The gifts included a tiny black leather jacket from one lesbian couple.)

It was at the hospital just after Sarah was born that they first ran up against the reality that their arrangement was highly unusual: only one person was permitted to visit with Nancy when she had the baby in the room. Amy decided to offer that opportunity to Doug, who was in New York specifically for the birth. "It was a really lovely gesture, but what it meant was that Amy never even got to hold Sarah until we got home," Nancy says. "It also meant that Doug was there a lot—and I really didn't *know* him at the time. I was feeling tired and physically awful, and this man would be there holding the baby, and I'd think, who is he? He and Amy meanwhile would get into these little arguments about silly things like what Chinese food to order."

Despite the initial tension and weirdness of being in such an intimate relationship with near-strangers, however, the adults have spent the year since the birth carving out an extremely workable arrangement. Their relationship is so steady, in fact, that Amy, Nancy, and Sarah are moving to New Mexico later this year. "We aren't making this move to become a nuclear family or anything like that, and we're not going to live with Doug and Bjorn," Nancy explains. "In fact, if Amy and I could afford a bigger apartment in New York and a private school education for Sarah, we would probably stay. But we like the Southwest, and we think it's a good place to start a business, which is something Amy has wanted to do for a long time, and which I'd like to help her with. And of course we realize that in Santa Fe we'll be able to rely on Doug and Bjorn to do a lot of the child care."

The four adults have as yet not had any serious disagreements: if anything, everyone has been on their best behavior during the weekends they've spent in New York and the two weeks they were together last fall in Santa Fe. "We had to learn that it doesn't take four people to get her out of the crib and into the car seat," Doug laughs. When they're all living in the same town, "maybe we'll have a *real* fight," he adds—although Amy claims that "we're all such reserved WASP types that we're more likely to sit around with a glass of wine and have a polite discussion."

Sarah bears her mother's last name, although her middle name is Doug's last name, and he's listed on the birth certificate as her father. (Friends argued with Nancy that she was handing Doug the ammunition he'd need to prove he was the father at a time when he hadn't established in writing that he had any obligation to the child—a deadly combination.) Technically Sarah is an "illegitimate" child, and according to Amy, "Nancy's mother entertains the hope that Nancy and Doug will get married. Of course," she adds with a Cheshire cat grin, "Doug is already married to Marta."

Their parents and siblings have greeted their gayness with varying degrees of acceptance, but Bjorn is the only one of the four adults whose family has refused to accept Sarah. "There's never been a problem with my being gay—I thought it was understood," he says. "But now, all of a sudden, the shit has hit the fan—and there's been a real lack of response and respect for my relationship to Sarah. The funny thing is that I think my family would come around if it were *my* biological child." Bjorn says that he doesn't really think of himself as a stepfather or coparent: "Doug and Nancy are the parents, and Amy is really the coparent. I'd like to be more like the grandfather or the uncle—someone who can *spoil* Sarah."

For Doug, the worst problem of fatherhood has been seeing so little of Sarah. "If she had come along a year earlier, I think we might never have moved so far away," he says. "I feel like I'm losing out on some of what's going on now, because I don't see her every day." If Amy and Nancy hadn't decided to move to New Mexico, he adds, he was planning to propose that Sarah spend at least a school year with him and Bjorn at some point.

In some ways, the most vulnerable adult in Sarah's family is Amy, since she *is* the coparent: the person who lives with Sarah and provides most of her financial support. But the law allows her no legal connection. Because Doug's name is on the birth certificate, Amy acknowledges, "legally, if something happened to Nancy, it would be up to Doug whether I could even see Sarah. I know that there are stepparents who are in my same situation, but they weren't there from the beginning." Doug and Nancy's wills specify that if they both should die, Bjorn and Amy will have custody of Sarah—but in real life, if any of the biological grandparents challenged the will, they'd stand a good chance of winning. Says Amy: "I know I'm risking a lot, but my own mother died when I was young, and I've always been completely aware that anytime, a person can lose everything. Your choice is either to never open yourself up again or to realize that you have to do it today—which is what I'm doing. Anyway," she adds, "I *love* her. I even love her when she shits on my cowboy boots."

Amy isn't sure yet what Sarah will call her when she starts to talk. "I'm not Mommy, but I'm *like* her other parent. It's a special relationship. Maybe we'll have to make up the name for it."

Nancy originally asked for no money from Doug, and in fact spurned his repeated offers to help out with the cost of the birth. She had been struggling with an unexpected but powerful postpartum feeling that she wanted to be the undisputed primary biological parent: "When she was born, I was suddenly hit with the reality of how much I was afraid of losing her—to anyone or anything," Nancy says. "I think now that it's the sort of free-floating anxiety that any new parent feels and has to work through, but at the time it attached itself to Doug, and the vulnerability I felt within our arrangement. On the one hand, Doug was just what I had been looking for, but he's *so* accomplished that it worried me—I think I was afraid that there was going to be some fierce sort of competition possible between us." Taking no money was Nancy's way of asserting her independence.

Amy had planned to support them all until Sarah was a year old, and then Nancy intended to go back to work. But when the time came, Nancy wasn't ready emotionally to leave Sarah all day. By then, Doug and Nancy had gotten to know each other better, and Doug finally persuaded her to accept child support. Doug and Bjorn have also rewritten their wills to provide for Sarah.

One of the questions that outsiders ask the adults most often is whether they want Sarah to grow up gay. (Most people who wouldn't be surprised if Jewish or Amish parents wanted Jewish or Amish children are nonetheless horrified at the possibility that a gay parent might prefer a gay child.) In fact, all four say they don't care if Sarah is heterosexual—not because they think it's better, but because all of them suffered as adolescents who weren't living up to *their* parents' ideas of proper sexual orientation. "The first thing children do without your permission is to pick their sex, and probably the second thing is to pick their sexual preference," says Doug.

The second most common question from the outside is whether they worry about Sarah suffering from discrimination because her parents are gay. Amy says that she imagines there might be limitations on where they can reside, and she knows there are plenty of people who don't accept them. "But we're all at the point where we know who *we* are and what our values are—that's just not an issue. For instance, I don't really care whether the pediatrician approves of my relationship. He just has to know that when I ask a question about what Sarah's eating, I get an answer, just the same as Nancy does. Anyway, I don't think we have to be perfect parents, just because we're gay."

She adds: "Sarah's not a social experiment—she's a child. When you're living as part of a relationship every day, it's not some sort of abstraction where you're trying to work out your ideology. It's your life. And this is ours."

Patricia J. Williams

My Best White Friend

My best white friend is giving me advice on how to get myself up like a trophy-wife-in-waiting. We are obliged to attend a gala fund-raiser for an organization on whose board we both sit. I'm not a wife of any sort at all, and she says she knows why: I'm prickly as all get out, I dress down instead of up, and my hair is "a complete disaster." My best white friend, who is already a trophy wife of considerable social and philanthropic standing, is pressing me to borrow one of her Real Designer gowns and a couple of those heavy gold bracelets that are definitely not something you can buy on the street.

I tell her she's missing the point. Cinderella wasn't an over-thirty black professional with an attitude. What sort of Master of the Universe is going to go for that?

"You're not a *racist*, are you?" she asks.

"How could I be?" I reply, with wounded indignation. "What, being the American Dream personified and all."

"Then let's get busy and make you *up,*" she says soothingly, breaking out the little pots of powder, paint, and polish.

From the first exfoliant to the last of the cucumber rinse, we fight about my man troubles. From powder base through lip varnish, we fight about hers.

You see, part of the problem is that white knights just don't play the same part in my mythical landscape of desire. If poor Cinderella had been black, it would have been a whole different story. I tell my best white friend the kind of stories my mother raised me on: about slave girls who worked their fingers to the bone for their evil half sisters, the "legitimate" daughters of their mutual father, the master of the manse, the owner of them all; about scullery maids whose oil-and-ashes complexions would not wash clean even after multiple waves of the wand. These were the ones who harbored impossible dreams of love for lost mates who had been sold down rivers of tears to oblivion. These were the ones who became runaways.

"Just think about it," I say. "The human drama is compact enough so that when my mother was little she knew women who had been slaves, including a

291

couple of runaways. Cinderellas who had burned their masters' beds and then fled for their lives. It doesn't take too much, even across the ages, to read between those lines. Women who invented their own endings, even when they didn't get to live happily or very long thereafter."

My best white friend says, "Get a grip. It's just a party."

I've called my best white friend my best white friend ever since she started calling me her best black friend. I am her only black friend, as far as I know, a circumstance for which she blames "the class thing." At her end of the social ladder, I am *my* only black friend—a circumstance for which I blame "the race thing."

"People should stop putting so much emphasis on color—it doesn't matter whether you're black or white or blue or green," she says from beneath an avocado mask.

Lucky for you, I think, even as my own pores are expanding or contracting—I forget which—beneath a cool neon-green sheath.

In fact, I have been looking forward to the makeover. M.B.W.F. has a masseuse and a manicurist and colors in her palette like Après Sun and Burnt Straw, which she swears will match my skin tones more or less.

"Why don't they just call it Racial Envy?" I ask, holding up a tube of Deep Copper Kiss.

"Now, now, we're all sisters under the makeup," she says cheerfully.

"When ever will we be sisters without?" I grumble.

I've come this far because she's convinced me that my usual slapdash routine is the equivalent of being "unmade"; and being unmade, she underscores, is a most exclamatory form of unsophistication. "Even Strom Thurmond wears a little pancake when he's in public."

M.B.W.F. is somewhat given to hyperbole, but it *is* awfully hard to bear, the thought of making less of a fashion statement than old Strom. I do draw the line, though. She has a long history of nips, tucks, and liposuction. Once, I tried to suggest how appalled I was, but I'm not good at being graceful when I have a really strong opinion roiling up inside. She dismissed me sweetly: "You can afford to disapprove. You are aging *so* very nicely."

There was the slightest pause as I tried to suppress the anxious rise in my voice: "You think I'm aging?"

Very gently, she proceeded to point out the flawed and falling features that give me away to the carefully trained eye, the insistent voyeur. There were the pores. And those puffs beneath my eyes. No, not there—those are the bags under my eyes. The bags aren't so bad, according to her—no deep wrinkling just yet. But keep going—the puffs are just below the bags. Therein lies the facial decay that gives my age away.

I had never noticed them before, but for a while after that those puffs just dominated my face. I couldn't look at myself for their explosive insolence—the body's betrayal, obscuring every other feature.

I got over it the day we were standing in line by a news rack at the Food Emporium. Gazing at a photo of Princess Diana looking radiantly, elegantly melancholic on the cover of some women's magazine, M.B.W.F. snapped, "God! Bulimia must work!"

This is not the first time M.B.W.F. has shepherded me to social doom. The last time, it was a very glitzy cocktail party where husband material supposedly abounded. I had a long, businesslike conversation with a man she introduced me to, who, I realized as we talked, grew more and more fascinated by me. At first, I was only conscious of winning him over; then I remember becoming aware that there was something funny about his fierce infatuation. I was *surprising* him, I slowly realized. Finally, he came clean: he said that he had never before had a conversation like this with a black person. "I think I'm in love," he blurted in a voice bubbling with fear.

"I think not," I consoled him. "It's just the power of your undone expectations, in combination with my being a basically likeable person. It's throwing you for a loop. That and the Scotch, which, as you ought to know, is inherently depoliticizing."

I remember telling M.B.W.F. about him afterward. She had always thought of him as "that perfect Southern gentleman." The flip side of the Southern gentleman is the kind master, I pointed out. "Bad luck," she said. "It's true, though—he's the one man I wouldn't want to be owned by, if I were you."

My best white friend doesn't believe that race is a big social problem anymore. "It's all economics," she insists. "It's how you came to be my *friend*—for once, she does not qualify me as black—"the fact that we were both in college together." I feel compelled to remind her that affirmative action is how both of us ended up in the formerly all-male bastion we attended.

The odd thing is, we took most of the same classes. She ended up musically proficient, gifted in the art of interior design, fluent in the mother tongue, whatever it might be, of the honored visiting diplomat of the moment. She actively aspired, she says, to be "a cunning little meringue of a male prize."

"You," she says to me, "were always more like Gladys Knight."

"Come again?" I say.

"Ethnic woman warrior, always on that midnight train to someplace else, intent on becoming the highest-paid Aunt Jemima in history."

"Ackh," I cough, a sudden strangulation of unmade thoughts fluttering in my windpipe.

The night after the cocktail party, I dreamed that I was in a bedroom with a tall, faceless man. I was his breeding slave. I was trying to be very, very good, so that I might one day earn my freedom. He did not trust me. I was always trying to hide some essential part of myself from him, which I would preserve and take with me on that promised day when I was permitted to leave; he felt it as an innate wickedness in me, a darkness that he could not penetrate, a dangerous secret that must be wrested from me. I tried everything I knew to please him; I walked a tightrope of anxious servitude and survivalist withholding. But it was not good enough. One morning, he just reached for a sword and sliced me in half, to see for himself what was inside. A casual flick, and I lay dead on the floor in two dark, unyielding halves; in exasperated disgust, he stepped over my remains and rushed from the room, already late for other business, leaving the cleanup for another slave.

"You didn't dream that!" M.B.W.F. says in disbelief.

"I did so."

"You're making it up," she says. "People don't really have dreams like that."

"*I* do. Aren't I a people, too?"

"That's amazing! Tell me another."

"O.K., here's a fairy tale for you," I say, and tell her I dreamed I was being held by Sam Malone, the silly, womanizing bartender on "Cheers." He was tall, broad-chested, good-looking, unbelievably strong. My head, my face were pressed against his chest. We were whispering our love for each other. I was moved deeply, my heart was banging, he held me tight and told me that he loved me. I told him that I loved him, too. We kissed so that heaven and earth moved in my heart; I wanted to make love to him fiercely. He put a simple thick gold band on my finger. I turned and, my voice cracking with emotion and barely audible, said, "What's this?" He asked me to marry him. I told him yes, I loved him, yes, yes, I loved him. He told me he loved me, too. I held out my hand and admired the ring in awe. I was the luckiest woman on earth.

Suddenly Diane Chambers, Sam's paramour on "Cheers," burst through the door. She was her perky, petulant self, bouncing blond hair and black-green eyes like tarnished copper beads, like lumps of melted metal—eyes that looked carved yet soft, almost brimming. She turned those soft-hard eyes on me and said, "Oh, no, Sam, not tonight—you promised!"

And with that I realized that I was to be consigned to a small room on the other side of the house. Diane followed me as I left, profusely apologetic with explanations: she was sorry, and she didn't mind him being with me once or twice a month, but this was getting ridiculous. I realized that I was Sam's part-time mistress—a member of the household somehow, but having no rights.

Then Diane went back into the master bedroom and Sam came in to apologize, to say that there had been a mix-up, that it was just this once, that he'd make it up to me, that he was sorry. And, of course, I forgave him, for there was nothing I wanted more than to relive the moment when he held me tightly and our love was a miracle and I was the only woman he wanted in the world, forever.

"Have you thought of going into therapy?" she jokes.

"As a matter of fact, I have," I say, sighing and rubbing my temples. "On average, we black women have bigger, better problems than any other women alive. We bear the burden of being seen as pretenders to the thrones of both femininity and masculinity, endlessly mocked by the ambiguously gendered crown-of-thorns imagery of 'queen'—Madame Queen, snap queen, welfare queen, quota queen, Queenie Queen, *Queen* Queen Queen. We black women are figured more as stand-ins for men, sort of like reverse drag queens: women pretending to be women but more male than men—bare-breasted, sweat-glistened, plow-pulling, sole supporters of their families. Arnold Schwarzenegger and Sylvester Stallone meet Sojourner Truth, the *Real* Real Thing, the Ace-of-Spades Gender Card Herself, Thelma and Louise knocked up by Wesley Snipes, the ultimate hard-drinking, tobacco-growing-and-aspitting, nut-crushing ball-buster of all time. . . . I mean, think about it—how'd you like to go to the ball dressed like a walking cultural pathology? Wouldn't it make you just a wee bit tense?"

"But," she sputters, "but—you always seem so *strong!*"

We have just about completed our toilette. She looks at my hair as though it were a rude construction of mud and twigs, bright glass beads, and flashy bits of tinfoil. I look at hers for what it is—the high-tech product of many hours of steam rollers, shine enhancers, body spritzers, perms, and about eighteen hundred watts of blow-dried effort. We gaze at each other with the deep disapproval of one gazing into a mirror. It is inconceivable to both of us that we have been friends for as long as we have. We shake our heads in sympathetic unison and sigh.

One last thing: it seems we have forgotten about shoes. It turns out that my feet are much too big to fit into any of her sequinned little evening slippers, so I wear my own sensible square-soled pumps. My prosaic feet, like overgrown roots, peek out from beneath the satiny folds of the perfect dress. She looks radiant; I feel dubious. Our chariot and her husband await. As we climb into the limousine, her husband lights up a cigar and holds forth on the reëmerging popularity of same. My friend responds charmingly with a remarkably detailed production history of the Biedermeier humidor.

I do not envy her. I do not resent her. I do not hold my breath.

Julia A. Boyd

Ethnic and Cultural Diversity: Keys to Power

WHAT IS PERSONAL IS ALSO POLITICAL

Difference is that raw and powerful connection from which our personal power is forged.

—LORDE, 1984, pg. 112

The woman of color's self-image, her confidence (or lack of it), as well as her perceptions of the world around her have evolved out of her personal experiences. Many of these experiences are rooted in myths and stereotypes surrounding her ethnic and cultural heritage and gender. Copeland (1981) states that negative feelings brought about because of these experiences are not always measurable, but assumptions can be made that these experiences do little to enhance a positive self-concept. From early adolescence to adulthood, women of color are inundated by media and social contacts that serve to instill the belief that to be different is societally unacceptable. It is obvious that commercial media presents images of women with flowing hair and strong European features as ideals of Western beauty. Even when women of color are used within the commercial context they are chosen to reflect characteristics, i.e., long straight hair, light coloring, thin lips, and noses, that often make them indistinguishable from women of non-color. From early childhood, children in our society hear and read stories and fairytales that are dominated by beautiful blond princesses and heroines who are often being rescued, fought for, and overall cherished. The message that our children receive is that attractiveness, success, and popularity are basically unattainable for females of color.

As Pratt (1984) states,

> The values that I have at my core, or my culture, will only be those of negativity, exclusion, fear, and death, and my feelings based in the reality that the group identity of my culture have been defined, often not by positive qualities, but by negative characteristics. (pg. 39)

Women of color continue to suffer the psychological damage of negative self-image, even today, twenty years after the onset of the Civil Rights movement, which served to enlighten the dominant culture to the plight of people of color. Slogans such as "Black Pride" and "Black Is Beautiful," among others, have not totally erased the psychological damage engendered in many Black women (Copeland, 1981, pg. 397).

ETHNICALLY DIFFERENT, YET CULTURALLY THE SAME

Our strategy is how we cope, how we measure and weigh what is to be said and when, what is to be done, and how, and to whom daily, deciding who it is we can call an ally, call a friend. We are women without a line. (Moraga, 1981, pg. 12)

How does the woman of color know she can trust her feminist therapist to be a friend and ally? Her reality is based in the constant struggle for survival, which demands that she be cautious. Generational teachings regarding trusting others outside the ethnic and cultural community have been strongly enforced by family and respected community members (Richie, 1983, pg. 20). From early childhood, women of color have been taught that personal disclosure outside the ethnic and cultural community is synonymous with treason. This strong devotion to non-disclosure has for many years silenced women of color in personal crisis. In order for the feminist therapist to effectively help women of color in therapy, the therapist must first understand the ethnic and cultural framework that supports the women of color's world. In order to illustrate this concept in concrete terms, I have chosen to include the following story I wrote as a miniature portrait of what this paper represents (Boyd, 1987).

THE GOSPEL ACCORDING TO ME

Yesterday during lunch Beth told me that I was her best friend. Now, I'll never understand why it is that this woman always chooses to get relevant when I'm trying to do justice to my stomach. Knowing Beth as well as I do, I know she was expecting some tactful response on my part. But it's tough being polite when you're hungry, and my stomach had been throwing some large hints to my brain and everybody else's within earshot all day about its empty state of affairs. So as I bit into my grilled cheese sandwich, I told Beth that I'd have to give the matter of her being my best friend a lot of thought, because having a best friend, someone who was really ace, numero uno in your life, deserved some heavy contemplation.

Thinking back on it, I guess I could have given Beth an answer during lunch. But how do you tell a white woman that it's still politically dangerous to have white folks for best friends, even if it is 198—. I mean now really! Mama always taught me that a dollar bill was a Black person's best friend, and so far as I know, Mama ain't lied to me yet. The gospel according to Mama states that a dollar bill don't give you no lip, it keeps food in your stomach, clothes on your back and a roof over your head. If you treat it right it multiplies and if you don't it disappears, but the bottom line is if you've got a dollar you've got a friend for life. I know Beth wouldn't understand Mama's logic because we come from two different worlds. It's not that I'm trying to discourage Beth, I really do like her. But having an ace partner means more to me than just sharing office space and having lunch together a couple times a week. I know that Beth made her comment sincerely. She wants me to notice that she's trying to bridge the gap, but what she doesn't understand is that it may take me longer to come over the water, because bridges have a way of not being stable when the winds blow too strong. As it is I've already got the neighbors talking because I've invited Beth to my apartment a couple of times. Wilda, my neighbor downstairs, almost broke her neck running up three flights of stairs to my place after Beth's first visit. It's not that Wilda's nosey you understand, it's just that she was concerned. Wilda knows that white folks driving 280Z's and wearing Klein jeans don't come around the projects very often and they never come in the building unless they're after something or somebody. I had one tough job on my hands explaining to Wilda that Beth really was "okay" and through Beth's volunteer work at the Women's Center she and I had gotten to be friends. Now Wilda, who is a whole lot like Mama in her logical thinking, feels it's her sworn duty to look out for me. And she will generally tell anyone within earshot, including me, that she thinks I'm a little strange but likable in my own fashion. But the look she gave me out of the corner of her eye let me know that now she really thinks I've lost all my street school'n. But like I said before Wilda preaches from Mama's gospel and Mama's Word states that you don't trust nobody two shades lighter than Black.

When I think about the pro's and con's of my friendship with Beth, both sides of the scale don't always equal out. Seventy-five percent of the time we get along pretty good: we believe in the same political causes even if our personal reasons are miles apart; we share similar interest in books, movies, and music; and we share the belief that going after what you want in life "is the name of the game." However, the other twenty-five percent of the time is what divides us. Beth would like to believe that as women and activists we are equals. She professes confusion when I speak about my Blackness being more than just skin color and hairstyle but a generational lifestyle that is rich in culture and value. Beth wants to form a friendship and bond with my womenness, the part of me which she can relate to as white woman that bears a striking resemblance to her feminist ideals. What she fails to understand is that in only identifying with that part of me she denies my existence as a whole person. I don't know about Beth, but I'm greedy. I want a whole friendship or none at all. Beth has the privilege to forget that she's white and middle-class and I have the right to remember that I'm Black folk ethnic. Our relationship as friends may never equal best, but at least it's a start to something better, and that's the Gospel according to Me.

This story points out some very real issues acted out in the therapy between women of color and white feminist therapists. While it was painful, I understood Beth's concept of me as a Black woman/feminist. Her assumptions were based on the limited interactions and information she had with people of color prior to our friendship. I could see the parallels in our shared cause, and the contradictions based in our realities of Black and White. Beth assumed that our parallel interest, feminism, would be enough to bridge the gap between our worlds. However, my assumptions about Beth, as a white woman/feminist were based on my reality (read survival) as a woman of color living in this society. Beverly Smith (1984, pg. 32) states, "It's impossible, I think to be a Black person in this country and not be deeply aware of white people. Part of our awareness is knowledge we need to survive." Joining the ranks of feminist leadership did not/could not erase the historical legacies that Beth and I brought to our relationship as friends. All too often therapists have entered the counseling relationship unmindful of the intrusion of their excessive, white, middle-class, cultural baggage (Smith, 1981, pg. 180). Therapeutically, the unaware feminist therapist will choose to believe that the struggles and values of the woman of color client should and will equal her struggles. *Often the values of the white feminist therapist overshadows the commitment and values of the woman of color, which would cloud the constructive nature of the therapy relationship.* An example taken from a woman participating in a Black women's support group illustrates this point.

> When I heard about this group I asked my therapist (a white woman) if I could attend. It seemed like all she was concerned about was the fact that I got raped. Hell! I know that was important, but that bastard got my last twenty-five dollars. That was all the money I had, till payday. I can deal with the rape later, but I won't have a job if I can't get back and forth to work. (Black rape victim, 1985)

In not recognizing the economic crisis as a major part of the client's concern, the white therapist alienated the client, thus making her value (the rape), the client's value. Elsie Smith (1981) reports that "white therapists hide behind the liberal facade of counseling, in trying to impose their values on their client" (pg. 141). Their racial and cultural perspectives are assumed to be those of their clients. In ignoring the ethnic and cultural differences, the white feminist therapist also ignores the realities. Those differences cannot be ignored in a therapeutic setting without diminishing the chance for effective healing.

ETHNIC AND CULTURAL SOURCES OF STRENGTH

As women, we have been taught either to ignore our differences or to view them as causes for separation and suspicion, rather than as forces for change.

—LORDE, 1984, pg. 112

Denial of differences and lack of educational awareness on the part of the therapist are two major reasons that women of color give for avoiding psychotherapy (Shipp, 1983). There is a very real fear that therapists will view ethnic and cultural behaviors and beliefs as pathologic, as opposed to legitimate survival responses. Women of color are acutely aware that much of the social research involving them has only served to perpetuate myths and stereotypes concerning ethnic groups. A prime example of distorted research that has caused a continuous backlash for Black women is the Moynihan Report (1965) in which the Black family was viewed as disintegrating due to the "matriarchal" family structure. Bell hooks (1981) points out quite eloquently in her book *Ain't I A Woman* that labeling Black women as matriarchs is analogous to labeling female children who are playing house and acting out the role of mother as matriarchs. In both instances *no real effective power exists that allows the females in question to control their destiny.*

Thus, Moynihan's report only serves to heighten the racist, socially accepted myth that Black females are unable to sustain interpersonal relationships. The so-called "Black matriarch" is a kind of folk character largely fashioned by whites out of half truths and lies about the involuntary conditions of Black women (Bond & Perry, 1975).

Women of color are not unaware of the socially accepted forms of labeling that are used to define their person and environment, and this awareness legitimizes their caution in seeking professional therapy. Feminist therapists are not exempt from bias in their attitudes and beliefs concerning women of color especially when their professional training has been designed to exclude ethnic and cultural normative values. The following case example helps to illustrate my point.

> A young Southeast Asian woman was court ordered to therapy for repeatedly shoplifting merchandise from a neighborhood grocery store. The young woman had been in this country less than a year and spoke minimal English. She was assigned to a white therapist who after several failed attempts to get the young woman to communicate her reasons for shoplifting informed the court that the client was withdrawn, uncommunicative, and appeared depressed. A young Asian paralegal working in the office at the time read the case and was able to shed some light on the problem. The Asian paralegal related that the item, repeatedly stolen from the store, sanitary napkins, was not openly displayed, or sold in public markets in the country of the Southeast Asian woman. The paralegal explained that in this woman's country, it was considered highly improper for women to publicly acknowledge their monthly menses. Purchasing the pads outright or explaining her reasons for taking this product would have caused this woman great embarrassment and public shame, not to mention a breach of her ethnic and cultural values on proper conduct.

The assigned therapist in this case overlooked critical information in her written assessment of this case. Thus, this Southeast Asian woman became an ethnic and cultural victim. The therapist's unwillingness to go beyond her training to gather necessary ethnic and cultural information led her to be ignorant of and thus insensitive to her client's value system.

CRISIS

In times of crisis or conflict, women of color will often cloak themselves in their ethnic and cultural traditions, looking to these traditions as a source of reawakening personal strength. By calling on the teachings and traditions of the ethnic culture, women of color gain a unique sense of personal power that is limitless. Every ethnic culture holds a key linked to the power of survival for the women of color. For the Latina woman it may be speaking only in her native tongue; the American Indian woman may turn to purification rituals; and the Black woman may take solace in religion (Bush & Babich, 1984). Another case example is used to understand this point.

> Recently a Native American woman who was brutally raped completed her healing and recovery process by retreating to her aunt's reservation and purifying her mind, body, and soul through a ritual meditation and sweat ceremony. This woman also sent her therapist (a white woman) a letter and a small bundle of sweet smelling sage to thank her.

For many women of color defining a sense of identity through rituals and traditional customs is paramount in developing a stronger sense of self individually and collectively.

DIVERSITY

Characterizing women of color into neatly packaged groups defined by customs and traditions might be an easy task, if the groups were not made up of individuals. Joyce Ladner (1971) in *Tomorrow's Tomorrow: The Black Woman*, points out that there is no monolithic concept of the Black woman, but there are many models of Black womanhood. This concept applies to all women of color. As women, women of color are distinct individuals who make choices as to the many ways in which they gain their strength. There are women of color who may not look to their ethnic and cultural traditions for subsistence. However, it is very likely that on some level such a woman will look to a source of comfort and/or nurturing that only her community or family of origin can offer. This attention to both group and individual needs may sound complex to a white feminist therapist. However being of one body yet sharing many voices is the daily life and strength of women of color.

BICULTURALISM AS SURVIVAL

In order to survive women of color have become masters in the art of being bicultural. Beverly Smith (1983), in her article *Some Thoughts on Racism* writes, "There is a lot of propaganda in this culture for the normality of the rightness of whiteness" (pg. 27). Generations of exposure to the socially accepted norms of whiteness have made it virtually impossible for women of color not to adopt specific behaviors, i.e., standards of beauty, language and mannerisms associated with white culture that would allow them to survive. In order to survive, Audre Lorde (1984) states,

> those of us for whom oppression is as American as apple pie have always had to be watchers, to become familiar with the language and manners of the oppressor, even sometimes adopting them for some illusion of protection. (pg. 114)

From an early age women of color learn the rudiments of ethnic culture at home and the crazy making double standards of social acceptance outside the home. Beginning in school young girls of color are introduced to *White Fairy Princess* or *Snow White* (Copeland, 1981). As these young girls grow into adolescence and adulthood they are repeatedly deprived of consistent models of women of color on which they can build solid images that reflect their ethnic heritage. For women of color learning to comply publicly with white standards has not been as much a choice as a dictate necessary for survival.

> "Sometimes you can hear them thinking in your bones."
> "They don't know this is my life they're playing with and I was born, knowing the rules."
> "Why do they play these silly head trip games, I don't trust any of them."
> "I'm afraid of God, dogs and the dark, in that order anybody else I'll fight." (Women of Color Support Group, 1987)

These quotes were taken from a women of color support group meeting. The subject was racial harassment on the job. Many of the women present had been seen individually by a white therapist who had referred them to the group after the women of color had started expressing pent up feelings of anger and rage at white employers. The continued challenge of being caught in a system that values only one set of standards is a constant burden for women of color. For the woman of color to openly fight back is an invitation to become a target of institutionalized racism designed in the form of rules and regulations to keep one in the proper place. The following example illustrates the sort of institutionalized racism that confronts women of color in daily work life.

> A Black city worker was disqualified from a higher paying non-traditional position, after she began taking the physical exercise portion of the test and noticed that the equipment was faulty. She pointed out to the test facilitator, a white female, the dangers of the equipment. The facilitator ignored her complaint and told her to quit complaining and complete the course like everybody else. When the Black woman refused due to the safety hazards involved she was disqualified. The Black woman filed a grievance and returned to her regular position. Due to the fact that her grievance was filed against her current employer she believed and rightly so, that she was singled out for continual covert harassment, that caused her to lose time from work, and eventually led her to seek therapy. In group the woman explained her situation and added that a white feminist group had offered her support which she refused. "After all," she explained, "just because they say they're feminist, that's no guarantee they'll understand my problem. They're white too."

This woman's sentiments are reflective of the feelings that many women of color share regarding white feminists. Women of color have been raised to see women of the dominant society as the standard by which they are measured. However, women of color are aware that the standards of measure are unequally balanced historically with the higher premium favoring whiteness. The term feminist, for many women of color has very little meaning, because as Barbara Smith (1984), points out, "people of color have profound skepticism that white people can actually be oppressed" (pg. 30).

JULIA A. BOYD
Ethnic and Cultural
Diversity: Keys to
Power

The master's tools will never dismantle the master's house.

—LORDE, 1984

Feminist theory and philosophy defined and written by white middle-class, college educated women in the '70s basically ignored the primary concerns of women of color. Bell hooks (1984) states, "White women who dominate feminist discourses today rarely question whether or not their perspective on women's reality is true to the lived experiences of women as a collective group" (pg. 65). By generalizing the need to end sexist oppression, feminist theoreticians assumed their experiences as women should/would cover the needs of all women. However, their perspectives did not reflect the experiences or history associated with women of color, who were bound by race and class (Giddings, 1984). Black women took personal affront to much of the feminist philosophy on the grounds that it equated white women's problems to the struggles of the Black experience (Smith, 1982). White feminists drew analogies between women and Blacks, making the assumption that Black women's experiences were unlike those of Black men (Hooks, 1981). It became exceedingly clear, to Black women, throughout the initial stages of the women's movement that the daily and historical contributions made by women of color were being downplayed or ignored. Black women and their sisters of color saw white feminists vying for the same (not equal) institutionalized racist oppressive power held by white males in this country. White feminists failed to recognize that feminism was not synonymous with freedom or fairness for women of color. Understandably, women of color felt cheated, thus victimized by a political move that was supposed to liberate and validate their reality. Akemi Kikumura (1981), in her book *Through Harsh Winters, The Life of a Japanese Immigrant Woman,* recalls the wisdom of her mother in saying,

> During my lifetime I hope that I can convince you that as long as you look Japanese, you are going to be Japanese. No one is ever going to say, Oh, look there goes an American. And you may never see Japan, but everyone is going to say, There's that Japanese girl. (pg. 93)

Women of color view feminism as yet another system in which they have to define and justify their reality, which makes it (feminism) just as oppressive as the traditional sexist patriarchal system.

Psychotherapy and counseling are primarily Western concepts based on the philosophical assumptions of life, liberty, and happiness for all members of this society (Sue, 1981). While these ideals are recognized as individual rights guaranteed by the Declaration of Independence, the Civil Rights movement of the 1960s gives clear evidence that this country, in reality, supports a monolithic set of values rooted in the traditional, white, middle-class, Puritan work ethic (Sue, 1983; Bush & Babich, 1983). These traditional values give little support or acknowledgment to those who are ethnically or culturally different. The Civil Rights movement provided the impetus for change, and raised the consciousness of the dominant society.

As the country began developing a new conscience towards ethnically and culturally different individuals, professionals in the field of psychotherapy began re-examining traditional concepts of therapy (Sue, 1983; Copeland, 1981). However, these attempts were hampered by the ethnocentric belief found in the white-dominated helping professions that ethnic and cultural should aspire to the Western dominant cultural standards of sameness. For therapy, as in the culture at large, ethnic and cultural diversity were sacrificed to the belief that assimilation into the dominant culture would solve the problems of people of color. Much of the literature written and taught by mental health professionals during the sixties and seventies reflected the bias in favor of assimilation by highlighting the negative aspect of non-white, non-middle class lifestyle. So while the social milieu was appearing to change, very little change was taking place within the traditional field of psychotherapy. In order for psychotherapy to meet the needs of women of color, the traditional models of treatment must be expanded to match or fit the ethnic and cultural lifestyle or experiences of the client. The woman of color who comes in to receive services should not be expected to defend or justify her lifestyle due to lack of knowledge or ethnocentricity on the part of the therapist.

THE REALITY OF FEMINISM IN TREATMENT WITH WOMEN OF COLOR

Feminism that denies the freedom of ethnic and cultural differences is not feminism; therapy that covertly denies the validity of a woman's ethnic and cultural experiences is not therapy. Innocence does not alter the reality (Hooks, 1981) for the large number of white feminist therapists who remain in a passive state of denial concerning the therapeutic needs of women of color. Many white feminist therapists forget that they were white long before they chose to become feminists or therapists. Being a feminist therapist does not negate the societal privilege that is inherent in being born white. In America, racist oppression runs deep and dies hard. It is nurtured by generations of "hand me down" hatreds (Smith, 1981). White feminists who exercise race privilege on a daily basis often lack awareness that they are doing so (Hooks, 1984). Unconscious cultural awareness or race privilege by the white feminist therapist is for the most part accepted and validated as being the norm in a society that promotes difference as being other or alien. Beverly Smith (1983), explains the common experiences of women of color by stating "I have the feeling that no one white understands our daily experiences" (pg. 27).

To understand is to obtain knowledge, and for white feminist therapists that understanding/knowledge must begin by recognizing that their personal relationship with the woman of color client is reflective of the larger world in which they both live. As a feminist, the therapist must recognize the balance of power between herself and her client are unequal. Her role as a therapist coupled with her politics as a feminist will place her in the responsible position of equalizing the division of power by becoming knowledgeable about her world and the world of women of color. The following example illustrates how I have attempted to go about this process in my own way.

Recently I had the experience of treating a young Southeast Asian woman for depression. She told me that she had been in treatment in the past, only to find that it had not been helpful. She explained that she had little hope that therapy would be helpful this time, but she had promised her physician that she would try once more. During our first interview, I obtained a full family history which included a detailed history of her family life prior to coming to the United States. In taking the history, I encouraged the woman to elaborate, which allowed me to gain some insight regarding her world as she experienced it. After the first interview, I began doing my homework, which was to network with other Southeast Asian women and to research material that would help me to know my client as a bicultural person. During subsequent sessions, as she related information concerning her depression, I was able to shape the therapy into a context that included some of her traditional ethnic values, such as family loyalty, and a circular mode of thinking concept of harmony between self and nature. In listening to this Southeast Asian woman, I was able to glean information regarding her lifestyle, her needs, her wants, and her disappointments, which were not the same as a Black therapist. However, I was able to recognize that her depression was in some part linked to an ethnic and cultural deprivation in living in the United States. By doing prior investigating and incorporating some of the above mentioned ethnic and cultural values into the therapy, effective, culturally literate treatment could take place for this woman.

In doing therapy with women of color, feminist therapists must recognize that they will again become students. The feminist therapist will have to learn about her client's world through the client's history, networking with agencies and individuals in the client's community and through researching relevant ethnic and cultural literature. Patricia Brown (1974) states that recognition of the client's ethnic identity strengthens the relationship between therapist and client. To ignore the meaning of the client's identity is to ignore the person; if that occurs treatment cannot take place. Only through recognizing that this person has a history and an identity that is completely different from one's own can one take an effective look at the symptoms presented. As therapists, many feminists have been quick to rely on the tools and tricks of the trade. The lessons of formal education have served their purpose well. They have seduced the therapist into the model of a monolithic value system regarding the correct approach to the psychotherapeutic process. Feminist therapists must stretch themselves beyond these limits in order to explore and shape treatment that will be more effective in the long run, as opposed to short-term solutions. Making the assumption that prior mental health training or feminist policies will transcend the necessity to comprehend the ethnic and cultural lines of survival for women of color will place both the client and effective treatment in serious jeopardy.

CHANGING DIRECTION

Now is the time for our women to lift up their heads and plant the roots of progress under the hearth-stone.

—HARPER, 1870, pg. 97

Feminist therapists have become pioneers in establishing previously uncharted courses in therapy. This practice must be continued in order for women of color to receive meaningful treatment. Initially, one of the most important dimensions of the counseling process is the ability to facilitate self-exploration and trust. Carkhuff (1969) refers to these facilitative dimensions as empathy, genuineness, positive regard, and concreteness. Along with Carkhuff's facilitative dimensions for providing effective treatment, the feminist therapist must be willing to examine her own beliefs regarding women of color in this society. She must be willing to analyze the myths, stereotypes, and misinformation that she has received in previous training and look at which of these have been erroneously applied to women of color. She must examine her biases in favor of the treatment modalities she has chosen to use. She must be willing to examine whether or not the framework and the concepts that she is currently using in the therapy process encourage ethnic and cultural sensitivity in the therapeutic setting. Feminist therapists must challenge and continue to challenge others in the field of psychotherapy regarding the treatment of women of color, as well as all women in the context of healing both emotionally and psychologically. As a feminist, the therapist will need to broaden her range of awareness in depth through reading, networking, and researching the lifestyles of women of color. She must teach others (feminists), and relearn the art of being a student in terms of ethnic diversity. In this way feminist therapists working with women of color will help their clients to receive effective professional mental health care.

CONCLUSION

Ideally therapy is the art of self-healing, which enables the client to draw on personal resources to empower and enrich her life. The traditional therapeutic process has denied women of color the value of self-empowerment by devaluing their ethnic and cultural identity. Women of color have the right to accurate, safe, and effective mental health treatment by feminist professionals who are ethnically and culturally literate. Ethnic and cultural literacy can only be accomplished if the feminist therapist is open to exploring ways in which traditional therapy can be ethnically and cultural sensitive, and thus, more diverse. Feminist therapists must be willing to broaden their perspective concerning the life-styles of women of color, and challenge traditional mental health modes of treatment. Feminist therapists can enable women of color to obtain the keys of personal empowerment, through sensitive ethnically and culturally diverse treatment.

References

BABICH, KAREN S., & BUSH, MARY T. (1983). *Cultural variations in psychosocial nursing.* Washington: University of Washington Press.

BOYD, JULIA A. (1987). The gospel according to me. *Backbone: Journal of Women's Literature, 4,* 59-61.

BULKIN, ELLY, PRATT, MINNIE, & SMITH, BARBARA. (1984). *Yours in struggle.* New York: Long Haul Press.

COPELAND, ELAINE J. (1981). Counseling black women with negative self concepts. *Journal of Non-White Concerns, 2* (9), 397–399.

GIDDINGS, PAULA. (1984). *When and where I enter: The impact of black women on race and sex in America.* New York: Bantam Books.

HOOKS, BELL (1981). *Ain't I a woman: Black women and feminism.* Boston: South End Press.

HOOKS, BELL (1984). *Feminist theory: From margin to center.* Boston: South End Press.

KIKUMURA, AKEMI (1981). *Through harsh winters: The life of a Japanese immigrant woman.* California: Chandler & Sharp.

LADNER, JOYCE A. (1971). *Tomorrow's tomorrow: The black woman.* New York: Doubleday & Company.

LORDE, AUDRE. (1984). *Sister Outsider: Essays and speeches.* New York: The Crossing Press.

MORAGA, CHERRIE, & ANZALDUA, GLORIA (Eds.). (1981). *This bridge called my back: Writings by radical women of color.* Massachusetts: Persephone Press.

SHIPP, PAMELA L. (1983). Counseling blacks: A group approach. *Journal of Personnel and Guidance, 8* (2), 108–111.

SMITH, BEVERLY (1983). Some thoughts on racism. *Aegis, 27,* 34–36.

SMITH, ELSIE (1981). Counseling the culturally different individual. *Journal of Non-White Concerns, 2,* (9), 141–147.

SUE, D. W., & SUE, D. (1977). Barriers to effective cross-cultural counseling. *Journal of Counseling Psychology, 24,* (5), 420–429.

SUE, S. (1983). Ethnic minority issues in psychology. *American Psychologist,* 583–592.

A Parent's Story

Jenny. An ordinary kid, from an ordinary family. Yet an extraordinary event changed our lives completely, and forever.

Mark. He appeared on our doorstep one evening in October 1985. I was tidying up the kitchen when I heard the doorbell ring, so I was the first one to reach the door. There he stood, a tall, blond young man, wearing blue jeans and a black leather jacket. With a charming smile, he asked, "Is Jenny home?" My first reaction was confusion. Who is this boy? Jenny had not mentioned that anyone, particularly a *boy*, was coming over. Then she came bounding down the steps, smiling, thrilled to see him. When I saw how excited Jenny was, I didn't have the heart to say no, to say that I really thought she was too young to have boys calling at the house.

That first evening, I guided them into the living room, where we all sat awkwardly, looking at each other. Jenny was far too shy to make casual conversation, and she was obviously far too taken with him. So my husband, Greg, and I kept the conversation going.

So Mark Smith came into our lives. Although Mark was very polite and answered all my questions about home and school, he was skillful at keeping the real Mark hidden. Later I would review the conversation and realize that I knew nothing about him.

For Jenny, the beginning of her relationship with Mark was a dream come true. Junior high had been an unhappy time in her life, a time when she found herself excluded. Her dream was to find acceptance in high school, to be popular and part of the crowd, and most of all, to find a boyfriend.

Her transition from girl to young woman was astounding to watch. Always a pretty child, Jenny, like so many kids, went through an awkward stage. She needed glasses at the age of ten, and with each passing year, the glasses became thicker. She also had braces on her teeth, and she grew taller, skinnier, and awkward. But by age twelve, she really started to change. First came contact lenses, which showed off her blue eyes, and she learned how to style her thick, blond hair. She developed a curvy shape and a sense of style and flair for clothes that was all her own. By the time she met Mark Smith, she was indeed a beautiful girl.

Her childhood attempts at sports were replaced by a love for dance. Through dance, she developed confidence and pride in her body. But her keen intellect was perhaps her most beautiful asset. A voracious reader since early childhood, Jenny continued that love with her studies. She was an honors student without much effort. Her talent for language was so great that by her sophomore year she was studying both French and Spanish. Her dream for her future was to utilize languages in a career, to live in Europe, to see the world.

Her interest in Mark was a bit of a mystery to me. Beyond his obvious good looks, I didn't see what the attraction could possibly be. In contrast to Jenny's love of learning, he was a poor student, uninterested in building for his future. Although my fervent hope was that he would go away to school, far away from Jenny, I was concerned enough about him to inquire about his plans after graduation now that he was in his senior year. I discovered that he had no plans. His parents had not spoken to him about his life after high school. My feeling was that he was just drifting through life. While Jenny was passionately interested in books, dance and her family, Mark's life centered on cars, his motorcycle and "riding around" with his friends. As I observed the differences between them, I knew it was just a matter of time before Jenny would tire of him and wish to be free.

Despite their age difference and lack of common interests, however, Jenny and Mark's relationship appeared to thrive. Apparently they were the talk of the school, the "perfect couple," so much "in love."

He called her daily, sometimes several times a day. They shared a locker at school and walked each other to class. They ate lunch together. He came over to our house about three nights a week. For a child of fourteen, it was pretty overwhelming. My rules were strict, but Jenny did not seem to mind. I think she knew she couldn't have handled a more intense relationship.

Some casual conversation with students employed in my office made me realize that Jenny and Mark might be discussing sex. So I said to Jenny one night in an offhand way, "Jen, if sex ever becomes an issue between the two of you, I hope you will talk to me about it first." The very next night she came to me! Without ever making eye contact, she told me she wanted to have sex with Mark and asked me to take her to a doctor for birth control pills. Horrified, I struggled to maintain my composure. I managed to stammer that I wanted to talk to some professionals first, to please wait for me to get her some help. I called every agency in the book, looking for someone who was skilled at talking to teenagers about the disadvantages of early sex. Finally I connected her with a teen from my office who felt comfortable talking about her own experiences. Jenny came home from that meeting and announced that not only was she not ready to become intimate, but that she also was going to break off her relationship with Mark completely. "I just want to be free, Mom," she told me. "I really envy my friends who don't have boyfriends." And so began the final phase of their courtship.

Mark ignored Jenny's attempts to break up. He still shared the locker, still walked her to class, still called. When she insisted that he stop, that she wanted to break up, he became more insistent, more possessive. The phone calls increased, the unannounced visits to the house more frequent. He would not move out of her locker. Because he made it so difficult, Jenny simply gave up and agreed to go back. When I questioned her, she said that she really cared for him and wasn't sure she wanted to end it. This on-again, off-again routine continued for the next several months, into the summer, until Jenny made the final break.

As Jenny increased her attempts to pull away, Mark intensified his actions to keep her locked in. He seemed to always know her plans. At first she would unwittingly tell him where she was going. Then, as she attempted to keep this information from him, he would turn to her girlfriends and find out about her activities from them. He was so skillful that, on one occasion, he showed up at a family reunion on her dad's side of the family, having been invited by Jenny's cousin with whom he had struck up a friendship. Her trips to the mall were marred by Mark's sudden appearance. Her weekly dance lessons were punctuated by his arrival, cunningly timed just a few minutes before I arrived to pick her up. The boys who expressed an interest in her were quickly squelched by a visit from Mark, who curtly told them, "She's my girl; leave her alone."

As Jenny grew more distant, he became more desperate. I realize now that he might have sat in the dark and watched our house at night. One night we decided on the spur of the moment to walk up the block for an ice cream cone. Outside our door, I noticed movement behind parked cars. Greg investigated and discovered Mark and his friend crouching behind the cars, watching our house. Another night, at midnight, I heard noises at Jenny's second-floor window. She and I looked out to see Mark standing below, throwing rocks at her window, yelling "Jenny, Jenny."

By August 1986, Jenny had had enough. Triumphantly, she called me at work one day and announced that she "had done it, really broken it off with Mark." She sounded happy, excited, relieved to be free. School would be starting in a few weeks, and Mark would not be there (he had graduated the previous spring). I never saw Mark Smith again. I thought he had gone away. The phone calls stopped. There were no more visits.

From Jenny's perspective, however, he never did go away. He just became more deceitful. She discovered that he was entering the school grounds and breaking into her locker, the same locker they had shared the year before. He would go through her things and read the notes her friends had written. She began to suspect that he was entering our home when we were gone; she told her friends that things in her room were often not as she had left them. Mark's picture, which she had put away in a drawer, kept reappearing on top of her TV. He left her threatening notes that hinted she "would not make it to homecoming" and desperate lines that said "I wish you would die." She told her friends about these things and even laughed the day of the homecoming parade, saying, "Well, I'm still in one piece." She never told me.

Friday, September 26, 1986, I woke Jenny to get her into the shower before I left for work. I hugged her and kissed her before leaving, as I always did. That morning I said "I love you, Jen," something I didn't always do. And she replied, "I love you too, Mom." We spoke briefly about the homecoming game that evening, and she asked if I could drive her to the dance or if she should ride with her friends. Then I rushed out the door. My day was uneventful. I was bored and had many things to do at home. I thought about asking my boss if I could leave work early, but I resisted the urge. I left work at my usual time and drove home thinking about the busy night ahead.

When I drove onto my street the first thing I saw were groups of neighbors standing in their yards, looking toward my house. Then I saw the ambulance, the police cars, the fire truck. I saw police officers running out of my house. I started shaking so violently that I could barely park my car. I ran out, shouting, "What is happening here?" I was stopped from entering my home and told that my daughter had been stabbed, but that "the paramedics are working on her." I watched as they carried her out on a stretcher and took her away in an ambulance. I hung onto a white and shaken Greg as he described walking into the house and finding Jenny "lying in a pool of blood." I sat in the hospital emergency room and heard them tell me that my daughter was deceased. Dead? Not Jenny. I just talked to her this morning. She is only fifteen. How can she be dead?

The days became a blur. Mark was arrested. He was tried and convicted of first-degree murder. At his trial, I learned the truth of my daughter's last months. I learned of the pressure he had put on her and his threats. I learned of the deception he forced her to participate in. I heard fourteen-year-old children describe their attempts to handle a situation adults could not handle. I saw the fear and guilt of her friends as they grappled with the thought that they could have saved her if only they had told someone what was going on. I learned that Mark had abused Jenny, slapping her and roughing her up frequently. I heard the kids say that it happens all the time at school, boyfriends hitting girl-friends, so they didn't think anything of it. I listened to a recreation of the last moments of her life: how she got off the school bus and entered our home alone to find Mark waiting for her, and how he stabbed her over sixty times with a seven-inch butcher knife, leaving her on the living room floor to be found by Greg, who came in from work carrying our one-year-old son. I heard the account of Mark's evening: how he had attended the homecoming football game with a date and how he laughed and ate and appeared very uncon-cerned that Jenny was dead.

Something rose up in me. Perhaps it started when I returned to work after her funeral. I realized that people expected me to carry on as if nothing had happened. They acknowledged my grief, but refused to mention the way my daughter died! I haunted the library, looking for books on the subject of teen dating violence. I remembered hearing a story, almost twenty years ago, of a young man shooting his girlfriend. Then I read of the Jennifer Levin murder in New York City. Can it be that this is happening all over, and no one is saying anything about it? Why hadn't other mothers spoken out, tried to warn me or warn Jenny of the danger?

My involvement began slowly. I read what I could find on the subject and talked to a lot of teens. My first speech was to a church youth group, a small gathering of teens who were laughing and kidding and poking each other. As I stood at the back of the room before I was introduced, I was terrified, thinking I would never hold their attention. I started out my talk by playing a portion of the song, "The Greatest Love of All." The words are about learning how to love oneself, finding self respect. As the song had recently been popular, the kids started swaying to the music and mouthing the words. Then I turned off the player and said, "I chose that song to play for you today because of the message of the words. I also chose that song to play six months ago at the funeral of my daughter, Jenny." Total silence! For the duration of my talk, not a soul moved. As I looked at the audience I could pick out who in that crowd was being abused by her boyfriend. I saw the looks that passed between friends. I saw the downcast eyes as I described Mark's behavior. Three years and hundreds of speeches later, I still see those things. I can pick out the ones whose lives I am describing.

On Jenny's sixteenth birthday, in an attempt to find some comfort in our grief, Greg and I attended a Parents of Murdered Children Conference. There I met two hundred parents who suffered as we did. In a group of parents who had lost a child to a boyfriend or spouse, I met Ellen Kessner, a writer who had also lost a child by murder. She asked me if she could write Jenny's story for publication. The *Redbook* article that followed (March 1988) educated thousands of parents nationwide. Suddenly teen dating violence became a household word. I was invited to appear on many TV shows. In our community, schools began including the subject in their curriculum.

Jenny is gone, a reality I must live with every day. Sometimes the grief is so overpowering that it seems I cannot survive it. But Jenny has touched so many. Her story has alerted parents and teens to the dangers of abusive relationships. She has saved many lives. And so I am able to say that she did not die in vain, that there was some purpose to her short life. It brings comfort, and it helps me go on. I'll never forget Jen. I miss her so much. I'll always love her.

June Larkin and Katherine Popaleni

Heterosexual Courtship Violence and Sexual Harassment: The Private and Public Control of Young Women

The song entitled 'I Used to Love Her' by the popular group 'Guns N' Roses' was playing as students entered the high school auditorium for an assembly on the topic of sexual harassment. The speaker began the presentation with the words of the song as one example of the violent and derogatory ways in which women are portrayed in popular culture. As she read the phrases which rationalized the killing of a female because her alleged 'bitching' and complaining had annoyed her male lover and murderer, many of the students (both male and female) began to laugh—but the young men also shouted comments that included 'Alright!', 'Go for it!' and 'Get her!'. The administrator, who initially had considered the assembly 'unnecessary', was forced to admit that there was a serious problem.

When sharing this story with other high school students we are often dismissed—the 'guys', we are told, were 'just kidding'. However, when young women were surveyed about issues they wanted to discuss at a retreat for female high school students 'girl-friend battering' was listed second among their concerns, surpassed only by the broader issue of violence against women (Toronto Board of Education, 1990). The priority these young women accorded this topic coupled with the fact that 61 percent of all women murdered in Ontario between 1974 and 1990 were killed by their male lovers (Crawford and Gartner, 1992) contradict the claim that the young men in the high school assembly were 'just kidding'. In Canada, the deaths of women at the hands of their male partners, for example Chia-Tsu, who was hacked to death with a meat cleaver; Valerie, who was tracked down and murdered; Sakina, who was beaten and then drowned in a bathtub; Pamela, who was killed with a chainsaw; Jacolena, who was doused with gasoline and set on fire; and Comfort, who was stabbed to death by her common-law partner, a year after she left him (Ontario Association of Interval and Transition Houses, 1990), are grim reminders of the warning inherent in the comments of these young men.

Our purpose in writing this article is to explore the impact of two forms of male violence—sexual harassment and heterosexual courtship violence—on

313

the lives of young women. In doing so we wish to address what Carol Gilligan (1990: 1) has identified as a 'startling omission', that is the absence of the voices of young women from psychologists' examinations of the problem of violence against women. In the words of Myrna Kostash (1989: 137):

> We have not heard these voices because they belong to people to whom we have not been accustomed to lending an ear: young females, frightened, demoralized, often poor and on their own . . . one can begin by listening.

The issue of violence in the lives of adolescent girls has received little attention in the vast feminist project of politicizing male violence against women. To date, recognition of the violence perpetrated against young women has focused primarily on the abuse perpetrated by trusted male adults. While the prevalence of child sexual abuse is alarming, with 16–50 percent of female children suffering physical and/or sexual abuse at the hands of men (Russell, 1986; Special Advisor to the Minister of Health and Welfare, 1990), we have yet to examine the full spectrum of abuse that permeates the lives of adolescent girls. It was our objective, therefore, to explore young women's experiences of violence both in the public sphere and in their most intimate heterosexual relationships. We wanted to understand from *their* point of view and reveal *in their own words*, the forms that the violence took, the conditions under which it occurred and the impact it had on their lives.

HOW WE CAME TO DO THIS WORK

This article has origins in two separate bodies of academic work. Katherine's research originated from her advocacy/counselling work with women survivors of incest, rape and other forms of male violence at the Sexual Assault Centre in Hamilton, Ontario, Canada. The service, a 24-hour crisis phone line, while geared to support adult women, was often utilized by adolescent girls, many of whom during the course of the conversation disclosed having experienced psychological, physical and sexual abuse at the hands of their heterosexual dating partners. The extent to which this is a hidden social and political problem became apparent as Katherine examined the literature on courtship violence and noted the absence of young women's perspectives on the issue. Rather, the voices of authority were those of family violence researchers who identified courtship violence as an interpersonal, interrelational, private problem (see, for example, Billingham and Sack, 1987; Henton et al., 1983; Laner and Thompson, 1982; Montgomery and Fewer, 1988).

June's interest in examining how young women experience sexual harassment stems from her work as Coordinator of the Women's Sexual Harassment Caucus at the Ontario Institute for Studies in Education (OISE). In her work with adult women she came to realize how many women had adjusted their academic and/or career plans because they were subjected to sexually harassing behaviour. Some women had quit jobs; others had dropped courses or changed universities. But it was not until her friend's daughter, a high school student, spoke of her experience of being rated on a scale of 1–10 by male students at her high school, of being pinched and grabbed and invited to join a group of guys in the back of a van, and of sitting in a classroom where a teacher continually reminded the students that women really *do* belong bare-foot and pregnant in the kitchen, that she began to wonder to what extent the experience of sexual harassment had altered the lives of girls and young women *before* they became adults. This concern was the impetus for her work.

We chose to integrate our work on sexual harassment and heterosexual courtship violence as a way of demonstrating the connections between the two forms of male violence and as a way of illustrating how young men's use of violence and harassment are played out both in the private and in the public spheres of young women's lives. Personal relationships, such as heterosexual courting relationships, are associations shaped by, dictated according to and experienced within, relations of power. The commitment to grounding inquiry in the arena of the 'private', therefore, makes it possible to understand broader political relations including males' harassment of females in the 'public' sphere. As Catherine MacKinnon puts it:

> . . . women's distinctive experience as women occurs within that sphere that has been socially lived as the personal—private, emotional, interiorized, particular, individuated, intimate—so that what it is to know the politics of women's situation is to know women's personal lives (MacKinnon, 1982: 534–5).

THE STUDY

In our investigation of young women's experiences of sexual harassment and heterosexual courtship violence we used interviews, which were conversational in style. Although a set of semistructured questions guided the interviews, for the most part the discussions were free-flowing and open-ended. The conversations allowed for a comprehensive expression of the young women's feelings and beliefs, and permitted the young women's experiences to surface 'whole, entire [and] complex' (Dubois, 1983: 11).

Katherine interviewed five young women who ranged in age from 17 to 21. At the time the interviews were conducted, four of the five women were attending a community college in a small city in Eastern Ontario, Canada. They were enrolled in traditional female, job-related, training courses: secretarial, child-care and fashion studies, as well as general social sciences. These young women volunteered to participate in the study following presentations Katherine made at the college. The fifth young woman, who had recently completed a life skills programme designed for street youth in Toronto, offered her participation when she was informed of the project by a staff member of the life skills programme. Generally, the young women originated from working-class backgrounds. Four were descended from Euro-Canadian heritage; one was of aboriginal ancestry. None of the girls had married. Some of the young women had experienced dating relationships with non-abusive boyfriends; others had involvement only with abusive dating partners. They had all survived forms of physical, psychological and sexual abuse by heterosexual courtship partners.

Katherine conducted two in-depth, conversational interviews with each of the five young women. She incorporated the concept of the 'right of reply' (Spender, 1985: 5) into her research to emphasize the contribution of the participants. The young women reviewed written transcripts of their interviews for

315

JUNE LARKIN AND
KATHERINE POPALENI
Heterosexual
Courtship Violence
and Sexual
Harassment: The
Private and Public
Control of Young
Women

possible omissions and misinterpretations and were invited to make additions and/or remove passages to which they objected. As Spender (1985) has noted, the 'right of reply' ensures that the participants have control over the research process and the data that are generated.

June interviewed female high school students who ranged in age from 16 to 20 and represented various geographical, racial, cultural and economic backgrounds. The young women attended schools in which the administration was committed to examining how sexual harassment and other forms of violence affected the lives of their female students. Prior to being interviewed the students kept a journal of their sexual harassment incidents over a 4-month period, and attended biweekly meetings in which they were encouraged to share their personal experiences. This process was an attempt to ensure that the students had the opportunity to develop a way of thinking about sexual harassment that was embedded in the events of their own lives, and it also gave the young women a chance to get to know June before they made a decision about being interviewed. In each school a teacher who acted as liaison between June and the young women organized and attended the group meetings and, in some cases, arranged the student interview schedule. The questions the young women were asked in the interviews were generated from information they had provided in their journals and in the group discussions. This was an attempt to ensure that the ensuing data were grounded in their personal experiences. Over 70 young women attended the large group sessions; 25 students requested a personal interview.

The documented accounts of these young women make visible the abusive behaviour that is part of the fabric of their everyday days. While our overall purpose is to provide a forum for young women's voices, we wish to situate our work in the larger context of the developing theories on female psychological development.

VIOLENCE AND THE PSYCHOLOGICAL DEVELOPMENT OF ADOLESCENT GIRLS

Carol Gilligan (1990), in her recent work with female students, reports that the sense of outspokenness and authority that is evident in young girls diminishes as they grow older. The confident 11-year-old is transformed into an apologetic, hesitant teenager who questions her own knowledge and her own sense of authority (Prose, 1990). Adolescence has been found to be a time when girls begin to 'contract' rather than 'expand', psychologically speaking. Clara Thompson noted this as early as 1942 when she reported that for boys adolescence was a period of opening up while for girls it was a period of shutting down (cited in Miller, 1984). According to Jean Baker Miller (1984), Freud argued that adolescent girls had to learn:

> . . . that they were not to use actively all of themselves and all of their life forces from a base centred in their own bodies and in their own psychological constructions. For Freud, this meant, of course, the derivatives of their sexual drive. Instead, these forces are to be turned now, to the use of others—men, in

the first instance and to the service of the next generation, childbearing (Miller, 1984: 8).

317

JUNE LARKIN AND
KATHERINE POPALENI
Heterosexual
Courtship Violence
and Sexual
Harassment: The
Private and Public
Control of Young
Women

Thus the sense of self of the adolescent girl is one that must defer to the needs and desires of others—particularly males. In contrast, Miller (1984: 9) notes that the adolescent boy:

> . . . is geared to developing 'himself' and a sense of his independent identity. The culture has made the heavy demand that he be so preoccupied. It has done so all along, but it does so at adolescence in an even more forceful way. He has also picked up the idea that the girl should adapt to him and he has not been encouraged to continue the development of the sense that he is primarily a boy in relationship with a primary responsibility for others and a desire to concentrate on the relationship between him and others.

Differences in the organization and development of males' and females' sense of self have implications for male–female interactions. Self-in-relation theorists propose that women's sense of self evolves in the context of important relationships in which the goal is the development of mutually empathic relationships (Jordan, 1984; Kaplan, 1984; Miller, 1984, 1986; Stiver, 1984; Surrey, 1984). Sex differences in relational styles have been reported in children as young as 3 years of age. Serbin et al. (1984) found that pre-school girls used polite suggestions to influence play partners while pre-school boys used direct commands. However, over a 2-year period boys became less and less responsive to polite suggestions so that girls became less successful in influencing the boys. As Maccoby (1990) has noted, the ways in which boys communicate with girls include commands, threats, boasts, heckling and exchange of derogatory remarks. In a review of studies on young girls' alleged 'passivity', compared with young boy's greater 'activity', Maccoby found that girls and boys were equally active in same-sex groups. However, the aggressive and demeaning ways boys communicated with girls in mixed-sex groups sent girls scurrying to the sidelines for protection while the boys continued their activities.

The pre-adolescent girl escapes much of this demeaning behaviour because she spends most of her time with other females. This may account for the more assertive and self-assured demeanour that Gilligan noted in the 11-year-old girls she interviewed. However, as she enters adolescence the young female is more vulnerable to abuse by males for three reasons. First, because women are taught that their value is determined by their ability to attract men, most heterosexual young women will perceive themselves as 'lacking at the very core when not in a relationship with a man' (Siegel, 1988: 117) and so they may opt to spend more time in mixed-sex settings. Second, boys as they grow older recognize their privileged position and realize that this position can only be maintained by force. Third, young women's sexual development becomes visible and young men begin to see them primarily as sexual beings:

> . . . as soon as women begin pubescent development they actually begin to see male behaviour toward them change. Adolescent girls are met with comments, glances, whistles . . . Fending off male sexuality, much of what is initially welcomed, the young girl also learns that she cannot always control sexual encounters she engages in. She also learns that if anything happens, she is to

blame . . . [she is] also aware that [she is] less physically powerful than men (Stanko, 1986: 2).

Researchers have found that the increased psychological trauma experienced by adolescent girls corresponds to the increased time they spend in cross-sex interaction (Maccoby, 1990). It appears that the development of male identity occurs at the expense of females' safety. As one young woman put it, in the process of becoming adolescents 'our lives [get] smaller and smaller, our days [get] shorter and shorter' (Herbert, 1989: 84). In the following section we examine how the experience of young men's violence contributes to the diminishing world of adolescent girls.

SEXUAL HARASSMENT AND HETEROSEXUAL COURTSHIP VIOLENCE

Sexual harassment and heterosexual courtship violence are part of the continuum of male violence that affects and restricts the lives of young women. Liz Kelly (1987) developed the concept of a continuum of male violence as a way of describing both the extent and the range of sexual violence in the lives of women and girls. We have adopted Kelly's concept of a continuum because it is useful in demonstrating that, although heterosexual courtship violence and sexual harassment are different forms of male violence, they share a common feature; that is, they are forms of diminishment, intimidation and force used by young men to establish and maintain their dominance over young women.

The terms sexual harassment and heterosexual courtship violence have only recently become part of the language we use to label male abuse. According to Kelly (1988: 139) naming involves 'making visible what was invisible, defining as unacceptable what was acceptable and insisting that what was naturalized is problematic'. Through the processes of keeping journals, participating in group discussions and/or interviews, and reviewing the transcripts of their interviews, the young women in both research projects began to develop a vocabulary with which to name their experience of male violence. For example, one young woman who participated in the study on sexual harassment wrote in her journal:

> My boyfriend wanted me to come over to his house to talk about our relationship. When I got there everything went smoothly for a while but then there came a point where he was becoming aggressive. At this point I was struggling for him to let go of me. When this occurred he lifted me up and carried me to the basement. I guess you could say he sexually harassed me . . . when I told my best friend she said it was date rape. He said it was all my fault. I know he was wrong because I said 'No' and he still forced his way inside of me. What could I have done? . . . I was helpless.

Given an opportunity and a language with which to label previously unnamed behaviour as abusive this young woman is beginning to identify the patriarchal themes of the injustice and power imbalance that pervade her intimate heterosexual relationship. More important than the accuracy of the label is her use of language which justifiably places the responsibility for the abuse beyond herself. This scenario highlights the need for young women to develop a vocabulary for the abuse that is perpetrated against them so they may become proficient in the language of their own lives.

319

JUNE LARKIN AND KATHERINE POPALENI
Heterosexual Courtship Violence and Sexual Harassment: The Private and Public Control of Young Women

Sexual harassment and heterosexual courtship violence operate to ensure that young women accept their position as an 'object' responsible for taking care of male needs through a three-part system of male control which includes acts of diminishment, intimidation and force. Acts of diminishment objectify and degrade young women through behaviour that includes criticism, rating and the display of pornographic material. Acts of intimidation, such as threats and surveillance, warn young women of the violent consequences should they challenge their ascribed position in relation to young men. And acts of force punish those young women who resist their assigned subordinate position. In the following section young women speak out about the ways they experience this three-part system of male control in the form of sexual harassment and heterosexual courtship violence.

Acts of Diminishment

Criticism was the most frequent means that young men used to diminish their girlfriends. Young men harshly criticized their girlfriends' choice of hairstyle, clothing, makeup, as well as permanent features such as physique, hair colour and complexion. In their dating relationships with young men, young women were consistently harassed to change their 'look' according to his preferences. As one young woman recalled:

> He didn't like the way I looked. I don't know what he was doing with me or I was doing with him. We didn't like each other very much. I wanted to look punky and he wanted me to look normal. So, for my birthday and things, he would buy me these sexy, little, normal clothes.

Young women are frequently diminished in public through the practice of being rated on a scale of 1–10 by young men. In one case, male students lined the school corridor and held up rating cards to evaluate female students who passed by. One young woman found that her objection to this behaviour resulted in the most extreme form of public diminishment: a score of 0:

> This guy and his brother went on with their sick way of having fun by rating young women as they passed by [them] in the hallway. I told the guy he was sexist and by rating young women as they passed by . . . he was making them uncomfortable. He said: 'Just for saying that, I give you a zero.'

The display of pornographic images operated to further diminish young women by reminding them that they are viewed primarily as sexual objects for the use and abuse of males. In the following scenario a young woman poignantly expressed the unequivocal relationship between pornographic images and violence perpetuated against women:

> I came across a stack of boards in the corner of the art classroom with graffiti written all over them. I expected to read 'So and so, 100% true love' or the names of people's favourite bands but as I looked at the graffiti I saw a picture of a naked woman (no arms, heads, calves or knees) with her legs wide open showing all her vagina, anal opening and breasts. I was shocked to see such explicit graffiti in my favourite class. I never thought anyone from our school

could draw such violent pictures of women in the classroom and not have anyone say or do anything about it. Other people must have seen it because the room is used by three other classes. [To me] that picture says 'Rape is OK, sexual abuse is OK' and this is what I'm scared of the most.

The experience of heterosexual diminishment for young women of colour was often racist. For example, young white women were generally rated higher than young Black women. This supports Dorchen Leidholdt's (1981: 20) assertion of a racial hierarchy 'in which women are rated as prize objects or despised objects according to their color'. In addition, comments typically levelled at young Black women reflected the stereotype of Black women's promiscuity and often resonated with the common pornographic image of a Black woman as 'a willing victim of her white master' (Mayall and Russell, 1993: 277):

> I hear Black girls like white guys' dicks.
> I hear Black girls are easy.

Acts of diminishment are often reinforced by young men's behaviour which young women experience as intimidation. Intimidating behaviour including surveillance, threats and sexual gestures are ways in which young men reinforce through fear their position of dominance over young women and through which young women become aware of the power of young men to control male–female relationships.

Acts of Intimidation

Young men intimidate their girlfriends by using surveillance tactics to closely monitor their girlfriends' behaviour, activities and access to other friends. Young women disclosed experiences of being spied on through windows, having their diaries, address books and mail read without permission, being telephoned countless times to verify their whereabouts and being visited unexpectedly at different events or in different places. The following passage typifies the degree of surveillance experienced by some young women:

> I met this woman R . . . she was a wonderful woman. I used to babysit for her occasionally. But K would phone seventeen times while I was babysitting. He would look in the windows when I was there with the kids because he thought I was having an affair with R. He just thought I was having affairs with everyone. He was possessive . . . more than I can even describe.

The wielding of threats of physical and sexual violence is a common practice used by young men to intimidate young women who challenge their male dominance:

> I was talking to this guy who sits beside me in class—he ended up calling me a 'bonehead'. I then said, 'You're the one who's a boner'. He said, 'You better shut up before I stick my dick up your arse so hard you won't be able to breathe'. He started to laugh.

Sexual gestures are another means of intimidation which young men use routinely to remind young women of their sexual and physical vulnerability:

> I was in the middle of a soccer game and somebody called me from the stands. I looked over because I thought it was someone calling me who knew me . . .

and this guy in the stands grabbed his crotch with his hands and moved it in the up and down motion. I turned my head and felt embarrassed because I had looked over. He must have gotten my name from someone in the stands. In some ways I felt a bit scared wondering if he was going to follow me.

The threat of further violence operates to thwart young women's resistance to much of the abusive behaviour they experience. For example, one young woman who threatened to pour her drink on a young man who had doused her with beer was warned: 'Do that, and I'll rape you.'

The third element in a system that enforces male dominance over young women is the use of force. Acts of force used by young men include not only the more extreme acts of physical battering and sexual assault, but also small acts of physical torment and sexual coercion.

Acts of Force

Young men physically torment their girlfriends by twisting their arms, pinching their bodies in many places, giving them shoves and poking their skin with sharp instruments, such as pen knives and pins. Being subjected to such physical torment was experienced as being terrorized:

He didn't hit me, but he would twist my arms or other mean things. Or he'd pinch me really hard when we were around other people. Then, I would yell at him and he would say, 'What's your problem?' He'd act as if he'd done nothing. And then, I'd look like a fool.

One young woman spoke about a friend who had been physically assaulted by a group of young men because she had refused to date one of their friends.

One of the guys had asked her out and she was right in the process of going steady with a guy so she said: 'No.' And a whole bunch of his friends were teasing her for a few weeks and then what happened was she was walking at lunch time by herself. [She was] going through the parking lot and these guys came right up to her. She didn't think much of it because she knew some of the guys but they followed her and started fondling her and eventually she was screaming and everything.

Fear of further verbal, physical and sexual harassment pressure some young women to engage in sex against their will.

I guess in all three relationships, there was a lot of forcing me sexually into doing what I didn't want to do. I'd do it just to get them off my back . . . basically I felt if I didn't, then I'd have to deal with him for the next couple of days making me feel bad . . . and it's . . . not worth the hassle. Go along with it and play the game.

Young men's practice of isolating young women in automobiles, especially after dark and in secluded settings, operates to intimidate young women to engage in sexual relations out of a belief that if they refuse to comply their physical and emotional safety may be compromised. Consider the case of one young woman who privately had promised herself to remain celibate for the first three months of any dating relationship. Her decision to break that personal contract, however, took effect following an evening car ride with her new

321

JUNE LARKIN AND KATHERINE POPALENI Heterosexual Courtship Violence and Sexual Harassment: The Private and Public Control of Young Women boyfriend to an isolated park. The young woman had sex not on the basis of her personal choice, but because she feared that, should she refuse, he might abandon her at midnight over three miles from home. The young man, therefore, used the young woman's fear of danger in the form of physical and/or sexual assault, as well as the uncomfortable likelihood of her having to respond to what she regarded as intrusive questions from her parents, as intimidation to secure what he wanted: sex.

'Playing the game' provides young women with some protection against the deleterious effects of young men's abuse. But, as we discuss in the following section, there is a large cost to young women forced to participate in the patriarchal 'games' used by young men to protect male dominance.

THE PSYCHOLOGICAL IMPACT

Acts of diminishment, intimidation and force affect young women in profound ways. First, they erode a young woman's personal sense of self. As Wise and Stanley (1987: 114) point out, the more subtle forms of abuse operate like a 'dripping tap' that slowly wears away young women's confidence and self-esteem. Second, acts of diminishment, intimidation and force threaten young women's sense of physical and psychological security. According to Stanko (1993: 161), 'women's lives rest upon a continuum of danger' so that 'the concrete knowledge that sexual danger can and does occur' evokes, in young women, a strong sense of anxiety and vulnerability. Much of their energy then becomes focused on developing safety precautions in their everyday lives. And third, the three-part system of violence and harassment results in the limitation of young women's personal development. Margaret Atwood describes young men's abusive behaviour as a way of reducing young women by 'cutting them down to size so they can be handled' (1988: 245). Indeed, the young women we talked to expressed concerns about fading into the background more often than they expressed enthusiasm abut their developing selves. As one young woman put it: 'Sometimes I feel like I don't exist.'

Young women's potential for self-definition is curtailed by their constant exposure to verbal criticism, a practice described by one young woman as psychologically distressing:

> There is something lacking in what he wants me to be. He doesn't understand that there are certain things that I like and enjoy. He likes me when I'm dressed up and looking the way he wants me to be—not myself. He was almost cruel in the way he would criticize me. It was hurtful because he was taking my personal little quirks . . . the way I like to dress and be and turning it around [to] look like it wasn't right or acceptable.

The experience of heterosexual courtship violence can damage a young woman's self-definition to the point at which she loses a sense of who she is. In fact, one young woman after having surveyed her dating history with males, poignantly analogized her loss of self to the loss of an old friend.

I almost feel like I lost my old self, like she's not here anymore . . . and I kind of miss her, sometimes. She was a fun person. I loved her.

As a consequence of young men's acts of intimidation many young women possess a threatened sense of security. The words of many young women reflect their threatened and unstable position given young men's social entitlement to violate and harass them:

I felt out of control, almost all the time, and it's a horrible feeling, it's a panicky feeling. You feel like they are the ones who are in control of everything, all the time. And there doesn't seem to be anything you can do.

After [a group of guys] did what they did to my friend I don't feel comfortable walking where they are in the school . . . I have to have at least one person with me or I'll take the longer route.

For one young woman the experience of harassing phone calls was so threatening that she was assigned an undercover police officer for protection.

This guy called up my house first and said: 'I went to school with her a year and a half ago.' My mother goes: 'Well, she's not at home. She's in school.' Then he called the school . . . and he talked to the vice-principal and said: 'Tell her I'm going to rape her and I'm going to kill her'; and so the vice-principal called my mother and told her to keep an eye on me . . . After that phone call the vice-principal thought I would have better protection if someone was with me all the time so in all my classes I had this guy sitting at the back of my shoulder and staring at me while I would do my work.

Boyfriends' acts of diminishment, intimidation and force operate to limit young women's personal development. For example, boyfriends' surveillance of their girlfriends' socializing with other young women, and subsequent accusations of lesbianism, resulted in many young women terminating friendships with other young women which had offered them enjoyment and support in times of crisis. Moreover, boyfriends' abusive behaviour eroded young women's psychological and emotional abilities to determine for themselves their own terms and boundaries for self-development. Enmeshed in relationships which encourage self-doubt and self-reproach, some young women put a definitive end to their involvement in such self-development activities as team sports, musical presentations and drama clubs.

The restriction of young women's activities in response to their fear and experience of males' abuse at school was evident as they envisioned how their school lives would be different if they studied in a harassment-free educational environment:

A lot of girls would excel in their school work . . . we could freely express how we feel about a subject because we wouldn't face the intimidation factor.

In a harassment-free school [girls] would feel able to strive to perform to their full level. They would be surprised what they can actually do. I think it would have a very big bearing on their performance in class and in sports.

[Girls] wouldn't be afraid that their answers were going to be cut down, they wouldn't be afraid about walking down certain halls at the school, walking by

323

JUNE LARKIN AND
KATHERINE POPALENI
Heterosexual
Courtship Violence
and Sexual
Harassment: The
Private and Public
Control of Young
Women

a certain bunch of guys that you know are going to say something or . . . that someone's going to reach out and grab your butt. I think I'd be even more out-going than I am now.

Every incident of violence experienced by young women contributes to their diminishing world. When young women have been stripped of their sense of self, when their personal growth has been stunted and when they live with a threatened sense of security, their ability to define who they are, their interests, desires and capabilities, and their personal boundaries, are seriously undermined. In this position, a young woman is not in control of her own self or of her own destiny. When young women's potential to determine and shape their own sense of themselves is jeopardized, as was the case with these young women, they are highly susceptible to losing their sense of self: 'I lost my old self . . . like she's not here anymore.'

The effects of heterosexual courtship violence and sexual harassment have implications for young women's status in the wider culture as well. The restrictions imposed on young women through the perpetual threat of male violence have the attendant consequence of limiting their power and control in the larger world, because so much of their behaviour is geared to securing their own safety. It is precisely this required pre-occupation with ensuring their own physical and psychological survival that precludes young women from focusing on the most important aspect of their personal development: themselves.

CONCLUSION

In addition to understanding the personal effects of these two forms of violence and coercion in perpetuating woman-abuse, we must be ever vigilant of the social promotion of men's violence against women. The theme of the song 'I Used to Love Her' which opened this article normalizes young men's right to exercise power, control and violence over young women in private relationships, as well as in the public arena. The male students' enthusiastic endorsement of the band's misogynist message is not anomalous. 'Guns N' Roses' ranks amongst the most popular heavy metal bands in North America, Great Britain and most parts of Continental Europe. And adolescents are the major consumers of heavy metal music.

In addition to being an instructional script promoting men's entitlement to violate young women, the song constitutes a blatant form of sexual harassment. The existence of a form of 'entertainment' which grants to young men the right to punish young women if they resist their ascribed role sends a powerful message to young women: to defy the authority of men is to risk the ultimate form of male violence: *death.*

References

ATWOOD, M. (1988). *Cat's Eye.* Toronto: Seal Books.

BILLINGHAM, R. and SACK, A. (1987). 'Conflict Tactics and the Level of Emotional Commitment Among Unmarrieds', *Human Relations* 40(1): 59–74.

325

JUNE LARKIN AND
KATHERINE POPALENI
Heterosexual
Courtship Violence
and Sexual
Harassment: The
Private and Public
Control of Young
Women

CRAWFORD, M. and GARTNER, R. (1992). *Women Killing: Intimate Femicide in Ontario, 1974–1990.* Oshawa: Women We Honor Action Committee.

DUBOIS, B. (1983). 'Passionate Scholarship: Notes on Values, Knowing and Method in Feminist Social Science', in R.D. Klein and G. Bowles (eds.) *Theories of Women's Studies,* pp. 105–16. London: Routledge.

GILLIGAN, C. (1990). 'Prologue', in C. Gilligan, N. Lyons and T. Hanmer (eds.) *Making Connections: The Relational World of Adolescent Girls at Emma Willard School,* pp. 1–5. Cambridge, MA: Harvard University Press.

HENTON, J., CATE, R., KOVAL, J., LLOYD, S. and CHRISTOPHER, S. (1983). 'Romance and Violence in Dating Relationships', *Journal of Family Issues* 4(3): 467–82.

HERBERT, C. (1989). *Talking of Silence: The Sexual Harassment of Adolescent Girls.* London: The Falmer Press.

JORDAN, J. (1984). 'The Meaning of Mutuality', Work in Progress Paper 23. Wellesley, MA: Stone Center Working Paper Series.

KAPLAN, A. (1984). 'The "Self-in Relation": Implications for Depression in Women', Work in Progress Paper 14. Wellesley, MA: Stone Center Working Paper Series.

KELLY, L. (1987). 'The Continuum of Sexual Violence', in J. Hanmer and M. Maynard (eds.) *Women, Violence and Social Control,* pp. 46–60. London: Macmillan.

KELLY, L. (1988). *Surviving Sexual Violence.* Minneapolis: University of Minnesota Press.

KOSTASH, M. (1989). *No Kidding: Inside the World of Teenage Girls.* Toronto: McLelland and Stewart.

LANER, M. and THOMPSON, J. (1982). 'Abuse and Aggression in Courting Couples'. *Deviant Behaviour* 3: 229-44.

LEIDHOLDT, D. (1981). 'Where Pornography Meets Fascism', *Women's International Newsletter* (15 March): 18–22.

MACCOBY, E. (1990). 'Gender and Relations: A Developmental Account', *American Psychologist* 45 (April): 513–20.

MACKINNON, C. (1982). 'Feminism, Marxism, Method and the State: Agenda for Theory', *Signs* 7(3): 515–44.

MAYALL, A. and RUSSELL, D. (1993). 'Racism in Pornography', *Feminism & Psychology* 3(2): 275–81.

MILLER, J. (1984) 'The Development of a Woman's Sense of Self', work in Progress Paper 12. Wellesley, MA: Stone Center Working Paper Series.

MILLER, J. (1986). *Towards a New Psychology of Women,* 2nd edn. Boston: Beacon Press.

MONTGOMERY, J. and FEWER, W. (1988). *Family Systems and Beyond.* New York: Human Sciences Press.

Ontario Association of Interval and Transition Houses (1990). *Balance the Power: Background Report Annual Lobby.* Toronto.

PROSE, F. (1990). 'Confident at 11, Confused at 16', *New York Times,* (7 January): 24, 40.

RUSSELL, D. (1986). *The Secret Trauma: Incest in the Lives of Girls and Women.* New York: Basic Books.

SERBIN, L., SPAFKIN, C., ELMAN, M. and DOYLE, A. (1984). 'The Early Development of Sex Differential Patterns of Social Influence', *Canadian Journal of Social Science* 14: 350–63.

SIEGEL, R. (1988). 'Women's "Dependency" in a Male-centred Value System'. *Women and Therapy* 7: 113–23.

SPECIAL ADVISOR TO THE MINISTER OF HEALTH AND WELFARE ON CHILD SEXUAL ABUSE IN CANADA (1990). *Summary Report: Reaching for Solutions.* Ottawa, Canada.

SPENDER, D. (1985). *For the Record.* London: The Women's Press.

STANKO, E. (1986). *Intimate Intrusions.* London: Routledge and Kegan Paul.

STANKO, E. (1993). 'Ordinary Fear: Women, Violence and Personal Safety', in P. Bart and E. Moran (eds.) *Violence against Women: Bloody Footprints,* pp. 155–64. Newbury Park: Sage.

STIVER, I. (1984). 'Beyond the Oedipus Complex: Mothers and Daughters'. Work in Progress Paper 26. Wellesley, MA: Stone Center Working Paper Series.

SURREY, J. (1984). 'Self-in Relation: A Theory of Women's Development'. Work in Progress Paper 13. Wellesley, MA: Stone Center Working Paper Series.

Toronto Board of Education (1990). *Needs Assessment: Leadership Retreat for Adolescent Girls.* Toronto.

WISE, S. and STANLEY, L. (1987). *Georgie Porgie: Sexual Harassment in Everyday Life.* London: Pandora Press.

PART SIX

Making Our Lifepaths

Because all the stories in this book involve some portion of a woman's lifepath, you may wonder why we have chosen to assemble a final section that focuses on girls and women at different ages. We have done so because we believe that these stories illustrate the complex interaction between women as actors and agents of change and the social forces that impinge on them. Gender-specific roles are brought into play as soon as a girl is born, and others become available as she moves through her life. They are modified by a woman's ethnicity, physical appearance, and abilities as well as by her age. But these potent social messages do not always enforce passivity. These stories illustrate the ways in which women resist and how such resistance may foster personal and societal change.

Sherry Gorelick is a professor of sociology and women's studies. She was, therefore, exquisitely aware of the meaning of the social signals elicited by her daughter as soon as she was born. These signals involve more than "simple" stereotypes of femininity. What does it mean when girls are sexualized by adults *only* when they are involved in encounters with males? Do you agree with Gorelick when she states that this kind of behavior devalues the bonds between females? Think about the consequences of many nonconscious encounters of the sort Gorelick describes. Do you believe that feminists make too much of a fuss over trivial matters?

Socialization into acceptable femininity is more problematic for women whose image does not fit the ideal created by our society. Nelly Wong's poignant poem describes how she longed to be "white." How might this desire have affected her ability to identify with other girls? How did it affect her relationships with white and Asian men?

Different roles are often assigned to women of color than to white women. Linda Grant, a sociologist, shows us how such roles may be assigned early in life. Unlike many of the readings in this book, this is not a single individual's story. Instead, Grant's intensive classroom observations enable her to identify consistent patterns of difference in the behaviors elicited from black and white girls in elementary school classrooms. Black girls assume the role of helper or caretaker, enforcer, and go-between. How are these roles defined? What do you think are the advantages and disadvantages of each role for the child who assumes it and for the classroom system as a whole? What is the role of racism in the assignment of these roles to black rather than white girls? These roles seem to be double binds; however, can you think of conditions under which social skills and academic achievement need not be incompatible?

Ellen Neuborne, a second-generation feminist and journalist, claims that social disapproval of assertive women has not disappeared. She exhorts young women to become aware of how insidiously they have been programmed to remain silent and invisible in the face of injustice. Her story is particularly frightening because it casts doubt on the idea of "sisterhood." How valid are Neuborne's criticisms of earlier feminist theories? What does she want feminism to teach her and others? Do you think the price she may have to pay for her outspokenness is worth it? We believe that her story provides an excellent vantage point from which to examine the consequences of individual versus collective activism.

Although some roles may be harmful to girls and women, rolelessness may be even worse. Women with disabilities have to be even more assertive than able-bodied women to avoid being invisible. However, disability is both real and socially constructed. It also affects women's perceptions of themselves as well as how they are perceived by others. Is it possible to view dependency as yet another kind of self-fulfilling prophecy? Several of Yvonne Duffy's respondents are very critical of the women's movement for not acknowledging their oppression, yet others believe that the movement has been beneficial to them. From the evidence they provide, what do you think? Do you think that feminism has an important role to play in this area?

Just as many women are likely to become disabled at some point in their lives, most women will become old (consider the alternative). Ursula Le Guin, a prize-winning science fiction writer, considers women's aging in terms of their biological and spiritual differences from men. Do you agree with her view that women have lost a great deal by denying important stages of their life cycle? A "crone" is an archetypal figure representing female wisdom. How does Le Guin believe that women achieve cronehood? Think about whether you have known any "crones" and what lessons they might have taught.

Shevy Healey, an activist who became a lesbian and a psychotherapist relatively late in life, presents us with a less romantic view of aging. She notes that whereas she was always proud of her various forms of "otherness" throughout her life, she found herself denying her own aging. Her negative perception of her aging self is another example of the consequences of internalizing harmful stereotypes. Ask yourself why aging stereotypes are particularly destructive to women. Do you agree with Healey when she states that telling older women they do not look their age is *not* a compliment?

But Healey's story can also be read as a very positive one. What does it mean for her and others that she is able to "name her experience"? How are issues of aging intertwined with other core issues in women's lives? What values did Healey reexamine as she grew older? Discuss some of these issues with some of the older women in your own life to see if they raise similar concerns. These kinds of discussions used to be called consciousness raising. They may tell you much about ageism as well as sexism in our society.

Healey's account seems to be a fitting place to end because it reinforces themes that recur throughout the lifespan. Language and interpersonal behaviors appear to be particularly important in shaping our views of ourselves and other women. Unfortunately, a feminist consciousness does not necessarily protect a woman from internalized sexism. These stories also show, however, that women can resist socialization into harmful roles and actively choose their lifepaths. They also indicate that individual change is important, but collective action may be even more effective. Finally, they suggest that we cannot rest in our past. What would you say to someone who argues that problems of social inequality have largely been resolved?

The Gender Trap

She was only 13 days old when we took her out for the first time, and the first encounter was a warning of those to come.

"Is girl?" our 81-year-old neighbor said in the elevator.

"Yes," we beamed.

"Congratulations. I have new great-grandson. One month old. Will be boyfriend for her."

My smile deteriorated. "Congratulations," I managed sullenly. He is old, I told myself. Old-fashioned. I have to be polite. Recognize cultural differences.

The next time we met, the conversation repeated itself verbatim. And the next. And the next. By the fourth or fifth time I lost my cool.

"She's only four weeks old, Mr. Shatgan. She doesn't need a boyfriend. She just needs to grow up!"

He seemed a bit taken aback by my anger. Perplexed, as though I were speaking in tongues. But the next time we met in the elevator, he offered the same match, and I matched it with my same impatience.

That November, she was two months old and we took her to Thanksgiving at my in-laws'. Her cousins, all boys, took great delight in playing with her, calling her by name, giving her toys, babbling at her. Billy, 4, and Jake and Peter, 11, spent much time dancing around her.

"That's good," my sister-in-law said. "She's learning to get the men dancing around her."

"Men?" I thought. "Gimme a break! They are all children. Billy is *four*!" The next year at Thanksgiving, the conversation repeated itself. Sonja Samia, my daughter, was 14 months old, and the "men" were 5 and 12. I thought to myself: "What if her cousins had been girls? The adults would have taken no notice whatsoever."

Absolutely right. Over the first couple of years of her little life, my daughter's encounters with female babies were treated by all onlooking adults as unimportant and uninteresting, or as what they really were: the meeting of two babies. Her encounters with male babies were, without exception, sexualized.

One afternoon, for example, I took her out to the park as usual. She was on top of the slide when another baby around the same age swaggered its wind-up-toy way past us. The child was dressed in a blue snowsuit with pink gloves, and my friend, a strong woman who is quite unconventional in many ways, asked the Number One All Important Question:

"Boy or girl?"

"She's a girl," the other mother smiled. "Hence the pink gloves."

"Oh," said my friend. Full stop. She turned back to me and picked up the conversation where she had left it.

Sonja Samia and the other little girl stared at each other fixedly for a long while, as children that age do, and then, as children that age do, Sonja Samia slid down the slide into my arms and the other little girl finished her cookie and toddled away.

Soon another little creature of my daughter's species staggered by, and Sonja Samia, at the top of the slide once again, fixed it in her gaze.

"It's a boy?" my friend asked the mother.

"Yes," the mother grinned, glancing at her little blue darling as the two babies stared each other down.

"Hey! Look at her!" my friend said of my daughter. "She's already got boys staring at her!"

"Sorry, he's already engaged," the mother proudly answered.

"They are babies," I said to my friend. "They are only babies!"

But it sounded like one hand clapping. No one even heard me speak. I never saw it fail: we could not be in the presence of a boy child without a match being made by some adult. The connotation, sometimes explicitly stated but most often implied, was that she would be lucky if she caught him.

Neither Sonja Samia nor the male infants could have cared less, of course. They were busy being babies. They drooled, fell down, stole cookies from each other, and poked each other's eyes, regardless of gender. It's the adults who were dreaming of lace and building porn castles in the sky.

It was not only my baby's encounters with *small* males that were sexualized by adults. They often sexualized her relationship with her father and de-sexualized her relationship with me.

When she was 11 months old, she took to crawling up to your face and putting her own face in it. She seemed to want to crawl down into your throat to see where the sound comes from. When she did this with me or with my female friends, everyone thought it was cute. When she did the same thing with her father, they called it French-kissing.

Once, her father was rolling around on the carpet with her, hugging and snuggling and giggling and laughing, and my friend whispered to me, "She's gonna have a powerful passion for men when she grows up."

"Why do you say that?" I asked.

"Just look at them!" she answered.

Days later, I was rolling around on the same carpet with her, hugging and snuggling and kissing and laughing. When I got up to go to the bathroom, she cried.

"She's crying for her mommy," my friends said.

They did not seem to think that she would have a powerful passion for women. At least it didn't occur to them to say so.

Her father and I cared for her equally. With the exception of breast-feeding, we did exactly the same things in the same way. We took her to day care and picked her up; we diapered her, fed her, put her to bed, played with her, snuggled her, and loved her. But when she cried for me, she was always seen as crying for her mommy, and when she cried for him, she was seen as wanting a man.

Children are erotic, so say psychologists, including feminist ones. The very *last* thing I would want to do would be to climb on a bandwagon of yet another emotional categorical imperative: women have been told too many times what we should feel, or what we do feel. So I will say only that I have experienced my daughter as very sensual, and so has her father. We are both absolutely clear, however, that we are her parents, her guardians, not her lovers.

But the world would not let him be simply her daddy. Traditional women saw miracles in his most ordinary fatherly behavior, such as when he bought socks for her. (*My* buying her socks was of course unremarkable, since I am her mother.) More modern women, those exposed to flashes of Freud and post-Freudian psychology, interpreted her father's relationship with her in quasi-romantic terms. In the eyes of the world he was either God the Father because he bought her socks, or Casanova because she loves him. He could not be simply Daddy. I, on the other hand, am merely her mother, no matter how she shows her love for me, and whether or not I buy her socks.

From the moment that we chose her name, in myriad microactions most of which are unconscious, we have been, willy-nilly, gendering our daughter. So has everyone else. (The men in my neighborhood will shadowbox with any apparently male toddler who staggers by, whether or not he is interested; they never shadowbox with female toddlers.) Yet many of the parents of boys of my acquaintance—even some feminist ones—are brand-new converts to biological determinism. Boys are more aggressive, they say. It's the testosterone. It explains so much.

So when my baby daughter tried to poke her finger in a new infant's eyes (to see how they work, I suppose), I would catch her hand and say, "No, not the eyes." When a little boy baby tried to do the same thing, his parent would catch his hand and say, "No, not the eyes," and then, more often than not, the parent would smile and say half-sheepishly, "Boys are so aggressive! No matter what I try to do . . ." But the smile was only half-sheepish because there was, I think, a thin streak of pleasure and relief. The little man had a little lion in him. The world was in order. Everything was normal.

Normal, the women's movement has shown us, is not good for women. When adults matched up my baby daughter with every passing male child, they devalued her and stereotyped her. Presumably it was only a joke. It was supposed to be cute. But it assumed that she was available and waiting, and it assumed that she would be indifferent to the specific character of the males who danced around her.

It also stereotyped sex. Adults endowed my daughter's encounters with any male creature who toddled by with a special emotional charge, as if to say, *This is important! It is about sex!* Adults regarded my baby daughter's encounters with other baby girls with inattention and indifference, even unto boredom, and in so doing they said, implicitly, "This is not important. They are only females. It is only about babies. It is not about sex."

And it is true: they *were* only babies. It was *not* about sex. But to recognize that only when the babies are of the same sex is to stereotype sex and to devalue the bonds among females. And the fact that women who are feminists also make these jokes about boys and not about girls does not lessen their effect in reinforcing sexism and compulsory heterosexuality.

These mating game stereotypes are profoundly reassuring to most people, as stereotypes always are to the people who apply them. They are perpetuated because whatever behavior fits the stereotype *fits* and whatever behavior does not fit is discarded. It becomes invisible, quickly forgotten. For if you are not the case that proves the rule, and you are not "the exception that proves the rule," then what will happen to the rule?

Better to believe—no matter how regretfully—that boys are naturally aggressive, and that every female longs for a male from when she is afloat in utero to the end of her life. So when boys act like Attila the Hun, adults nod their heads sadly and smile. They are smiling because they are relieved. Everything is in its place, in order. Better a stereotype of an oppressive order ("Boys are naturally aggressive"; "girls are easier to handle"; "every woman needs a man") than ambiguity, with its scent of unknown changes, its frightening possibilities.

How could I be so rude and ungrateful as to rail at my poor old neighbor's mating game? He was only expressing his culture—*our* culture—the harmless assumptions and gentle jokes of daily life. To criticize the mating game is to be a spoilsport, humorless, picky. To question it seems trivial, a petty violation of the normal.

I do not know what Sonja Samia will be when she is 20 years old, or 30, or 50. Will she be bisexual, lesbian, or straight, a feminist or a femme fatale?

She was, at 15 months, a very determined and self-determining little person. She would look around the room, decide what she wanted, purse her little mouth, and pursue it like a park hound stalking a squirrel. Her sureness of what she wanted and needed caused me some short-term exasperation but much long-term joy and deep-down pride. It's still the best thing about her. I aim to do everything I can to make sure that she keeps and deepens that sure sense of her own self. I am determined to encourage her to know herself as an interconnected social being, knowing and appreciating her own feelings, thoughts, and desires, whatever they may be.

As she tries to find her own path in life, however, she must pick her way through a minefield of other people's hungers, stereotypes, and fears. It is not a kid's game: it is a silent tyranny of daily life.

By the time Sonja Samia reached eight years old, her father and I had divorced. The mating game jokes among the adults have decreased temporarily, chiefly, I believe, because older girls and boys play separately. The business of rigging the mating game—and it is big business indeed—has shifted to the dreammaking machines: the idiot box and the video store.

There the Disney empire skillfully reaches through little girls' eyes, forming and fondling their fantasies. Beauty falls in love with the Beast (no matter how beastly he may be), the Little Mermaid has no female friends, and no one ever suggests that Sleeping Beauty might one day be awakened by a *princess*. That would be against all the rules. As a result, the third-grade girls now take up the mating game jokes on their own, teasing each other over who is most favored by the boys, no matter how lackluster those boys may be.

But, thankfully, theirs is also the post-Stonewall generation: Some of them have openly gay uncles or lesbian mothers. The heterosexist assumptions of the 1990s are nowhere near as suffocatingly absolute as the silence of the 1950s. There's no telling what kind of world these children, including Sonja Samia, will make when they are old enough to find their own way to love.

Nellie Wong

When I Was Growing Up

I know now that once I longed to be white.
How? you ask.
Let me tell you the ways.

> when I was growing up, people told me
> I was dark and I believed my own darkness
> in the mirror, in my soul, my own narrow vision

> > when I was growing up, my sisters
> > with fair skin got praised
> > for their beauty, and in the dark
> > I fell further, crushed between high walls

when I was growing up, I read magazines
and saw movies, blonde movie stars, white skin,
sensuous lips and to be elevated, to become
a woman, a desirable woman, I began to wear
imaginary pale skin

> > > when I was growing up, I was proud
> > > of my English, my grammar, my spelling
> > > fitting into the group of smart children
> > > smart Chinese children, fitting in,
> > > belonging, getting in line

when I was growing up and went to high school,
I discovered the rich white girls, a few yellow girls,
their imported cotton dresses, their cashmere sweaters,
their curly hair and I thought that I too should have
what these lucky girls had

> > when I was growing up, I hungered
> > for American food, American styles,
> > coded: white and even to me, a child
> > born of Chinese parents, being Chinese
> > was feeling foreign, was limiting,
> > was unAmerican

when I was growing up and a white man wanted
to take me out, I thought I was special,
an exotic gardenia, anxious to fit
the stereotype of an oriental chick

    when I was growing up, I felt ashamed
    of some yellow men, their small bones,
    their frail bodies, their spitting
    on the streets, their coughing,
    their lying in sunless rooms,
    shooting themselves in the arms

when I was growing up, people would ask
if I were Filipino, Polynesian, Portuguese.
They named all colors except white, the shell
of my soul, but not my dark, rough skin

    when I was growing up, I felt
    dirty. I thought that god
    made white people clean
    and no matter how much I bathed,
    I could not change. I could not shed
    my skin in the gray water

when I was growing up, I swore
I would run away to purple mountains,
houses by the sea with nothing over
my head, with space to breathe,
uncongested with yellow people in an area
called Chinatown, in an area I later learned
was a ghetto, one of many hearts
of Asian America

I know now that once I longed to be white
How many more ways? you ask.
Haven't I told you enough?

Linda Grant

Helpers, Enforcers, and Go-Betweens: Black Females in Elementary School Classrooms

SCHOOLS AND SOCIAL PLACEMENT

Students attending public schools in the United States learn lessons that go far beyond the formal curriculum. Through the informal curriculum (sometimes termed the hidden curriculum) they learn about status relationships among persons of various race-gender groups in society (Chesler and Cave 1981; C. Grant and Sleeter 1986; L. Grant 1984, 1985; Sadker and Frazier 1973). The hidden curriculum consists of routine, everyday interchanges that provide students with information about the placement of persons of various race-gender groups. The informal social roles that students come to assume in schools closely parallel adult roles deemed appropriate for persons of their race-gender configurations.

Schools are important sites for learning about social rankings related to race, gender, and class, even though they operate under the rhetoric of "equal opportunity" (Bowles and Gintis 1976). For many students, attending a desegregated public elementary school provides their first sustained contact with children of other races (and other socioeconomic classes). Impressions thus formed may be long-lasting. The transmission of status arrangements through schooling occurs despite dedicated educators' efforts to provide race- and gender-equitable learning environments (C. Grant and Sleeter 1986; Guttentag and Bray 1976; Schofield 1982).

I concentrate here on effects of schooling on the social placement of Black females, whose experiences in schools, as in other domains of social life, have been underexplored (Allen 1979; Davis 1971; Hare 1980; Luttrell 1989; Murray 1975). Available research suggests that Black girls' experiences in school differ significantly from those of other race-gender students (see, e.g., Hare 1979, 1980; Irvine 1985; Scott-Jones and Clark 1986). Black girls achieve more highly than Black boys but more poorly than White students. They have higher self-esteem than White girls but lower self-esteem than Black males. Black females' schooling experiences cannot be wholly understood by extrapolating from research on girls or research on Blacks (Hare 1979).

337

LINDA GRANT
Helpers, Enforcers,
and Go-Betweens:
Black Females in
Elementary School
Classrooms

TABLE 1. Percentage of Black Students and Teacher Race, Six First-Grade Midwestern Classrooms

Teacher Name[a]	Teacher Race	Blacks Pupils in Classroom[b] (%)	School District[a]
Maxwell	White	22	Glendon
Avery	White	21	Glendon
Delby	White	22	Ridgeley
Todd	Black	59	Ridgeley
Horton	Black	29	Ridgeley
Douglas	Black	96	Ridgeley

[a]All teacher and school district names are fictitious.
[b]Includes only those students enrolled in the classroom for 80 percent or more of the total observation period.

I suggest that complex, subtle processes in schools encourage Black girls, more so than other students, to assume distinctive roles: helper, enforcer, and go-between. These roles develop their social skills more than their academic abilities. In doing so, they encourage Black females toward adult roles stressing service and nurturance. Skills developed via these roles are consistent with occupational roles in which Black women currently are overrepresented (for example, nurse and teacher's aide). These roles do not stress the intellectual skills and individual attainment associated with high-status professional positions, such as lawyer and political leader.

SETTING AND METHODS

This study is based primarily on observations in six desegregated first-grade classrooms in working-class communities near a large Midwestern city. Enrollment ranged from 21 to 96 percent Black. Three had White teachers (Maxwell, Avery, Delby) and three had Black teachers (Todd, Horton, and Douglas). (All teacher and student names are fictitious). Table 1 shows specific characteristics of each room.

I observed each room from twenty to thirty hours over several months. I also interviewed all teachers but Avery at the conclusion of observations. (More information on settings and data collection is provided in L. Grant 1984, 1985).

These data are supplemented by in-progress observations in four first- and second-grade rooms in a desegregated rural Southern primary school. Table 2 provides information on these rooms. Black enrollment ranges from 30 to 92 percent in each room. The first-grade teachers (Carson and Hilton) are White; the second-grade teachers (Jordan and Parker) are Black.

Numerical data cited below are from the Midwestern schools only. Examples of Black girls' classroom roles come from both settings. Despite geographical and time separations in these two settings, classroom roles played by Black females are remarkably consistent. Furthermore, in both settings Black girls took on similar roles in White-teacher and in Black-teacher rooms.

TABLE 2. Grade Level, Academic Track, Percentage of Black Students, and Teacher Race of the Southern Primary School Classrooms

Teacher Name[a]	Teacher Race	Grade Level	Track Level[b]	Black Pupils in Class-rooms (%)
Taylor	White	1	Middle	74
Hilton	White	1	Low	92
Jordan	Black	2	High	30
Parker	Black	2	Middle	65

[a]All teacher names are fictitious.

[b]Classes at each grade level were tracked as high, middle, or low on the basis of standardized test scores and teacher recommendations. Each room was subdivided into two to four ability-graded reading groups.

BLACK GIRLS' CLASSROOM ROLES

The Helper or Caretaker

Helpers or caretakers provided nonacademic aid in classrooms, mostly to peers but occasionally to teachers. I distinguish between academic helpers, those providing academic aid, and helpers or caretakers, who provided nonacademic assistance. Caretaking or helping included helping peers locate lost materials or providing comfort to an emotionally distressed child. As I have reported elsewhere (see Grant 1985), tutoring was provided primarily by White students. In all classrooms, Black girls were overrepresented relative to their proportions of enrollment, as helpers. Furthermore, they provided nonacademic help to diverse race-gender peers, sometimes interrupting their own academic work or risking sanctions to do so.

Sandra (Black), in Jordan's class, exemplified the helper. She often returned early from recess to sweep the classroom floor. Jordan praised her efforts and occasionally asked her to carry out additional tasks, such as sweeping up sand in the hall. Jordan confirmed that Sandra's sweeping of the room was voluntary and referred to her as "our little housekeeper."

Celeste (Black), in Todd's room, stationed herself near the door to help peers on and off with outerwear. When Celeste was absent, other children tried to play her role but were rejected by classmates and told by Todd to sit down. Gloria (Black), in Carson's room, was the informal monitor who ensured that students left each afternoon with the correct coats, lunch boxes, and schoolbags.

Helpers sometimes became so concerned with aiding others that they neglected their academic work. Juliette (Black), in Avery's room, often failed to complete assignments because she ran errands for tablemates (finding lost crayons, getting tissues from the teacher's desk, etc.). Todd described Meredith (Black) as "bright but an underachiever." She also characterized her as a "busybody," too often abandoning her work to help with or check on someone else's. In a sixty-five-minute observation period, Todd reprimanded Meredith eleven times for stopping work on math to carry out tasks such as helping a friend search for a barrette and settling a noisy verbal dispute between two boys at the next table.

Helpers occasionally gave up privileges, or risked sanctions, to aid peers. Marvin (Black), in Hilton's room, cried because a punishment forced him to sit on the pavement adjacent to the playground rather than participate in recess games. Sheila (Black) voluntarily relinquished participation in games to comfort Marvin for the entire thirty-minute period. Millie (Black), in Horton's room, defied Horton's angry "Get back to that seat NOW" and continued to approach Horton to tell her that tablemates Gregory (Black), Cynthia (White), and Adam (White) lacked marker pens for an assignment. The students got the needed materials, but Millie lost her free-time activity privilege for defying the teacher's command.

The willingness to risk reprimands to aid a peer was a distinctive characteristic of Black girls. White females often helped peers, though their efforts tended to concentrate on a narrow range of close friends rather than on the diverse students aided by Black girls. White girls rarely persisted in helping when teachers threatened sanctions.

The helping and caretaking activities of Black girls likely contributed to other students' social comfort in the classroom and aided in maintenance of order and peace. Nevertheless, these actions had costs that might diminish intellectual achievement and favorable evaluation. Academic work was interrupted, and teachers occasionally reprimanded the helpers.

The Enforcer

A second role overplayed by Black girls, relative to their enrollment, was that of self-appointed enforcer. Without explicit requests from teachers, the girls urged peers to comply with class or school rules. Black girls enforced more than other students in all Midwestern and Southern rooms.

When teacher Parker left the room briefly to greet a parent, she told students to "stay seated and be quiet." Nevertheless, several students left their seats. When Gerald (White) walked past Pamela (Black), Pamela rose, placed her hands on his shoulders, gently kicked the back of his legs, told him to "move it," and pushed him several feet back to his desk. She then pointed a finger at Steven (Black) and threatened: "You're next." Steven quickly took his seat. She then shook her head sternly at Renee (White), who had started to rise but sat down in response to Pamela's action.

Enforcements appeared to have many motivations. Some appeared to be genuine attempts to aid the teacher. Cheryl (Black), in Delby's room, was near tears when classmates ignored her pleas to be quiet, as Delby had requested. Sometimes enforcements seemed to be bids to gain the teacher's favorable attention, as when Juliette (Black), invariably called Avery's attention to her enforcements. Some appeared to be attempts to protect peers, as when Camille (Black), in Maxwell's room, told classmates to "look busy" when she perceived that Maxwell was ready to move around the room to check work.

Enforcers typically restated teacher messages, often exaggerating the teachers' threats about consequences of noncompliance. When Horton warned that students not completing work would be unable to see a movie, Angela (Black) told inattentive and nonworking classmates Clifton (Black) and Yvonne (Black) that the teacher had threatened to "cut their fingers off" if they did not complete their work on time.

339

LINDA GRANT
Helpers, Enforcers,
and Go-Betweens:
Black Females in
Elementary School
Classrooms

The enforcer role could be risky. Some peers resisted enforcements, as when Joel (White), in Jordan's room, slapped Ramona (Black) when she reminded him to keep hands off science experiment materials, as the teacher had requested. Teachers often reprimanded self-appointed enforcers, as when Douglas told Carolyn (Black) to "get back to your seat where you belong" when the child attempted to have peers return books to a shelf.

Enforcers demonstrated considerable knowledge of, and loyalty to, classroom roles. Whatever their motivations, successful enforcements served social control functions in the classrooms and minimized overt resistance to teacher rules. Successful enforcements also revealed that Black girls had substantial influence with peers of diverse race-gender attributes. It is not clear, however, that teachers were cognizant of this effect. Most ignored or discouraged enforcements.

The Go-Between

The most complex, but also the most influential, role assumed by Black girls was that of the go-between. Camille (Black), in Maxwell's room, was a go-between. An excerpt from field notes illustrates the scope of the role:

> Camille responds to Felix's (Black) appeal that he needs a replacement for a broken shoelace, comes to his side, then contacts the teacher. When Maxwell becomes engaged in a conversation (with a White female from another grade who came with a message), Camille goes to see George (White) to see if he has a shoelace in a box of odds-and-ends he keeps on his desk. He does not. Camille relays a request from George to Babs (White) to borrow a marker pen, then hammers out the details of the trade between George and Babs when they disagree. Camille scowls at Bradford (White) as he tries to trip her in the aisle, tells him to mind his own business, then giggles with Penny (White) as she laughs in response to Camille's remark to Bradford. Camille repeats her request to Maxwell, coming to the teacher's desk, then suggests that Maxwell send Sylvia (White) to see if the special education teacher in the adjoining room has a shoelace. Maxwell agrees and Camille calls to Sylvia as she leaves: "And it doesn't matter what color." Enroute to her own desk, Camille tells Gary (White) to pick up his coat from the floor so it does not get dirty and stepped on. She responds to a hand motion from Tobin (Black) for help in reading a word, which she gives. Camille whispers to Sarah (Black), who smuggles her a handful of jellybeans. Camille, at her desk, shares some jellybeans with Clarissa (White). Camille is called to Maxwell's desk to relay a message to Felix to see the special education teacher to get a shoelace. Camille thanks Sylvia for running the errand when the teacher says nothing to her, then goes to stand at the corner of Maxwell's desk, where Maxwell looks at her and says, "Camille, what are you doing up here? It's time for math."

Camille's actions in the ten minutes covered above involved one-third of the class, plus the teacher. She provided links and transmitted influence from teacher to student, student to teacher, and student to student. She, like the other go-betweens, had easy access to the teacher and high status in the class. Camille often was chosen by peers to give out treats or lead games.

Not all rooms had go-betweens. In the Midwest schools they did not appear in the Black teachers' classrooms. In the Southern school, however, go-betweens emerged in both White teachers' and Black teachers' rooms. Where the role existed, it inevitably was filled by a Black female.

Mona was the go-between in Jordan's room. Jordan usually made participation in recess contingent on completion of work. Mona engaged in complex negotiations with adults and students around this issue. At the beginning of the seven-minute excerpt below, Mona has finished work and reads an enrichment book. Christopher and David across the aisle have been working off and on a math assignment, frequently interrupting their work for mock sword fights with small plastic rulers used in their work.

341

*LINDA GRANT
Helpers, Enforcers,
and Go-Betweens:
Black Females in
Elementary School
Classrooms*

> Christopher (White) and David (Black) complain to Mona (Black) that Jordan warned them that they would have no recess if they do not complete math worksheets in the next six minutes. Mona tells Christopher: "Well, you two been screwing around." Christopher tells her: "I didn't have no recess yesterday either." Mona tells him, "Gimme that," and grabs his worksheet. David stands over her desk. Jordan tells David: "Sit down, please, I think you've got work to do." Mona goes to Jordan for a whispered conversation and apparently gets her approval to work at a back table with the boys. Mona tells them: "I ain't done this one yet. I don't know how." She then goes to Gail (White), who tells her: "Go away." Mona tells Gail, "You're a bitch," then goes to Anita (White), who gives help. Mona returns to the table and writes an answer on Christopher's paper. David copies this. The recess bell rings, and Christopher groans: "We ain't finished. We ain't going to get to go out." David puts both hands over his eyes in an exaggerated gesture of frustration (but then giggles at Christopher and Mona). As the rest of the class leaves , Mona goes to Jordan, who talks with Ms. Kyle (White), a teacher's aide from another room. Mona asks: "If they get done before ten minutes, can they have part of their recess? They're getting it now." Jordan smiles, then says: "What do you think, Ms. Kyle?" Ms. Kyle nods in the affirmative, and Jordan says, "Well, okay, but have them bring [their papers] to me before they go off [a paved area near the playground]." Christopher overhears and clasps his hands together over his head in a "victory" gesture, and David laughs and slaps him gently across the back. As Jordan puts papers in a cabinet near the door, Mona asks Ms. Kyle the answer to the next problem. Ms. Kyle and Mona return to the table to work with the boys as Jordan [on playground duty] leaves. They complete the work in about two minutes. The boys grab papers and run off, with David calling out: "OKAY." Ms. Kyle tells Mona: "That was nice of you," and puts her arm around Mona as they leave the room.

Mona displayed the same pattern of multiple contacts with teachers and peers visible in Camille's actions. She interacted easily with students and teachers and persisted in the face of obstacles. Although other students negotiated with teachers, Black girls were virtually the only ones to negotiate about matters not directly related to themselves or their needs. Mona's actions produce a positive outcome for her classmates (recess time) and for the teacher (completion of work by students who do not always do so). To play the role, Mona has relinquished some of her own work and leisure time.

Erving Goffman (1959) believes that go-betweens operate in many social settings. He labels the actions of a go-between in social encounters as a "discrepant role." It makes sense, he argues, only when one considers the go-between's position as a constituent member of two or more "teams" that have few positive ties. The go-between maintains a delicate balance, sometimes involving subtle distortions of one group's orientation to the other, so that a closer relationship between the teams is possible. Playing the role successfully requires access to both groups and extensive knowledge of their operating norms. It also requires the willingness to take personal risks in the interests of social harmony.

Commonalities Among the Roles

The three roles characteristically assumed by Black girls put a premium on social, rather than academic, skills. Helpers, enforcers, and go-betweens frequently neglect academic work to meet the needs of others in the room. This brings them disproportionate amounts of praise from teachers for social actions, but also causes a relative neglect of their academic work. Teacher praise skewed toward social deeds rather than academic work likely strengthens Black girls' tendencies to stress social skills as the primary mode of attainment. In a cyclical fashion teachers' tendencies to see Black girls primarily in terms of social behaviors (see below) increases over time.

EMERGENCE AND MAINTENANCE OF ROLES

Understanding the complex dynamics by which Black girls' roles emerged and were maintained in classrooms requires consideration of teachers' perceptions of these students, teacher–student interactions, and peer interactions in the desegregated rooms. Some authors have argued that minority parents, more so than White parents, socialize their children, and especially their daughters, to take care of peers (Ladner 1971; Lewis 1975). Black girls may arrive at school primed for service roles. The school environment reinforces this predisposition. Helpers, for example, usually first performed their roles spontaneously. Over time, teachers and peers increasingly looked to them to perform certain tasks. When Sandra was absent one day, Jordan told students: "Things just won't be as tidy today."

Teachers' Perceptions

Interviews with five of the six observed Midwestern teachers provided information on teacher perceptions. Teachers were asked: "Tell me about [child's name]'s academic skills and performance" and "Tell me about [child's name]'s relationships with other children in the class." The open-ended questions allowed discernment of the direction of assessments as well as criteria teachers believed relevant in evaluating students of each race-gender group. When interviewed, teachers had no standardized achievement test data, except for a few students referred for special testing.

Academic Skills Ratings

Black girls' academic skills were rated as average or slightly below average compared with the other three race-gender groups in these classes. Of the twenty-six Black girls assigned to the five interviewed teachers, 23 percent

343

LINDA GRANT
Helpers, Enforcers,
and Go-Betweens:
Black Females in
Elementary School
Classrooms

were rated as high, 42 percent as average, and 35 percent as low or below average. Black girls' skills were rated most similarly to White males and were lower than those of White females but higher than those of Black males. Avery, who was not formally interviewed, mentioned spontaneously that one of her three Black female students was average in academic skills, while the other two were below average.

Even though skills of White males and Black females were similarly rated, teachers' assessments of White boys differed in one important respect. For 20 percent of the White boys rated average and 11 percent rated below average, teachers commented that these students were immature. Teachers thought their performances might improve with time. They did not make such comments about any Black female student. Evaluations of Black females differed from those of other students in another important respect. Unlike children of all other race-gender configurations, no Black female was singled out as having outstanding skill in a specific area—athletics, music, art. The "ho-hum" quality of most teachers' assessments of most Black girls is reflected in Maxwell's comments about Carrie: "She's about average in everything. Her work habits are good. She's very neat and quiet . . . no problem at all. She can take care of herself. She usually doesn't have much to say." Only one Black girl was labeled by her teacher as "one of my brightest students," an accolade usually given only to White students.

Also reflected in the evaluations was a concentration on social skills ("neat and quiet"), even when teachers were asked to discuss academic skills. Delby's comments about Nancy are another example: "She's an average student, I would say, but oh, what a helper. She always keeps her eyes on things, picks things up, helps out other [students] who don't understand work or are having some problem. She is always asking: 'What can I do to help?'"

Teachers sometimes suggested that Black girls' social rather than academic skills might be most critical to success in school, as was apparent in Todd's comments about the low-achieving Doris: "It takes her longer to learn things than most children. . . . Other children help her out a lot because Doris is such a pleasure to have in the class. She is always smiling, always trying, always being kind to other people. [Classmates] have a lot of patience with her. . . . They don't treat her the way they treat [other low achievers]. I think that will be pretty important to her later on."

Teachers' responses to the questions about academic skills were coded point by point for each child, and ratios of academic to nonacademic criteria mentioned for various race-gender children were compared. Examples of academic criteria were "He's very good in science" and "She has trouble reading." Examples of nonacademic criteria were "She's always beautifully dressed" and "He's got a strong rebellious streak." Some teachers (for example, Horton) made mostly academic comments about students, while others (for example, Delby) relied more heavily on nonacademic criteria. Nevertheless, every teacher used higher ratios of nonacademic criteria when evaluating Black females than other groups. This suggested that for this group, teachers were more attentive to students' nonacademic behaviors and attributes than their academic skills. Assessments of White girls in most rooms relied on nearly equal proportions of academic and nonacademic criteria, while assessments of boys of both races stressed academic criteria.

Teachers made the most extensive comments about the academic skills of unusually high achievers (mostly White students) or unusually low achievers (predominantly Black males). They viewed high achievers as reflecting favorably upon teachers, while low achievers threatened to expose them as poor instructors or to disrupt the class. The average, shy, quiet Black females fell outside these groups, and they attracted only limited teacher attention, a pattern observed in other studies (Byalick and Bershoff 1974; Irvine 1985).

Social Skills Ratings

Teachers commented that Blacks girls were mature, self-sufficient, and helpful. They also identified White girls as mature, labeling them cognitively mature and "ready for school." For Black girls the assessment of maturity did not translate into expectations of high academic performance in the same way that it did for White girls. Teachers did not see Black girls as cognitively mature. Instead, they described them as having a precocious social maturity that was detrimental to academic performance. Douglas praised six-year-old Edna for feeding and dressing three preschool siblings each morning so that her mother, a nurse working the night shift, could sleep. But Douglas added: "Of course, all that responsibility doesn't give her much time to concentrate on [school work]."

Teachers pointed to Black girls' preoccupation with adult roles, viewed by teachers as a distraction from work. At recess these children played house, portraying family members, cooking and cleaning, and primping for dates with imaginary boyfriends. At sharing time they bragged of assuming adultlike roles, such as preparing a large meal. Maxwell noted that a group of Black girls often were inattentive to lessons because "they're passing around lipstick or giggling about who kissed whom on the bus yesterday."

The precocious maturity of Black girls also was observed by Joyce Ladner (1971) in a study of Black teenagers living in a housing project. She found that most Black girls lived in adult worlds at young ages. Parents gave them adult-level knowledge and responsibilities, the first to shield them from harsh realities of their environment and the second to provide help to parents in meeting their own multiple roles. Rather than seeing these qualities as assets, teachers in this study viewed them as impediments to learning.

Teachers identified fourteen of the twenty-six Black girls as generous and helpful to teachers and peers. These qualities were noted twice as often in reference to Black girls as to other students. Such attributes seemed to be the most reliable means for Black girls to capture teachers' favorable attention.

Teacher–Student Interactions

There were two components to teacher–student interactions: behaviors initiated by teachers and behaviors initiated by students.

Teacher Behaviors

As was the case for all race-gender students, teachers' behaviors toward students were partially consistent, and partially inconsistent, with their evalu-

345

LINDA GRANT
Helpers, Enforcers,
and Go-Betweens:
Black Females in
Elementary School
Classrooms

ations of them. In subtle ways teachers encouraged Black girls to pursue social contacts rather than press toward high academic achievement. This was observable through track placements, responses to academic work, and feedback for behavior.

All teachers in the Midwest schools used ability groups for reading instruction. After the first two weeks of observation, groups became quite stable, with less than 4 percent of students (none of them Black females) changing groups. In the Southern schools 5 percent of students changed groups. The three Black girls involved all moved downward. Midwestern teachers identified groups as composed of students reading above, at, and below grade level. Black females most often were placed in at-grade-level groups (48 percent); 21 percent were in above-grade-level groups, and 31 percent were below grade level. These distributions closely paralleled placements for all students, regardless of race-gender status, except that Black girls were more often in at-grade-level and less often in above-grade-level groups. Consistent with teachers' assessments of ability, Black girls were placed lower than White girls, higher than Black boys, and similarly to White boys. Black girls had very similar group placements in the Southern school. Group placements usually paralleled teachers' assessments of students' skills, but often White girls—and occasionally also a few Black girls—were placed in higher groups in doubtful cases because teachers believed they behaved well. Avery, uncertain whether Diana (Black) belonged in an average or a lower group, decided on the former because "She tries hard, helps other children, obeys, and sets a good example."

Counts of teachers' praise and criticism for academic work showed no particular pattern of favoritism for any race-gender group across the six Midwestern rooms. Black girls received average, and in some rooms slightly greater than average, amounts of praise for day-to-day work. The three Black teachers were somewhat more apt to praise Black girls' academic work than were the White teachers. In comparison with other students, Black girls received slightly more qualified praise, suggesting that work fell short of the best in the room (e.g., "That's a fine printing paper, much better than yesterday's."). Black girls in most rooms received less criticism for academic work than most students, although teacher criticism sometimes is important in pressing students to do their best work.

Black girls never received a significant type of praise reserved almost exclusively for White girls. Teachers assigned white girls high-responsibility academic tasks, such as tutoring or orienting a new student to class work. Of twenty-two such special assignments, eighteen went to White girls. Designating White girls as trusted aids may have overridden routine praise and marked these children as particularly competent in the eyes of peers. Such assignments often were mentioned by children when discussing which peers were "smart." The qualification of praise, and the exclusion of Black girls from special tasks implying academic competence, suggested that teachers did not view them as the most able students in the room.

Feedback patterns suggested that teachers were especially sensitive to the social behaviors of Black females. Behavioral feedback was defined as teacher praise or criticism for actions unrelated to academic work (e.g., "I like the way Rhonda [Black] is standing quietly in the lunch line."). In three rooms

(Maxwell's, Horton's, Avery's) Black girls received substantially more behavioral praise than other students. In Delby's and Douglas's rooms they received considerably fewer reprimands for behavior than other student groups. In all rooms they received substantially fewer reprimands for behavior than Black males did. There were no systematic relationships between teacher race and feedback patterns to Black girls for behaviors. Black girls received disproportionately high ratios of praise for behavior from most teachers.

Student Behaviors

Teachers' behaviors toward Black females created certain opportunities for some Black girls to gain visibility and teacher praise via social actions. Teachers' behavioral praises were asymmetrically distributed among Black girls. In each White teacher's classroom in the Midwest, one Black girl received the most praise. This child was the go-between. The go-betweens who emerged in the four Southern classrooms also had atypically high ratios of teacher praise. Black teachers' classrooms in the Midwestern schools (Horton's, Todd's, and Douglas's) did not have go-betweens, although they contained identifiable enforcers and helpers.

Black girls were uniquely situated in their classes for the go-between role. Their position in what Bruce Hare (1975) terms the "psychological and academic middle ground" gave them experiences in common with those of all other race-gender groups. Their relative freedom from teacher monitoring, in comparison with Black males, gave them both opportunity and motivation to play the role. For some, peer involvements were alternative sources of reward. The go-between had ready access to the teacher's sphere of influence and to peer networks but was probably not perceived as having exclusive allegiance to either. The role also is consistent with themes in parental socialization of Black daughters (Ladner 1971; Lewis 1975; Lightfoot 1979; Reid 1972).

By playing the go-between role, Black females likely made important contributions to the social integration of desegregated classrooms. By avoiding exclusive commitments to tight peer groups but maintaining weaker ties with many peers, the go-between wove a pattern of loose connections that Mark Granovetter (1973) argues contributes to social integration of a collectivity.

The enforcer role also is logically related to Black girls' locations vis-à-vis teachers and peers. Enforcement was an alternative to high academic achievement for teacher recognition. Since teachers only rarely counted Black girls among the highest achievers in their classes, enforcement was the most successful means for garnering teacher praise. Enforcement also could benefit peers if it kept them out of trouble with the teacher. It worked only when students had substantial social power in peer networks and were willing to risk retaliation from classmates. As I have reported elsewhere, Black girls were less likely than White girls to be intimidated by aggression or threats of aggression from peers (L. Grant, 1983). This meant that Black girls were more likely to enforce rules on peers directly. White girls either ignored classmates' infractions or told teachers about their misbehaviors.

It is unclear to what extent teachers in the Midwestern and Southern classrooms encouraged helper, enforcer, and go-between roles and to what extent they evolved from parental socialization and preschool experience stressing

347

LINDA GRANT
Helpers, Enforcers,
and Go-Betweens:
Black Females in
Elementary School
Classrooms

social skills and loyalty to peers. Both likely are important. Since this study collected no data on preschool socialization, consideration of the issue can be only speculative. Teachers seemed to reinforce the roles. Five of the six teachers in the Midwestern schools called on Black girls almost twice as frequently as any other race-gender group to help peers in nonacademic matters, whereas White girls were their usual choice for help with academic tasks, such as tutoring. All teachers in the Southern school except Parker also overselected Black girls as helpers. Parker was equally likely to select Black and White girls (relative to enrollments in her room) as helpers and chose Black girls as tutors slightly more often than White girls. Critical in the go-between and enforcer roles was Black girls' orientations toward teachers. These ranged from apple-polishing to wary avoidance, but mostly fell in between. Although generally compliant with teacher rules, Black females were less obviously tied to teachers than White girls and contacted teachers only when they had reason to do so. In each room a contingent of White girls spent a great deal of time with teachers, prolonging questions into chats. Black girls' contacts were briefer, more task-oriented, and often on behalf of a peer rather than self. Black girls risked reprimands in many cases to get aid for peers. Overall, in the Midwestern rooms from 32 to 47 percent of Black girls' approaches to teachers (depending on room) were on behalf of peers. This compared with no more than 17 percent for children of other race-gender groups in any room. Black girls' tendency to interrupt their academic work to seek aid for peers was a behavior rarely observed in other students.

Black girls spontaneously took on aspects of the three roles, especially that of the go-between. When Camille was ill for a week, another Black girl attempted to become the go-between—Camille's role. Teacher Maxwell rebuffed Helene's efforts, however. When Camille returned, she resumed her duties with no apparent communication with Maxwell about the matter.

Black Girls' Relationships with Peers

Black girls' ties with classmates were logically related to their relationships with teachers and to themes in preschool socialization. These children's peer relationships also were critical to their assumption of the distinctive classroom roles.

Black girls had the most extensive, most egalitarian peer ties of any race-gender group (L. Grant 1983). Although they rarely instigated physical or verbal aggression, they were less apt than White girls to be intimidated by aggression or threats. Black girls thus appeared more powerful and less exploited in peer networks than other students.

Extent of Contacts

In all the Midwestern rooms except Delby's, Black girls had more extensive peer contacts than any other race-gender group. Most Black females crossed race and gender lines more readily than did other students. This finding is contrary to some research with older students, which suggests that Black girls are more isolated than other students (D'Amico 1986; DeVries and Edwards 1977; Patchen 1982; Schofield 1982). Although this study cannot wholly account for the discrepancy, some speculation is possible.

Janet Schofield found that emerging romantic and sexual interests and normative patterns of male-female recreational activities limited cross-racial ties of female junior high students more so than those of boys. Sexuality was not an issue for first graders. Furthermore, first-grade girls played in large groups. They had not yet moved into the tight, small cliques that Schofield found most common among the teenagers. Larger-group activities encourage cross-racial interaction.

Second, many previous studies have been conducted in schools where Blacks and Whites differed markedly in social class and achievement. In schools used in this study, Black and White students were of common social class origins, and Black girls were most often in middle academic tracks, where they had contacts and common experiences with diverse peers.

Third, these rooms had greater-than-token proportions of minority students, and their dynamics thus probably differed from rooms where one racial group was an extreme majority. James Rothenberg (1982) has suggested that nearly equal proportions and multiple status lines diminish the importance of any one characteristic, such as race or gender, as an interaction barrier.

Helping Behaviors

Black girls gave substantial academic help to peers. Academic aid was given and received in nearly equal proportions. This contrasted to patterns for White girls, who gave much more academic aid than they received. Black girls gave somewhat more care than they received in return, but their caring activities were more likely to be reciprocated than were those of White girls. Also, as noted earlier, Black girls helped diverse race-gender peers, rather than concentrating on close friends, as other students did. These activities likely maintained the extensive social ties and social influence needed to carry out the distinctive classroom roles. Unlike White girls, Black females received nearly as much aid and care as they dispensed. These variations resulted from different patterns of within-race, cross-gender interactions. Black males and females aided one another reciprocally. However, White girls gave from 62 to 75 percent of help and 68 to 75 percent of care (depending on room) when interacting with White males.

Aggression

All Midwestern teachers forbade physical and verbal aggression, but each room had its share of pushings, name-callings, and hair-pullings. Depending on the room, from 58 to 89 percent of physical aggression involved males only. Black males were only slightly more likely than White males to be involved in these incidents. Less than 4 percent of physical aggression involved girls only. Thus, most physical aggression involving girls was cross-gender. Males initiated from 59 to 90 percent of physical aggression (depending on the room).

In most rooms Black girls were only slightly more likely than White girls to be involved in aggression, but the responses of Black girls were different. White girls usually backed down, complied, withdrew, or—very occasionally—complained to the teacher. Aggression or threats thus were used by other students to exercise power over them. Such tactics were less effective with

Black girls, who fought back verbally or physically against more than half the aggression they encountered. Their retaliation rate was far above the 14–25 percent rate for White girls in the six rooms, but far below that for boys of either race.

349

LINDA GRANT
Helpers, Enforcers,
and Go-Betweens:
Black Females in
Elementary School
Classrooms

Racist and Sexist Remarks

Black girls were the sole victims of the six racist remarks by White males recorded in five Midwestern rooms. A Black girl was the target of the only racist remark recorded in the Southern school. Although such remarks were rare, they were dramatic and captured the attention of all classroom actors when they occurred. Five of the six came in nearly identical circumstances. After the teacher had complimented a Black girl for her work, a White boy of lower achievement made a racist remark. Just after Avery's compliment to Diana (Black) for her work, Bruce (White) asked her, "When are you going to fatten up, like most Black ladies?" Black girls also were targets of four of eight sexist remarks, a slight overrepresentation.

The pattern seemed an example of what Schofield (1982) termed "appealing to one's strong suit." White boys, perhaps threatened by the Black girls' academic skills, appealed to their seemingly irrelevant statuses of whiteness and maleness to put Black females in their place. Thus, Black girls sometimes risked sanctions from peers for high academic achievement.

Overall, however, Black girls had more egalitarian peer relationships than did White girls. This might have resulted from teacher practices, norms that evolved among peers, or preschool socialization. The latter probably was the strongest influence, although this study cannot directly address the issue. Peers influenced Black girls to give aid and care, for example, by asking them to do so more often than other children. Peers were important supporters of the go-between role by looking to Black girls to take messages to teachers. Black girls' reputation among peers for not backing down probably contributed to successful performance of the enforcer role. The patterns also are consistent with themes in parental socialization of Black girls, including helping peers and fighting to protect one's interests. In these rooms peer interchanges, as well as teacher–student contact, put a premium on Black girls' social, rather than academic, skills.

IMPLICATIONS OF CLASSROOM ROLES

I have drawn a complex, not always consistent, portrait of Black girls' experiences in desegregated classrooms. Conclusions must be cautious, since I studied only a limited number of classrooms. Many of the issues raised—such as the genesis, prevalence, and maintenance of the go-between role—deserve further research attention.

This study provides evidence that Black girls' classroom roles differ from those of other children. In schools Black girls occupy a "place" that is established by the interaction of multiple forces, including parents, teachers, peers, and societal norms about appropriate roles for persons of certain race-gender statuses. The "place" Black girls occupy is, in Goffman's terms, "not a material thing to be possessed and then displayed" but, rather, "a pattern of appropriate conduct, coherent, embellished, and well articulated" (1959:75).

The roles probably contribute to classroom social order. The go-between, and to a lesser extent the helper and the enforcer, weave ties between many peers, enhancing social integration. The cost may be enhancement of social skills at the expense of academic development. While social skills sometimes give Black girls academic benefits (for example, placement in higher reading groups in doubtful cases), they are learning relational modes of achievement and social skills. In schools and societies that reward individual achievement, they may be disadvantaged in the long run.

Since my research to date has covered only the first and second grades, implications for adult roles are less clear. Emphasis on Black girls' social rather than academic skills, which occurs particularly in White-teacher classrooms, may point to a hidden cost of desegregation for Black females. Although they usually are the top students in all-Black rooms, they lose this position to White students in desegregated rooms. Their development seems to become less balanced, with emphasis on social skills. These skills assuredly are helpful in high-status adult roles, but the lesser attention to Black girls' academic work may discourage them from gaining credentials to enter such positions. Black girls' everyday schooling experiences seemingly do more to nudge them toward stereotypical roles of Black women than toward alternatives. These include serving others and maintaining peaceable ties among diverse persons rather than developing one's own skills.

Schools are by no means the only contributors to Black girls' socialization. There are important overlaps in Black girls' experiences in school and in other spheres of social life, such as parental socialization. Nonetheless, classroom life supports the channeling of Black girls toward stereotypical roles. This occurs through selective reinforcement of students' entering predispositions. Actions of teachers and peers, and responses of Black girls, seem only minimally influenced by students' abilities and aptitudes or by teacher ideologies. Rather, they are products of teachers' and students' transmission of societal expectations. Blocking infiltration of such expectations from society requires, first, a recognition of the subtle ways in which they filter into school life and, second, intervention in aspects of school life that limit rather than enhance options for students of all race-gender groups.

References

ALLEN, WALTER. 1979. "Family Occupational Status and Achievement Orientations Among Black Females in the U.S." *Signs* 4: 670–680.

BOWLES, SAMUEL, and HERBERT GINTIS. 1976. *Schooling in Capitalist America.* New York: Basic Books.

BYALICK, ROBERT, and DONALD BERSHOFF. 1974. "Reinforcement of Black and White Teachers in Integrated Classrooms." *Journal of Educational Psychology* 66: 473–480.

CHESLER, MARK, and WILLIAM CAVE. 1981. *A Sociology of Education: Access to Power and Privilege.* New York: Macmillan.

CRAIN, ROBERT, and RITA MAHARD. 1978. "Desegregation and Black Achievement: A Review of Research." *Law and Contemporary Society* 42: 17–56.

CRAIN, ROBERT, RITA MAHARD, and RUTH NAROT. 1982. *Making Desegregation Work: How Schools Create Social Climates.* Cambridge, Mass.: Ballinger.

351

*LINDA GRANT
Helpers, Enforcers,
and Go-Betweens:
Black Females in
Elementary School
Classrooms*

D'AMICO, SANDRA. 1986. "Cross-Group Opportunities: Impact on Interpersonal Relationships in Desegregated Middle Schools." *Sociology of Education* 59: 113–123.

DAVIS, ANGELA. 1971. "The Black Woman's Role in the Community of Slaves." *Black Scholar* 3(4):2–15.

DeVRIES, WILLIAM, and KEITH EDWARDS. 1977. "Student Teams and Learning Games: Their Effects on Cross-Sex Interaction." *Journal of Educational Psychology* 69: 337–343.

GOFFMAN, ERVING. 1959. *The Presentation of Self in Everyday Life.* Garden City, N.Y.: Anchor Doubleday.

GRANOVETTER, MARK. 1973. "The Strength of Weak Ties." *American Journal of Sociology* 78: 1360–1380.

GRANT, CARL, and CHRISTINE A. SLEETER. 1986. *After the School Bell Rings.* London: Falmer Press.

GRANT, LINDA. 1983. "Gender Roles and Status in Elementary Children's Peer Interactions." *Western Sociological Review* 14 (Fall): 58–76.

———. 1984. "Black Females' 'Place' in Desegregated Classrooms." *Sociology of Education* 57: 98–111.

———. 1985. "Race-Gender Status, System Attachment, and Children's Socialization in Desegregated Classrooms." Pp. 57–77 in *Gender Influences in Classroom Interaction,* edited by Louise Cherry Wilkinson and Cora Bagley Marrett. New York: Academic Press.

GUTTENTAG, MARCIA, and HELEN BRAG. 1976. *Undoing Sex Stereotypes.* New York: McGraw-Hill.

HARE, BRUCE. 1985. "Black Girls: A Comparative Study of Self-Perception and Academic Achievement by Race, Sex, and Socioeconomic Background." In *Beginnings: The Social and Affective Development of Black Children,* ed. Margaret B. Spencer et al. Hillsdale, N.J.: Erlbaum.

IRVINE, JACQUELINE JORDAN. 1985. "Teacher–Student Interactions: Effects of Student Race, Sex, and Grade Level." *Journal of Educational Psychology* 78: 14–21.

LADNER, JOYCE. 1971. *Tomorrow's Tomorrow: The Black Woman.* Garden City, N.Y.: Anchor Doubleday.

LEWIS, DIANA. 1975. "The Black Family: Socialization and Sex Roles." *Phylon* 36: 221–237.

LIGHTFOOT, SARA. 1979. *Worlds Apart: Relationships Between Families and Schools.* New York: Harper Colophon.

LUTTRELL, WENDY. 1989. "Working-Class Women's Ways of Knowing: Effects of Gender, Race, and Class." *Sociology of Education* 62: 33–46.

MURRAY, PAULE. 1975. "The Liberation of Black Women." Pp. 351–363 in *Women: A Feminist Perspective,* edited by Jo Freeman. Palo Alto, Calif.: Mayfield.

OGBU, JOHN. 1978. *Minorities and Caste.* New York: Academic Press.

PATCHEN, MARTIN. 1982. *Black-White Contact in Schools.* West Lafayette, Ind.: Purdue University Press.

REID, INEZ. 1972. *"Together" Black Women.* New York: Emerson Hall.

ROTHENBERG, JAMES. 1982. "Peer Interactions and Classroom Activity Structures." Ph.D. dissertation, University of Michigan.

SADKER, MYRA, and NANCY FRAZIER. 1973. *Sexism in School and Society.* New York: Harper & Row.

SCHOFIELD, JANET. 1982. *Black and White in School.* New York: Praeger.

SCOTT-JONES, DIANE, and MAXINE CLARK. 1986. "The School Experiences of Black Girls: The Interaction of Gender, Race, and Socioeconomic Status." *Phi Delta Kappan* 67: 520–526.

Ellen Neuborne

Imagine My Surprise

When my editor called me into his office and told me to shut the door, I was braced to argue. I made a mental note to stand my ground.

It was behind the closed door of his office that I realized I'd been programmed by the sexists.

We argued about the handling of one of my stories. He told me not to criticize him. I continued to disagree. That's when it happened.

He stood up, walked to where I was sitting. He completely filled my field of vision. He said, "Lower your voice when you speak to me."

And I did.

I still can't believe it.

This was not supposed to happen to me. I am the child of professional feminists. My father is a civil rights lawyer. My mother heads the NOW Legal Defense and Education Fund. She sues sexists for a living. I was raised on a pure, unadulterated feminist ethic.

That didn't help.

Looking back on the moment, I should have said, "Step back out of my face and we'll continue this discussion like humans."

I didn't.

I said, "Sorry."

Sorry!

I had no idea twenty-some years of feminist upbringing would fail me at that moment. Understand, it is not his actions I am criticizing; it is mine. He was a bully. But the response was my own. A man confronted me. My sexist programming kicked in. I backed off. I said, "Sorry."

I don't understand where the programming began. I had been taught that girls could do anything boys could do. Equality of the sexes was an unimpeachable truth. Before that day in the editor's office, if you'd asked me how I might handle such a confrontation, I never would have said, "I'd apologize."

I'm a good feminist. I would never apologize for having a different opinion.

352

But I did.

Programming. It is the subtle work of an unequal world that even the best of feminist parenting couldn't overcome. It is the force that sneaks up on us even as we think that we are getting ahead with the best of the guys. I would never have believed in its existence. But having heard it, amazingly, escape from my own mouth, I am starting to recognize its pattern.

When you are told you are causing trouble, and you regret having raised conflict, that's your programming.

When you keep silent, though you know the answer—programming.

When you do not take credit for your success, or you suggest that your part in it was really minimal—programming.

When a man tells you to lower your voice, and you do, and you apologize—programming.

The message of this programming is unrelentingly clear: Keep quiet.

I am a daughter of the movement. How did I fall for this?

I thought the battle had been won. I thought that sexism was a remote experience, like the Depression. Gloria had taken care of all that in the seventies.

Imagine my surprise.

And while I was blissfully unaware, the perpetrators were getting smarter.

What my mother taught me to look for—pats on the butt, honey, sweetie, cupcake, make me some coffee—are not the methods of choice for today's sexists. Those were just the fringes of what they were really up to. Sadly, enough of them have figured out how to mouth the words of equality while still behaving like pigs. They're harder to spot.

At my first newspaper job in Vermont, I covered my city's effort to collect food and money to help a southern town ravaged by a hurricane. I covered the story from the early fund-raising efforts right up to the day before I was to ride with the aid caravan down South. At that point I was taken off the story and it was reassigned to a male reporter. (It wasn't even his beat; he covered education.) It would be too long a drive for me, I was told. I wouldn't get enough sleep to do the story.

He may as well have said "beauty rest." But I didn't get it. At least not right away. He seemed, in voice and manner, to be concerned about me. It worked. A man got the big story. And I got to stay home. It was a classic example of a woman being kept out of a plum project "for her own good," yet while in the newsroom, hearing this explanation about sleep and long drives, I sat there nodding.

Do you think you would do better? Do you think you would recognize sexism at work immediately?

Are you sure?

Programming is a powerful thing. It makes you lazy. It makes you vulnerable. And until you can recognize that it's there, it works for the opposition. It makes you lower your voice.

It is a dangerous thing to assume that just because we were raised in a feminist era, we are safe. We are not. They are still after us.

And it is equally dangerous for our mothers to assume that because we are children of the movement, we are equipped to stand our ground. In many cases, we are unarmed.

The old battle strategies aren't enough, largely because the opposition is using new weaponry. The man in my office who made a nuisance of himself by asking me out repeatedly did so through the computer messaging system. Discreet. Subtle. No one to see him being a pig. Following me around would have been obvious. This way, he looked perfectly normal, and I constantly had to delete his overtures from my E-mail files. Mom couldn't have warned me about E-mail.

Then there is the danger from other women. Those at the top who don't mentor other women because if they made it on their own, so should subsequent generations. Women who say there is just one "woman's slot" at the top power level, and to get there you must kill off your female competition. Women who maintain a conspiracy of silence, refusing to speak up when they witness or even experience sexism, for fear of reprisals. These are dangers from within our ranks. When I went to work, I assumed other women were my allies.

Again, imagine my surprise.

I once warned a newly hired secretary that her boss had a history of discrimination against young women. She seemed intensely interested in the conversation at the time. Apparently as soon as I walked away, she repeated the entire conversation to her boss. My heart was in the right place. But my brain was not. Because, as I learned that day, sisterhood does not pay the bills. For younger women who think they do not need the feminist movement to get ahead, sisterhood is the first sentiment to fall by the wayside. In a world that looks safe, where men say all the right things and office policies have all the right words, who needs sisterhood?

We do. More than we ever have. Because they are smooth, because they are our bosses and control our careers, because they are hoping we will kill each other off so they won't have to bother. Because of all the subtle sexism that you hardly notice until it has already hit you. That is why you need the movement.

On days when you think the battle is over, the cause has been won, look around you to see what women today still face. The examples are out there.

On college campuses, there is a new game called rodeo. A man takes a woman back to his room, initiates sexual intercourse, and then a group of his friends barges in. The object of this game is for the man to keep his date pinned as long as possible.

Men are still afraid of smart women. When Ruth Bader Ginsburg was nominated to the Supreme Court, the *New York Times* described her as "a woman who handled her intelligence gracefully." The message: If you're smarter than the men around you, be sure to keep your voice down. Wouldn't want to be considered ungraceful.

A friend from high school calls to tell me he's getting married. He's found the perfect girl. She's bright, she's funny and she's willing to take his last name. That makes them less likely to get divorced, he maintains. "She's showing me she's not holding out."

In offices, women with babies are easy targets. I've seen the pattern played out over and over. One woman I know put in ten years with the company, but once she returned from maternity leave, she was marked. Every attempt to leave on time to pick up her baby at day care was chalked up as a "productivity problem." Every request to work part-time was deemed troublemaking. I sat just a few desks away. I witnessed her arguments. I heard the editors gossip when she was absent. One Monday we came into work and her desk had been cleaned out.

Another woman closer to my age also wanted to work part-time after the birth of her son. She was told that was unacceptable. She quit. There was no announcement. No good-bye party. No card for everyone in the office to sign. The week she disappeared from the office, we had a party for a man who was leaving to take a new job. We also were asked to contribute to a gift fund for another man who had already quit for a job in the Clinton administration.

But for the women with babies who were disappeared, nothing happened. And when I talked about the fact that women with babies tended to vanish, I was hauled into my boss' office for a reeducation session. He spent twenty minutes telling me what a great feminist he was and that if I ever thought differently, I should leave the company. No question about the message there: Shut up.

I used to believe that my feminist politics would make me strong. I thought strong thoughts. I held strong beliefs. I thought that would protect me. But all it did was make me aware of how badly I slipped when I lowered my voice and apologized for having a divergent opinion. For all my right thinking, I did not fight back. But I have learned something. I've learned it takes practice to be a strong feminist. It's not an instinct you can draw on at will—no matter how equality-minded your upbringing. It needs exercise. You have to think to know your own mind. You have to battle to work in today's workplace. It was nice to grow up thinking this was an equal world. But it's not.

I have learned to listen for the sound of my programming. I listen carefully for the *Sorrys,* the *You're rights.* Are they deserved? Or did I offer them up without thinking, as though I had been programmed? Have you? Are you sure?

I have changed my ways. I am louder and quicker to point out sexism when I see it. And it's amazing what you can see when you are not hiding behind the warm, fuzzy glow of past feminist victories. It does not make me popular in the office. It does not even make me popular with women. Plenty of my female colleagues would prefer I quit rocking the boat. One read a draft of this essay and suggested I change the phrase "fight back" to "stand my ground" in order to "send a better message."

But after falling for the smooth talk and after hearing programmed acquiescence spew from my mouth, I know what message I am trying to send: Raise your voice. And I am sending it as much to myself as to anyone else.

I've changed what I want from the women's movement. I used to think it was for political theory, for bigger goals that didn't include my daily life. When I was growing up, the rhetoric we heard involved the theory of equality: Were men and women really equal? Were there biological differences that made men superior? Could women overcome their stigma as "the weaker sex"? Was a woman's place really in the home?

These were ideas. Important, ground-breaking, mind-changing debates. But the feminism I was raised on was very cerebral. It forced a world full of people to change the way they think about women. I want more than their minds. I want to see them do it.

The theory of equality has been well fought for by our mothers. Now let's talk about how to talk, how to work, how to fight sexism here on the ground, in our lives. All the offices I have worked in have lovely, right-thinking policy statements. But the theory doesn't necessarily translate into action. I'm ready to take up that part of the battle.

I know that sitting on the sidelines will not get me what I want from my movement. And it is mine. Younger feminists have long felt we needed to be invited to our mothers' party. But don't be fooled into thinking that feminism is old-fashioned. The movement is ours and we need it.

I am one of the oldest of my generation, so lovingly dubbed "X" by a disdainful media. To my peers, and to the women who follow after me, I warn you that your programming is intact. Your politics may be staunchly feminist, but they will not protect you if you are passive.

Listen for the attacks. They are quiet. They are subtle.

And listen for the jerk who will tell you to lower your voice. Tell him to get used to the noise. The next generation is coming.

Yvonne Duffy

. . . *All Things Are Possible*

. . . As Differently Abled women in the latter part of the twentieth century, what can we do to support one another as we strive for self-actualization? How do we handicap ourselves and each other? What is our role in the women's movement? How do we fit into society as a whole?

I recently received in the mail a paper entitled "Disabled Women: Sexism Without the Pedestal" (Fine and Asch, 1981) in which the term "rolelessness" is used to describe the status of Differently Abled women in society. Whereas Differently Abled men have the choice of identifying either with their disability or with their maleness—a more positive image—according to the authors, women have no real option, since both identities are seen as equally powerless. To what extent is this true?

Because of her specific physical condition (systemic lupus), Dahtee sometimes must use a wheelchair and at other times can walk unassisted; from this unique vantage point, she has been able to study how the same persons' attitudes toward her changed according to whether she was Differently Abled or able-bodied:

> Before I was disabled, I was always very popular . . . very strong personality, infectious laugh, good listener as well as a good talker, and I knew how people responded to me then. . . . And then, when I was disabled, I went through these amazing realizations of how people treat disabled people. . . . I was always so used to people being respectful of my intelligence and my knowledge, and suddenly, I had people leaning down and slowly articulating into my face, "Are you all right, dear?" type of things. . . . I was not allowed to be respected. . . . I did not feel that anybody could see any of the beauty in me.

With nothing else changed but her legs' physical ability to carry her around, Dahtee's status vacillated between that of a pretty, well-educated, young woman and a mentally impaired illiterate. She was fortunate in possessing a strong sense of self. For those of us whose egos may not have been so fully developed when we became Differently Abled or who have faced this

357

kind of oppression since early childhood, finding suitable roles is bound to be more difficult, however. For example, Connie L. stated,

> I have no role in society and feel really rotten about it . . . this is perhaps the hardest and most devastating question . . . because it has forced me to confront myself and how I have allowed myself to diminish to a point where I hardly feel I exist anymore.

Anet emphasized that we must make an effort toward self-determination:

> One thing that is disturbing to me is how easy it is for people with disabilities to give up their right to make their own decisions and to control their own lives. Somehow, we are convinced very early in our disability, whether the disability occurs to us as a child or in mid-adulthood, . . . that we are totally dependent, helpless, and this is just not true. . . .
>
> Eight years of isolation in San Francisco taught me how easy it is to get into an attitude of helplessness, of just deciding that there is no cure for the situation of isolation. It takes a lot more aggressiveness and assertiveness than we really want to have, to get out and be a member of society, to find answers for our needs. They just don't exist at home. . . . If I want to take a class in art, I should be able to do that and not just say, "Well, it's too much of a hassle to cope with transportation getting there. . . ." We just have to fight the ease with which we can slip into an apathetic state, so it entails changes in behavior patterns that many times create problems.

There is an interesting parallel here in the dependent wife who relies on her husband to make all her decisions, to supply her with opinions on all major issues, and, in fact, to define her world for her. Sanctioned by a large segment of society, this cocoon type of existence becomes more and more comfortable as one relinquishes her mind and heart to the control of another, and this can be a very difficult mold from which to break away.

Taking responsibility for one's own life is risky; one may make poor decisions and have to live with them without shifting blame to anyone else; one may be faced with tremendous challenges, physically, mentally, and spiritually.

What are the rewards? To determine one's own existence can be exciting. The book from which this article is taken could never have been written, for example, if twelve years ago, I had not relinquished my easy, dependent existence with an aunt and uncle to try living independently in Ann Arbor. It has not been easy, and I still don't feel quite as self-determining as Colleen Moore, a California paraplegic, who said, "I know I can create the events of my life as I wish." But I continue to grow more self-reliant even as my physical abilities weaken, because independence is a state of mind, not a state of body, and even my worst days are better than those comfortable eons I passed doing nothing more strenuous than crocheting and watching T.V.

Do we take a back seat to Differently Abled men? Thinking back over the years to the numerous committees, boards, task forces, etc., on which I have served with other Differently Abled persons, the most vocal, the most assertive, the most adamant about the need for change, I recall, have been women. This trend appears to be continuing in the younger generation; one of my helpers, who served at a camp for Differently Abled children last summer, observed that the female children were usually the most assertive.

Women have emerged as early leaders in the struggle for equality waged by other minorities. Harriet Tubman and other black women who risked their lives daily so that others could take the Underground Railroad to freedom come first to mind. Perhaps those who suffer double oppression are first to recognize the necessity of liberation and, being already at the bottom of the totem pole, have the least to risk by speaking against the system.

As many of us become leaders and spokeswomen in our movement for equal rights, what can we do to support each other as we all seek the roles, traditional or non-traditional, best suited to us? Anet and Lola expressed their thoughts on this subject:

> There really needs to be more thought put into how disabled people can become independent. And there has to be more discussion of philosophy of independence that is not connected at all with the number of things a person has to be dependent upon. That is, independence really starts within you. . . .
>
> I've known many attendant/disabled person relationships that I would call very unsatisfactory because the disabled person doesn't think of the attendant as an employee but . . . as a caretaker or parent figure, getting back to the opposition between philosophies of self-reliance and caretaking. These are two philosophies that are directed at the disabled, and I don't think [she] is getting enough of the self-reliance philosophy. . . .
>
> We need to counsel newly disabled and children who are disabled on self-reliance and decision-making in evaluating where we are in life and what our status is in connection with the rest of society and learning how to improve it.
>
> [Lola] would like to see more handicapped people in the various media, more active, less stereotyped portrayal . . . not just as main characters but also . . . supporting roles, bit parts—how about a handicapped secretary or neighbor, a handicapped woman sitting in a bar or restaurant that the main character walks into.
>
> Also, it has occurred to me that I've never seen a handicapped person on a game show. Do they think we don't like money? . . . I've never seen anyone handicapped doing a commercial. We buy all that stuff too.

Certainly, economic pressure is a valid tool, used with varying success by other minorities. Two things are important to remember when boycotting products and services to protest discrimination. First, sufficient numbers of persons must participate in order to make a financial impact; so it is a good idea to enlist the support of relatives, friends, and classmates, etc. Second, the proprietors should be informed of the reasons you and others are boycotting them as well as the changes you expect them to make.

How do we further handicap each other in our mutual struggle for full acceptance? Although stereotyping, a natural strategy we all use to put some order into a chaotic world, does not have to be prejudicial, it all too often locks us into others' expectations of us. It is essential that we examine our own attitudes regarding persons with other specific physical conditions to be sure that we are not hindering them from attaining their full potential.

Dahtee related her growth in self-awareness upon suddenly becoming Differently Abled:

> I remember being just amazed when I realized my own stereotypes and my own prejudices against disabled people. That was the greatest learning experience for me when . . . I realized that . . . here I was sitting in a wheelchair with

my own personal problems, and I knew nothing about the deaf world. I knew nothing about the blind world—cerebral palsy scared me to death—wouldn't allow myself to give them the intelligence that I so wanted people to give me.

She went on to explain how her world expanded as she overcame her bigotry:

I've gotten very involved with sign language, in going for my certification as an interpreter because one of the men that I met and became sweethearts with was a deaf man . . . so I began using sign on a daily level for communication . . . because I was seeing him all the time, and I began to really respect this beautiful language system, with the beautiful, honest concepts and grammar—everything about it.

Patting ourselves on the back because we are farther along the road to independence than others with similar physical conditions is a form of snobbery we can all do without, for, certainly, in diminishing the accomplishments of others, we diminish ourselves. Expressing how she felt about this tendency was Rebecca Burns:

I bitterly hate the feeling of stigma I have among other handicapped people because I live with my mother. I feel that they think I'm backward, and I hate the feeling of having less confidence in some ways than some of my peers.

Several respondents felt alienated from the women's movement. Having suffered more serious discrimination as a result of being Differently Abled than being women, they thought that most feminists neither understood nor even acknowledged this problem. Mary James said,

Disabled women are the symbol of the most major form of "oppressed people" in this country, but I don't feel the women's movement is doing any recognizing of this. I am definitely a feminist but have no allegiance with women's groups. Their . . . problems seem so trivial as compared to those of the disabled women.

Michelle felt "left out. . . . I am a feminist—radical probably—but I see that as a separate part of my life from disability . . . there is no arm of the movement concerned about disabled women." Deena remarked, "We do fit in but only on the outside like some sort of mascot."

Personally, I feel that there is little genuine concern displayed for Differently Abled women except by some lesbians in the women's movement. Besides being more conscious of the sexual myths and taboos that can hurt us all, lesbians often seem more politically aware of other minority movements than other feminists. The Michigan Women's Music Festival stands as an illustration of how we can be accommodated at meetings and gatherings with minimal financial expense when planners are sensitive to our needs and creative about meeting them.

The following women discussed the discrimination we face and how they felt the women's movement was benefiting us:

Connie L. described the evolution of her thinking about our relationship to the women's movement:

At first, though I've always considered myself a supporter of the feminist movement, I felt rather isolated from it. I could understand their outrage at being judged wholly or primarily on the basis of their sex, but my problem was having people recognize that I had a sex.

As time went on though, I felt disabled women fit well into the women's movement. The need to fit into a particular mold in order to be considered a "real woman" was lessened by the movement . . . a sensitizing of men, a reevaluation of what they considered important in a woman and a relationship, couldn't help but make life better for disabled women. And, of course, the more wide open the choice of life styles, the better it is for us highly "irregular" types; so I think disabled women could not only benefit from the changes but have a lot to offer in helping to bring them about.

Jenny Jones, a paraplegic since birth, spoke.

We, in a way, have a double problem. Once you buck the disability, then you're next bucking the fact that you're a woman. I don't think I've had the discrimination because I'm a woman because they never saw beyond the disability, which may also be the factor in the fact that they don't know you.

Added Martha Merriweather,

We have to fight architectural barriers, attitudinal barriers, employment barriers . . . in addition to all that, we're also women. I think this takes a great deal of endurance, stamina, determination, but I intend to pursue it to the best of my abilities. I have wondered when I receive my degree in journalism, where I will go from there. Will I be accepted even though I am handicapped? I would hope that my personality is strong enough, that my skills are sharp enough, . . . that I am going to get the job that I want when the time comes.

Carol Sea, a social worker, thought the women's movement had been especially beneficial to us by helping others

realize that individuals should do the jobs that they are best at doing rather than doing jobs that they think they are supposed to do. In other words, because of the shift in the emphasis of women being homemakers, . . . in my relationship with my partner, I can go out and earn money at an intellectual job . . . and my partner could stay home and do the manual stuff.

Mae Evans summarized,

Before I was disabled, I had a comfortable identity as a wife, mother, and community leader. . . . I thought "women's rights" were for others who had not lucked into a good life situation. After paraplegia, things were different. I lost my comfortable identity because I could no longer function in that role. I had to find some other way to operate, but there was no other way because I was no longer able to do the things that a female person "does" to be worthwhile. When I went into therapy for postparaplegia depression, I became angry that the depression was not caused by the leg loss; it was caused by my original low self-esteem which prevented me from accepting leg loss. I discovered that I had been a victim of cultural attitudes on women and didn't even know it.

Disabled women can learn from the women's movement how they have been held back by things other than their own disabilities. We may not be able to improve our personal physical situation, but we can change how we and others feel about our being women.

Reciprocal relationships in which we are able to give as well as receive are generally more satisfying, and this is no less so in our liaison with the women's movement. Pooh Grayson noted,

> Disabled women are good problem-solvers, good managers, and have endless determination, or they don't survive. Those of us who have made a life of our own would be a great asset to the women's movement.

Mae Evans went a step further:

> Able-bodied women can learn from the disabled, who have had to learn this before they can truly cope, that the physical body is not as important as the person who lives inside; that one is first, a person and second, a female; that sex is less important than sexuality, and individuality is more important than these two; and that every woman who is honestly involved in her own personal growth is making a contribution to the women's movement whether she is aware of it or not.

What were the major concerns of the Differently Abled women in this study? Certainly, the desires they expressed, financial and emotional security, sexual happiness, barrier-free access to the community, and legal rights, are no different than those of most able-bodied women. Overwhelming all other concerns, however, even when they appeared to be talking about something else, has been the need to be fully accepted as women rather than as asexual objects of pity. Sally Smith related:

> I am new in the community . . . , and I'm also newly married. One of my bigger concerns is that I be accepted as one of the housewives . . . rather than a poor disabled female . . . I do not want this type of concern/sympathy, and I find it very difficult to become one of the girls. In fact, it has been impossible so far. . . . I would like to be more a person—me, Sally Smith, the person—rather than me, that poor girl in the wheelchair.

Woodie stressed:

> First and foremost, I want people to know that I'm a person regardless of whether I have a disability. I have wants and needs and fears; I'm happy and I'm sad just like anybody else. I'm not immune to feelings and because I do have feelings I am a person. . . .
>
> Secondly, I'm a woman. I do consider myself liberated—if not physically liberated, legally liberated, . . . spiritually liberated. Being a woman is very important to me. . . .
>
> Last but by no means least, I am a disabled woman. That also brings with it a few added concerns, but my disability is *not* the biggest most important thing in my life. I do not want people to judge me simply because I am disabled.

Woodie would probably agree with Martha Merriweather, who said,

> I love people who accept me for what I am—people who forget the fact that I'm in a wheelchair and will bring a chair to the table at dinner for me and then apologize and say, "Oh gee, I forgot." I find that extremely complimentary.

Indeed it is. My ideal person will do whatever is necessary to help me function independently, then, will forget about my specific physical condition and treat me as me—lover, friend, writer, or whatever I am in relation to that person.

When *we* can forget about being Differently Abled, I am convinced that it helps others to do so. Forgetting about it does not mean being passive or giving up the fight for accessible buildings and transportation, equal opportunities for employment, and legal rights. On the contrary, we must become even more assertive about obtaining these; having them will render us more independent and, thus, make it easier to concentrate on others rather than on ourselves and our limitations. Being more creative in finding new methods of doing things may help us forget about it for longer periods of time. Becoming better organized in daily activities may mean less time with an attendant; everyone needs some time alone every day to think and dream.

Most of all, forgetting the specific physical condition does not mean ignoring or failing to accept its existence. The period of solitude each day is particularly essential in truly coming to grips with it, for in really accepting the limitations, whatever they may be, while still striving to realize one's full endowment lies the key to full personhood.

Becoming a full person and not just *"a poor girl"* is not easy; it takes a lot of effort, but then most worthwhile achievements do. In closing, Elizabeth Mark and Deena gave us a glimpse of the rewards. Elizabeth Mark says,

> I love so much. There is not much I hate. Maybe other women who are disabled will realize, as I did, that there is love in our world—you just have to push yourself to your potential.

Deena contributed:

> I don't have any more hates since I just made the miraculous discovery that I accept myself as what I am, and I am loved more for the right reasons because of this discovery.

Ursula K. Le Guin

The Space Crone

The menopause is probably the least glamorous topic imaginable; and this is interesting, because it is one of the very few topics to which cling some shreds and remnants of taboo. A serious mention of menopause is usually met with uneasy silence; a sneering reference to it is usually met with relieved sniggers. Both the silence and the sniggering are pretty sure indications of taboo.

Most people would consider the old phrase "change of life" a euphemism for the medical term "menopause," but I, who am now going through the change, begin to wonder if it isn't the other way round. "Change of life" is too blunt a phrase, too factual. "Menopause," with its chime-suggestion of a mere pause after which things go on as before, is reassuringly trivial.

But the change is not trivial, and I begin to wonder how many women are brave enough to carry it out whole-heartedly. They give up their reproductive capacity with more or less of a struggle, and when it's gone they think that's all there is to it. Well, at least I don't get the Curse any more, they say, and the only reason I felt so depressed sometimes was hormones. Now I'm myself again. But this is to evade the real challenge, and to lose, not only the capacity to ovulate, but the opportunity to become a Crone.

In the old days women who survived long enough to attain the menopause more often accepted the challenge. They had, after all, had practice. They had already changed their life radically once before, when they ceased to be virgins and became mature women/wives/matrons/mothers/mistresses/whores/etc. This change involved not only the physiological alterations of puberty—the shift from barren childhood to fruitful maturity—but a socially recognized alteration of being: a change of condition from the sacred to the profane.

With the secularisation of virginity now complete, so that the once awesome term "virgin" is now a sneer or at best a slightly dated word for a person who hasn't copulated yet, the opportunity of gaining or regaining the dangerous/sacred condition-of-being at the Second Change has ceased to be apparent.

Virginity is now a mere preamble or waiting-room to be got out of as soon as possible; it is without significance. Old age is similarly a waiting-room, where you go after life's over and wait for cancer or a stroke. The years before and after the menstrual years are vestigial: the only meaningful condition left to women is that of fruitfulness. Curiously, this restriction of significance coincided with the development of chemicals and instruments which make fertility itself a meaningless or at least secondary characteristic of female maturity. The significance of maturity now is not the capacity to conceive but the mere ability to have sex. As this ability is shared by pubescents and by postclimacterics, the blurring of distinctions and elimination of opportunities is almost complete. There are no rites of passage, because there is no significant change. The Triple Goddess has only one face: Marilyn Monroe's, maybe. The entire life of a woman from 10 or 12 through 70 or 80 has become secular, uniform, changeless. As there is no longer any virtue in virginity, so there is no longer any meaning in menopause. It requires fanatical determination now to become a Crone.

Women have thus, by imitating the life-condition of men, surrendered a very strong position of their own. Men are afraid of virgins, but they have a cure for their own fear and the virgin's virginity: fucking. Men are afraid of crones, so afraid of them that their cure for virginity fails them; they know it won't work. Faced with the fulfilled Crone, all but the bravest men wilt and retreat, crestfallen and cockadroop.

Menopause Manor is not merely a defensive stronghold, however. It is a house or household, fully furnished with the necessities of life. In abandoning it, women have narrowed their domain and impoverished their souls. There are things the Old Woman can do, say, and think which the Woman cannot do, say, or think. The Woman has to give up more than her menstrual periods before she can do, say, or think them. She has got to change her life.

The nature of that change is now clearer than it used to be. Old age is not virginity, but a third and new condition: the virgin must be celibate, but the crone need not. There was a confusion there, which the separation of female sexuality from reproductive capacity, via modern contraceptives, has cleared up. Loss of fertility does not mean loss of desire and fulfillment. But it does entail a change, a change involving matters even more important—if I may venture a heresy—than sex.

The woman who is willing to make that change must become pregnant with herself, at last. She must bear herself, her third self, her old age, with travail and alone. Not many will help her with that birth. Certainly no male obstetrician will time her contractions, inject her with sedatives, stand ready with forceps, and neatly stitch up the torn membranes. It's hard even to find an old-fashioned midwife, these days. That pregnancy is long, that labor is hard. Only one is harder, and that's the final one, the one which men also must suffer and perform.

It may well be easier to die if you have already given birth to others or yourself, at least once before. This would be an argument for going through all the discomfort and embarrassment of becoming a Crone. Anyhow it seems a pity to have a built-in rite of passage and to dodge it, evade it, and pretend nothing has changed. That is to dodge and evade one's womanhood, to pretend one's like a man. Men, once initiated, never get the second chance. They never change again. That's their loss, not ours. Why borrow poverty?

Certainly the effort to remain unchanged, young, when the body gives so impressive a signal of change as the menopause, is gallant; but it is a stupid, self-sacrificial gallantry, better befitting a boy of twenty than a woman of forty-five or fifty. Let the athletes die young and laurel-crowned. Let the soldiers earn the Purple Hearts. Let women die old, white-crowned, with human hearts.

If a space ship came by from the friendly natives of the fourth planet of Altair, and the polite captain of the space ship said, "We have room for one passenger; will you spare us a single human being, so that we may converse at leisure during the long trip back to Altair, and learn from an exemplary person the nature of the race?"—I suppose what most people would want to do is provide them with a fine, bright, brave young man, highly educated and in peak physical condition. A Russian cosmonaut would be ideal (American astronauts are mostly too old). There would surely be hundreds, thousands of volunteers, just such young men, all worthy. But I would not pick any of them. Nor would I pick any of the young women who would volunteer, some out of magnanimity and intellectual courage, others out of a profound conviction that Altair couldn't possibly be any worse for a woman than Earth is.

What I would do is go down to the local Woolworth's, or the local village marketplace, and pick an old woman, over sixty, from behind the costume jewelry counter or the betel-nut booth. Her hair would not be red or blonde or lustrous dark, her skin would not be dewy fresh, she would not have the secret of eternal youth. She might, however, show you a small snapshot of her grandson, who is working in Nairobi. She is a bit vague about where Nairobi is, but extremely proud of the grandson. She has worked hard at small, unimportant jobs all her life, jobs like cooking, cleaning, bringing up kids, selling little objects of adornment or pleasure to other people. She was a virgin once a long time ago, and then a sexually potent fertile female, and then went through menopause. She has given birth several times and faced death several times— the same times. She is facing the final birth/death a little more nearly and clearly every day now. Sometimes her feet hurt something terrible. She never was educated to anything like her capacity, and that is a shameful waste and a crime against humanity, but so common a crime should not and cannot be hidden from Altair. And anyhow she's not dumb. She has a stock of sense, wit, patience, and experiential shrewdness, which the Altaireans might, or might not, perceive as wisdom. If they are wiser than we, then of course we don't know how they'd perceive it. But if they are wiser than we they may know how to perceive that inmost mind and heart which we, working on mere guess and hope, proclaim to be humane. In any case, since they are curious and kindly, let's give them the best we have to give.

The trouble is, she will be very reluctant to volunteer. "What would an old woman like me do on Altair?" she'll say. "You ought to send one of those scientist men, they can talk to those funny-looking green people. Maybe Dr. Kissinger should go. What about sending the Shaman?" It will be very hard to explain to her that we want her to go because only a person who has experienced, accepted, and acted the entire human condition—the essential quality

of which is Change—can fairly represent humanity. "Me?" she'll say, just a trifle slyly. "But I never did anything."

But it won't wash. She knows, though she won't admit it, that Dr. Kissinger has not gone and will never go where she has gone, that the scientists and the shamans have not done what she has done. Into the space ship, Granny.

Confronting Ageism:
A MUST for Mental Health

Old age crept upon me and caught me unawares.

Like most women, I had never thought about my own growing old. When I was young I felt invincible. In my 30's I was too busy struggling through my life to think about any future. I do remember thinking longingly of "retirement" but that was because I didn't like my life very much and felt powerless to change it.

In my 40's and 50's, with my life exploding in many new directions, I felt, in my heart of hearts, that I was beating the clock. I first began my college education at age 43 and not too long thereafter got divorced after some 22 years of marriage. I continued and finished my undergraduate work while my only child was herself away at college. Deciding to go for broke, at 47 I left Southern California where I had lived most of my adult life to go to graduate school in Ohio, and at 54 I finally got a Ph.D. in clinical psychology. At 50 I made another drastic life change when I fell in love with a woman and came out as a lesbian.

With so much going on for me, I did not feel in sync with my peers and fooled myself into thinking, when I thought of age at all, that it was "a state of mind," nothing else. The experience of being out of sync was, in fact, what felt most familiar.

My mother, father, and I arrived in this country from Poland in 1923. Within six months my father died, and at age 24 my mother was left alone without any close family to raise a two year old child. I started kindergarten not knowing a word of English, and my sense of shame and alienation was more profound when my first name was arbitrarily changed by the school registrar. My own name was too "foreign" sounding; thus Sheva became Evelyn.

Although almost all immigrants were poor, we were in an especially impoverished category. At the height of the Great Depression when my mother got sick and could no longer bring home even the four dollars a week she was earning we were forced to go on county welfare to survive.

I was out of sync even as a Jewish child raised in a Jewish ghetto, for my mother was a revolutionary and an atheist. I was the only child I knew who ate bread on Pessach (Passover), and who "on principle" did not say aloud the Pledge of Allegiance to a government which hypocritically claimed to be for liberty and justice for all, while favoring the rich at the expense of the poor. At five I proudly marched with my mother, a garment worker, on my first picket line. I clearly remember running with her down an alley to escape the Philadelphia mounted police, who, with horses rearing and stomping, charged into the picket line of mostly women and children in an attempt to break the strike. By age eleven I was a seasoned Junior Pioneer leader wearing my red bandanna and marching in picket lines and May Day Parades. From the rebellious tom boy to the high school rebel, I was an "expert" in knowing what it felt like to be other than the mainstream, while at the same time having a strong sense of place and solidarity with my own political comrades.

The closest I came to being mainstream was when I finally got my Ph.D., but by then I was an "out" lesbian and feminist—both of which did not exactly clothe me in respectability.

Surely then, with all of my previous experience of otherness, I could be expected to make a relatively easy transition to the otherness experienced so acutely by old women. Absolutely not so. I continued through my 50's steadfast in my delusion that age, *my* age, was irrelevant. More and more in social circles I experienced myself as the "older" woman in the group, but coming out as a lesbian at 50 and having a wonderfully exciting decade only promoted my sense of myself as an exception. It is true that I began to fret about my outward appearance more than I ever had. The wrinkles, loose flesh, the changes in my body left me worried and split. How could my body feel so charged and sexual, my self be so full of plans and dreams and energy, while at the same time it was registering the signs of growing old? Although I never dyed my hair, by now a lovely steel gray, I did seriously consider a face lift. Only at the last minute did I acknowledge to myself that it would take more than surgery to help me resolve my internal split about my own aging.

My growing external change of status forced my growing internal discomfort to reach more conscious levels. My first intimations of what age stereotyping was all about occurred when I moved into a new community and was shocked to find myself addressed by younger people, with the ritual respect reserved for—not Mother—but Grandmother, at a time when my own grandchild had not yet been born. I began to work only part time and this meant increasing isolation from colleagues and work-related sources of respect. I found also that younger professionals who were meeting me for the first time and knew that I too was a professional assumed a respectful rather than collegial stance, while those who knew nothing about me most often ignored me completely.

My own mother and step-father, now in their early 80's, seemed to be having increasing health difficulties, but I must admit, strange as that seems to me now, I simply did not pay much attention and blithely assumed that they would go on as always, at least until some far-off future. My world changed radically and shockingly when my step-father died unexpectedly after surgery, leaving my mother alone, in failing health and total panic. Suddenly I found myself solely and increasingly responsible for my mother's care, a task which took enormous energy and struggle.

When she died some two years later at age 85, no amount of preparation helped me to experience my new position in the world, feeling orphaned at 63! I became the oldest living member of my very small family. In a way I could not foresee I was catapulted into an active awareness of my own mortality, my own vulnerability, myself as an old woman.

There ensued a series of struggles and learnings which I think are relatively typical, though at the time I thought were unique. The invisibility I experienced as an old woman felt much different from all the experiences of otherness I had ever known. Being subject to special oppression was certainly familiar enough. What was different this time, however, was how I felt inside as I experienced this oppression. Whatever fear I had experienced in being "other" throughout my life, I had always felt a core of strength and pride in who I was and what I stood for—in my poor and working class background, my Jewishness, my atheism, my foreignness, my political radicalism, my being a girl, a woman, a lesbian. Now, I was attempting to deny my otherness by denying my own aging, a denial that masked the tremendous fear I felt about being an old woman, about being "over the hill," for I had internalized the ageist stereotype that my life was all but over and I did not want it to be! Neither did I want to be part of a group stigmatized as ineffectual, useless, ugly, asexual, whining, passive, lifeless, sick, dependent, powerless—the antithesis of everything I had tried to be and make of my life.

What a dilemma: hating and dreading what being old represented, while each year becoming more clearly identifiably old. All I really wanted was to hold back the clock by some magical act of will. Truth is, I think I tried that—for a while convincing myself that if only I exercised the right way, ate the right food, lived the right kind of pure and glowing life, I would "beat" old age. I never, as yet, questioned the validity of my ageist assumptions. My fears were reinforced by watching my mother grow old and die, an old age that was full of denial and fear of the changes occurring in her body and her life, and rage at what she considered the whittling away of her self and the ending of a life that felt unfulfilled.

Looking back on that time, only now can I see how hard I was working to deny my feelings and my confusion. It was, of course, not possible to deal with a problem that I refused to identify, for I was doing what all oppressed groups try to do; I was trying to pass—to myself at least. Knowing that I felt inside a continuity with the person I always was, instead of realizing that growing old does not mean dropping off a precipice, I decided I felt "young" inside. But no matter how automatic and unconscious this universal practice of passing for younger is, it remains a deeply alienating experience. Begging the question, refusing to acknowledge my age did nothing but rob me of the core of strength I needed to sustain and guide me through this great life change, crossing the bridge between mid-life and old.

Finally, the reality of my life forced me to go beyond denial and into acknowledging and coping somehow with my unaccustomed and unwanted status of being an old woman. In the beginning of this struggle I found myself wavering between rage—at the patronizing dismissals meted out to me in many different forms, and anxiety and foreboding about my future.

Having just turned 70, I can look at my last decade and chart my progress to a rich and rewarding old age. I am able to view my own process within the context of the political, not simply the personal. This pushes me to share my experience in the hope that it can be useful to other women learning to grow up to be old. But although I think the issue has universal significance, denial about the process is so ingrained that it seems somewhat daring, even brave, to speak in detail about my own struggles to explore the dimensions of being an old woman. For the most part, neither books nor songs are written about the every day, heroic and ordinary lives of old women. Talk about being old by the old is a conversational taboo. Interestingly, only young and mid-life women feel free to speak easily and insultingly of their dread of coming into my time of life.

I owe a huge debt to Barbara Macdonald and the book she wrote with Cynthia Rich, *Look Me In The Eye—Old Women Aging and Ageism* (1991). When I read and reread this book I felt a profound and exhilarating relief. For in writing about her own life Macdonald had also named my experience and made me feel sane, less alone and less fearful. It reminds me of the excitement of discovery we women experienced in the early days of the women's movement when we learned through our consciousness raising groups as nothing else could teach us, that what was happening in our lives was not a matter of individual flaw or problem but a common experience of oppression.

So, too, has this time of my life been a sorting, testing, learning, both as I become more mindful and attentive to my own experience and as I share with other old women and learn from our common experience. Yet this ongoing process is complex and I often feel muddled and overwhelmed. When that happens, I long to find some systematic simple way, because I am that kind of a person, to categorize and define the various components of my experience.

Am I dealing, in any given instance, with the ageism, sexism, heterosexism, or anti-semitism of our society? Am I being "too" sensitive? Certainly as an old Jewish lesbian I can expect to and mostly do get treated in certain predictable ways in our oppressive mainstream culture, but my dismay is more acute when I experience the same slights, the same invisibility in my own special lesbian and feminist community. Since old women, lesbian or heterosexual, are invisible in our society, it is easy to grow used to that condition and sometimes the only clue I have that I am in the world but not part of it is an uneasy delayed reaction I have to my own invisibility. It is not always clear at first.

Or am I dealing not just with external ageism but a response that arises from my own internalized ageism, buttressed by the sexist and heterosexist models of aging I have from my mother and her generation?

Or, finally, can I trust that my response is actually coming from inside me, from my own body of life experience?

Sometimes there seems almost no area of behavior and emotion in which I can totally trust my first reaction. In almost every part of my life I am forced again and again to examine my ageist expectations, not because I necessarily want to do so from some intellectual curiosity, but because if I do not do this, false expectations and assumptions cloud and diminish my ability to actually experience my life.

I think often of the most important model I've had—my own mother and her unfulfilled old age. I have to remind myself that her life and my life have been vastly different, that the times in which we both lived, the options we had and choices we made were vastly different. I remind myself also of the research that points out that in old age there is greater heterogeneity than at any other developmental stage, which provides even less basis for the existing stereotypes about old women. Yet these cultural assumptions harden into oppressive dogmas. Ageism, primarily a woman's issue, is the extension of the sexism, heterosexism, racism, and rampant consumerism of our multi-corporate society. Old women, outliving men in greater numbers, have lost their special capacity for service to the patriarchy. They no longer function as ornaments, lovers, domestics, bearers and rearers of children, or as economic drudges in the work place. To quote Copper (1988), "The ageism which old women experience is firmly embedded in sexism, an extension of the male power to define, control values, erase, disempower and divide."

The expressions of ageism are many. A core area of my ongoing examination of my own aging is my self and my relationship to my body. This is a most complex relationship, encompassing issues of illness and wellness, fear of incapacity and actual disability, loss of independence and acceptance of interdependence, the intricate relationship of my body and appearance to my sense of self and self-esteem, my own standards and politics of beauty, and more. The interrelationship and the complexity of all of these issues make them difficult to untangle. I find comfort in reminding myself that I am not dealing with trivialities but with the core issues that we all face throughout our entire lives. The fear of aging, reaching phobic proportions among white skinned women of European background, has grave repercussions for women as they experience their own aging. My greater urgency to confront these issues is my conviction that my health, well being and life itself rest on finding my way through the swamp of the ageist myths and assumptions.

My appearance was the first indicator I could see of my own aging. The face lift that I didn't get compelled me instead to examine my assumptions about beauty and appearance. It forced me to begin specifically to confront the basic assumption underlying ageism, that youth is good, desirable, and beautiful; old age is bad, repulsive and ugly. Otherwise every time I look in the mirror I must feel contempt and aversion for how I look, or avoid looking altogether because, by patriarchal standards of beauty, I will find no beauty there. The most frequent "compliment" given to old women is "you don't look your age." Consider for a moment that what is really being said is that if you did look your age you would look ugly. There is an erosion of the self which occurs when who you are is everywhere made synonymous with unattractiveness and undesirability.

I was thrilled to read Cynthia Rich's article on Ageism and the Politics of Beauty (1988), which challenges us to look at how we arrive at our ideas about beauty and to reconsider the "mysteries of attraction." For unless we examine these "mysteries" we may well exclude, to our impoverishment, whole categories of women as attractive, particularly those who are disabled or old. Rich says, "Our task is to learn, not to look insultingly beyond these features to a soul we can celebrate, but instead to look at these bodies as parts of these souls—exciting, individual, beautiful."

My first big stretch then was to examine my own conditioned notions and reconsider more open ways to experience beauty. Most helpful to me in this process is the greater reliance I have been developing on my own senses, rather than on preconceived ideas. Skin that is old and wrinkled is soft and lovely, and as I touch my own skin and that of my lover I feel deep pleasure. Letting go more and more of my conditioning makes it possible for me to look with a clearer more loving vision at myself and the other old women around me. A shift, not yet complete, is taking place.

My relationship to my body has always been somewhat problematic. I have lived much of my life in my head and was trained, even more so than most women, to ignore my body's demands either for rest or attention. With growing psychological sophistication I talked about and regularly included in my practice as a therapist the notion of making friends with one's body. However, outside of sporadic frenzied efforts, I myself continued largely to ignore my body, and seemed to be able to do so with impunity since for the most part I was blessed with good health.

But starting in my 60's, my body no longer permits me to ignore her; she has begun to speak most loudly on her own behalf. Although I've always eaten too quickly and too much, for the first time I began to develop digestive problems. My vision, even with glasses, has become strained, and I've had laser surgery for glaucoma in both eyes. I have found that it takes me longer to recuperate, either after hard work or a transient illness, and I get downright cranky with insufficient rest. In other words, my body is showing some wear and tear after a long and arduous life. Certainly an acceptable proposition in a sane society and one that can be lived with, particularly since so many of us have paid such lip service to the need for women to attend to ourselves and our bodies with kindness and care, not only to others.

But in our culture, one of the first ageist assumptions is that to be old automatically means to be in some state of failing health and decrepitude, physical, mental, or both, and, further, to be in this state means to be valueless and a non-person. It is no wonder, then, that women from their thirties on begin to lament their failing physical abilities, as if the standard set in the teens and 20's are the normative standards for life. My experiences with health limitations were so tied in with ageist expectations that at the first signs of what turned out to be a relatively mild condition I had a life crisis. I will not ever forget the absolutely unreasoning fear I felt the night I finally called the paramedics for what I thought was probably gas, but "given my age" could perhaps be chest pains, and signal the "beginning of the end." I'm not sorry I called the paramedics that time, or the time after. What I see in retrospect is that my fears, fed by the ageism of the medical establishment, were in large part due to my ageist expectations that my body was supposed to give out.

That incident provided me with some first-hand education about the rampant ageism of the medical establishment. I was referred from one doctor to another, experiencing a range of attitudes from the paternalistic "what do you expect at your age" to the downright incompetent in which, despite all medical information that *less* rather than *more* medication is indicated with age, I was, without diagnosis, prescribed heart medication to take for the rest of my life "just in case." Only after I became very much sicker (from the side effects of the medication) and after many expensive intrusive tests was it determined that nothing much was wrong with me that could not be controlled simply by proper diet and exercise. Of course a part of me felt foolish. But the havoc created by this series of events impressed upon me as probably nothing else would have how crucially my own welfare depends upon my confronting and challenging ageism, the ageism of the medical establishment as well as my own internalization of it. I was forced as well to learn in a new way how I must indeed listen to and attend to my body.

Medical research shows that there is no reason that most of us cannot remain in relatively good health until all but the very last stages of our life, particularly if we take proper care of our bodies. With age our bodies do demand more time and attention, and for the most part we learn to live with that greater demand. Like any other stage of life, there is a downside to old age, and I believe this is it. For all of us, young and old, our worst fear is what will happen to us in the event of chronic or severe illness in a society without adequate universal health care coverage, with a medical establishment that is racist, ageist, and sexist to the core, and with disability a social stigma. We are all haunted by the specter of being warehoused into nursing homes should we become disabled through accident or illness and unable to care for ourselves. We are taught to hate and fear disability and the disabled, and our society has tried to isolate and segregate the disabled, both young and old.

In addition, given that old age in white western European culture is thought of as a disease rather than a stage of life, it is not surprising to find that problems of living arising from greater fragility are reduced to medical problems requiring medical solutions. The medicalization of old age means that government funding gets funnelled through the medical establishment into nursing homes, vastly more expensive for the consumer and vastly more profitable for the provider than home health care.

The whole issue of possible disability raises another new area for reevaluating long held beliefs and attitudes. I have worked hard to become self-reliant and independent, and my ability to be "my own" person and do it "on my own" has been a source of pride for me. Lesbians, who do not look to men to be taken care of, place a high premium on that quality and have much difficulty in asking for help. Now, as an old woman, I am forced to reexamine the value I have placed upon personal independence at the expense of interdependence. There is much stretching to do in knowing that I am not diminished by asking for help. Should I become chronically disabled, I know I will face more critically the ongoing struggle to maintain an intact sense of myself while relying more upon others.

One thing is certain, our society makes interdependence difficult, for we live in a society segregated by race, ethnicity and age. Before I became conscious of my own ageism, I assiduously avoided anything that had to do with "old," including activities at our local Senior Center. As I began to acknowledge and accept my aging, I also began eagerly to seek out the companionship of old women, in my local neighborhood and in the lesbian community. It didn't take me long to know that the best of my learning and growth could take place here with these old women, as together we confronted the gripping issues of our lives.

Without any apparent loss of the energy and excitement of my youth, I once again became an activist, as one of the founders and organizers of the First West Coast Conference and Celebration of Old Lesbians (1987), as well as of the national Old Lesbians Organizing for Change (OLOC), which grew out of the Second West Coast Conference in San Francisco (1989). Lesbians, this time old lesbians, are once again in the forefront, on the cutting edge of the struggle for women's liberation.

We did an enormous amount of hard work to clarify our purpose and our goals as we hammered out a policy to confront the ageism within our lesbian community as well as the larger community. The uncompromising nature of our struggle was set from the start when we limited our group to old lesbians sixty and over, and when we insisted on calling ourselves OLD. The age limit exists so that old women have the opportunity to speak for ourselves, for, as an OLOC brochure (1992) says, "we are especially sensitive to those who see themselves as committed to the old, doing 'good' for the old, speaking for us. That is ageism!"

The insistence, for the first time, on 60 as an exclusive limit for belonging made 60 plus an important and empowering time in women's lives. I pointed out in my welcoming talk at the First West Coast Conference that important and painful as the problems of mid-life women may be, "to lump aging from 40 to 90+ is once again to trivialize the problems of old women—and once again to defer to younger women. We are expected to be available to nurture young and mid-life lesbians. Instead we boldly say 'No, this is our space.' We take this strong stand to affirm ourselves."

The "O" word is probably more dreaded than the "L" word. I have never yet attended a group, as either leader or participant in which the issue has not come up. Why use that word. I will never forget one group in which an old lesbian talked about how disgusting, revolting, and actually nauseating that word was. Yet we old lesbians again stood firm, accepting none of the euphemistic substitutes that came pouring in.

The OLOC brochure says that although "Old has become a term of insult and shame . . . we refuse the lie that it is shameful to be an old woman." We are neither "older" (than whom?) nor "elder," nor "senior." We name and proclaim ourselves as OLD for we no longer wish to collude in our own oppression by accommodating to language that implies in any way that old means inferior, ugly or awful. For to the degree that old women deny our own aging we cripple our ability to live. By naming ourselves old, we give up the attempt to pass. And as we break our silence, we empower ourselves and each other.

The excitement of this struggle is enormous. There were approximately 200 old lesbians attending each of the West Coast Conferences, and within a year when OLOC began to issue a Newsletter the mailing list grew to over 700 names. Now there are clusters of old lesbians meeting in at least 14 states, with plans for some of us to caravan around the country to meet and organize additional old lesbians. There is no question that old lesbians want to network with each other and share their experiences so that they can become a force in changing the ageism of our society.

Such an exciting endeavor! I often feel astonished at how rich in exploration and discovery my life is. This is not what I expected. This self of mine, that I always characterized at its best as a seeker after truth, is still in there doing her thing! And I am surprised, for I believed the same things we were all taught about what it means to be old.

I am learning better than ever before just how political the personal is. Never has my political life been so intertwined with my personal thrust toward clarity and resolution. I believe that our work has impact, that I have impact as we old lesbians continue to organize and make ourselves visible.

As part of our active engagement with life I and my partner are constantly building our friendship circle, a community of old and new friends and comrades, based first on our own special group of old lesbians but extending intergenerationally to many women. For our community of women strengthens and sustains us.

I have always wanted to live a mindful life, and I believe that my ongoing process of checking the dimensions of my own reality keep me mindful, alert and aware.

I am bemused when I think of my many fears about growing old. I was even afraid to retire and waited an extra year because I wasn't sure that I would have either enough to do or enough money to do it with. Although money is not abundant, I am fortunate that it is an occasional rather than a chronic worry. Since we hear only the down side of growing old, I was unprepared for my life as it is now. It is different from what I expected. Not until I stopped working could I even begin to imagine the exhilarating sense of freedom which unstructured open-ended time makes possible, a delicious experience I am having for the first time in my life.

How could I expect that my old age would be so full of life and love and excitement? All the ageist cliches depict old age as a static time, and the major gerontological theories reinforce those cliches, categorizing old age as a time of disengagement, when the biological clock winds down and the spirit and psyche withdraw. I do not dispute that such characterizations may be true for some. That is not the way, however, I am experiencing my life. I am not unaware that my body is moving closer to dying, and that at the time of my actual dying, if the process is natural and not precipitated by trauma, I may indeed have a different agenda.

For now, however, my life is very much in process, full of opening new doors while looking back at old and treasured experiences. My past gives my present a richness and a backdrop for the exploration which is happening in the present. Almost every value and belief I have held is up for reexamination and reevaluation.

In speaking of my old age, I once declared with some disappointment that I have not miraculously arrived at a state of grace or of wisdom, that I am still in process. This, then, is perhaps the greatest miracle of all. That so long as there is life, there is the possibility of growth and change. Old age provides no guarantees but death. However, it does provide us with a special gift, the final challenge and the final opportunity to grow up.

References

COPPER, B. (1988). *Over the hill, Reflections on ageism between women.* Freedom, CA: The Crossing Press.

MACDONALD, B. & RICH, C. (1991). *Look me in the eye—old women aging and ageism.* San Francisco, CA: Spinsters Book Company.

OLOC Brochure (1992). OLOC, P.O. Box 980422, Houston, TX 77098.

RICH, C. (1988). Ageism and the politics of beauty. In Macdonald, B. & Rich, C. (1991) *Look me in the eye—old women aging and ageism* (pp. 139–146), San Francisco, CA: Spinsters Book Company.

Afterword

By now you have read many women's stories. We hope you have discovered that women are not all alike. Their stories differ, depending on so-called objective variables such as sexual orientation, age, ethnicity, and social class circumstances. These variables are beginning to be explored by social and developmental psychologists (especially those interested in a multicultural perspective). But personal history is also transformed by the meaning of such variables for each woman. Think about what it means to be a lesbian mother, a black intellectual, or an old activist when these labels have contradictory meanings in our society.

How do self-definitions influence a woman's behavior? This question is especially important when the self appears to contradict what the social system says a woman ought to be. How can a woman's sense of self—her individual identity—be represented by psychology? As feminist psychologists, we wrestle to reconcile individual subjectivity and group data. We are especially concerned with the question of the place of the individual's story in psychology.

Although these questions have not yet been answered, we believe that the individual life story contributes to traditional psychology in a number of ways. We will summarize a few ideas we have thought about and invite you to provide some of your own.

First, we believe these stories are important because they can be used to disrupt the idea that psychology has created universal laws of behavior. They suggest that groups of women are no more alike or different than are women and men. They argue that psychology must move beyond its traditional laboratory context if it truly wants to understand human beings. We believe that psychology must also look at how meaning is constructed and conveyed.

The value of these stories does not depend, however, on whether they are "true." All stories, including our own, are both "true" and "untrue" at the same time. They enrich more official histories by filling us in on the conscious meaning of events in women's everyday lives. But, they also show us how a

377

woman's experience of her own life can be changed and reinterpreted depending on later circumstances.

Second, many of these stories tell us about how women change as they come to understand the power of social categorization. Rejecting the categories set out for them in advance, the women who speak in this volume have taken for themselves the "power to name" by claiming the right to describe—and reinterpret—their own experience. Some of them also speak for other girls and women who might not have had a voice without their help. Their stories tell us that naming is a privilege of individuals as well as society and that it is never too late to rename.

Third, these stories tell us that differences among women need not be a source of divisiveness. Telling each other our stories can become a source of community—one that has become lost as society has become more technical and urbanized. We ask you to continue your experiences with this book by asking others around you for their stories. Listen to personal histories from both closely related women such as your mother or grandmothers and women who are very different from yourself.

We hope you have enjoyed these personal histories and feel that you have gotten to know many of the women who have narrated them. A few of these women were famous in their own time and have been forgotten. Others are very unlikely to be known by anyone except their relatives and friends. They teach us that every woman does not and cannot deal with her reality in the same way, and they force us to be careful in making judgments about the "best" way to cope. Many of them do, however, suggest that communal strategies may be more useful than individualistic ones.

Finally, these stories help us to ask, Where do we go from here? Stories are important because they validate other women's struggles and because they have important lessons to teach each of us. The future is not necessarily an improvement on the past, and all change is not necessarily progress. These stories warn us that if we forget our histories we may be doomed to repeat them!

Credits

Part One

p. 15: Furumoto, L. (1979). Mary Whiton Calkins (1863–1930): Fourteenth president of the American Psychological Association. *Journal of the History of the Behavioral Sciences, 15,* 346–356.

p. 26: "'How can a little girl like you teach a great big class of men?' the Chairman Said, and Other Adventures of a Woman in Science," by Naomi Weisstein, in S. Ruddick and P. Daniels (eds.), *Working it Out,* pp. 241-250. Copyright © 1977 by Naomi Weisstein. Reprinted by permission of the author.

p. 33: Source: Mary Crawford, from *Ms. Magazine,* August 1981, pp. 86-89. Copyright © 1981. Reprinted by permission of the author.

p. 38: The following is reprinted from *Talking Back* with permission from the publisher, South End Press, 116 Saint Botolph Street, Boston, MA 02115.

Part Two

p. 47: From Judith Ortiz Cofer, *The Latin Deli: Prose and Poetry.* University of Georgia Press, 1993. Copyright © 1987-1993 R.R. Bowker. All rights reserved. Reprinted by permission of the University of Georgia Press.

p. 55: Source: "'Opening' Faces: The Politics of Cosmetic Surgery and Asian American Women," by Eugenia Kaw, in N. Sault (ed.), *Many mirrors: Body image and social relations.* Copyright © 1994. Reprinted by permission of Eugenia Kaw.

p. 74: From Michelle Fine (ed.), *Disruptive Voices: The Possibilities of Feminist Research.* Copyright © 1992. Reprinted by permission of The University of Michigan Press.

p. 95: Source: M. Crawford & M. Gentry (eds.), *Gender and thought,* pp. 175-187. Copyright © 1989. Reprinted by permission of Mary Crawford, Ph.D.

p. 107: "The Other Body," by Ynestra King, *Ms.,* March/April 1993. Reprinted by permission of Ms. Magazine, © 1994.

p. 112: Reprinted by permission of Sage Publications Ltd and Diana E.H. Russell from Alice Mayall and Diana E.H. Russell, "Racism in Pornography," *Feminism & Psychology,* Vol. 3, No. 2. Copyright © 1993.

p. 119: From OUTRAGEOUS ACTS AND EVERYDAY REBELLIONS by Gloria Steinem.

Part Three

p. 129: "The Rape of Mr. Smith," by Unknown, from *Women Helping Women: Volunteer Resource Manual,* by Rape Crisis Services, Urbana, Illinois.

p. 131: "If Men Could Menstruate," by Gloria Steinem, *Ms. Magazine,* October 1978. Reprinted by permission of the author.

p. 133: Copyright © 1996 by The New York Times Co. Reprinted by Permission.

p. 135: From "Feminist Theory and Standardized Testing" by Phyllis Teitelbaum in GENDER/BODY/KNOWLEDGE edited by Alison M. Jaggar and Susan R. Bordo. Copyright © 1989 by Rutgers, The State University.

p. 145: Reprinted by permission of Jeremy P. Tarcher, Inc./The Putnam Publishing Group from "Are We Having Sex Now or What?" by Greta Christina from THE EROTIC IMPULSE: Honoring the Sensual Self edited by David Steinberg. Copyright © 1992 by David Steinberg.

p. 149: Reprinted by permission of Sage Publications Ltd from Carol Nagy Jacklin, "How My Heterosexuality Affects My Feminist Personality," *Feminism & Psychology,* 2. Copyright © 1992.

p. 152: "Coping with Rape: Critical Perspectives on Consciousness," by Michelle Fine, Ph.D., *Imagination, Cognition, and Personality, 3,* 1983-1984, pp. 249-267. Used by permission of the publisher, the Baywood Publishing Co., Inc.

p. 165: "Invisibility is an Unnatural Disaster: Reflections of an Asian American Woman," by Mitsuye Yamada from *This Bridge Called My Back: Writings by Radical Women of Color.* Copyright © 1983 by Cherrie Moraga & Gloria Anzaldua. Used with permission of the author and Kitchen Table: Women of Color Press, P.O. Box 908, Latham, NY 12110.

p. 170: Reprinted from Gender Outlaw, by Kate Bornstein (1995) with permission of the publisher, Routledge, New York.

Part Four

p. 191: From MAKING WAVES by Asian Women United of California. Copyright © 1989 by Asian Women United of California. Reprinted by permission of Beacon Press, Boston.

p. 199: Abridged from Shellee Colen "With Respect and Feelings", Voices of West Indian Child Care and Domestic Workers in New York City. Copyright © 1985 Shellee Colen.

p. 219: APPROXIMATELY 13 PAGES from WOMEN CREATING LIVES: IDENTITIES, RESILIENCE, AND RESISTANCE edited by C.E. FRANZ AND A.J. STEWART. Copyright © 1994 by Westview Press. Reprinted by permission of Westview Press.

p. 231: APPROXIMATELY 19 PAGES from WOMEN CREATING LIVES: IDENTITIES, RESILIENCE, AND RESISTANCE edited by C.E. FRANZ AND A.J. STEWART. Copyright © 1994 by Westview Press. Reprinted by permission of Westview Press.

p. 249: "An Academic Woman as a Token: A Case Study," by Janice D. Yoder, *Journal of Social Issues,* Volume 41, No. 4, 1985, pp. 61-72. Copyright © 1985. Reprinted by permission of The Society for the Psychological Study of Social Issues.

p. 260: From WHERE THE GIRLS ARE: GROWING UP FEMALE WITH THE MASS MEDIA by Susan J. Douglas. Copyright © 1994, 1995 by Susan J. Douglas. Reprinted by permission of Times Books, a division of Random House, Inc.